Railroads of Indiana

The wooden caboose is now railroad history, like the conductor's waved "highball" starting this Nickel Plate freight into the night from Frankfort in 1943.   *Photo by William Rittase—Jay Williams collection*

Railroads of Indiana

RICHARD S. SIMONS

AND

FRANCIS H. PARKER

INDIANA UNIVERSITY PRESS
Bloomington & Indianapolis

■

The paper used in this publication meets
the minimum requirements of
American National Standard for
Information Sciences—Permanence of Paper
for Printed Library Materials,
ANSI Z39.48–1984.

Manufactured in the United States of America

Library of Congress Cataloging-in-Publication Data

Simons, Richard S.
Railroads of Indiana / Richard S. Simons and
Francis H. Parker.
p.   cm.
Includes bibliographical references and index.
ISBN 0-253-33351-2 (cl : alk. paper)
1. Railroads—Indiana—History.   I. Parker, Francis H.
(Francis Haywood), date .   II. Title.
HE2771.I6S56   1997
385'.09772—dc21   97-21579

3   4   5   02   01   00   99

■

To James A. Bistline, retired general counsel and
assistant to the president of the
Southern Railway:
a respected official in the rail industry,
a reliable friend of the rail enthusiast.
And to our favorite rail travelers,
Carol and Richard Parker,
Rosmarie and Charlotte Simons,
and Jeff Smith.

■

Contents

Preface

This book is an effort to explain and trace the development of Indiana's railroads from their inception in 1832 to the present and to examine closely nearly all phases of their operation. To our knowledge this is the first attempt, other than anecdotal, to cover this topic so broadly and intensively.

Yet we regard it only as a beginning. We hope that it will serve as a reference base and to inspire those who wish to expand further Indiana's store of railroad knowledge. Although we have made strenuous efforts to ensure accuracy, no doubt some errors have crept in, and we shall be grateful to any reader who will call them to our attention.

Included are line-by-line descriptions of the 15 major rail systems which operated during the first half of this century. As a benchmark we have chosen the mid–1940s, before the era of mega-mergers which consolidated most of Indiana's railroads into three major systems, and potentially still further into two. Maps for each system generally show them as they were at that time, although also including previously abandoned branches which were specifically part of that system. Each system description includes a corporate family tree which shows origins, acquisitions, and relationships, but usually does not include out-of-state predecessors or merger partners or transition, construction, or non-operating corporations. Modern switching roads and spin-off short lines are combined in a single chapter, since the line between the two has blurred. Distances usually are rounded to the nearest mile throughout the book. As a comparative yardstick, the number of passenger trains operated by each line during the national peak period of railroad activity, which was World War I, is contrasted to the post–World War II numbers, when the final decline of passenger service began.

Although this book is a joint effort, Francis H. Parker was primarily responsible for chapters 1 through 7 and chapter 14. Richard S. Simons wrote chapters 8–10, 12–13, and 15–21. Chapter 11 was a joint effort.

No book of this scope would be possible without the generous help of many persons recognized in the rail and related fields. Several went to great lengths to provide critical information that had eluded us, and they responded so promptly and with such enthusiasm that they obviously viewed our project as their very own.

These included James A. Bistline, Alexandria, Va.; Thomas G. Hoback, Indianapolis; Janet Moran, Hammond; Howard Pletcher, Fort Wayne; Robert L. Reid, Evansville; Wiley W. Spurgeon, Muncie; Dr. Clay Stuckey, Bedford; the late Thomas W. Tobin, Marion; and Richard Wallis, Wheaton, Ill.

We are indebted, also, to helpful railroad officials including Chris J. Burger, president of Central Railroad of Indianapolis, and his predecessor, Henry E. Weller, Jr.; H. Terry Hearst, president, and Harold F. Parmly, vice-president, Chicago SouthShore and South Bend Railroad; Richard L. Neumann, general manager, and Phillip G. Wilzbacher, director of marketing, Indiana Southern Railroad; Thomas G. Quigley, vice-president, Indiana Rail Road; William G. Prime, Madison Railroad director; and John Michael, chief dispatcher of the former Erie Railroad. Short line presidents made our task easier by returning questionnaires promptly and completely.

Several authors in the rail field gave us their personal assistance. They included Victor M. Bogle, Indiana University–Kokomo; H. Roger Grant, Clemson University; Peter T. Maiken, Beloit, Wis.; Jerry Marlette, Indianapolis; and David P. McLellan, Mishawaka.

Illustrations have come from many sources. Particular assistance in researching their collections for relevant photographs was given by Jonathon Bremer, Muncie; M. D. McCarter, Camp Verde, Ariz.; Harold A. Miller, Marion; and Jay Williams, Indianapolis. George Wesselhoft helped prepare the maps.

Others, all bound by a common interest in railroads, devoted time, support, and wise counsel. They include Victor A. Baird, Fort Wayne; Ed

Breen, Marion; Phil Brooks, Indianapolis; William E. Ervin, Hartford City; Demosthenes P. Gelopulos, Valparaiso University; David Goldzwig, Dayton, Ohio; David W. Hayes, Hardinsburg, Ky.; Steve Jones, Wabash; Otis E. Marks, Kokomo; Jack Miller, Wabash; Craig Pressler, Noblesville; Wes and Shirley Ross, Lexington, Ky.; Walter Sassmannshausen, Fort Wayne; Jeff Smith, Olympia, Wash.; John Martin Smith, Auburn; Jeff Strombeck, Mishawaka; Jeremy Taylor, Metamora; Fred Wouster, Mexico; and State Representative Dean Young, Hartford City, and his staff.

Many libraries provided valuable assistance. They include the Indiana Historical Society and Indiana State Libraries; Marion Public Library, particularly Mary Leffler of the reference department and Barbara Love, head of the Indiana room; Ball State University Library, especially Paul Stout and Barbara Lowe in the map collection; Willard Library, Evansville; Huntington and Crawfordsville Public Libraries; University of Chicago Regenstein Library, particularly Michael D. Brown; Northwestern University Transportation Library, Evanston, Ill.; and Mark Cedeck, St. Louis Mercantile Library. Paula Corpuz of the Indiana Historical Society also was helpful.

To these persons and institutions, we are grateful for their interest and generous assistance.

—Francis H. Parker,
Muncie

—Richard S. Simons,
Marion

Railroads of Indiana

A Southern Railway train wends its way through a forested setting at Lincoln State Park in Spencer County. Hoosier Southern Railroad now owns the line. *Photo by Richard S. Simons*

Introduction: The Railroad and Indiana

IN 1832 the Indiana legislature chartered eight possible railroad lines connecting the state to its neighbors, to the Ohio River, and to Lake Michigan. In 1838 the first train left North Madison carrying dignitaries on an inspection trip fifteen miles to Graham's Ford, and the railroad age in Indiana was launched.

In the 160 years that followed, Indiana and its railroads have grown and changed, each dependent on the other. In the early years railroads were a state initiative, a matter of pressing internal improvements to support the growth of population, cities, and agriculture. Without economic transportation to move crops to market, the rich lands of the Indiana interior were valueless. Generations of citizens and legislators struggled with the problem of financing and building canals, roads, or railroads to support settlement and move the crops to market. State government was seen as the only entity capable of financing the necessary improvements.

The first Indiana railroads were feeders to existing water transportation, with one end anchored either at the Ohio or the Wabash & Erie Canal. By the Civil War this had changed, as railroads linked with each other in growing transportation chains. Indiana benefited by its location, as railroads had to cross it to connect the east with he western gateways at Chicago and St. Louis. Indianapolis emerged as the first major inland city not connected to water transportation.

In the decades following the Civil War railroads acquired unquestioned dominance in long distance transportation. Growing population density provided the market for additional rail lines, and rail lines became the necessary precondition for growth of cities and towns. Railroads brought fuel and raw material to support Indiana's shift toward a manufacturing economy, and their location largely determined where industries were located in Indiana's growing cities.

In later years railroads became corporate monoliths, competing for territory and control as they held unquestioned sway over the transportation of the state. They reached a peak in mileage and passenger service around the First World War, and remained relatively stable through the second World War, from which they emerged optimistically looking forward to new levels of passenger and freight service and new locomotive technologies. By the 1950s the optimism was fading amid uneasy signs that the railroads were overextended and ill-prepared to cope with new competition from interstate highways, long-distance trucking, and jetliners.

In the decades since 1960, the rail system of Indiana has been drastically reorganized. Again an issue for public policy, the rail system of Indiana, like that of the northeast generally, appeared headed for collapse in the 1960s, and was transformed by a combination of federal intervention, large-scale mergers, and drastic reductions in mileage. By the 1990s, Indiana railroading was dominated by only three major systems, and by the time this book is published there may be only two. Abandoning their traditional role as an all-purpose transportation system, railroads have concentrated increasingly on wholesale transportation—the transportation of bulk commodities over long distances between major terminals and shippers. They have regained a measure of economic health, and have developed new transportation niches, especially in intermodal and in auto shipments. Ironically, their marketing success, combined with the almost-obsessive contraction of facilities, has led again to a concern about railroad capacity, and to a fear that the railroad plant may have shrunk too far to adequately support the role which railroads may be called on to play in the future.

Most Hoosiers have missed the current resurgence of rail traffic, since the link that the average citizen has with railroads has been broken. Since the 1960s rail employment has plummeted, the passenger train and the train station have all but disappeared, and few people now either ride railroads or know anyone who works for one. Railroads have seemingly become invisible, even as their freight traffic volume grows.

Approaching a new century, with three decades of railroad turmoil and reorganization behind us, is an appropriate time to pause and look back at the history of the railroads in Indiana thus far. A generation is now passing which grew up knowing railroads as they once were—as the unquestioned backbone of passenger and freight transportation in the state, and as a major employer in their own right. Once-familiar corporate names are becoming distant memories, and the physical remains of their presence are steadily eroding. The time seems ripe for an overview.

The subject has not been ignored, to be sure. Indepth studies have been done of individual railroads, most notably of the Monon and the Nickel Plate, two railroads whose interest to Hoosiers and railroad enthusiasts alike has probably outweighed their overall significance on the national railroad scene. Detailed corporate histories have been done or are underway for other railroads, and a rich enthusiasts' literature has covered the details of rolling stock and operations, especially those of more recent years. What has been hard to find is an overview of Indiana railroading generally. A useful but somewhat anecdotal work by George Rainey, himself a railroader, was published in 1969 but is now dated and difficult to find. Elmer Sulzer's classic account, *Ghost Railroads of Indiana,* was written in 1970, but the abandonments of which he wrote have since been dwarfed by more recent changes.

This book began with the frustration of the authors trying to find an overall handbook and guide to the railroads of Indiana. We have tried to pull together their history in three successive components. First is a chronology and overview, looking at the railroad system as a whole as it has evolved through five successive eras: 1830–1860; 1860–1900; 1900–1930; 1930–1960; and 1960 to the present. These eras make sense to us, and we hope will make sense to the reader, in understanding the broad themes of Indiana railroad history, and in noting the commonalities among railroads within each era. Second is a brief synopsis of individual railroad systems, tracing their corporate and physical growth and transition. Third is a section devoted again to commonalities, focusing on specific services, facilities, incidents, and personalities.

A note is in order about our grouping of lines. Railroaders have long memories, and the language of railroading is replete with everyday references to systems now long-deceased. Commonplace examples in Indiana include the Panhandle, the Vandalia, the Big Four, the Clover Leaf, and the Lake Erie and Western, none of which, strictly speaking, has existed as a corporate entity for the last 60 years. More recently, older railroaders stubbornly refuse to acknowledge that they actually worked for the Norfolk and Western or Norfolk Southern rather than the Wabash or Nickel Plate on which they had first hired out. The rule book might say Norfolk Southern, but the belt buckle still said Nickel Plate. When it came to the ill-fated merger of the Pennsylvania and the New York Central, surely it was asking too much psychologically to ignore a century of bitter rivalry and proud company loyalty.

Our response has been to group systems as they were during the first half of the twentieth century, during the period of greatest stability for the railroads. We have chosen a date of 1940 as our reference point in organizing the corporate histories, after the turmoil of the nineteenth century with its constantly shifting names and alliances, but before the waves of mergers which have successively erased almost all the traditional corporate identities since World War II. Accounts of individual rail lines will be found grouped under the corporate framework as it was at that time, and the earlier history of the line will lead up to that point. Subsequent references to individual rail lines, such as accounts of the current crop of railroad short lines or the evolution of the "super-systems," will trace their history only back to that reference date, and it will be assumed that anyone interested in the earlier history can find it within the individual railroad history.

The book is intended as a reference for the general enthusiast of Indiana railroads or Indiana history. We hope to provide an overall understanding of the role that railroads have played, and the elements of their physical fabric, rolling stock, and operations in each of the eras outlined above. We also hope to provide a reference for those curious to determine the origins and subsequent history of specific pieces of track. The Indiana landscape today is a jigsaw puzzle of former rail lines, their geometry starkly in contrast to the orthogonal mile-square grid of section lines in northern Indiana or the rolling unglaciated landscape of southern Indiana. The railroad geometry cuts across these landscapes, visible either as the glistening rails of active railroads or the inexplicably straight lines of embankments or tree lines marking a former rail line. In some cases the alignment of a string of towns betrays the linear geometry of a now-vanished railroad. In many towns a corridor of railroad-related uses and spaces marks the passage of a now-vanished railroad. Constantly encountered on any drive across the state, these railroad geometries raise provocative questions of origins and evolution. We hope that this book provides some answers. Using a wide array of map sources we have tried to compile an accurate all-time map of Indiana railroads, plotted on a system by system basis. For those interested in following specific current or abandoned lines on the ground, a useful complementary source is the detailed *Railroad Atlas of North America—Great Lakes East*, compiled by Mike Walker and published in 1997 by Steam Powered Publishing.

Another purpose of the book is to note and encourage the growing railroad preservation movement, a largely volunteer effort to record, preserve, and even operate aspects of Indiana's railroad heritage. Throughout the state, communities and individuals have devoted sweat, money, and ingenuity to restoring railroad depots, cars, or locomotives, as well as the photographs, maps, and paper evidence of vanished railroads. Scattered and often struggling, these groups collectively are preserving the historic artifacts through which we can better understand our railroad history. Probably more endangered are the priceless recollections of retired railroaders, the older men and women who operated the railroads before the technological and organizational innovations of recent years swept so much away. We hope that this book will encourage the greater understanding and preservation both of railroad artifacts and their oral history.

Railroads play a key role in Indiana's economic development even today, though that role is much less visible to the average citizen or consumer. The technology and the industry of railroads have absorbed the energies of generations of creative Hoosiers, whether in developing the pioneer railroads, operating the great systems in their heyday, looking to their dynamic and changing future, or preserving the artifacts and memories of railroad history. We hope this book adequately represents their efforts.

Pioneer railroads commonly used scrip to help finance construction. This example was issued for Indiana's first road, the Madison and Indianapolis, in 1845. The drawing depicts a Baldwin 4–2–0 locomotive like the M&I's 1837 Madison or 1839 Indianapolis. *Indiana Historical Society, Negative C6522*

2

Beginnings: 1830–1860

ON NOVEMBER 29, 1838, Governor James Wallace and state legislators joined fellow Hoosiers on the first steam train in Indiana. At eight miles an hour the dignitaries rode from North Madison to Graham's Ford, inaugurating service on the first fifteen miles of the state-financed Madison and Indianapolis Railroad. Pulling them was an English locomotive, the Elkhorn, built in 1836 for a pioneer Kentucky railroad and borrowed for the occasion. The M&I's own first locomotive had been lost at sea, thrown overboard en route from Philadelphia to New Orleans during a storm.[1]

The years between 1830 and 1860 were the formative years of Indiana railroading. Remote from us chronologically, and woefully lacking in photographic record, the era is a fascinating study of problem solving and new technology. Hoosiers for the first time learned what a railroad was and how to build one. They laid the framework for a century of railroad dominance that followed.

THE INTERNAL IMPROVEMENTS PROBLEM

The M&I's lost locomotive was a commentary on the difficulty of travel in 1838. It was American-built, but its delivery to Hoosier soil from Philadelphia required a sea trip to New Orleans and an upriver journey to Madison. Indiana crops in most areas had equally difficult journeys to reach eastern markets—a severe disadvantage to settlement and development of the state. Away from the rivers, settlements like the new Indiana capital were at an even greater disadvantage. The borrowed Elkhorn, everyone hoped, was the first step in linking the interior of Indiana to waterways and canals leading to the vital eastern markets. Little did inaugural participants know that it would be nine long years before the whistle of a steam engine was heard at the Indianapolis end of the new railroad.

The need for transportation facilities—"internal improvements" in the language of the day—was already evident by the 1820s. When Indiana became a state in 1816 its population was less than 135,000. Most settlers had arrived by crossing the Alleghenies and rafting down the Ohio, to establish farms and communities in the valleys tributary to the river. The Ohio had seen steamboats since 1812, and by 1832 steamboats were regularly ascending the Wabash to Lafayette. Crops were shipped downriver by flatboat from Gosport on the White River, and from Lafayette on the Wabash. River navigation, however, led downriver to New Orleans and the Gulf, away from the East Coast markets.

Settlement in the central part of Indiana had become possible with the 1818 New Purchase Treaty with the Indians, but travel was still possible only by foot or horseback. When the Indiana General Assembly, convening in Corydon in 1820, decided to locate a new state capitol in the interior of the state, they directed their commissioners to select a site with the "advantages of a navigable stream and fertility of soil, while [keeping in mind] the geographical situation of the state." When they finally convened at Indianapolis in 1825, it was a one-street village of only six hundred inhabitants, with an unreliable stage service and poor roads. When the steamboat *Robert Hanna* finally ascended the White River to Indianapolis in April 1831, it was stranded all summer before it could return downriver. No steamboat would successfully follow it.[2]

Besides the rivers there was the National Road, first proposed to Congress in 1808 by U.S. secretary of the treasury Albert Gallatin. Under construction since 1811, the National Road was completed through Centerville and Wayne County, Indiana, by 1827. In 1829 Congress appropriated money for constructing the road east and west from Indianapolis. Washington Street, the widest street in the Hoosier capital, had been laid out 120 feet wide to accommodate the coming road.[3] Any road, however, was limited in its capacity to handle crops or heavy cargoes.

Hopes were turning to two new transportation modes: the well-tested but capital-intensive canals, and the relatively untried railroads. New York State's Erie Canal had proven a technological and economic success, collecting $1,000,000 in tolls even before it was opened from end to end in 1825.[4] Ohio had followed with an 1825 bond issue "to provide for the internal improvement of the State of Ohio by navigable canals."[5] By 1827 the Ohio and Erie Canal was opened between Cuyahoga Falls and Cleveland, and by 1832 canals linked Lake Erie and the Ohio River, connecting the state, via Lake Erie and the Erie Canal, to the Eastern Seaboard. When finally completed in 1848, the Ohio state canal system would include 1,015 miles of waterway, connecting in two places with canals into Indiana.

Railroad technology was less familiar. Horse-powered tramways were common in Great Britain by 1800, hauling coal short distances from mines downhill to canals. Commercially viable steam engines had served these tramways since 1813, but the first steam-operated common carrier,* the 25-mile Stockton and Darlington, had only opened in 1825. By 1828 tramways were in use in Pennsylvania, taking anthracite coal short distances from mines to canals. On one of these tramways, the imported Stourbridge Lion, a typical English tramway engine, became the first operating railway locomotive in America.

A much bolder proposal was launched on July 4, 1828, when the "first stone" was laid in Baltimore for the new Baltimore and Ohio Railroad—a stunning proposal to link the Atlantic Coast and the Ohio Valley with 380 miles of untested railroad technology, across rough and largely unsurveyed terrain. Charles Carroll of Carrollton, the last surviving signer of the Declaration of Independence, turned the first spadeful of soil. "I consider this," he said, "among the most important acts of my life, second only to my signing the Declaration of Independence, if even it be second to that."[6] By 1830 the line was open for passengers and freight between Baltimore and Ellicott's Mills, Maryland, 13 miles. Despite a trial run of the steam engine Tom Thumb

---

*Common carrier lines are those operating under a public charter. In return for the grant of public powers such as eminent domain, common carriers are regulated and required to handle all freight and passengers offered under existing tariffs. Private roads typically serve only a single customer, and do not offer their services to the public.

in 1829, service began with horses. In December 1830, the South Carolina Railroad became the first common carrier railroad in the U.S. operated by steam power, followed on August 9, 1831, by the first run of the De Witt Clinton from Albany to Schenectady in New York.

Ohio Valley states looked to these eastern pioneers for inspiration. Michigan chartered the Pontiac and Detroit Railway Company in July 1830, although the first 13 miles did not open until 1838. In Ohio the Mad River and Lake Erie Railroad was incorporated February 5, 1832, and completed in 1838 from Sandusky to Bellevue. The Erie and Kalamazoo Railroad was incorporated in 1833 to build 33 miles from Toledo to Adrian, Michigan. Completed October 3, 1836, it opened with steam power, the first railroad in the Midwest to do so. Kentucky in 1830 chartered the Lexington and Ohio Railroad, opened January 30, 1834, for 28 miles between Lexington and Frankfort. Horses and an unsuccessful homemade steam locomotive were replaced by British steam locomotives built in 1836.

Canals or Railroads?

Indiana followed Ohio's canal lead in 1827, when Congress granted the state alternate sections of land for a canal to link Lake Erie with the Ohio via the Wabash River. Groundbreaking occurred in 1828 in Fort Wayne, although construction did not begin in earnest until 1832. After many delays, the Wabash and Erie would open to Peru in 1837, Lafayette in 1843, Terre Haute by 1848, and Evansville by 1853. The completed canal, 464 miles from Toledo to Evansville, was the longest in the country. It was successful in reorienting Indiana's trade from the Mississippi to the East and in promoting the settlement of the area, but financially it was a failure. Construction costs were $6,500,000, $3,000,000 of which came from proceeds of land sales. Net operating revenues over the canal lifetime were only about $1,300,000. The portion below Terre Haute was lightly used and was abandoned in 1860, with portions of its towpath subsequently supporting a railroad.

America's first Union Depot, built in 1853 on the site of the present Union Station train shed, served the six roads then entering the city. Five tracks extended the length of the interior; four roads had designated tracks while two shared the fifth. *Indiana Historical Society, Bass Photo Collection, Negative 5881*

In 1832, buoyed by the railroad agitation among Indiana's neighbors, the Indiana legislature chartered eight railroad companies on February 2 and 3, 1832, following Michigan by only three days, and preceding Ohio by two. Five of these were to connect Indianapolis with the Ohio River or its tributaries at points, respectively, of Harrison, Lawrenceburg, Madison, Jeffersonville, and New Albany.[7] The other three would connect the Falls of the Ohio with Lafayette, Lafayette with Lake Michigan, and Richmond to Hamilton, Ohio.

Although railroads would later follow almost all of the chartered routes, none of the original charters was actually realized. One did, however, produce actual construction. The charter for the Lawrenceburg and Indianapolis authorized a route through Shelbyville, and just east of Shelbyville, on July 4, 1834, a 1¼-mile stretch of railroad was opened for service with one horse-drawn car run-

ning on wooden rails. A state historical marker on Route 44 in Shelbyville commemorates the site of this short-lived demonstration railroad.

By 1835, preliminary exploration was underway on a second of the 1832 railroad charters, that connecting Madison to Indianapolis. As with the Shelbyville project, however, private capital was not available to launch the project. If a railroad was to be built in Indiana, it appeared, public financial support would be the necessary precondition. As the federal government retreated from its early support for the National Road, the advocates of internal improvement turned to Indiana state government for support. In January 1835, the Committee on Canals and Internal Improvements presented a report listing the comparative merits of canals versus railroads. Canals were cited for their permanence, relative cheapness of construction, and ability to carry heavy agricultural loads. It was also noted that the canal water could be used for hydraulic power as well, producing revenue and benefiting the community. Railroads were cited for their speed, their ability to operate year round, and the ability to use steam power advantageously. Cost comparisons seemed to indicate that although canals would be more expensive to build, canal construction would involve local materials with the consequent recirculation of money locally, whereas much of the money expended in railroad construction "must of necessity be sent out of the country, and when completed, the farmers must be dependent on a monopoly for the transportation of the fruits of their toil."[8]

The Committee on Canals and Internal Improvements recommended the construction of canals wherever possible. The result was a heroic, if wildly unrealistic, commitment of state funds for internal improvements, primarily for canal construction but including one important railroad project. On January 27, 1836, Governor Noah Noble signed "An Act to Provide for a General System of Internal Improvements" (Indiana Legislature, General Laws of the State of Indiana, 1836). The act created a Board of Internal Improvements and an Internal Improvements Fund, and authorized borrowing to the amount of $10,500,000 for completion and extension of the Wabash and Erie ($1,800,000), a Central Canal ($3,500,000), the Whitewater Canal ($1,400,000), a highway paralleling the Ohio River ($1,350,000), a railroad from Madison on the Ohio to Lafayette on the Wabash by way of Indianapolis ($1,300,000), and other smaller projects.[9] The board was to make loans, use those loans as collateral for Indiana bonds, and use the interest earned to finance roads, railroads, and canals. The act provided for a "Rail Road" or "McAdamized Turnpike" between New Albany and Crawfordsville.[10]

The 1830s: Starting the Madison Railroad

With the promise of state funding in hand, work began in earnest on the line from Madison to Indianapolis. Although Madison was the second largest city in the state (1830 population of 1,752 for Madison and 2,079 for New Albany), it was about the closest river point to the small settlement at Indianapolis. In 1837 work started on the line northwestward from North Madison and on the Madison Hill, rising 413 feet through the Ohio River escarpment to the relatively level terrain a mile north of town. It was expensive and slow,

involving cuts through solid rock to depths of 100', plus two embankments each nearly 100' high.[11]

Work went faster on the relatively level terrain beyond North Madison. In May 1838 rail laying began on the 15-mile segment between North Madison and Graham's Ford Bridge, to be completed that November. Completion of this line, short and unfinished as it was, called for a celebration and it was here, on November 29, 1838, that the borrowed Elkhorn pulled the first steam passenger train in Indiana. By June 6, 1839, five more miles between Graham's Ford Bridge and Vernon were opened to traffic, and a second locomotive, again ordered from Philadelphia, entered service April 1 of that year.

Further construction was delayed by the collapse of the publicly funded internal improvements system. With no tax resources behind the program, interest charges were met by further borrowing. Further borrowing became impossible in depressed conditions following the panic of 1837, and $3,000,000 was lost with the failure of financial agents. The ambitious public internal improvements program ground to a halt.

Indiana was not alone. On March 20, 1837, Michigan, with a population smaller than Indiana's, bonded herself for $5,000,000 to build two canals and three railroads. Michigan purchased the assets of private companies already begun. Work was halted by the panic of 1837. Michigan, like Indiana, was subsequently to prohibit state aid for internal improvements in its 1850 Constitution.[12]

The 1840s: On to Indianapolis

Little did the dignitaries on that first trip in 1838 guess that it would be nine years before the railroad to Indianapolis was finished, and that the noble state enterprise by that time would have given way to private companies. Besides the line to Indianapolis, the 1840s saw completed only a 16-mile branch from Edinburg to Shelbyville, and the start of work on several more. Indiana's population in 1840 was 685,866; in 1850, 988,416—an increase of over 40%. It must have been a frustrating decade for railroad advocates, but it paved the way for the extraordinary explosion that was to follow in the 1850s.

In 1841 the Madison incline was finished, to become an operating headache for generations of future railroaders. With an average grade of 5.89%, it was too steep for regular locomotives, and ascending freight cars were pulled up the incline by eight tandem-hitched horses. Cars descended by gravity, with predictable results. On March 28, 1844, a descending passenger train, with a locomotive on the lower end, was overtaken by a loaded wood car let loose at the top, smashing the passenger car, killing four passengers, and injuring 10 or 12 more.[13]

On June 1, 1841, the line was completed 27.8 miles from Madison. Another 28 miles were partially graded and bridged by 1842, but the state was financially exhausted and unable to complete the work. It had built well, with T rail from England and substantial stone bridges, but the costs of construction and the Madison hill had greatly exceeded revenues. Between 1836 and 1842 the state expended over $1.6 million on the line, while receiving only $62,000 in income. Completion by public funds was impossible, and on January 28, 1842, the legislature passed an Act providing for the completion of construction of all or any of the public works of the state by private companies. The Madison and Indianapolis was turned over in February 1843 to a newly formed private Madison and Indianapolis Railroad Company. The state retained a stock interest in the railroad, and the final transfer of deed to the railroad did not occur until 1856. At that time it was estimated that the private company had paid a total of $65,832 to acquire a property on which the state had expended over $1,600,000.[14]

After 1842 the private Madison and Indianapolis obtained local subscriptions, largely paid in land and produce, and managed to borrow eastern capital.[15] Construction resumed under private ownership, facilitated by economies in construction. By 1844 the line had reached Columbus, 45 miles from Madison and halfway to Indianapolis. By 1845 it was to Edinburg, and by 1846 to Franklin, 65 miles away. In anticipation of its arrival, and as a sign of the agitation for railroads generally, an Indianapolis weekly, the *Locomotive,* began publication in 1845 to report on railroads and other doings of interest. It would last until 1860.[16]

On October 1, 1847, the last rail was laid in Indianapolis, 86 miles from Madison. The ensuing celebration that day was duly reported:

> At about 3 o'clock in the afternoon, the belching forth of the loud mouthed cannon announced the time for the approach of the cars from Madison. Such a collection of people as thronged the grounds adjacent to the depot has not been witnessed in these parts since Tippecanoe times. They were there by acres, stretching far out along the railroad, some upon trees, stumps, fence mounds, and everything which tended to raise one squad above another. Soon a dark spot in the distance was descried by those picketed upon the furthest outposts; then was heard the shrill whistle of the locomotive, echoing through hoary forests and o'er verdant fields and shout answering to shout as the two iron steeds puffing and snorting majestically turned the curve in the road a short distance from town, followed by two long trains of passenger and freight cars, completely filled with human beings, the ladies waving their white handkerchiefs and the men and boys using their lungs in answering back the long, loud huzzas from the people awaiting their approach.[17]

Following a "pleasure ride" to Greenwood and back, the first train departed for Madison. The Reverend Henry Ward Beecher, who rode it, described his car as "a mere extempore wood-box, used sometimes without seats for hogs, but with seats for men, of which class I happened to be one."[18]

A new era was opened: "For the first time manufacture for other than domestic consumption became a possibility, and the agricultural products of the region became sensitive to the movements of outside markets. In a few weeks wheat advanced from 40 cents a bushel to 90 cents."[19] Homes, warehouses, and a brick Depot Hotel sprang up around the Indianapolis depot in an area previously unsettled outside the original mile square. The railroad prospered, with sixteen locomotives delivered by 1849.[20] Receipts climbed from $22,110 in 1843 to $60,053 in 1845 and $212,090 in 1848. They were to climb still higher, but changes in state legislation and corporate competition were also to bankrupt the road in 1852, an early victim of the continually changing railroad environment.

In 1849 the 16-mile Shelbyville Lateral Branch Railroad was completed between Shelbyville and the Madison and Indianapolis at Edinburg. Work was begun on four other lines, including one renamed from an original 1832 charter and three chartered between 1847 and 1849. Many more were chartered, primarily with the prospectus of connecting the Indiana interior with navigable water. As Victor Bogle summarizes the period:

> When the railroad fever first hit the Hoosier State, waterways were the accepted mode of transporting bulky materials over long distances. The initial purpose of the railroad was to supplement the waterway system. Since the state's population was weighted toward the Ohio River, towns along its banks had a

strong priority as terminals for the earliest chartered roads. Of the hundred or so authorized before 1850, twenty-five were to have points on the Ohio as one of their terminals. Almost this many more were to touch the Wabash and Erie Canal, while others were to tie in the northern portion of the state with the natural waterway supplied by the Great Lakes. A few of the more ambitious routes, most notably the one to be followed by the New Albany and Salem Railroad, attempted to link all three of these east-west waterways.[21]

The 1850s: The Railroad Explosion

By late 1849 Indiana had completed barely over 100 miles of railroad. By March 19, 1851, however, the *Indiana State Sentinel* reported that "the cars were running on two hundred and forty-five miles of railroad in Indiana, and it was expected that five hundred miles would be in operation by the end of the year."[22] After decades of frustration, the 1850s saw a remarkable burst of activity. Concentrated primarily in the first half of the decade, Indiana achieved a rail network covering the entire state, linked to the East Coast, the Great Lakes, and Chicago. Indiana became a railroad state, and the railroad became the central fact in Indiana's growth and development. In a real sense, all subsequent additions were just to fill in the framework created in the remarkable burst of construction in the 1850s.

Railroad construction proceeded outward from existing railroads or waterways. From Shelbyville, railroads opened to Knightstown (26 miles) and Rushville (18 miles) in 1850. From Franklin, a line opened to Martinsville (26 miles) in 1852.[23] From Indianapolis lines headed north and northeast. The Peru and Indianapolis, heading for a canal connection at Peru, was completed to Noblesville by March 1851. The Indianapolis and Bellefontaine Railroad opened to Pendleton in 1850, Chesterfield in 1851, and Muncie by mid–1852. By the end of December 1852, its tracks were completed to Union (now Union City) on the Indiana-Ohio state line, to meet an Ohio connection underway from Dayton.

Canals were the supply lines for the railroads which would ultimately replace them. Starting in Lafayette in 1851, the Lafayette and Indianapolis reached Indianapolis in 1852, with rails and locomotives delivered from the East on the recently completed Wabash and Erie Canal.[24] The Crawfordsville and Wabash Railroad, building 26 miles

between Crawfordsville and a Wabash River landing one mile south of Lafayette in 1851–52, probably received its sole locomotive by canal as well. The Terre Haute and Richmond began construction in 1851 with two locomotives delivered at Terre Haute by canal and two more at Indianapolis arriving from the East via canal to Cincinnati, via river from Cincinnati to Madison, and via railroad from Madison to Indianapolis.[25] By May 1852, the line was continuous between Indianapolis and Terre Haute, 73 miles.[26]

From the Ohio River at New Albany, the New Albany and Salem completed 35 miles to Salem in 1851, followed by 20 more to Orleans the same year. From nearby Jeffersonville, the Jeffersonville Railroad built 26 miles of track from the Ohio riverbank to Vienna in 1851, reaching Columbus (and competition with the Madison road) in the fall of 1852.

Northern Indiana, after years of fruitless effort, received rail connections in the 1850s from two competing Michigan projects, the Michigan Central from Detroit and the Michigan Southern from Monroe, with a connection to Toledo. Both railroads had begun under the Michigan Internal Improvements program, aiming to connect their respective terminals with Lake Michigan. By the 1850s both of them had redefined their target as the rising new community of Chicago, but to reach Chicago both Michigan roads had to cross Indiana.

As early as 1835 an Indiana legislator had proposed a charter for a grandly named Atlantic and Pacific Railroad, and the company had been formally organized May 25, 1835, as the somewhat more modestly named Buffalo and Mississippi.[27] As with many other projects, sufficient funding had not been raised, but the company was still alive in 1851, its charter rights now confused with two newer companies, the Northern Indiana (to build east from La Porte), and a separate Northern Indiana in Ohio, presumably with the same mission to build west from Toledo.

The Michigan Central, already stretching from Detroit across Michigan to New Buffalo by 1849, extended its line into Indiana at Michigan City by October 1850. Negotiations with the New Albany and Salem permitted the Michigan Central to build across northen Indiana on the NA&S's charter in return for financial aid to the latter road. While these negotiations were underway the Michigan Central's rival, the Michigan Southern, building from Toledo, reached the Indiana state line about ten miles east of Elkhart by late summer 1851.

Working in Indiana, the Michigan Southern promoters acquired the charters of both the Northern Indiana and the Buffalo and Mississippi.[28] Concerned at being left off the route, Goshen supporters of the former Buffalo and Mississippi secured the promise of a branch line from Elkhart in return for the charter transfer. By October 1851, the Michigan Southern had built 25 miles in Indiana to reach South Bend, and by the following year had added the obligatory 10.1-mile branch to Goshen.[29]

The two Michigan rivals prepared to race to Chicago. The Michigan Central built west around the Lake Michigan shoreline, while the Michigan Southern struck west from Elkhart through La Porte. In late February 1852, the Northern Indiana and Chicago completed the Michigan Southern's entrance into Chicago over five miles of track owned jointly with the Chicago, Rock Island and Pacific. Three months later the Michigan Central's line entered Illinois, for a connection with the Illinois Central into Chicago. Northern Indiana was now connected by rail to the east and to Chicago. Construction now started south from Michigan City on the northern end of the New Albany and Salem. By December of 1852 much of the grading between Michigan City and Lafayette was in place, and 30 miles of completed track stretched almost a third of the way to Lafayette.

Public support for railroads continued during the 1850s, but the emphasis shifted from state to local level. Despite the prohibition on state financing of private corporations, public aid at the local level continued and expanded. In 1851 Allen County citizens authorized the county commissioners to raise $100,000 to purchase stock in the proposed Ohio and Indiana Railroad. The needed money would be raised by sale of county bonds with interest paid through property taxes.[30] Other cities and counties supported railroads as well:

> Particularly after 1845, the promoters of a large number of railroad projects appealed for aid to the interests of competing cities and counties. Sometimes these pleas were rejected—Indianapolis's Marion County, for example, voted against a subscription to the Madison road—and the sums involved were not so great as they were to be in later decades. Yet before the Civil War, railroad aid was given by some sixteen counties and ten cities, to an amount that may be estimated at about $1,750,000. This local aid made a significant contribution to the rapid development which gave to the state more than 2,100 miles of railroad in 1860 and which had already fulfilled the ambition of an early

governor to make Indianapolis the "Radiating Rail Road City."[31]

By the end of 1852 Indianapolis was connected to the Ohio River at Madison and Jeffersonville, to the Ohio border at Union City, to Terre Haute, and to Lafayette, with another line heading north toward the canal at Peru. Crawfordsville and Lafayette were linked by rail, and the New Albany and Salem project was moving north from the Ohio and south from Lake Michigan. Two lines linked the northern part of the state with Detroit and Toledo to the east, and with Chicago to the west.

Railroad construction in Ohio strengthened Indiana's ties to the East. In July 1853, the Bellefontaine and Indiana, stretching east from Union City on the state line, completed a chain of roads from Indianapolis to Cleveland and the East. By December 1853, the Indiana Central was completed from Indianapolis to Richmond and the Ohio line, with connections to Dayton. Forming a continuous railroad chain from Dayton to Terre Haute, it made redundant a long piece of the National Road.

The 27-mile New Castle and Richmond, completed in 1853, became the first link in a Chicago-Cincinnati route diagonally across Indiana. By October 1853 Indianapolis was linked to the Ohio River at Lawrenceburg with the completion of the Lawrenceburg and Upper Mississippi Railroad (renamed in 1850 from the Rushville and Lawrenceburg). A locomotive had been delivered by boat at Lawrenceburg in September 1852, and crews building west had met those building east somewhere west of Shelbyville. The completed line was immediately renamed the Indianapolis and Cincinnati, though it would not enter Cincinnati until the following year.

Unable to secure a trackage rights agreement over the M&I, the Jeffersonville began building a parallel line to the M&I between Columbus and Indianapolis, and by late 1853 had built ten miles from Columbus to Edinburg before the M&I conceded to share its monopoly and grant trackage rights from Edinburg to Indianapolis. The 23.8-mile Columbus and Shelby Railroad also opened from Columbus in 1853, competing with the 1849 Shelbyville Lateral Branch Railroad and leading to its abandonment—the first route in the state to be permanently abandoned.

In 1853 the New Albany and Salem reached Bedford and Bloomington. From Michigan City the

NA&S reached Lafayette, creating, with the 1852 Lafayette and Indianapolis, a continuous line of rails from Indianapolis to Lake Michigan and Chicago.

In 1854 the Peru and Indianapolis was finished to Peru. The New Albany and Salem project was also completed, the longest railroad in the state to date, 288 miles from New Albany to Michigan City under a single corporate ownership. Evansville was connected by rail in November 1854, when the Evansville and Crawfordsville opened between Evansville and Terre Haute. For the first time the railroad was directly supplanting a waterway, for Evansville, Vincennes, and Terre Haute all were open to steamboat navigation. The railroad also offered direct competition for the Wabash and Erie Canal, whose extension from Terre Haute to Evansville had only opened the year before. Poorly built and lightly used, the canal between those cities would only last until 1860 in the face of railroad competition.

The Wabash and Erie Canal aided its new rival one more time in 1854 when it delivered the first locomotive in Fort Wayne for construction on the Ohio and Indiana Railroad from Crestline, Ohio. Part of a chain of railroads receiving financial assistance from the growing Pennsylvania Railroad, the completion of the Ohio and Indiana to Fort Wayne in October 1854 linked northern Indiana to the East Coast by rail for the first time, and marked the first incursion of what would become the Pennsylvania System into Indiana. The initial purpose seemed to be to extend on westward to Peoria and Burlington, Iowa, but the destination was soon changed to the growing rail junction of Chicago.[32]

In southern Indiana, construction was underway by 1854 on the great Ohio and Mississippi project, intended to shorten the distance between Cincinnati and St. Louis by about one-half compared to the circuitous water route. A Cincinnati-built locomotive arrived at Lawrenceburg by flatboat for early construction, and by April of 1854 a bridge across the Miami River connected Lawrenceburg by rail to Cincinnati. Shop facilities were established outside Aurora, Indiana, and by June 6 the rails were already in Seymour, one-third of the way across Indiana. The Miami River bridge also afforded a rail connection for the Indianapolis and Cincinnati, previously terminated at Lawrenceburg. The connection was plagued by the recurring gauge problem, since the new Ohio and Mississippi had chosen a 6' gauge, not yet shared by any railroad in any of the three states through which it would operate.

The Indianapolis and Cincinnati laid a third rail from Lawrenceburg into Cincinnati on the O&M, with the I&C to share one-fifth of their through traffic receipts with the O&M.

By the close of 1854 over 1,400 miles of railroad were in operation in Indiana. Indiana ranked fifth in completed railroad mileage.[33] This completed perhaps the most remarkable four years in Indiana railroad history, dramatically changing the state from an isolated rural economy to one directly linked both internally and to outside markets by rail.

Railroad building in the later 1850s was slowed by the financial panic in 1857, but nevertheless saw the addition of a third and fourth line across the state to Chicago and three lines completed to St. Louis. By 1855 the Lake Erie, Wabash and St. Louis was completed from Toledo to New Haven, Indiana, and by 1856 the railroad paralleled the Wabash and Erie Canal all the way to Lafayette. Canal towns became railroad towns as terminals and yards were constructed in Fort Wayne, Peru, and Lafayette. By late 1855 packet lines ceased to operate on the canal and by 1857 canal boat clearances at Fort Wayne and Lafayette were only one-fourth of those in 1854.[34]

In 1856 a connection between Indianapolis and St. Louis opened when the Terre Haute and Alton completed its line between Terre Haute and the Mississippi River at Alton and across from St. Louis. In southern Indiana the broad-gauge Ohio and Mississippi built its final 65 miles in Indiana, from Mitchell to Vincennes, in 1857, and opened the entire 340 miles from Cincinnati to the Mississippi river bank opposite St. Louis the same year. A grand excursion left Baltimore June 1, 1857, with celebrations all along the line commemorating the so-called American Central Route between Baltimore and St. Louis.[35] Although advertised as a through route, the excursionists, like the passengers and freight who would follow, had to contend with three different railroad gauges, a river crossing by ferry, and a carriage ride between stations across Cincinnati, not to mention the final river crossing at St. Louis.

Still building west, the Wabash completed its connection from Lafayette across Illinois to St. Louis in late 1857, opening a third Indiana connection to that city.[36] In northern Indiana, the chain of roads encouraged by the Pennsylvania pushed on toward Chicago. The Fort Wayne and Chicago, incorporated in 1852 to extend the work of the

Ohio and Indiana, built 19 miles of line from Fort Wayne to Columbia City by 1856. Consolidated and reorganized as the Pittsburgh, Fort Wayne and Chicago Railroad Company in May 1856, it pushed on to Plymouth, halfway across the state, by the end of the year. Two years later the line was in Chicago, reaching Chicago December 25.[37] In March of 1858, with the completion of a bridge in Pittsburgh, a complete through line of rails now existed from Philadelphia to Chicago. Although viewed as a feeder to the expanding Pennsylvania system, the connection was not yet secure, as events after the Civil War would demonstrate.

The existing Northern Indiana Railroad, part of a line from Toledo through South Bend to Chicago, opened a shorter second route between Toledo and Chicago, connecting to the 1852 spur line between Elkhart and Goshen. By May 1856, now formally titled the Michigan Southern and Northern Indiana Railroad, the line was completed to Butler, Indiana.[38] By early 1857 it was completed through Noble County.[39] By 1858 it was open throughout from Toledo to Elkhart, commonly known as the Air Line Route to distinguish it from the nine-miles-longer "Old Road" between those two points.

With the exception of the New Albany and Salem line between the Ohio and Lake Michigan, the bulk of new construction in this decade was oriented east and west, as the growing eastern railroad network reached out across Indiana en route to the western gateways at Chicago and St. Louis. Besides the NA&S only two major north-south lines were initiated during this decade, and neither was completed. Both sought to link Cincinnati and Chicago. From the north, the Cincinnati, Peru and Chicago proposed to build a 220-mile road from a point on the Indiana border near Chicago to Cambridge City, where connection would be made to another projected line to Cincinnati.[40] Incorporated June 23, 1853, the CP&C opened 28 miles of 4'10" gauge track in 1855, connecting the Michigan Southern and Northern Indiana at La Porte with the Fort Wayne and Chicago at Plymouth. Further construction ceased until after the Civil War.[41] From the south another railroad with similar professed intentions was reaching northwest across Indiana toward Chicago. From Richmond, already on the Indiana Central line to Indianapolis, the Cincinnati and Chicago Railroad extended the line of the New Castle and Richmond on to Logansport by 1857, but did not complete a connection to Chicago. This and the east-west oriented Air Line in

northeastern Indiana were the last major construction in Indiana of the 1850s.

By the eve of the Civil War, 71 of Indiana's 92 counties had rail connection with the outside world. Instead of isolated lines linking city and waterway, Indiana was part of an interconnected northeastern railroad network. Benefiting by her strategic location, Indiana was connected to Chicago, St. Louis, Louisville, Cincinnati, Columbus, Detroit, Toledo, Pittsburgh, and Buffalo. Continuous lines of rails extended to Philadelphia, Baltimore, and New York. Canals and waterways were no longer important. The railroad was to be the driving force in Indiana's economy. As summed up in a Fort Wayne newspaper: "There can be no place justly entitled to the appellation 'city' unless she has a Railroad, and now that Fort Wayne has a completed Railway, this with her vast wealth, her central position, her water power, manufacturing facilities and fertility and extent of adjacent territory, and her population of 8000 justly entitles her to the name."[42]

Indianapolis as a Hub

Stimulated by the arrival of the Madison and Indianapolis in 1847, Indianapolis emerged as the first major city whose growth depended entirely on railroads rather than water transportation. From 1840 to 1850 Indianapolis population tripled (2,692 to 8,091), overtaking Madison (3,798 to 8,012) and pulling almost even with New Albany (4,226 to 8,181). From 1850 on there would be no contest, as the capital with its new inland transportation far outstripped the older river towns. By September 1849, an Indianapolis newspaper, the *Locomotive,* was advocating that the city should be known as "The City of Railroads."[43] By the end of 1853 Indianapolis was the hub from which seven railroads radiated, reaching the Ohio River in three places, the Wabash in two, and the borders of both Ohio and Illinois.

A factor in this success was the linking of the railroads via the Indianapolis Union Railway in 1850, and the opening of the first Union Depot in the country in 1853, allowing convenient transfer of passengers from train to train at a single facility. In this Indianapolis was well ahead of other cities such as Cincinnati, where local merchants felt that trade would prosper if railroads were forced to unload and reload their cargoes and passengers. For years both passengers and freight had to connect in Cincinnati via wagons through the city streets.

The original Madison and Indianapolis depot faced on South Street, then $1/4$ mile outside the settled district. In the spring of 1849, with the Peru and Indianapolis and the Indianapolis and Bellefontaine both commencing construction from Indianapolis, the question of depot facilities became a public issue. The new roads converged at the northeast corner of the Indianapolis land donation (now the corner of Massachusetts and 10th). From there, the two roads proposed to lay a track through the central part of town, along the streets. Objections were raised, and a citizens' meeting was held at the courthouse on March 3, 1849 "to discuss the propriety of admitting a track to be laid within the city proper."[44] The Peru and Bellefontaine roads agreed the following month to run a common track south "through Noble's pasture," outside the eastern boundary of the built-up area, and then to curve across the National Road and down along Pogue's Run to a connection with the Madison Road, through the unbuilt and irregularly laid out southeastern corner of the original town plat. They sought and were granted permission to straighten Pogue's Run, and by late 1849 had effected a connection with the Madison Road.

By this time a meeting of joint committees from the Madison, the Bellefontaine, the Peru, and the newly proposed Terre Haute and Richmond had agreed on the desirability of a more formal connection. By the end of 1849 the joint committee had purchased a site for a new "Union Depot," two blocks northwest of the original Madison Depot, on the south side of Louisiana Street and inside the original town plat. Tracks were laid in 1850, and the depot opened for use September 28, 1853. It was a brick structure 120 by 420 ft., and five tracks ran lengthwise through its interior. The Madison, Terre Haute, Lawrenceburg, and Central (from Richmond) lines each had an individual track, while the Bellefontaine and Peru roads shared a track.[45] The tracks converging on the depot now formed a railroad corridor along Louisiana Street and along Pogue's Run, lined by the individual freight depots and engine facilities of the various roads. The Bellefontaine road at first went its own way, with a brick depot and shops built in 1851 in the northeastern part of the city, reached by a track down the diagonal of Massachusetts Avenue. This was sold in 1853 and new freight and engine facilities were built along Pogue's Run, convenient to the Union De-

pot. The Lafayette and Indianapolis, not mentioned in the allocation of Union Depot tracks, entered Indianapolis at its northwest corner, and built a freight depot at North Street and the canal in 1852–53. A connecting track was later built south along the canal and Missouri Street, one block inside the original town boundaries, to reach the Louisiana Street railroad corridor and the Union Depot.

The basic railroad geography of Indianapolis was established. As later roads arrived after the Civil War they appended themselves to the armature of lines established in 1849–53, and radiated outward, with their respective yards and engine houses at various locations outside the central city. Freight houses remained centrally located until they were abandoned in the 1970s and 1980s, and the successor to the 1853 Union Depot still survives in its new guise as a festival marketplace and hotel. With minor subtractions the railroad corridors established by 1853 still exist in central Indianapolis, although the Lafayette road's connection along the canal, long since replaced as a through route, was removed in the 1980s as part of the canal and state office reconstruction project.

TECHNOLOGY, ARCHITECTURE AND INNOVATION

As railroads were built, an entire technology was being invented, often out of necessity. Trained engineers were few, and the limited English precedents seldom applied in a country of vast unpopulated distances rather than existing cities and markets. The period from 1830 to the Civil War saw initial decisions about location and construction which would shape the railroads for the remainder of their existence.

Routes and Alignment

Early railroads emulated canals in seeking level alignments for horses or locomotives, interspersed with short inclined planes analogous to locks on the canal. It was believed that locomotives could not draw loads uphill, and inclined planes permitted cars to be drawn uphill by cables and stationary power. Planes were used on the Baltimore and Ohio, the Philadelphia and Columbia, the Mohawk and Hudson, and the Lexington and Ohio in the early 1830s. In Pennsylvania the Allegheny Portage

Railroad used planes to cross the backbone of the Alleghenies.

The Madison hill in Indiana, with its 5.89% grade and its straight but costly alignment, followed the inclined plane model, although stationary engines were never installed. The timing was ironic. Four months after surveys were let on the Madison line, a Norris locomotive, the George Washington, successfully surmounted a 7% inclined plane near Philadelphia with a small payload, demonstrating the railroad's ability to deviate from the water level-with-planes alignment of the canal builders.[46] Had the lesson of the George Washington been available, the search might have been made initially for an alignment suitable for locomotive haulage, and the Madison hill track might never have been built. As it was, the hill was early recognized as a mistake, and $309,479 was spent between 1852 and 1855 in an attempt to build a new 4.75-mile entrance to Madison bypassing it. One of the two tunnels initiated on this unfinished line was actually bored through and can still be seen near Madison in Clifty Falls State Park.[47]

Fortunately for the engineers, Indiana's topography generally did not pose challenges equivalent to the Madison hill. Easy grades and alignments were generally available, although some alignment decisions would later haunt the railways, prompting costly rebuilding. A few railroads, like the White Water Valley (1860s), were doomed as through routes by the sharp curves they inherited along with their canal right-of-way, placing them at a disadvantage in speed and capacity.

Unlike British railways, which were typically built with two tracks at the outset (one for each direction), Indiana railways, like most early American railways, were built with a single track for economy. Trains were scheduled to meet each other at specific sidings, with complicated rules to deal with late trains or other irregularities. Operations were facilitated when telegraph lines were built along the railroads. Used at first for commercial messages only, telegraph train orders were first sent on the Erie Railroad in 1851, and by 1853 the Madison and Indianapolis had begun using telegraph orders to expedite train movements. The telegraph increased the capacity of single-track lines, and before the Civil War only the most heavily traveled railroads found it necessary to add additional tracks. The Lake Shore line had just begun double-tracking between Elkhart and Chicago by 1857.[48]

Gauge and Track

Early railroads were seen as self-contained links between two cities, or between a city and a waterway. Even when railroads connected, cars and locomotives remained on the individual railroads, while passengers and freight changed. Management procedures were not yet in place to handle the interchange of equipment, and technological incompatibility among different roads often made it impossible. Chief among these problems was track gauge (width between inside railheads). Early tramways in England and the U.S. followed a variety of gauges, but by 1830 the majority of British railways had settled on 4'8½" as a standard, one which was copied in the U.S. by the fledgling Baltimore and Ohio and by other eastern railroads.[49] South of the Ohio River, however, 5' gauge predominated. New Jersey railroads followed a 4'10" gauge, as did early Ohio railroads anticipating connections to the East and New Jersey.[50] In 1848 the state legislature of Ohio made 4'10" the official Ohio gauge, though not all railroads conformed.[51] The Erie Railroad, built across New York State, adopted the odd gauge of 6', in part to preclude connections which might divert traffic to other states.

In Indiana, the Madison and Indianapolis and its connections were built to the 4'8½" standard, as were the Lafayette and Indianapolis and the Indianapolis and Bellefontaine. In 1855, however, the I&B changed its gauge to 4'10" to accommodate a connecting Ohio line.[52] Across southern Indiana, the Ohio and Mississippi operated a 6' gauge, shared at the time only by the Erie Railroad.[53] Although not critical in an era when passengers and freight routinely changed trains anyway, the gauge differences epitomized a range of technological differences which would have to be sorted out as the rail network matured after the Civil War.

Early English and American track sometimes used stone "sleepers," supporting cast iron rail segments. Kentucky's Lexington and Ohio, opened in 1832, used longitudinal limestone sills with a strap-iron running surface.[54] Timber, however, soon became a more widely used alternative. In Indiana the Shelbyville demonstration line, opened in 1834 without benefit of trained engineers, was constructed of "timber of various kinds, six by eight inches, and twenty feet long, and completely covered with earth."[55]

The Madison road, when opened in 1838, was

Early builders sometimes were forced to overcome rough terrain. This was Little Tunnel, one of 18 in Indiana, two miles west of Tunnelton, Lawrence County. The broad-gauge Ohio and Mississippi Railroad, now CSX, built it in 1857, but daylighted it in 1899.   *Lester Sloan—Robert F. Smith collection*

built as one would build a barn frame, with a continuous line of 10 x 10" timbers buried in trenches, connected by 6 x 8" cedar crossties at intervals of four feet.[56] The ends of the crossties were framed into the longitudinal timbers, and fastened to them by locust pins.

Buried timbers, or timbers overlaid with crossties, were subject to rapid deterioration. By 1832 Robert Stevens in New Jersey developed the simpler system of using crossties alone, with rail directly attached, placed in a bed of dirt or (preferably) stone for drainage, and held in alignment by the rails themselves.[57] The track structure floated in its bed, and required constant realignment, but was simple and cheap to build. It gradually became the standard, but the reliance on lengthwise foundation timbers evidently continued at least until 1849, as illustrated by a report of the Indianapolis and Bellefontaine chief engineer:

I have provided for ballasting the entire road with gravel to the depth of one foot, upon which longitudinal sills 3x12" will be placed under each rail throughout the entire track. Upon those sills, cross ties $7\frac{1}{2}'$ long, or large enough to square six feet, will be placed at an average distance of three feet from centre to centre. Upon the cross ties the iron will be secured in the ordinary way by chairs and spikes, the track to be filled with gravel to the tops of the cross ties.[58]

Railroad rails themselves were of iron, either "bar" rails or T rails. Bar rails were flat strips of iron—usually 5/8" x $2\frac{1}{2}$", spiked through holes in their face onto longitudinal timbers. The rail was simply a bearing surface, with structural strength offered by the support timber. T rails, invented in 1830 by the resourceful Mr. Stevens, combined a rounded railhead with a thinner web for vertical rigidity, and a flat base to spread weight to the crosstie.[59]

Bar rail was cheap but troublesome; prone to curl under the weight of the rolling wheels, work loose, and writhe upwards in potentially lethal "snakeheads." After a bad accident in 1844 one Michigan road attached iron plates to the bottom of cars to prevent snakeheads from impaling the passengers. Despite its faults, bar rail was often economically necessary. The Madison and Indianapolis began with T rail, but when state construction gave way to private building after 1843, the line was completed to Indianapolis with 21-lb. bar rail in short lengths.[60] An 1839 European visitor, having visited the Madison and Indianapolis as well as other completed American roads, defended the cost advantages of the bar rail, provided that speeds would be limited to 12 or 15 mph.[61] The Peru and Indianapolis was completed from Indianapolis to Noblesville in 1851 with strap rail, to be replaced with 50-lb. T rail in 1856. Forty-five miles of the New Albany and Salem were laid with bar rail, to be replaced in the 1850s by T rail.[62]

When they could afford it, Indiana railroads preferred T rail. The Indianapolis and Bellefontaine was built with T-rail on the main track, but bar rail on sidetracks.[63] President Smith of the Indianapolis and Bellefontaine Railroad estimated the cost of the 83 miles of road "ready for the cars" as ... $8,700 per mile for the T rail or $5,953 per mile for flat bar.[64]

Iron rail was often imported from England. The Madison and Indianapolis was laid initially with T rail weighing 45 lbs. to the yard, imported from Wales, and delivered upriver to Madison from New Orleans.[65] The Indianapolis and Bellefontaine used 60-lb. rail, also imported via New Orleans. The Lafayette and Indianapolis began construction at Lafayette in 1851 with 55-lb. wrought iron rail from Wales, delivered from New York through the Erie Canal, Lake Erie, and the Wabash and Erie Canal.[66]

Locomotives

By the time Indiana entered the railway age, the steam locomotive was accepted as the standard motive power for railways. Indiana's first railroad, the 1834 demonstration line at Shelbyville, was horse powered, but the officers already recognized the advantages of steam:

> The road in every respect is calculated for the use of locomotive power—and the speed and cheapness of that power over every other, will no doubt occasion it to be adopted on this road as it has on almost every other of any extent in the United States and in Europe. It would, therefore, be proper at once to save the expense of a horse path. This is estimated to cost three hundred dollars per mile, and supposing the road to be ninety miles long, twenty-seven thousand dollars may be saved. A sum sufficient to procure all the locomotive power necessary for a long time. And it will likewise supersede the outlay of capital that would otherwise be necessarily invested in horses. In addition to these advantages, if steam alone should be used, the intermediate space between the rails need not be so entirely filled with earth as is required by the horse path, and thus the rails, at least, may be made to last many years longer than they would do were they brought into immediate contact with the earth.[67]

It is possible that some of the officers had even seen a steam locomotive by this time, for two mechanics, Joseph Bruen and Thomas Barlow, had built a miniature steam locomotive in Lexington, Kentucky, in 1826 or 1828. Large enough to pull a car and several passengers, it was exhibited in Louisville and throughout Indiana and Ohio.[68]

The Madison road opened in 1838 with locomotives, although horses handled cars on the Madison hill until 1847. The Elkhorn, the first steam locomotive on Indiana rails, was British, a Planet-class locomotive, built in 1836 by Robert Stephenson of England for the Lexington and Ohio Railroad in Kentucky. Based on a prototype built for the Liverpool and Manchester in 1830, it was a popular design in England and was copied by early American locomotive builders. A simple four-wheeled design, its two axles were mounted in a rigid wooden frame. The front axle, with wheels about 3' in diameter, was not powered. The rear axle, with driving wheels 5' in diameter, was forged like a modern crankshaft, and driven by rods from two steam cylinders mounted between the front wheels.[69] It probably weighed about eight tons.

The rigid Planet design was successful on track built to solid English standards, but was less suitable on hastily built and undulating American track. The solution, found by an American designer in 1832, was to substitute a flexible four-wheeled swiveling truck in place of the rigid front axle of the Planet. The resulting 4–2–0 locomotive was better suited to uneven American track, and quickly became popular. The Baldwin Locomotive Company, after starting with a Planet copy in 1832, quickly adopted the new design, which remained popular through the 1830s. The Madison and Indianapolis' second and third locomotives, like the one originally ordered but lost at sea, were Baldwin 4–2–0 engines. Delivered in 1839 and 1841, they were named the Madison and the Indianapolis respectively. They powered the M&I for its first three years.

The 4–2–0 design, while flexible, was limited by its single driven axle. The next evolutionary step was to add another driving axle, creating a more powerful 4–4–0. First developed in 1837, the design quickly so dominated American locomotive practice that it became known as the "American Standard" or simply "American" type. Of the 25 locomotives reported owned by the Madison and Indianapolis by 1855, most were 4–4–0s.[70] The 4–4–0 predominated on other Indiana roads for which we have pre–Civil War records, augmented by an occasional 4–6–0 with smaller drive wheels for heavy freight. The majority of early Indiana locomotives were from eastern builders, including Baldwin, Rogers, Norris, Mason, and Hinkley.[71] At least 39 were from Cincinnati, however, where five separate locomotive builders flourished between 1845 and the panic of 1857.[72] Cincinnati-built engines were ordered by the M&I, Indianapolis and Cincinnati, Ohio and Mississippi, New Albany and Salem, Peru and Indianapolis, and Evansville and Crawfordsville.[73] Apparently, no locomotives were built in Indiana before 1860, although a locomotive firm was established in Aurora, Indiana, perhaps in conjunction with the O&M shops located there.[74]

The Madison and Indianapolis, with its vexing inclined plane, replaced horses with two cog-wheel locomotives in 1847 and 1850, both of 0–8–0 design. One set of cylinders drove the eight powered wheels, while a second set, placed vertically over the boiler, were connected to a cog wheel which engaged the rack rail in the center of the track. Expensive to maintain and and prone to disastrous failure, the system lasted until after the Civil War.[75]

Early locomotives were not expected to be fast. An 1856 timetable for the New Albany and Salem shows an express and a freight in each direction daily. The express took 16 hours to cross Indiana, averaging a little more than 15 mph. The freights took 30 hours southbound and 35 northbound, averaging about 10 mph. They beat the freight wagons and canal boats, and that was the point.

Cars

The first freight cars for the M&I came from the East via New Orleans. They were four-wheel affairs with a five-ton capacity, or 25 to 30 hogs.[76] The first passenger coach, built by Thomas L. Paine & Son in the fall of 1838, was about 30' long and very plain, with hand brakes controlled by levers.[77] The M&I set up its own car shops in North Madison, which provided the majority of the M&I equipment as well as building for other roads in the Midwest. Freight cars were simple wooden structures, easily built by local carpenters using wheels, axles, and other castings from outside suppliers. Four-wheeled cars soon gave way to eight-wheeled, riding on a flexible four-wheeled truck at each end. As with the evolving locomotive designs, the flexible truck cars proved better suited to uneven track than the rigid four-wheelers.

By 1852 M&I passenger trains were carrying express cars and an elaborate ladies' car in addition to ordinary coaches.[78] Crude sleeping cars, first introduced in Pennsylvania in 1837, were available in Indiana in the 1850s. In 1858 a sleepless night in one such car crossing Indiana may have inspired a Chicago contractor named George Pullman to perfect the improved sleeping car which would bear his name following the Civil War.[79]

Depots and Facilities

Early American railroads appropriated existing buildings or designs for their depots, while groping for an architecture better suited to their unique functional requirements. Unlike the stagecoach, which could pull up to the door of an inn, the train required a platform for boarding several cars at once, plus shelter for passengers waiting to board.

The most distinctive depot type to emerge before the Civil War was the "train barn," a rectangular building with one or more tracks entering through an end door and running the length of the building interior. This design probably originated with English prototypes. At a period when American railroads were importing British rail and locomotives, and when England was the recognized leader in railroad technology, it is not surprising that English designs should have inspired American imitations.

The first depot in Indianapolis was a modified train barn design, with an interior track used for unloading freight cars, while passengers boarded from a track alongside the building, protected by wide overhanging eaves. The Indianapolis *Locomotive* described it as follows:

> The depot house is brick, substantially built; the first building is 50 feet square and two stories high. This is occupied as offices, rooms for clerks, board of directors, ladies sitting room, & c. It is finely finished and is a handsome looking house. The ware-house extends 350 feet from the front building, and is 50 feet wide; this building is brick, with a covered roof—the eaves extending about ten feet beyond the walls on each side, affording protection from the sun and rain. The cars run through the centre of the entire building, and in the ware-house, on either side of the cars, is ample room for storage.[80]

In Indianapolis, the railway opened its first depot on the south side of South Street, between Pennsylvania and Delaware and separated from the settled part of town by Pogue's Run. A two-story brick office and waiting room fronted on South Street, with a 350-foot-long brick freight shed extending south. A track for freight cars ran the interior length of the building, while passenger trains stopped to one side. Broad eaves extended ten feet on either side of the freight station to provide shelter.[81]

The first Indianapolis depot of the Lafayette road was also of this type. The Indianapolis Union depot, opened in 1853, was a notable train barn example.

A brick structure, 120 x 375 feet, it contained five separate tracks running the length of the interior, each designated for use by a specific railroad.[82] It lasted until 1887. The New Albany and Salem built a number of brick train barn–style depots. One, at Gosport, remained in depot use until the 1970s. Remarkably, the original New Albany depot, constructed about 1850, survived until 1995, though long out of railroad service.

Locomotive repair and maintenance created a need for other unique railroad structures. Smoke from the engines soon made it apparent that the engines should be housed somewhere other than in the depot, and the need to turn the locomotives at the end of their trip quickly led to the turntable, a wooden or iron bridge structure capable of pivoting around its center. Since early locomotives were short, the turntable was seldom longer than 50 feet, and could be accommodated within the building structure. Individual tracks or "stalls" radiated from the turntable. Records are not clear on early engine depots, so we cannot say for sure when these were first used in Indiana. Both New Albany and North Madison acquired enclosed "roundhouses," as these came to be known, but probably not until after the Civil War.

3

Expansion and Consolidation: 1860–1900

O N OCTOBER 19, 1874, Baltimore and Ohio construction crews building their new railroad through northwestern Indiana reached the Michigan Central Railroad at Willow Creek (present-day Portage) in Porter County. Although they held court orders permitting them to cross the Michigan Central at grade, the B&O workers and officers, and the Porter County Sheriff, were met by ditches, barricades and a large force of armed men, and by Michigan Central trains stoutly obstructing the crossing point. Unable to disperse the men or arrest their leaders, the sheriff called for help from Indianapolis. The next day, under protection of Indiana militia and Gatling guns dispatched by Governor Hendricks, the B&O was finally able to complete its crossing and reach its Chicago destination without bloodshed.[1]

Though bloodless, the Willow Creek battle epitomized Indiana railroading after the Civil War. No longer a publicly promoted "internal improvement," railroads were now aggressive private companies vying to expand and dominate. Indiana's rail network was largely completed in this era, while still changing rapidly in technology and organization. Railroad names and alliances changed so often that by 1893 the *Official Guide of the Railways* felt compelled to list, in 11 pages of closely packed small type, the names of 2,300 *former* railroad companies in the U.S. Unquestionably the dominant transportation force in Indiana, railroads totally supplanted both canals and roads for intercity transportation. Railroads and cities grew together, and Indiana developed an industrial base to match its agricultural beginnings.

By 1900 rail lines served all but three Indiana counties. Two of these, Switzerland and Ohio counties, would never see rail lines. Both were on the banks of the Ohio, well favored by river transportation, but they became transportation backwaters in

the age of railroads. By the turn of the century few areas in Indiana were over ten miles from a rail line. The rail network was far more integrated physically and economically than in 1860. Physical links were completed, including bridges across the Ohio and Wabash. Railroads were standardized. A uniform track gauge and compatible standards for wheels, couplers, and brakes permitted cars to move from one system to another, and accounting practices encouraged car interchange rather than reloading freight at the boundaries of each railroad's property. New "fast freight" lines and sleeping car companies provided equipment which traveled freely among railroads. Standard operating rules permitted railroad labor itself to move more freely from one line to another, and gave rise to the "boomer," the itinerant railroad worker who moved from line to line as whim and traffic demands dictated. For railroad labor it was a time of organization and struggle, with epic strikes which reverberated through Indiana and the East generally.

Growing railroad networks fostered the growth and transformation of Indiana, and tied its economic fortunes more tightly to the national economy. A historian has noted: "In general, the early railroads commercialized existing local economies and broadened them into regional economies. They largely accomplished this in the 1850s. After the Civil War the railroads forged the regional economies into a national one."[2]

Natural resources, like coal or limestone in southwest Indiana and natural gas in east central Indiana, were exploited and developed by expanding rail lines. Belt lines within Indiana cities opened new sites for industrial expansion. City maps of this period show a profusion of rail spurs cutting through the street gridiron to support factories and stockyards. The railroads were the lifeline that tied local economies to the nation. In some cities the railroads were themselves the economy, and communities vied for the location of railroad repair shops and division points.

THE CIVIL WAR

The Civil War demonstrated the strategic importance of railroads to the Union victory. Supplies from northern industries could readily reach the armies in the field, and the armies themselves, if necessary, could be rapidly repositioned by rail. On at least five occasions Union Army regiments of 450 or 500 men were transferred across Indiana on the Ohio and Mississippi.[3] In 1863 Indiana railroads participated in the movement of 20,000 men from the Army of the Potomac to the aid of Union forces at Chattanooga. The troops rode railroads of three different gauges, and marched across the Ohio River twice on temporary pontoon bridges. Entering Indianapolis on the Indiana Central from Columbus, Ohio, they marched across town to trains of the Jeffersonville, Madison and Indianapolis, and were delivered to Jeffersonville for another march across the river to Louisville and more waiting trains. The entire army, including 100 carloads of equipment and ten batteries of field guns, was transferred from the East to Chattanooga in 11 days—four less than planned. They were followed a few weeks later by an army payroll of $2,000,000 in cash, packed in a heavy wooden box and shipped as a regular express shipment between Cincinnati and Louisville on the O&M and JM&I.[4]

President Lincoln himself rode by train through Indiana en route to his inauguration in 1861. Leaving Springfield, Illinois, he changed trains in Lafayette and arrived in Indianapolis to be greeted by a crowd of 30,000 and a 34-gun salute honoring the 34 states in the Union. He left Indianapolis the next morning, his 52nd birthday, on the Indianapolis and Cincinnati Railroad, making short speeches at Shelbyville, Greensburg, Batesville, and Lawrenceburg on his way to Cincinnati and Washington.

Four years later Lincoln returned, a martyred hero, on perhaps the most epic train journey in American history. On a special train operating under military orders, his slow cortege retraced much of the inaugural journey, greeted by throngs of mourners. In New York it was estimated that three quarters of a million people followed his procession from Union Square to the railroad depot. On some divisions the same engines and engineers that

had pulled his train to Washington pulled him home to Springfield for burial.

The "long black train" entered Indiana on the Indiana Central from Columbus, Ohio, at 3 A.M. on April 30, 1865. In Richmond, where it was reported that 10,000 people stood bareheaded in the rain to watch, the governor and a party joined the train. At Indianapolis by 7 A.M. Lincoln's casket was removed to the State Capitol where thousands could pay their respects. At midnight the journey resumed over the Lafayette and Indianapolis to Lafayette, leaving there at 4 A.M. over the Louisville, New Albany and Chicago to Michigan City. Through the night, residents of town after town turned out to watch the train. In Westville, Indiana, a historical marker, erected 100 years after the event, states simply: "On Monday, May 1, 1865, shortly before 8 A.M., the train bearing the body of President Lincoln stopped briefly at this site." The train arrived in Michigan City through an arch of evergreens, and then turned west over the Michigan Central toward Chicago. The railroads that had taken Lincoln to Washington, and that had helped him preserve the Union, were taking him home to Springfield.

NEW CONSTRUCTION, 1860–1899

In 1862, spurred partly by the need to cement the western states to the Union cause, Congress voted land grants and loans for the construction of the transcontinental railroad. With the Civil War over, officers and soldiers alike turned from fighting to railroad building. When the rails of the Union Pacific and the Central Pacific met at Promontory Summit, Utah, in 1869, a new railroad boom period had started:

> The furious construction pace set by the transcontinentals proved contagious, and within two years, after a rapid and steady growth, the new mileage of railroad put in operation during the single year was more than 7,300. During the panic of the early seventies, however, new construction slowed down to a mere 1,700 miles in 1875.
>
> In the latter half of the decade, as the country gradually recovered from the depression, construction of new mileage kept pace with the general revival. In 1882 a new peak was reached: in 12 months more than 11,500 miles of new line had been opened. From that record total there was a sharp drop the following year to about 6,600 miles, itself a figure which would have seemed phenomenal a dozen years before. The

The Reuben Wells, named for its designer, was the first locomotive to work the Madison Hill without cog wheel assistance. The heaviest locomotive in the world when built by the JM&I shops in Jeffersonville in 1869, it is now displayed in the Children's Museum in Indianapolis. *Drawing from the British journal* Engineering, *Feb. 12, 1869*

rapidity with which the country's railroad system developed is emphasized by the fact that whereas in 1865 there was one mile of track in operation for every 1,000 of population, twenty years later there was one mile for every 450 of population. While the population of the country has, very roughly, doubled, the railroad mileage had approximately quadrupled.

Partly because of the rapid growth that had already taken place, partly for other reasons, in the late eighties and early nineties construction of new mileage again diminished. By 1893 the total mileage of the country was 176,461 and the railroads stood ready to serve beyond the economic capacity of the country to support such service adequately.[5]

New railroad construction in Indiana followed these national peaks and slumps from the Civil War to the panic of 1893, after which little was added until the turn of the century. Indiana mileage increased from 2,163 miles in 1860 to 3,177 in 1870 and 4,454 in 1880.[6] General patterns of construction may be traced from decade to decade.

1860—1869

Little construction occurred during the war years. The Evansville and Crawfordsville built from Terre Haute to Rockville in 1860 but could get no farther. On the opposite side of the state the Cincinnati and Indianapolis Junction entered Indiana as far as Connersville in 1862 before stalling until after the war. From 1860 to 1866 state railroad mileage grew by only 54 miles.[7] The "Junction" and its subsidiaries were able to push from Connersville west to Indianapolis by 1869, and from Connersville north to Muncie by 1869. From Indianapolis the Indianapolis, Crawfordsville and Danville pushed west to Danville, Illinois, by 1867, and the Indianapolis and Vincennes connected its named cities by 1869. The Ohio and Mississippi built a branch from North Vernon into Jeffersonville in 1869. Across northern Indiana the Chicago and Great Eastern and other roads built a connecting series of lines from Union City, Ohio, all the way to Chicago in 1867 and 1868, all of which were consolidated in 1868 into the Columbus, Chicago and Indiana Central.

1870–1879

The 1870s saw an intensification of the rail network in northern Indiana, further connections across state lines including the first bridge across the Ohio to Kentucky, and initial rail development of the coal fields of southwestern Indiana. Most projects were completed before the financial panic of 1873.

The Baltimore, Pittsburgh and Chicago was completed across northern Indiana in 1874 and the Peninsular Railway, subsequently the Chicago and Lake Huron, was built from Michigan as far as Valparaiso in 1873.[8] A series of north-south connections was built in northern Indiana. The Evansville, Terre Haute and Chicago connected Terre Haute and Chicago, and formed friendly connections to Evansville as part of what would later be called the Evansville route. The Fort Wayne, Jackson and Saginaw, the Grand Rapids and Indiana, the Cincinnati, Richmond and Fort Wayne, the Cincinnati, Wabash and Michigan, and the Terre Haute and Logansport all built lines approximating their corporate titles, even if the Cincinnati connection was indirect. The same could not be said for the grandly named Lake Erie, Evansville and Southwestern, which managed little more than 17 miles of construction from Evansville to Boonville by 1873.

Two lines angled across northeastern Indiana, the Detroit, Eel River and Illinois, and the Toledo, Delphos, and Burlington. An additional line crossed the state from east to west, built by the Lafayette, Muncie and Bloomington in 1872 and 1876, and the Fremont and Indiana in 1879. Yet another intended cross-state line, the Cincinnati and Terre Haute, started construction at two ends, but by 1871 had built only 26 miles east from Terre Haute and 10 miles west from Greensburg. The

fragments were never connected, and both were later absorbed into projects with quite different purposes. It was typical of this entire period, when ambitions and speculation often outstripped the actual need for railroads.

Indianapolis, already well served, acquired only one additional line during this decade, when the Indianapolis and St. Louis opened in 1870 closely paralleling the earlier Terre Haute and Richmond between Indianapolis and Terre Haute.

Railroad construction in southern Indiana was sparse compared to that in the north. A branch was built to French Lick, Evansville was connected to St. Louis, and a start was made on construction east of Evansville, including the disconnected Cincinnati, Rockport and Southwestern from the river port of Rockport inland to Jasper. Completed in 1878, it was the last piece of line built initially as a feeder to water transportation. From this time on, every new piece of track would be added to the already existing network.

July 1871 saw the end of the broad gauge in Indiana, when the 6' gauge Ohio and Mississippi narrowed its line to standard. The Louisville Division, built only five years before, was narrowed in one day, followed a week later by the narrowing, in one day, of 340 miles of main line. This move toward standardization was shortly followed by the quixotic narrow-gauge movement, vigorously promoted in the 1870s as the low-cost alternative for railroad construction. The Toledo, Delphos, and Burlington, entering Indiana from Ohio in 1879, was built to a track gauge of 3'. It was originally promoted to form a connection with the 3' gauge Havana, Rantoul and Eastern, which had barely crept across the state line from Illinois in 1877, but the two lines would never meet. The Indianapolis, Delphi and Chicago was completed between Delphi and Rennsselaer in 1878, but never got close to Indianapolis until after its gauge had been widened to standard. The 3' gauge Bedford and Bloomfield, built through the hills of southern Indiana in 1877, came closer to approximating the conditions under which a lightly built line might make sense, but in Indiana, as in the rest of the country, the narrow-gauge movement was an aberration in a system which was striving for uniformity and integration.[9]

Contraction of the money supply, overextension of rail mileage, the political scandals of the Grant administration, and the collapse of the investment banking firm, Jay Cooke and Company, triggered the panic of 1873. This six-year depression lasted longer and was more intense than any that America had yet suffered. Railroad construction slowed, unemployment approached the 3 million mark, and hundreds of businesses failed. Rate wars, followed by wage cuts for railroad labor, led to the Great Strike of 1877, focused on the lines of the Pennsylvania Railroad. In Pittsburgh, state militia fired on strikers, killing 20 and unloosing a riot which destroyed 104 locomotives, 2,000 railcars, and the PRR depot and roundhouse. In Chicago street fighting between police and workers killed 40 to 50 people. Ten died in Baltimore. Federal troops, moving into city after city, finally imposed calm, but the country was shaken both by the specter of labor as a potentially revolutionary force, and by labor's realization of the powers arrayed against them.[10]

1880–1889

Three lines were completed to Chicago: the Chicago and Grand Trunk Railway in 1880, the New York, Chicago and St. Louis in 1882, and the Chicago and Atlantic in 1883. The first was a consolidation of short lines which had been operating as the Chicago and Lake Huron, plus 30 miles of new construction west of Valparaiso. The Chicago and Atlantic was the western outpost of the Erie Railroad System, while the NYC&StL, soon nicknamed the Nickel Plate, provided a friendly connection at Buffalo for the Lackawanna and the Lehigh Valley. From Evansville the Evansville and Indianapolis was diverted from its Indianapolis intention and headed toward Brazil in 1885, forming connections with lines built variously by the Chicago and Great Southern, the Chicago and Indiana Coal Railway, and others, reaching as far as La Crosse for a connection with the Chicago and West Michigan, finished in 1882, which reached New Buffalo, Michigan.

Indianapolis received two new connections to Chicago. The Cincinnati, Lafayette and Chicago was completed in 1872 from Lafayette to Kankakee, Illinois, with trackage rights into Chicago over the Illinois Central. The second link was the completion in 1883 of the Chicago and Indianapolis Air Line Railway, crossing the Louisville, New Albany and Chicago, with which it immediately merged, at the small town of Monon.

The 1880s saw the high water mark of the narrow-gauge movement in Indiana. The Toledo, Cincinnati and St. Louis built a narrow-gauge line from Frankfort west to St. Louis in 1882, acquired the connecting Frankfort and Kokomo, narrowed it

from standard to narrow in 1881, and put on narrow-gauge express trains between Toledo and St. Louis in the summer of 1883. Part of the so-called Grand Narrow Gauge Trunk, the last completed link in a 1,642-mile line projected from Toledo, Ohio, to Laredo, Texas, was finished in August 1883, only to see the system collapse in foreclosure.[11] On June 26, 1887, the narrow-gauge line from Toledo to Frankfort was converted to standard gauge, followed in 1888 and 1889 by widening the line from Frankfort to East St. Louis. In 1895 the former Bedford and Bloomfield was widened, and the last vestige of the misguided narrow-gauge era disappeared.

The Louisville, New Albany and St. Louis was completed across southern Indiana in 1882, picking up and connecting existing lines to reach Evansville, Rockport, and Cannelton. A minor connection off the LNA&StL, the Louisville, New Albany and Corydon was also finished in this decade. Of all the railroads built in Indiana during the 1880s, the seven-mile-long LNA&C is unique as the only one still operating under its original name in 1996!

1890–1899

Fewer lines were added in the 1890s, and those mostly in the years before the depression of 1894. In 1890 the Evansville and Richmond, falling short of Richmond, opened 101 miles of line between Elnora and Westport in southern Indiana, to be linked in 1900 from Elnora to Terre Haute. In 1891 the Cincinnati, Wabash and Michigan built 38 miles of line between Anderson and Rushville, filling the last gap in a line from North Vernon to Benton Harbor, Michigan. In 1893 the Wabash constructed yet another east-west line across northern Indiana, linking Detroit and Chicago. In 1894 the Indiana, Illinois and Iowa Railroad, already in place from Kankakee to North Judson, extended its line from North Judson to South Bend, creating an outer belt bypass around Chicago between the New York Central lines at South Bend and the Santa Fe at Streator, Illinois. Other additions in this decade were short, like the Elkhart and Western, completed in 1893 from Elkhart to Mishawaka.[12]

LINE IMPROVEMENTS

Although overshadowed by the miles of new construction, railroads were also beginning to upgrade

The Coe Adams, an American-type (4–4–0) built in 1874, was the first locomotive on the Frankfort and Kokomo Railroad. The road was converted to narrow gauge in 1881 and reconverted to standard gauge in 1887. *Richard S. Simons collection*

their earlier construction, correcting mistakes where possible and investing in line improvements to better handle the increasing volume of traffic. Most of these improvements were incremental—filling in a trestle, replacing track and bridges. By 1890 the entire Lake Shore & Michigan Southern was doubletracked, and third and fourth tracks were added in many locations by the turn of the century.[13] Some improvements involved new line construction. An example was the 1875 cutoff around Lawrenceburg built by the Indianapolis, Cincinnati and Lafayette, shortening the through route by six miles and reducing the original line to a branch into Lawrenceburg.

The CCC&StL—the Big Four—built a bypass around the southern city limits of Anderson in the early 1890s, including a new yard at the crossing of the Cleveland Division (Cleveland-Indianapolis) and the Michigan Division between Louisville and Benton Harbor, Michigan. The new line was almost a mile shorter than the original Bellefontaine line route through Anderson, but passenger trains continued to use the old route to reach the passenger station downtown. Between 1891 and 1894 the Louisville, Evansville and St. Louis built its shops one mile south of Princeton, Indiana, served by a new bypass line around the city.[14]

The Monon made numerous improvements at the end of the century. On January 3, 1898, the CI&L incorporated a subsidiary, the Indiana Stone Railroad Co., to build 9.4 miles of new main line along Clear Creek south of Bloomington. Two miles longer than the original main line through Smithville, the new route reduced the grade against traffic from 83 feet per mile to 26.4 feet.[15] It was completed September 1, 1899. An 1897 study recommended substantial rebuilding of the poorly built line between Hammond and Monon. Construction which followed eased a number of curves but required a 963-foot-long floating wooden trestle across a bog just south of Cedar Lake.[16]

Competition for passenger traffic to the 1893 World's Columbian Exposition in Chicago stimulated some improvements. In 1893 track pans were first installed on each of the four main line divisions of the LS&MS, as well as on the Michigan Central. Track pans had first been used in the East in 1870, and permitted suitably equipped locomotives to scoop up water without stopping. Dramatic and expensive to maintain, they illustrated the competitive lengths to which railroads were willing to go to speed their premier schedules.[17]

CONSOLIDATION OF THE BIG SYSTEMS

The post–Civil War era saw the rise and dominance of a few large systems in Indiana, replacing a multiplicity of locally promoted and financed projects. The Pennsylvania System and the New York Central System, through multiple subsidiaries, spread their networks in competitive fashion throughout Indiana through construction or acquisition. Eastern carriers like the B&O, the Erie, and the Canadian Grand Trunk extended their systems, each sending one or more lines from the Eastern Seaboard across Indiana in search of western connections. A group of midwestern carriers— the Lake Erie and Western, the Wabash, the Nickel Plate, the Clover Leaf, and the Chicago and Eastern Illinois—established their niches in between, and sometimes in competition with, the dominant systems. North and south through the state went Indiana's own railroad, the Monon, while in the interstices of the system were those hopeful, optimistic, or downright hopeless properties built during the surge of construction from 1865 to 1900.

It was an era of frequent and bewildering corporate realliance and change, but the dominant pattern was the amalgamation of small railroads into larger ones. As Allen Trelease has noted, "In 1850 hardly any railroad could afford to build or operate a line more than 200 miles long. In 1880 hardly any railroad could afford not to. Those that could not grow were absorbed by those that could."[18]

Until shortly after the Civil War most railroads had been local corporations, owning at most a few hundred miles of track which often connected with other lines at the terminals. But in 1869 Cornelius Vanderbilt gained control of the Lake Shore and Michigan Southern; he united it with his New York Central and thereby formed a through trunk line from the Atlantic seaboard to Chicago and the West. As noted by a corporate historian:

> The advantages to be derived from having a long trunk line under one ownership, rather than controlled by several separate and diverse interests, soon became manifest and a new era had begun. The larger companies quickly expanded their systems by absorbing smaller roads. The history of the Pennsylvania system in the eighties typifies this phase of development. In 1880 the system represented an amalgamation of forty-four smaller companies, operating 3773 miles of track. During the next ten years 29 more companies were absorbed, at least one every year and never more than four in any single year. Through these acquisitions by 1890 the parent company had increased its mileage to about 5000.[19]

By the 1890s, following a period of bewildering name changes and alliances, the outlines of the big systems had become apparent in Indiana—systems which would remain essentially intact for the next half century. The 1893 *Official Guide of the Railways* indicates many names that would remain recognizable until 1960. Grouped together in the Guide were the constituent parts of the Vanderbilt empire, including the New York Central and Hudson River, the Lake Shore and Michigan Southern, the Michigan Central, and the Cleveland, Cincinnati, Chicago and St. Louis Railway, all of which but the first served Indiana. The competing Pennsylvania system included the Pennsylvania Railroad System east of Pittsburgh, and two components making up the Pennsylvania Lines west of Pittsburgh. The "Lines West," as they were often called, included the lines operated by the The Pennsylvania Company, notably the Pittsburgh, Fort Wayne and Chicago Division, and the separate lines of the Pittsburgh, Cincinnati, Chicago and St. Louis Railway

Company focused on Indianapolis, Richmond, and Logansport. Separate vassals of the Pennsylvania empire were the Vandalia line (west of Indianapolis and from Terre Haute to South Bend) and the Grand Rapids and Indiana north from Fort Wayne.

In this era the Baltimore and Ohio had completed its own line to Chicago and acquired the Ohio and Mississippi to St. Louis (soon to be merged with the existing Baltimore and Ohio Southwestern). The Chicago and Erie was part of the Erie Lines, while the Wabash, Chicago and Grand Trunk, Louisville and Nashville, Elgin, Joliet and Eastern, and Monon were all in recognizable mid–twentieth century form. The New York, Chicago and St. Louis existed, as did the Lake Erie and Western and the Toledo, St. Louis and Kansas City. Although the latter two would disappear into the NYC&StL in 1922, they were still colloquially separated for decades after that.

Unfamiliar names in 1893 include "The Evansville Route," an amalgamation of four roads in western Indiana. Only one of these, the Chicago and Eastern Illinois, would still exist in 1950, in a changed configuration. With the exception of the C&EI, most major systems in Indiana in 1893 remained easily recognizable for the next 70 years, before disappearing in successive waves of late twentieth century mergers.

THE CHANGING PUBLIC ROLE: FROM PUBLIC ACTION TO PUBLIC SUBSIDY

Railroad expansion after the Civil War was the province of private capital, though often assisted by local bond issues. The state role in Indiana railroad development was terminated with the failure of the 1836 Improvements Act. Following financial collapse in the 1840s, Indiana adopted a constitutional provision barring state aid to railroads, but this did not apply to counties or municipalities. Federal land grant support for railroads, although active in Michigan, Illinois, and throughout the West, did not exist in Indiana. County and local governments were the active supporters of railroad projects in the decades after the Civil War, both through direct subsidies and through the loan of public credit to railroad enterprises. "Between 1865 and 1875 subscriptions or donations were ordered in eighty-nine municipal or county elections, and similar action was taken by forty-three townships and two cities

between 1876 and 1886, with the total voted exceeding $6,000,000."[20] Indeed, local subsidies continued into the twentieth century, with North Judson and Peru both voting aid for the approaching Cincinnati, Richmond and Muncie by 1902. The motive, as Goodrich has noted, was survival and commercial competition, winning for the community a place in a railroad network whose broad outlines were determined by the private corporations. Prospective railroads would often canvass the route, surveying or suggesting multiple routes until communities vied to support the line.

Financial contributions could literally be a matter of life or death for the community which was served or bypassed, but the contributions did not constitute public planning in the same sense as the 1836 Internal Improvements program.[21] In some cases local contributions were seen as direct stimuli to local employment. In 1876, when the proposed Indianapolis Belt Railway project was stalled following the financial panic of 1873, the mayor of Indianapolis delivered a message to city council, advocating that the city undertake the work. As he later wrote, it would "not only furnish work for our laboring population during the savage year of 1876 but also relieve our streets. It would also bring here an immense cattle business and lay down a great taxable property."[22] Work was commenced with the loan of $500,000 of the city's credit. When a land dispute stalled construction again in 1877, the mayor again took action to restart it in the midst of a threatened "bread or blood" demonstration by unemployed workingmen and their wives.[23]

In Indiana the decision, following the bad experience of the 1840s, was for public bodies to simply subsidize, but not to own, the private railways. Indiana concurred with most other states in this, although there were exceptions. Nearby Cincinnati, hampered by an 1851 Ohio Constitution prohibiting public support for private corporations, proceeded to build the Cincinnati Southern Railway to Chattanooga as a public corporation.[24] Authorized in 1869 and finally completed in 1880, the railway's 334 miles were almost entirely outside the bounds of Ohio. In North Carolina, the state-owned North Carolina Railway remains public property to this day, although leased to the Norfolk Southern and its predecessors ever since 1871.[25] Indiana remained committed to private initiative and public support with little accompanying public oversight. In fact, during the late nineteenth century, as the movement grew for railroad regulation, Indiana was one of the last to take action, not establishing a state railroad commission until 1905.

TECHNOLOGY, ARCHITECTURE, AND INNOVATION, 1865–1900

The post–Civil War era moved railroad technology from its earlier experimental stage to a mature and sophisticated standard. It also saw the advent of standardization in gauge, equipment, and operations, permitting the railroad network to function as an integrated physical network even though comprised of multiple competing owners.

Railroad Gauge

Railroad track gauge was an obvious candidate for standardization. With four different track gauges in Indiana by the Civil War, it was obvious that the network could not be truly unified. Troop movements during the war were hampered, and postwar movement of freight would be increasingly limited by this physical discrepancy. When the Pacific Railway was authorized by Congress in 1862, its gauge was set at 4'8½"—the dominant gauge in the North. When the Confederate states, with their preponderance of 5' gauge lines, were defeated three years later, the stage was set for national uniformity of gauge, opening the way for physical integration of the railroad system.

So long as speeds were low, minor differences in track gauge could be accommodated using wheels with unusually wide treads. Freight cars of the new "Fast Freight" lines were fitted with these wheels, as were special movements like Lincoln's funeral train. Wider gauges—5'0" and 6'0"—were beyond the reach of compromise wheels and required an actual change of wheels. Locomotives and passenger cars were not likely to leave their own systems and posed no problem.

By 1869 large portions of the unique "Ohio gauge"—4'10"—were narrowed, leaving mostly the trivial difference between 4'8½" and 4'9".[26] The Ohio and Mississippi, with its isolated 6' gauge system, was narrowed in 1871, only seven years after finally becoming part of a continuous 6' gauge system between New York and St. Louis. The O&M's entire 340-mile main line was narrowed in a single day by 2,727 men, divided into 68 teams, each responsible for five miles of track.[27] In 1880 the Erie itself, originator of the unique 6' gauge, succumbed

to necessity and narrowed its tracks to standard. When the Erie subsequently built across Indiana it was as a standard-gauge railroad.

Connections to the south opened another gauge problem. The Ohio River bridge at Jeffersonville, completed in 1870, opened a through route for its two owners—the standard-gauge Jeffersonville, Madison and Indianapolis and the 5'0" gauge Louisville and Nashville. A steam hoist system in Louisville lifted each car arriving from Indiana so that its own trucks could be removed and replaced with wide-gauge trucks for travel farther south.[28] A similar system on the L&N served Evansville, which was linked to Kentucky by a bridge in 1885. The actual transfer of trucks was quick, but it imposed a massive inventory problem keeping track of each car's original trucks and reuniting them with the car when the cars returned to their own system. The problem was finally solved when the L&N, in concert with other southern 5' gauge roads, narrowed 2,000 miles of its line to standard on a single day in 1886.[29]

By the 1890s the gauge problem was essentially solved. Although the *Official Guide to the Railways* still felt compelled to identify the gauge of each railroad in 1893, the vast majority were either 4'8½" or 4'9". In Indiana the Pennsylvania system components were the main 4'9" holdouts, but the nominal half-inch difference was not a deterrent to interchange. With the formation of the American Railway Engineering Association around 1893, the 4'8½" standard was generally accepted.[30]

Steel

A major technological change in the post–Civil War era was the shift from wood to iron, and later from iron to steel, in many areas of railroad construction. Throughout this period wooden bridges were regularly replaced by metal. The Terre Haute and Richmond, which had built a wooden bridge across the White River in 1851–52, replaced it with iron in 1866.[31] The White Water Valley Railroad had built a series of wooden truss bridges in 1867; these were replaced with iron truss bridges by the end of the century, with the replacements themselves largely hand-me-downs from other lines being upgraded.

Steel replaced iron for new railroad rails shortly after the Civil War. By the end of the century steel had largely replaced iron for locomotive and structural production, and was poised to replace wood for car body production. Iron rails were subject both to wear and to deformation, a problem exacerbated by heavy Civil War traffic. By the early 1860s the Pennsylvania Railroad was replacing rails on some sections every six months. Steel, a harder and more durable metal, became available as an alternative after the first Bessemer steel plant was built in 1860 in Sheffield, England.[32] Steel was twice as expensive as iron initially, but lasted eight times as long. In 1863 the Pennsylvania Railroad ordered 150 tons of new steel rail for trial in areas of heavy traffic, and by 1873 some 627 track-miles of steel rails weighing 67 lbs. per yard had been laid on Pennsylvania main lines.[33] Already, some 25 other American railroads were also using steel in quantity.[34]

Success prompted domestic steel production, beginning in 1867. The Cambria Iron Works entered steel rail production in 1871, followed by Andrew Carnegie's new high-production Pittsburgh plant in 1875. From that time on, rail imports became insignificant, and the railroads and the new American steel industry marched in tandem. The price of steel fell below that of iron in 1883 and virtually superseded it thereafter. By 1880 30% of the nation's track mileage was steel, climbing rapidly to 80% in 1890.[35]

Indiana railroads followed suit. By 1875 the Indianapolis, Cincinnati and Lafayette had $27\frac{1}{2}$ miles of steel rail, and was laying more.[36] By 1895, rail replacements eliminated the last iron rails on the Monon in Indiana.[37] Within that time frame most of Indiana's railroads switched from iron to steel, beginning with the main lines and trickling gradually down to the branches and the side tracks.

Steel also became the preferred structural material for bridges. The Eads Bridge across the Mississippi at St. Louis, opened in 1874, was the first major steel span in the U.S. By the turn of the century steel had replaced both iron and wood as the most economical material for bridges. It was also poised to replace wood in railroad car construction, although that revolution did not take hold until after 1900.

Locomotives

From the Civil War to 1900, the most prevalent locomotive design remained the 4–4–0 or American Standard for general service, supplemented by the 2–8–0 or Consolidation type, introduced in 1866, for heavy freight service. The Pennsylvania alone built 800 class R 2–8–0s starting in 1885, and all but the smallest of Indiana roads had their share for freight service. Other common engine types introduced during this period included the 2–6–0 or Mogul type, typically used on lighter and faster freight trains than the 2–8–0, and the 4–6–0 or "tenwheeler" type, built with both large driving wheels for passenger service and small ones for freight.

The American type continued as the typical all-purpose engine on smaller railroads, and dominated the passenger business until well into the 1890s. A star of the 1893 Chicago World's Fair was the New York Central and Hudson River Railroad's 4–4–0 No. 999, which had created a sensation in May 1893 by reaching a speed of 112.5 mph between Batavia and Buffalo. With high 86" drive wheels meant for speed rather than power, the 999 was a purpose-built racer. Its clean-lined design illustrated an evolution in locomotive esthetics as well as function. Victorian decorations and excesses were replaced by an elegant and balanced simplicity, lasting for only a few years into the early twentieth century. Although subsequently modified, the 999 still demonstrates some of this elegance at the Museum of Science and Industry in Chicago.

The heyday of the 4–4–0s was almost over by the 1890s, as heavier trains demanded more power and steam capacity. The LS&MS 4–4–0s heading the new Exposition Flyer, a fast 19-hour train between New York and Chicago in 1893, were the last of that type to be ordered by the road. Among the 62 locomotive exhibits at the World's Fair were three ten-wheelers (4–6–0s) ordered for Indiana railroads. In 1899 16 Brooks ten-wheelers were introduced by the LS&MS on fast passenger trains across Indiana. At 86 tons each, they were then among the heaviest express engines in the world.

In addition to purchases from commercial builders, some railroads built locomotives in their own repair shops. The Jeffersonville shops of the JM&I built 28 locomotives between 1860 and 1881, including the Reuben Wells, a 0–10–0 tank engine designed specifically for the troublesome Madison hill. Weighing 55 tons, the Reuben Wells was the heaviest engine of its day when finished in 1868, and survives today in the Indianapolis Children's Museum.

Railroads also pursued standardization of engine designs, unlike the earlier practice of buying unique individual engines from a variety of builders. In 1868 the Pennsylvania Railroad prepared designs for eight standard classes of locomotives for passenger, freight, and switching service, each des-

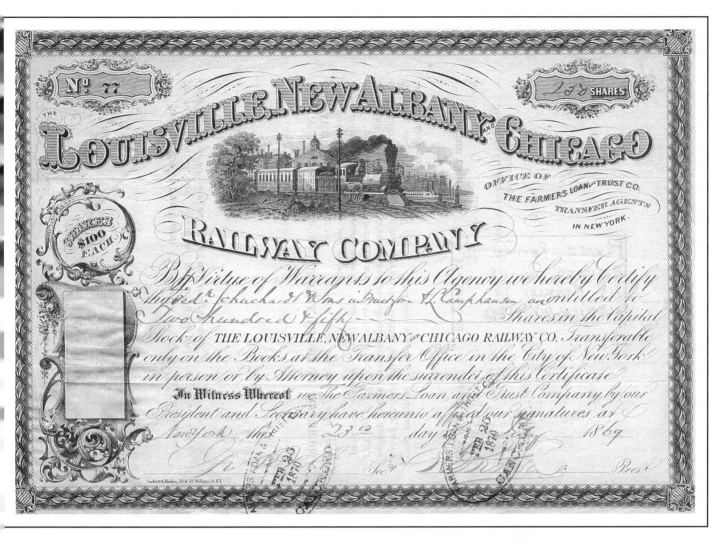

This Louisville, New Albany and Chicago Railway certificate of 1869 confirms the transfer of 258 shares of stock, valued at $100 each. The road, later the Monon, operated as the LNA&C between 1869 and 1897.
Richard S. Simons collection

ignated by a letter of the alphabet.[38] Engines built to these designs were ordered from outside builders or built in the company's own shops, including those at Fort Wayne and Logansport. Between 1867 and 1897 the Pittsburgh, Fort Wayne and Chicago company shops in Fort Wayne built a total of 321 locomotives of various standard designs. The Columbus, Chicago and Indiana Central, under lease to the Pennsylvania's Pittsburg, Cincinnati and St. Louis Railway, built locomotives in Logansport, Indiana, from at least 1874 to 1887, using plans (and possibly some castings) from the parent Pennsylvania RR shops in Altoona. A 45-ton 4–6–0 freight engine, built in Logansport in 1882 to a standard

Pennsylvania freight design, survives today in a museum in Baltimore, the second of only two Indiana-built steam locomotives to survive.[39] The Wabash in Fort Wayne and the B&O in Garrett also may have built locomotives.

One thing the late nineteenth century locomotives had in common was the absence of any trailing wheels behind the drivers. Weight was carried primarily on the drivers, and the need to keep axle weights within the capacity of the light rails at the time limited the total weight of the locomotive. The capacity of the firebox was also limited by the narrow space available between the driving wheels. By the end of the nineteenth century a few wide fireboxes had been built by raising the boiler and firebox above the wheels, but this was only possible with low-drivered engines like the 2–8–0. A more promising innovation, the addition of a trailing truck, was slow to appear. Although Baldwin displayed a new 2–4–2 wheel arrangement at the 1893 fair, appropriately named the Columbia type, it did not become popular. The next step in locomotive evolution had to wait for the turn of the new century.

Cars

Freight and passenger cars grew in size from the Civil War to the turn of the century, and increased in variety and complexity. Throughout this period, however, basic car construction was of wood, augmented by iron truss rods as tension elements. Wheels, axles, and hardware were iron, but even in passenger and freight car trucks the bolsters and other structural elements were usually wood. The advantage of wood was ease of construction and repair. The disadvantage was rapid deterioration and structural weakness, but in an era of abundant wood, cheap labor, and short trains these were not major flaws.

The most common freight cars were the simple boxcar and gondola. The boxcar, with its sliding side doors, was the all-purpose carrier for everything from grain to machinery. The gondola, simply a flatcar with stakes supporting low sides and ends, could carry coal or rock, and with the addition of underbody doors or hoppers could be unloaded by gravity. In addition, more specialized cars were appearing. Stock cars with open slatted sides for ventilation carried livestock to the slaughterhouses of Chicago. Tank cars with a cylindrical tank on a flatcar carried the new petroleum products of Pennsylvania and Texas. Shortly after the Civil War the caboose appeared, with accommodations for the train crew and a distinctive cupola from which to watch the freight train for overheated journals or other problems.

The refrigerator car first appeared in Indianapolis in 1860, when a newspaper noted a car's arrival with five tons of fresh fish and fruits. It was reported that the car left with a load of fresh beef, and that several such cars were being built in Indianapolis under Lyman's patent for a local provision dealer.[40] George H. Hammond, the founder of the meat packing industry in Hammond, made his mark in railroad history in 1869 when his firm began to operate its own ice-cooled refrigerator cars to ship dressed beef.[41] The refrigerator car was the basis for centralization of meat packing in cities like Chicago, and for the viability of marketing fresh produce hundreds of miles from where it was grown.

The Janney or knuckle coupler was introduced in 1868, replacing the previous link-and-pin coupler, reducing slack action and break-in-twos in trains, and saving fingers for generations of trainmen to come. The Master Car Builders Association adopted the Janney style coupler as standard in 1882, paving the way for other industry standards to facilitate car interchange. The Westinghouse air brake, first demonstrated in 1869, was applied to all LS&MS passenger cars by the end of 1871.[42] Automatic air brakes for freight cars were applied starting in 1877, replacing the need for brakemen riding the car tops, permitting safer train control, and also permitting the operation of longer freight trains.[43] Like the knuckle coupler, it became an industry standard to facilitate interchange.

Railroad cars were built both by the railroads themselves and by outside builders, and constituted a substantial manufacturing activity in Indiana during this period. With car construction primarily of wood, freight cars could be constructed with the same skills needed for barn or wooden bridge construction. Critical castings and forgings, including the wheels, axles, couplers, and brake equipment, could be purchased, so cars could be assembled by even the simplest of facilities. Railroad car shops were constantly repairing wooden cars damaged by heavy loading, rough handling, wrecks, and simple weather and deterioration; often there was little to distinguish between the heavier repairs and simply starting over with a new car. Railroad repair shops were quite capable of building new railroad cars, and a number did. It was calculated that between 1882 and 1887, 12,823 freight cars were built by the Pennsylvania Railroad's Fort Wayne Shops.[44]

In addition to railroads themselves, a number of car builders were active in Indiana during this period. Some were small, like the Cambridge City Car Co. in that city from 1868 to 1871.[45] Others were larger, like the Indianapolis Car Company (1870–1900), with 45 construction stalls, each capable of holding two cars.[46] An entire neighborhood in eastside Indianapolis grew up around the company, which later moved to an extensive site on Hadley (later Kentucky) Avenue adjacent to the Indianapolis Belt Railway.

Two of the largest car companies were at opposite

ends of the state: Haskell and Barker in Michigan City, and the Ohio Falls Car Co. in Clarksville. Haskell and Barker began freight car construction in 1852, and by the time they incorporated in 1871 had already produced 15,000 cars. The company grew steadily. By 1910 3,500 men were producing 10,000 cars annually. With 34 buildings on 116 acres of land it claimed to be the largest freight car plant in the world.[47] It was sold to Pullman in 1922 and continued production, in steel, until 1971.

The Ohio Falls Car and Locomotive Company, founded in 1864, experienced financial setbacks and a disastrous fire in 1872. It was rebuilt by 1875, with a complex of at least 17 brick buildings on a large site. It produced thousands of cars for the rest of the century, and continued car production after its sale to American Car and Foundry in 1899. Although adapted to other uses the complex remains today, designated as the Ohio Falls Car and Locomotive Company Historic District.

Passenger Cars

Passenger cars, of largely wood construction, increased in size from the Civil War to 1900, with the development of six-wheel trucks for heavier cars, car vestibules in place of open platforms, and improved heating and ventilation. The majority of passenger cars were straightforward day coaches, baggage cars, or combination baggage-coach cars, but by 1870 sleeping cars were listed on a number of Indiana roads, including Pittsburgh to Indianapolis, Cleveland to Indianapolis, New York to Louisville (via Cambridge City), Columbus, Ohio, to Chicago and St. Louis, Cincinnati to St. Louis, and Louisville to Chicago. Parlor cars for day travel complemented the sleeping cars, and served as a de facto class distinction in a country which could not quite bring itself to designate cars by class. The first dining car, named the Delmonico, appeared on the Chicago and Alton in 1868. In November 1880 a dining car built by Pullman was added to the O&M's evening passenger train at Milan, Indiana, and carried into Cincinnati. It was said to be the first dining car to enter Cincinnati.[48]

Passenger car construction was more intricate than freight cars, and required skilled finish carpenters, but the same shops that produced freight cars generally produced passenger cars as well. An especially elegant example was built by the Pennsylvania's Fort Wayne shops in 1869:

One of the most elegant silver palace cars we have seen came to the city yesterday from the shops of the Pittsburgh, Fort Wayne, and Chicago Railroad Company, at Fort Wayne, Indiana, where it was built. The car is built on the Pullman patent and embraces all the latest improvements. The exterior is finished in magnificent style, painted bright and beautiful, and so highly finished as to faithfully mirror objects about it. The car rests on two staunch six-wheel trucks, supplied with the best of eliptic springs. . . . The bottom of the car has double flooring of heavy timber and lighter boarding running transversely. The floors are carpeted with the richest moquet in bright light colors, in keeping with the elegant upholstery of the silver armed seats. Along the ceilings are bars of silver the full length of the car, and here and there are ornamental designs in silver to please and relieve the eye. The lamps are all silver, and of fine cut glass. The entire woodwork is oiled black walnut, with gold trimmings. The windows are of fine plate glass, and between every pair is an adjustable table which can be set up firmly for writing purposes, reading, card playing or games between passengers vis-a-vis. The mirror between the windows is so constructed that by pushing a spring it disappears and a lamp in a neat little silver cove is brought.

The berths are perfectly arranged, and would seem to render a sleepless night impossible. Altogether the car is a gorgeous specimen. Mr. Wm. Wadington, the master builder of the Fort Wayne establishment, designed it, and superintended its construction. It cost about $18,000, and is intended to run on the Pacific Railroad.[49]

Although this "Silver Palace Car" did not run in Indiana, similar ones did, including cars built for the growing Pullman Palace Car Company. George M. Pullman had constructed his first custom-made sleeping car, the Pioneer, in 1864. As reported in the press of the era:

In 1867 Mr. Pullman formed the Pullman Palace Car Company and devoted it to carrying out an idea which he had conceived, of organizing a system by which passengers could be carried in luxurious cars of uniform pattern, adequate to the wants of both night and day travel, which would run through without change between far distant points and over a number of distinct lines of railway, in charge of responsible through agents, to whom ladies, children, and invalids could be safely intrusted.[50]

The Pullman Company evolved both as a builder of cars and an operator of cars. In 1880 it erected what was termed "the most extensive car works in the world" at the new planned industrial community of Pullman, 14 miles south of Chicago. In competition with Pullman was the Wagner Palace

Car Company, whose cars were used on the Vanderbilt railways, including the Big Four and LS&MS. Both Pullman and Wagner advertised the availability of special private, hotel, and hunting cars in the June 1893 *Official Guide,* but Pullman was eventually to triumph, the name becoming virtually synonymous with railroad sleeping cars for the next half century.

Passenger trains were brightly hued in the early post–Civil War years. Big Four trains in this era were painted orange, with deep maroon letter boards.[51] The New York–Chicago "Fast Mail" inaugurated on the LS&MS in 1875 used white cars with buff letter boards and gold lettering, and for years the road painted passenger cars a yellowish cream.[52] The Pennsylvania opted early for a darker and more practical Tuscan red. In the late 1890s the Wagner palace cars were painted chocolate brown, followed by coaches on the LS&MS. In 1898 it was reported that all passenger equipment of the NYC, Lake Shore, Michigan Central and Nickel Plate lines would be painted a uniform olive color with gold striping, a color which would dominate railroading until streamliners appeared in the 1930s.[53]

Interiors were ornate, with the fussiness of the early postwar "Silver Palace Cars" giving way in the 1890s to a simpler but more graceful esthetic. Wooden carbuilding appeared at its best in those private cars built for railroad executives and business tycoons, and one of the best of these survives today in Indiana. A private car built in 1898 for Henry Flagler, a founding partner of Standard Oil and developer of much of Florida's east coast, is displayed at the Indiana Transportation Museum in Noblesville. Restored to its original beauty, the interior is replete with satinwood-paneled walls and hand-carved white mahogany, with a fireplace in the dining room.

DEPOTS AND BUILDINGS

As railroads grew, they developed a range of specialized building types to meet their evolving needs. Most common of the railroad buildings, and most visible in the Indiana community, was the depot. The railroad depot was the point of contact between the railroad and the community, and the community's link to the outside world. It was the entry point for newcomers, the meeting point for those returning, and the place of arrival for the U.S.

mail. With its telegraph connections it was also the communication center for messages in an era before widespread telephone use.

Depots evolved into a range of customary types, tailored in size and function to meet specific community needs. These included simple waiting shelters, combination passenger-freight depots for small towns, and separate passenger and freight depots for larger communities. Most numerous in Indiana were the combination depots, typically 16 to 20 feet wide and between 40 and 60 feet long, depending on the expected volume of business. The combination depot was divided lengthwise into three rooms, with passenger waiting room and freight room at the two ends, separated by the agent's/operator's office. The roof, supported by ornamented brackets, had wide overhangs to protect waiting passengers. Most combination depots were wood, and styles reflected the domestic architecture of the period—simple Italianate designs with tall narrow windows and board and batten siding in the '70s and '80s, or more ornate Stick and Queen Anne styles in the '80s and '90s. A number of these depots have survived as museums or in private uses. Very few remain in railroad use.

A typical depot feature was the bay window in the office, where the operator's desk and telegraph key were located. A train order signal, usually a semaphore, was mounted outside and controlled by the agent/operator, who was simultaneously train operator, ticket agent, freight and express agent, and usually the commercial telegraph agent as well. As operator he (in a few cases, she) transmitted telegraph train orders from the central dispatcher to the train crews. Some orders could be picked up on the fly. One of the minor dramas of railroading was the sight of the operator poised at trackside with a message hoop raised as a speeding train bore down. Without flinching, the operator had to stand close enough to the train for an engineman to extend a gauntleted hand, scooping up the hoop and order. Repeated a second time for the conductor on the caboose, the performance was especially dramatic at night and was one of the pleasures of small-town depot watchers ensconced on the platform express wagon.

Towns of more importance, such as courthouse towns, rated separate passenger and freight depots. The passenger station might have separate waiting rooms for men and women (in practice the distinction was really between smoking and non-smok-

Indianapolis Union Station, with its distinctive Romanesque tower, replaced the original structure in 1888. A $30 million renovation in 1986 converted it into a festival marketplace, but by 1997 the city, by then the owner, was still seeking an economically viable long-term use.   *Indiana Historical Society, Negative 824*

ing), and might even aspire to internal plumbing. The passenger depot also included an express room or a small separate express building, since express shipments, along with baggage, rode on the passenger trains. Passenger depot styles followed those of combination depots, but were larger and more ornate. Separate freight depots had raised floor levels for easy access to boxcars. Purely functional, the freight depot often resembled a large combination depot with the office at one end. Sometimes former combination depots were relocated and converted to freight depots. Built on a heavy timber frame, it was an easy job to jack the building up, move it sideways onto a freight car, and transport it short distances along the tracks as needed.

Passenger, freight, and combination depots were needed in large numbers, and railroads in this era developed individual standards for them. The personality of each railroad was marked by its building styles as much as its equipment. A series of standard designs for the Pittsburgh, Cincinnati, Chicago and St. Louis "Panhandle Lines" were published in an 1893 reference book, and examples built to these plans still exist in Indiana.[54]

Less common depot types included the L-shaped "Junction" depot design found where two railroads crossed, with separate offices and freight rooms joined by a common waiting room where the two wings met. Other depots were combined with grain storage, where the railroad itself served as a grain collection agent, or were combined with hotels. A rambling two-story junction depot–hotel in Vincennes evolved to serve the O&M and Evansville and Crawfordsville, and even included a pool room!

Large city terminals, custom designed to fit circumstances, frequently comprised two separate structures, the depot proper—or "headhouse" containing the offices, waiting room, baggage facilities, restaurant, etc.—and the train shed covering the tracks and platforms. The two structures, although attached, often represented very different solutions. The train shed was a functional engineering solution while the headhouse was a more consciously "architectural" solution.

Indianapolis is a prime example. The 1853 train barn structure of the Indianapolis Union Station was replaced in 1888 by an imposing Romanesque headhouse, designed by Thomas Rodd, which survives to this day. Attached to it was an iron-arched train shed (since replaced), of very different design, covering the tracks on the site of the former train barn.

Other Railroad Structures

Railroads evolved other standard building types in this era. Interlocking towers, two stories high, sprouted at junctions and important control points. From his elevated vantage point an operator, using mechanical levers connected to long rods, could throw signals and track switches within several hundred yards of the tower. Mechanical interlocking mechanisms prevented clear signals unless track was properly aligned for a non-conflicting movements. Almost extinct in Indiana, the few active towers in 1997 include IU tower at Indianapolis Union Station, Hulman tower in Terre Haute, and State Line tower in Hammond. None of these structures dates from before the turn of this century, and it is doubtful if any late nineteenth century examples survive in Indiana.

Water tanks to serve the steam locomotive's huge thirst were located at frequent intervals along railroad lines, often near a depot or other stopping point. Usually of wooden construction, tanks were equipped with a spout for rapid discharge into the locomotive tender. Alternatively, a water tank might supply several standpipes through large diameter underground lines, each standpipe located at a probable locomotive stopping point. A characteristic accent in the steam-era railroad landscape, we know of no railroad water tank still standing in Indiana.

Roundhouses, the characteristic structures associated with steam locomotive servicing, were located at terminals and division points, and contained tracks radiating from a revolving turntable. Early turntables, no more than 50 feet long, could be housed entirely within a structure resembling a large round barn with a central clerestory. North Madison in early post–Civil War days had such a building, similar to one which remains today as the centerpiece of the Baltimore and Ohio museum in Maryland. As locomotives grew between 1860 and 1900, turntables became too long to contain within a building, and the roundhouse became a segment of a circle. At large terminals the roundhouse might completely surround the turntable, as in several Indianapolis roundhouses. In early years all engines were stored in the roundhouse. In later years its function was limited to engine servicing or light repairs. At smaller engine terminals a rectangular engine house might be separate from the turntable. A rectangular engine house from this period survives in Fort Wayne, but the surviving round-

A string of late nineteenth century wooden freight cars occupies an Evansville and Terre Haute Railroad siding in Terre Haute. Behind the wooden passenger cars are the massive roundhouse and car repair shops of the Vandalia Railroad. *T. H. Martin—Jay Williams collection*

houses at Frankfort, Washington, and Princeton were built or heavily modified after 1900.

Associated with roundhouses at important engine terminals were the backshops for handling heavy repairs. The larger backshops were equipped with traveling cranes capable of lifting and moving an entire locomotive. The shops contained parallel tracks, reached from outside by a traversing transfer table. The same design was used for car shops, including both railroad shops and commercial car builders. As a design the backshop evolved into this form in the late nineteenth century, but the few surviving Indiana examples are from the twentieth.

Section houses, located every five to ten miles along the track, held the tools and handcar used by section crews responsible for track maintenance. Like other small railroad maintenance buildings, coal sheds, and yard shanties, they were usually built to standard designs and formed a background of railroad facilities now almost totally vanished. The crossing watchman's shanty, still common in Indiana up through World War II, formed an additional friendly point of contact between railroad and local community.

OPERATION

Railroad operating patterns grew as traffic volume increased in the postwar years. As routes became increasingly longer, there was a need to divide them for operational purposes. Drawing on military analogies, President J. Edgar Thomson divided his sprawling Pennsylvania Railroad into several operating "divisions" and gave their superintendents responsibility for daily operations. Division superintendents reported to a general superintendent, who in turn reported to the president of the railroad.[55] The Pennsylvania's system was widely emulated by other railroads in the United States after 1860. Each division was approximately 100 miles long, a reasonable run for a steam locomotive between servicings, and often a long day's run for a freight crew. Engines, crews, and cabooses changed at each division point, cars and engines were repaired, and freight trains were switched and reassembled. Often the railroad became the economic base of the town (see chapter 14).

Public timetables by 1868 indicated a typical pattern of two to four passenger trains per day in each direction, usually designated Express, Mail, or Accommodation. A variety of through cars, including sleepers, indicated that interchange agreements were gradually replacing the insularity of early railroads. By 1893 principal routes were carrying six to ten passenger trains each way per day, with other lines carrying three or more. A distinction between main and secondary lines was more evident by 1893 in the type of accommodation offered, with diners, sleepers and parlor cars on the more important routes. Principal trains were beginning to carry names, and roads vied to promote their services. The C&EI-E&TH "Evansville Route" advertised their "Chicago and Nashville Limited—a solid vestibuled train with elegant coaches and Pullman Sleepers. Entire train heated by steam from the engine and lighted by Pintsch gas. This train carries also a Luxurious Dining Car."[56] The Pennsylvania Company listed its New York and Chicago Limited as an "extra fare" train, the precursor of flagship trains of the twentieth century. Trains on the Big Four included the Southwestern Limited, a name that would survive for more than 70 years.

A major impetus to recreational travel was the World's Columbian Exposition in Chicago, attracting 27 million visitors in 1893. New trains handled the crowds, including the Exposition Flyer on the LS&MS, the Columbian Express on the Pennsylvania, and the World's Fair Special from Nashville on the Evansville Route. The Big Four even changed its timetable herald to include "World's Fair Route."

Freight operations, while not as dramatic as the premier passenger runs, were what paid the bills. The interchange of freight cars became an effective reality after the Civil War, stimulated by traffic bottlenecks during the war. Observing the huge pile-up of freight in Pittsburgh in 1863, caused by a break in gauge at that point, a shrewd businessman saw the potential in through traffic. His Union Transportation Company started in 1864 with 1,000 boxcars with broad tread wheels, capable of handling gauges from standard to 4'10". The new line guaranteed delivery from New York to Chicago in just six days, and shippers paid 25 cents per hundredweight extra for such astonishing speed.[57] With their distinctive markings the cars became better known as the Star Union Line, and led to competing private "fast freight lines" whose cars operated through over several railroads.

Railroads themselves were not slow to recognize the value of through traffic. In September 1867 the Master Car Builders Association was formed. Among its chief concerns was the formulation of rules and procedures for dealing with interchange cars.[58] By 1875 the private fast freight lines were largely dead, taken over by the railroads themselves or rendered redundant by the universal acceptance of freight car interchange.[59] The Union Transportation Company was sold to the Pennsylvania in 1873 to become their house line, which by 1888 operated a fleet of 10,000 cars.[60] Other private car lines emerged under the control of shippers, notably the Chicago meat packers. George Hammond, after working with a separate shipper line, began operating his own refrigerated meat cars, and by 1885 had 600 cars in service.[61] The Merchants Despatch Transportation Company, beginning as a private fast freight line about 1857, was acquired by the New York Central and its subsidiary roads in 1871, and by 1880 had shifted its traffic base from dry freight to refrigerated freight.[62]

Rate wars between rival rail empires were the stuff of late nineteenth century buccaneering capitalism. Rate discrimination between large shippers and small, and between major cities and captive on-line points, fueled the demand for railroad regulation. The establishment of the Interstate Commerce Commission in 1887, and of state railroad commissions in many states in this era, marked a new phase in relations between the railroads and the public. They also recognized the extent to which the railroads dominated the transportation and indeed the economic lives of countless communities during these years when the railroad system finally came of age.

The Twentieth Century Limited, inaugurated in 1902, was famous for 65 years for luxury, glamour, and speed. Pulled by a high-drivered 2–6–2, it speeds past La Porte on the Lake Shore and Michigan Southern (later New York Central) during the first decade of the century. *La Porte County Historical Society*

4

The Era of Dominance: 1900–1930

THE EARLY TWENTIETH CENTURY was the high point for Indiana railroads in mileage, employment, and passenger service. In 1920 Indiana railroads reached a main-line mileage of 7,426 miles, their all-time high.[1] Railroads dominated intercity transportation to a degree now hard to imagine. World War I severely tested railroad capacity and witnessed the temporary control of the railroads by the federal government. New lines were built, even as the weakest lines were already being abandoned, with more than 164 miles scrapped between 1911 and 1920.[2] In general, however, railroads remained assured and dominant throughout the three decades between 1900 and the Great Depression.

FINISHING THE NETWORK

The first decade of the twentieth century saw the last major additions to Indiana's railroads. In 1906 the Indianapolis Southern completed 89 miles from Switz City to Indianapolis. In 1906 the Chicago, Indiana and Southern completed 109 miles between Indiana Harbor and Danville, Illinois, all but ten of them in Indiana. In 1907 the Chicago, Cincinnati and Louisville completed 230 miles across Indiana, the last and shortest route to be completed between Cincinnati and Chicago. Each of these would soon be absorbed by larger systems. Other through lines completed in this era were the 1903 Pere Marquette extension from Michigan through Michigan City to Porter, and the Southern Indiana from Terre Haute into Illinois, completed in 1906 to form a line between Chicago and the Indiana coal fields.

Other lines served to better integrate existing systems. A Wabash cutoff between New Haven and Butler in 1902 connected existing lines and rerouted through traffic. The 41-mile Indianapolis

and Frankfort gave its parent Pennsylvania access to Indianapolis from the north. Completed in 1918, it was the last major addition to any main line railroad in Indiana.

Branches completed in these years were the Monon's 1907 extension from Wallace Junction to Victoria in the southwestern Indiana coal fields, the Southern's 1907 extension from Jasper to French Lick, and the Big Four line to Evansville in 1911. Extensive in mileage but of purely local interest was the 1905 St. Joseph Valley between Elkhart and Columbia, Ohio. Other short lines of only local interest were the Chicago and Wabash Valley (1901), the Cincinnati, Bluffton and Chicago (1903), the Evansville and Ohio Valley (extensions 1908 and 1911), the Evansville, Suburban and Newburgh, the grandly named New Jersey, Indiana and Illinois (South Bend to Pine, 1905), and the tiny 6.5-mile Ferdinand Railroad (1909).

Little remained to be built after 1910. In 1911 the Evansville, Mt. Carmel and Northern linked its named cities, and soon served as a Chicago-Evansville connection of the Big Four system. In 1918 the Indianapolis and Frankfort opened between Ben Davis, just west of Indianapolis, and Frankfort, providing its parent PRR with a direct connection from Chicago and Logansport into Indianapolis. In 1927 the Algers, Winslow and Western constructed coal lines east from Oakland City. Not becoming a common carrier until 1931, it was the last newly constructed common carrier in Indiana.

THE INTERURBANS

Separate from the steam railroad system was Indiana's electric interurban system, built largely in the first decade of the twentieth century. By 1895 13 Indiana cities had electric streetcar systems, several with short extensions outside city limits. By 1898

Anderson and Alexandria were linked by electric rail lines, one of several claimants for the title of Indiana's first interurban.[3] On the first day of 1900 the first interurban car entered Indianapolis, and a burst of construction activity was underway. By the end of 1900, 678 miles of interurban were in place, and by 1908, almost 1,800 miles were in place. The Indianapolis Traction Terminal opened in 1904 on Market Street one block from the State Capitol. Its arched train shed spanned nine tracks to accommodate the almost 400 cars which entered the city daily. By 1914 interurban mileage peaked at 1,825 miles, second only to Ohio for the highest mileage in the nation.[4] Thirteen lines radiated from Indianapolis, connecting to Louisville, Richmond, Muncie, Fort Wayne, Peru, Lafayette, Terre Haute, and intermediate cities. Interconnected lines reached into Ohio, Kentucky, Michigan, and Illinois, while a smaller isolated network centered on Evansville. Every Indiana city of over 5,000 population except Bedford, Bicknell, and Bloomington was either on an interurban line or had electric streetcars.[5]

The interurbans often paralleled the steam railroads, and competed with them primarily for local passenger and freight traffic. They provided frequent, convenient service, but were in turn vulnerable to the even greater convenience of the automobile and motor truck. The story of the Indiana interurbans has been told elsewhere, but the system's heyday was over by 1930.[6] Consolidated into one major company in 1930 and 1931, most remaining lines were abandoned in 1941. The South Shore line, upgraded in the 1920s to electric railroad status and modernized again in the 1970s, remains as the last survivor of the remarkable Indiana interurban system.

UPGRADING THE MAIN LINES

As the Indiana rail network reached the limit of its expansion, more attention focused on investments to improve the capacity of existing lines. The Big Four relocated about 14 miles of its Cincinnati-Indianapolis line, which climbed out of the Ohio Valley from Lawrenceburg up the winding valley of Tanner's Creek toward Sunman. The overall grade was reduced, 19 bridges eliminated, and the distance shortened by major earthworks and a new line higher above the valley floor.[7] New bypasses took the Big Four out of city streets in Batesville and Pendleton, leaving portions of the old mains to

serve local industries. In 1929 the Evansville, Indianapolis and Terre Haute Railway, controlled by the Big Four, built a cutoff outside Washington, Indiana, shortening the line.[8]

In 1901, the Southern Indiana built a one-mile spur into Seymour to serve a new station and connect with other railroads. The B&O across southern Indiana was extensively rebuilt in 1901 with line relocations near North Vernon, Osgood, and Shoals. A new tunnel east of Shoals shortened the line by almost $1\frac{1}{2}$ miles, eliminating seven bridges and more than 360 degrees of curvature.[9] Almost seven miles of new line were located between Osgood and Pierceville in 1901, reducing track mileage by almost a mile but requiring a new viaduct 109 feet high across Laughery Creek. Four miles were relocated just west of North Vernon.

The PCC&StL upgraded parts of its line between Richmond and Terre Haute, including replacing about seven miles west of Brazil with a straighter and shorter alignment. The eastern part of the line through Cambridge City was elevated around 1910, the Cambridge City end of the connecting branch from Columbus was abandoned, and a new $4\frac{1}{2}$-mile extension of the branch built to a new junction just west of Dublin.

In 1903–04 the Big Four changed its Chicago Division entrance into Indianapolis, building a five-mile cutoff from New Augusta south to the Peoria and Eastern, and demoting the old line behind the State Capitol to an industrial spur.[10] In 1913 work began on several miles of elevated approaches to Indianapolis Union Station, to reduce congestion and accidents at street crossings near the station. Trains used the new elevated station starting in 1918, but completion of the train shed was delayed by material shortages during World War I. The new train shed was grafted on to the 1888 headhouse, and was built on the site of two previous train sheds.

The parallel Pennsylvania and Wabash RR tracks through Fort Wayne were elevated above street grade starting in 1912, and a new depot completed for the Pennsylvania in 1914. In 1929 the New York Central and the Grand Trunk Western joined in a grade separation project in South Bend, involving almost three miles of elevated double track, a new bridge over the St. Joseph River, and a new Art Deco Union Depot.[11]

Main lines were relaid with heavier rail and bridges, capable of supporting heavier and faster trains. The C&EI completed doubletracking its main line from Chicago to Clinton, Indiana, by

Doubletrack action east of Fort Wayne in the early twentieth century. A Pennsylvania Lines 4–4–2 passes Mike Tower with a passenger train, as the caboose of a freight train recedes down the opposite line. Razor-sharp ballast edge testifies to the labor-intensive activity of the track crews. *Jay Williams collection*

Big Four local train to Cincinnati pauses at Metamora sometime around World War I. Branch lines like this former White Water line were now far removed from the heavy action of the main lines.   *Whitewater Valley Railroad collection*

1906. The B&O and the Erie across northern Indiana were both doubletracked by 1913.[12] The Big Four was largely doubletracked between Union City and Indianapolis around 1910. The Indianapolis–Richmond and Chicago–Logansport–Union City lines of the PCC&StL were doubletracked during this period, with some grade separations.

Block signal systems, either manual or automatic, increased track capacity by permitting trains to safely follow one another more closely on the same track. Following a series of deadly train wrecks in 1906, the General Assembly in 1911 passed legislation enabling the Indiana Railroad Commission to require block signals.[13] By 1909 196 miles of line in Indiana, on the Michigan Central and the LS&MS, were equipped with automatic block signals, and another 1,419 miles of line on nine different systems were protected by manual block signals.[14] It was estimated that when the signaling ordered by the commission was installed, 64% of the mileage in the state would have block signals.[15] The Erie installed automatic block signals as it doubletracked, as did the Big Four on its Indianapolis–Terre Haute line.[16] Single-track lines also benefited from automatic block signals, including the LE&W line into Indianapolis, shared by LE&W and Pennsylvania Railroad trains until 1918.

As line improvements were concentrated on the more heavily used lines, the difference between main lines and branches became more pronounced. Main lines with heavy rail, new bridges, and automatic signals supported the fast and heavy through trains. Lesser lines could support only smaller locomotives, and frequently were the recipient of castoff rail and bridges from the rebuilt main lines.

IMPROVED FACILITIES

New engine servicing facilities, repair shops, and freight classification yards were built during this period on most major lines. Between 1918 and 1922 the Pennsylvania Panhandle Lines built a new 100-acre yard on the eastern edge of Richmond, about the same time as the new Hawthorne Yard on the east side of Indianapolis.[17] The C&EI opened a new and larger yard just north of Evansville in 1928.

In 1906 the Michigan Central opened Gibson Yard in Hammond, where the MC crossed the Chicago, Indiana and Southern. It was a hump yard, one of five in Indiana by 1912.[18] Hump yards, introduced in the East as early as 1882 on the Pennsylvania Railroad, expedited train classification. As incoming trains were pushed across the hump, cars were uncoupled to run by gravity into separate classification sidings. Elkhart on the LS&MS and Logansport on the PCC&StL had two separate hump yards each to classify eastbound and westbound cars, and a second hump would later be installed at Gibson. Humps would also be built at the Pennsylvania's Richmond and Hawthorne yards after World War I and at the New York Central's yard in Indianapolis.

Early hump yards were labor intensive. Hump riders rode each car, applying hand brakes to keep it under control. To improve safety and efficiency, the Indiana Harbor Belt installed the world's first mechanical car retarders on the North Hump of Gibson Yard in 1924.[19] Air-activated retarders applied friction to the car wheels, slowing them to the desired degree. Parts of this original installation are now in the Smithsonian Institution in Washington.[20] Mechanical car retarders became the preferred standard, though Hawthorne Yard in Indianapolis was still using car riders in 1950.

New and larger depots, engine servicing, and shop facilities were built on all the major lines through Indiana. Existing roundhouses were replaced or enlarged, with longer turntables to handle larger locomotives. The Pennsylvania, LS&MS, and Michigan Central main lines across northern Indiana were speeded up through the installation of track pans, permitting steam locomotives to scoop up water under way and eliminating time-consuming water stops. The Pennsylvania built track pans 4.6 miles east of Hanna about 1911.[21] By 1913 the LS&MS had ten track pans between Buffalo and Chicago. Over the years the NYC had pans in Indiana at Corunna, Grismore (two miles northwest of Ligonier), Lydick, and Chesterton. By 1913 there were 14 pans on the Michigan Central between Buffalo and Chicago, including one at East Gary.[22] All pans were on doubletracked lines, with separate pans for each direction.[23]

TECHNOLOGY, ARCHITECTURE, AND INNOVATION

Steam Power

Between 1900 and World War I a new generation of steam locomotives replaced the 4–4–0 and other small nineteenth-century designs in main-line service. Common to the new designs were higher capacity boilers and fireboxes. A new design feature, a trailing truck, was added to carry the weight of the firebox, which was moved behind the driving wheels to gain greater width and depth.

First to appear were the 4–4–2 Atlantic and 2–6–2 Prairie type. In 1898 the Wabash purchased five Baldwin Atlantics.[24] They were followed by the Michigan Central and the Big Four in 1901. Atlantics were also used in Indiana at least by the Pennsylvania, New York Central, C&EI, C&O of Indiana, Monon, P&E, IC, and Clover Leaf. Graceful and high-drivered, Atlantics had steam capacity to haul light trains at high speed. In 1905 a Pennsylvania 4–4–2 set a reputed world's record of 127.1 mph for a short distance while hauling the Pennsylvania Special between Crestline and Fort Wayne. Atlantics soon proved too light for long trains of heavy steel cars, although Pennsylvania and Wabash Atlantics handled the short Detroit Arrow, one of the fastest passenger trains in the country, on a 295-mile, 5-hour schedule in the 1930s.[25]

The less common 2–6–2 Prairie was used primarily by two roads in Indiana. Starting in 1900 the LS&MS built 81 2–6–2s for heavy passenger service. Although powerful and fast, their two-wheel leading trucks were considered to lack track holding ability at speed. The Wabash bought 90 2–6–2s in 1906–07, some of which lasted until after World War II.[26] Both LS&MS and Wabash later rebuilt a number of 2–6–2s into 4–6–2s. The Milwaukee Road used 2–6–2s on their Indiana lines, but these were smaller-drivered locomotives intended primarily for freight service.[27]

The 4–6–2, or Pacific type, was destined to become the most common steam passenger engine of the twentieth century. First built in 1902 for the Missouri Pacific Railroad, the 4–6–2 combined the stable four-wheel leading truck of the Atlantic with the powerful six driving wheels of the Prairie. The Michigan Central and the Big Four introduced Pacifics in 1904, followed in 1907 by the LS&MS. Hundreds more Pacifics were introduced on the several NYC lines, including five built in the Big Four's new Beech Grove Shops in Indianapolis.[28]

The Pennsylvania lines acquired 227 K–2 class Pacifics between 1910 and 1913, followed by 425 heavier K–4 class Pacifics between 1914 and 1928. The K–4s, sometimes doubleheaded, handled Pennsylvania passenger trains across Indiana until the end of the steam era, while the K–2s were common on secondary lines. Pacifics were adopted as standard passenger power by most Indiana lines, including the NYC, PRR, B&O, NKP, Wabash, Erie,

Pere Marquette, Monon, Southern, C&EI, L&N, GTW, and P&E.

The 4–6–2 Pacific was followed by the 2–8–2 Mikado, a logical outgrowth of the 2–8–0 Consolidation. Consolidations remained common well into the twentieth century for slow freight, as demonstrated by the fact that over 3,000 Consolidations were built for the Pennsylvania after 1905; but for faster main-line freight they gave way to the 2–8–2. Named for a first example exported to Japan, the first Mikado for U.S. use was built in 1902, and Indiana railroads were acquiring them soon after 1910. The LS&MS ordered its first 2–8–2s in 1912 (the same year the Southern and Wabash did) for fast freight service, and had them delivered with tender scoops to pick up water from track pans.[29] The Mikado design proved so successful that the New York Central, having acquired 977 relatively modern 2–8–0s between 1903 and 1910, rebuilt 462 of them into Mikados between 1912 and 1918, the most extensive locomotive rebuilding program in the history of steam railroading.[30] The rebuilt engines used the same wheels, sometimes the main frame, and many parts of the old engines, but added new cylinders, larger boilers and fireboxes, and the supporting trailing truck. Used in Indiana on the NYC, the Big Four, and the Indiana Harbor Belt, they could move freight significantly faster than the original engines.

Mikados became the predominant freight locomotive design of the twentieth century. Starting in 1914 the Pennsylvania built 574 L–1-class Mikados, sharing an identical boiler with the more famous K–4 Pacific. The New York Central ordered successively heavier classes of Mikado, and other Indiana roads acquired them in large numbers for main-line freight trains. The B&O, C&O, NKP, Erie, L&N, GTW, Pere Marquette, Monon, Southern, Wabash and C&EI all used sizable numbers of Mikados in Indiana. During World War I the United States Railroad Administration (USRA) developed 12 standard locomotive designs, of which the most popular was the light Mikado, which was widely used in Indiana. A 1918 USRA Mikado built for the LE&W was restored and returned to service in 1988 by the Indiana Transportation Museum.

Other steam engine designs appeared in smaller numbers in this era. The 2–10–2 Santa Fe type, powerful but slow, was extensively used in Indiana by the Pennsylvania, and in small numbers by the Pere Marquette and the Monon (Wabash and B&O, which also owned them, seldom used them here).

Smoky scene at PRR 7th Street crossing in Terre Haute in 1926 reflects the clutter of urban rail yards, with tower, crossing watchman's shanty, and position-light signal. In the background are the PRR train shed and the turreted Union Station, with C&EI train shed at right angles beyond.   *Jay Williams collection*

Three 0–8–8–0 Mallet compounds worked the Elkhart hump yard starting in 1914, apparently the only articulated steam locomotives regularly working in Indiana.[31]

The 4–8–2 or Mountain type evolved from the 4–6–2, first as a passenger engine for steeply graded lines, and later as a fast freight engine for flat lines like those across northern Indiana. The New York Central acquired 4–8–2s starting in 1916 and named theirs for the Mohawk River, part of the NYC Water Level Route. They eventually became the NYC standard main-line freight engine, but also handled passenger trains if needed. "Mountains" were built throughout the 1920s and eventually saw service in Indiana on the NYC, Pennsylvania, Wabash, B&O, L&N, and GTW.

In 1922 the Lima Locomotive Works, of Lima, Ohio, added a high performance boiler to an existing New York Central heavy Mikado design, creating an engine which could handle trains almost twice as fast with a 22% saving in coal. To this design, Lima in 1925 added a 50% larger firebox, carried by a four-wheel trailing truck, creating a new 2–8–4 locomotive. The prototype was sold to the Boston and Albany, and was named the Berkshire type in honor of the Berkshire mountains which the B&A crossed. Lima coined the trade name "Super Power" to describe engines built following its principles. Between 1927 and 1929 the Erie Railroad bought 105 Berkshires for freight service, the precursors of similar engines built later for the NKP and Pere Marquette in Indiana.

Adding a larger firebox and four-wheel trailing truck to a heavy Pacific created a new Hudson class, introduced on the New York Central Lines in 1927. Between 1927 and 1932, 145 J1 Hudsons were built for the NYC and 50 for the Michigan Central and Big Four. Named for the Hudson River section of the NYC Water Level Route, the Hudsons were both powerful and graceful in appearance. They became synonymous with passenger travel on the NYC system, whose publicity department projected their image extensively in their advertising. On level Indiana terrain they could handle 18 steel passenger cars—three cars more than the Pacifics they replaced. The smaller NKP acquired eight 4–6–4s in 1927 and 1929, and the Wabash later rebuilt 2–8–2s into 4–6–4s for World War II passenger service.[32]

Internal Combustion Beginnings

The 1920s witnessed the evolution of self-propelled gas-electric cars, the precursors of dieselization. Combining electric motors like the interurbans with an on-board, gasoline-driven power plant, they were built by traditional interurban builders and by a newcomer, the Electro-Motive Corporation. EMC, which built 400 cars between 1924 and 1932, was not initially a manufacturer, but rather a packager of car bodies, gas engines, and components from various builders. The cars worked, and the per-mile cost was less than half as much as the steam trains they replaced.[33] EMC, later purchased by General Motors, would become the most important force in dieselization in the era which followed.

Steel Cars

The 1900–1930 era was characterized by new and heavier steel freight and passenger cars. By 1900 railroads sought larger capacity freight cars than could be constructed with existing wood technology. The price of steel construction fell due to increased steel production, while wood prices rose due to forest depletion. The first production steel hopper cars were built by the Pressed Steel Car Company of Pittsburgh in 1897, followed in 1898 by 1,000 hoppers for the Pennsylvania.[34] The new cars had a rated capacity of 50 tons, 15 tons higher than the previous standard wood hopper car design of 1895.[35] By 1904 the Pennsylvania had 20,000 steel hoppers, and soon many railroads had similar designs from a number of builders.[36]

The transition from wood to steel construction was rapid. In 1900 21% of the new freight cars built nationally were steel or steel framed; in 1910 92% of new cars were steel.[37] By 1915 steel cars were a majority of the total U.S. fleet, and by 1920 steel cars were almost double the number of wood cars.[38] The transition from wood to steel was accompanied by an increase in freight car capacity. On the Pennsylvania average capacity increased from 30.7 to 54.2 tons.[39]

The change to steel passenger cars lagged a few years behind freight cars, but accelerated dramatically after 1910. The Pennsylvania Railroad experimented in 1892 with steel ends on baggage-postal cars, encouraged by the U.S. Post Office, whose Railway Post Office clerks worked in the vulnerable cars right behind the engine in passenger trains.[40] Steel frames were introduced on the Pennsylvania in 1898.[41] By 1905 steel underframes were becoming common on otherwise wooden cars, stimulated by the need for stronger cars to reduce wreck dam-

The USRA light Mikado, designed during World War I, was used as a standard freight locomotive by a number of Indiana roads. Wabash 2218, built in 1918 and seen at Wabash in 1931, exemplified the breed.　*Photo by C. L. Harper—M. D. McCarter collection*

age and fatalities. The same year the Pennsylvania built its first all-steel coach, stimulated in part by need for fireproof cars in the tunnel then being built under the Hudson River approaching New York City's Pennsylvania Station. In 1907 the Pennsylvania RR began construction of its steel P70 coach in Altoona—a design which remained standard throughout the heavyweight era of the teens and twenties.[42]

So many passenger trains negotiated tunnels approaching their respective New York terminals that both the Pennsylvania and the New York Central were driven to supply large fleets of steel cars. By 1918 62% of the Pennsylvania's vast fleet of pass-

enger equipment was steel, and by 1933 the last wooden passenger cars had disappeared from the roster.[43] The Baltimore and Ohio also converted rapidly to steel equipment. In 1911–12, B&O purchased 78 steel passenger cars. More followed, and by 1917 nearly three-quarters of all B&O passenger traffic moved in steel cars.[44]

Heavyweight riveted steel passenger cars were built until the early 1930s. Weighing up to 80 tons, they had concrete floors for noise deadening and ride quality. They continued the wooden era practice of a clerestory roof for ventilation and light, although some cars were converted to air conditioning beginning in the 1930s. Conservative and

Interiors of heavyweight cars like the Balthasar
Club emulated the conservative elegance of fine hotels.
Jay Williams collection

comfortable, passenger trains of the heavyweight era were generally painted an olive or "Pullman green" except on the Pennsylvania, where a deep Tuscan red predominated. Shiny when new or in premier passenger service, ordinary cars acquired a deep indeterminate tone after continual subjection to soot, brake shoe dust, and right-of-way grime.

Steel construction required new plant investment, which was only possible with size. The Ohio Falls Car Company in Clarksville, along with 14 other car builders, was merged into the new American Car and Foundry Company in 1899. Pullman absorbed other builders, including Haskell and Barker of Michigan City in 1922. Pullman and ACF dominated passenger construction and a good share of freight car business until after 1930.

Pullman Cars

Nothing symbolized the heavyweight standard era more than the heavyweight Pullman car. In 1910 the Pullman Company, dominant in passenger car construction and in monopoly control of sleeping car operations, began producing all-steel sleeping cars in place of the handcrafted wood sleepers of the previous period. Five hundred steel Pullmans were built in 1910 alone. Between 1910 and 1930, the Calumet Shops of the Pullman Company built well over 8,000 "heavyweight" Pullmans, and by 1926 three-quarters of the Pullman fleet consisted of all-steel sleeping, parlor and club/lounge cars, utilizing a standard 80-foot body. The cars were ponderous, with poured concrete floors and six-wheel trucks, and their riding comfort exceeded anything built before or since. Floor plans and accommodations varied widely, but almost half of the cars were standard "12–1" sleepers, with 12 open sections of facing seats which converted into upper and lower berths, and one drawing room convertible to three berths. The open sections were separated by bulkheads but open to the central aisle. Privacy at night was provided by canvas curtains, which also absorbed noise. Stepping from a daycoach into a Pullman, one noticed a pronounced hush, reinforced by a polite sign reading, "Quiet is requested for the benefit of those travelers who have retired." Men's and women's washrooms were at opposite ends of the car, except for private facilities for the drawing room. The standard Pullman was the backbone of the sleeping car business,

and few communities of any size in Indiana were not served by them.

Heavyweight Pullmans were standardized, and essentially the same cars were found on all trains offering sleeping accommodation. Prestige trains like the Twentieth Century or the Broadway included cars with a higher proportion of closed rooms, and their cars would be the most recent productions from the Calumet Shops, but their external appearance was identical to that of the humble set-out sleeper serving Indianapolis, Fort Wayne, Evansville, or Muncie. The Pullman Company maintained a universal high level of comfort, shrouded for the most part in anonymous "Pullman green"—a dark olive green chosen for its ability to hide soot and grime. The cars were named rather than numbered, in name series which reflected their assigned service or their specific configuration.

Buildings and Depots

The period 1900 to 1930 was the last period of concentrated railroad depot construction in Indiana. In the late teens the Interstate Commerce Commission ordered valuation surveys of all U.S. railroads. These exhaustive physical inventories, conducted on Indiana railroads generally between 1916 and 1919, reveal the rail system at its peak mileage and dominance. Indiana railroads had close to 1,500 depots at this time, including many built after the turn of the century as replacements for destroyed or obsolete depots on older lines. Depots continued to follow the functional categories developed in the previous period, but naturally adopted newer styles in place of the Italianate, Stick, or Queen Anne styles of 1860–1900. Small-town depots, whether in wood or in brick, reflected the indirect influence of Richardsonian and Craftsman styles.[45] Larger structures were more deliberately architectural, including such Neoclassical designs as at Richmond (1902), Gary (1910), and Fort Wayne (1914). The last major depot in Indiana was the Art Deco one at South Bend (1928–29). Built as part of a comprehensive track elevation project, it was designed by Fellheimer and Wagner, New York

Central house architects and designers of the massive Cincinnati Union Terminal. In Indianapolis and other larger cities, freight houses of brick or concrete frame construction replaced the older wood structures, and the interurbans evolved a range of depots and substations fitting their unique needs.

Railroad coaling towers, roundhouses, turntables, and repair shops grew during this period to accommodate larger equipment. Construction was substantial, with the result that the structures sometimes long outlived their working lives. Concrete coaling towers built during this period survived into the 1990s in Evansville, Frankfort, Lafayette, Michigan City, and Peru, unused for more than 30 years after last fueling their last steam engines. Repair shops were rebuilt or expanded from older facilities, but in the Indianapolis suburb of Beech Grove the CCC&StL created a massive new locomotive repair shop to serve its entire system. Constructed largely between 1907 and 1913, Beech Grove employed over 5,000 people during its peak in World War II.[46] It remains active in the 1990s as Amtrak's systemwide car repair shop.

PASSENGER AND FREIGHT SERVICE

The 1900–1930 era saw the absolute peak of passenger traffic on Indiana railroads, both in ridership and in number of passenger trains operated. Freight tonnage had not yet peaked, but given the smaller tonnage carried per train the total number of freight trains was probably also at a peak. It was estimated in 1910 that about 200 trains arrived in Indianapolis each day, while the Indianapolis Belt handled more than a million freight cars each year.[47]

Passenger and freight operations between 1900 and 1930 saw a growing difference between the main lines and the branch lines. Main lines, with heavier rail, double tracks, and new signaling, had the capacity to handle more and heavier trains pulled by heavier locomotives, and saw a heavier volume of long distance trains. Branch lines saw local freights and passenger trains, the life blood of small communities before the rise of automobile and truck competition.

Passenger Service

Early in this century passenger trains operated almost as many miles in Indiana as freight trains,

though freight contributed 70.7% of railroad revenue and passenger traffic 27.6%.[48] Main-line passenger service was dominated by the extra-fare name trains, and most famously by the New York Central's Twentieth Century Limited and the Pennsylvania's Broadway Limited. Inaugurated on identical 20-hour schedules on the same day in 1902, both trains were equipped until 1910 with wood and then with heavyweight steel Pullmans and railroad-owned dining cars, and with such amenities as barber shops and train secretaries.[49] They competed for the lucrative New York–Chicago first-class business, and paused in Indiana primarily to change locomotives. During the 1920s the Twentieth Century ran regularly in two or more sections, reaching a peak of seven successive eastbound sections on January 7, 1929.[50] Steam-hauled throughout this era, the New York Central's Hudsons became almost synonymous with the train when introduced in 1927.

Other New York–Chicago extra-fare trains included the Lake Shore Limited and Chicago Express on the NYC, the Wolverine, Mohawk, and Michigan Central Limited on the Michigan Central, and the Pennsylvania Limited, Manhattan Limited, and Metropolitan Express on the Pennsylvania, while New York–St. Louis extra-fare trains included the Central's Southwestern Limited, the Pennsylvania's St. Louisan, and the B&O's National Limited, inaugurated in 1925.[51] Indicating the volume of first-class travel, other trains, though not extra-fare, carried Pullmans only and accommodated no coach passengers. The Pennsylvania introduced a Washington-Chicago extra-fare train, the Liberty Limited, in 1923, the same year the B&O inaugurated its Capitol Limited between the two cities.[52]

Though overshadowed by the extra-fare trains, all main lines through Indiana carried fleets of named trains in these peak passenger years, usually with a mixture of coaches, Pullmans, parlor cars and diners, and mail and express cars. The Erie's Erie Limited competed between New York and Chicago with the Nickel Plate, whose Nickel Plate Limited offered joint service with the DL&W to New York starting in 1929.[53] Pullman cars were everywhere, and were the standard vehicle of travel for longer trips. In 1929 the Pullman Co. operated 8,842 cars and carried 33,434,268 passengers. The average passenger's trip was 420 miles.[54]

Between 1900 and 1930 long-distance trains began service through Indiana from Chicago to

Florida, starting with the Dixie Flyer in 1908. The Dixie Flyer used the C&EI through Terre Haute, and what was then the E&TH from Terre Haute to Evansville.[55] It was joined in 1913 by the seasonal all-Pullman Dixie Limited.[56] Service expanded with the Florida boom of the 1920s. The Dixie Flyer became two sections, one being all-Pullman, and the Dixie Limited became year-round.[57] The competing Southern Railway inaugurated the Cincinnati-Florida Royal Palm in 1921 and the Ponce de Leon in 1924, both trains having Big Four connections across Indiana to Chicago.[58]

The Michigan Central, GTW, Pere Marquette, and Wabash trains competed across northern Indiana, some with long-distance Pullman connections to the East. Even the Clover Leaf, a distinctly secondary line due to its narrow-gauge origins, hosted a named train, the Commercial Traveler, inaugurated in 1901 between St. Louis and Toledo to serve the Pan-American Exposition at Buffalo that summer.[59] The Monon, with its own trackage entirely in Indiana, operated trains over trackage rights into Louisville and Chicago, and offered joint service between Cincinnati and Chicago in cooperation with the B&O and its predecessors.

Secondary lines throughout Indiana, limited by lighter rail and weaker bridges, typically offered unnamed accommodation passenger service during this era, although a surprising number of routes saw through Pullman cars or joint services. Only in the 1920s did automobiles and paved roads cut into the local passenger traffic, but most secondary lines continued passenger service until the Depression. Among the first substantial abandonments of passenger service was the 1929 removal of NKP passenger trains between Fort Wayne, Muncie, and Connersville.[60]

Freight Service

Freight trains, composed of new steel-framed cars and more powerful locomotives, grew longer in the first part of the century. In 1911 the average Indiana freight train comprised 25 cars.[61] According to 1909 Indiana legislation, any train over 50 cars required six crew members rather than the normal five.[62] A 1912 source distinguished "ordinary slow freight" and "fast freight service," the latter composed primarily of package or perishable freight moving between railroad freight houses rather than between private shippers.[63] Examples of fast freight were two trains from Boston to Chicago, one each handled by the LS&MS and the MC. Leaving Boston at 8:00 and 8:30 P.M., they arrived in Chicago at 6:30 and 8:15 A.M. the third day.[64]

Average freight speeds were slow. Tests conducted in 1904 on the Baltimore and Ohio Southwestern across Indiana assumed three categories of freight trains: "common freights" scheduled at 9 mph, "semi-quick dispatch freights" averaging 15 mph, and "quick dispatch freights" averaging 19 mph.[65] Most freight trains were reclassified at each division point yard, creating further delays. In 1926 a New York Central official boasted about the "main-tracking" of freight trains, with eastbound trains made up at Elkhart and avoiding intermediate yards to run through to Buffalo, Syracuse, and Albany, but it was clear that this was an unusual practice.[66]

Terrain also slowed freight trains. In southern Indiana tracks climbed across watersheds, and even in flat central Indiana lines climbed in and out of river valleys. In steam days this usually meant adding and removing helper engines for specific grades. Steep grades out of the Ohio River Valley required helper engines on the New York Central at Lawrenceburg, the B&O at Cochrane, and the Southern at New Albany. Grades on one or both sides of the Wabash River Valley required helpers on the New York Central at Wabash, the Nickel Plate at Peru, the New York Central and the Nickel Plate at Lafayette, and the Clover Leaf at Cayuga. Other helper grades included the B&O at Connersville (Whitewater River) and at Washington (White River), and the Monon north out of Bloomington, among others (this in addition to the common steam-era practice of "doubleheading"—using two locomotives for extra power over the entire run). Timetable location names like "doubling track" on the Illinois Central in Brown County testified to the even slower practice of uncoupling freight trains and dragging them to the top of a hill in two or more sections, a practice also used by the Monon and by Southern Railroad coal trains into French Lick.

Larger shippers—mines, factories, grain elevators, fuel dealers—had their own freight sidings and were switched directly, creating a corridor of industrial uses clustered near the railroad station. In an era still dependent on rail access, long spur tracks or belt lines opened up additional land for industries in a number of Indiana cities and small towns. Smaller firms shipped or received freight through the railroads' own freight houses, and in the larger towns railroads continued to replace and expand their freight houses to handle the growing volume. Small shipments—"LCL" or less-than-carload-lots—would be consolidated into cars heading for other freight houses or for local service on particular lines. Much freight required rehandling, and loss and damage were factors which would increasingly haunt the railroads as alternatives became available. Carloads destined for a single shipper could be loaded or unloaded at railroad "team tracks," although the teams and wagons which lent their name to these facilities gave way steadily to the new motor truck. Throughout this period the motor truck was still largely a feeder, rather than a competitor, to the railroads.

PUBLIC ACTION

If railroads were organizationally more stable in this era than in the years before the turn of the century, it was partly due to increased public scrutiny. In 1904 the U.S. Supreme Court ruled that the Northern Securities Company, James J. Hill's financial device for monopolizing transportation in the Northwest, was a conspiracy in restraint of trade and a violation of the Sherman Antitrust Act.[67] What has been characterized as "helter-skelter consolidation on the railroads' own terms," so characteristic of the previous era, was replaced by public scrutiny of mergers, primarily through the Interstate Commerce Commission.[68]

In 1905 the Indiana legislature authorized the establishment of the Indiana Railroad Commission to be responsible for regulating intrastate railroad rates and passenger and freight car service.[69] Although lagging behind many states in this regard, the agency was a relatively strong one, with power to alter rates it considered unfair.[70] Following a series of high-fatality train wrecks in Indiana the Commission was also given responsibility for a series of railroad safety regulations. The Commission annual reports deal judiciously with a series of local complaints ranging from overcrowded excursion trains to inadequate station facilities. In 1913 the Railroad Commission was replaced by a broader based Public Service Commission, with supervision over all public utilities as well as railroads.[71] In 1909 the General Assembly, reflecting the numerical strength and political power of railroad labor, passed the first of several full-crew laws which continued to affect railroad operations for at least 50 years.

During the emergency of World War I, Indiana railroads, like those throughout the country, were operated directly by federal control. With railroad freight backed up for hundreds of miles from East Coast ports, and a perceived lack of coordination among railroads, the railroads were brought under the control of the United States Railroad Administration, which operated the railroads from December 28, 1917, to March 1, 1920.[72] Unpopular with railroad management, the USRA was criticized for wage settlements which escalated operating costs after the war.[73] It left a lasting legacy in the form of well designed standard locomotives and freight cars, an alternative to each railroad designing its own equipment. USRA locomotives were used by many Indiana railroads, and were so well liked that duplicates were ordered after the return of the railroads to their owners in 1920.

In returning railroads to private control, the federal Transportation Act of 1920 authorized a stronger regulatory role for the Interstate Commerce Commission, and commissioned a study of possible railroad consolidation. The resulting plan, prepared by Harvard professor William Ripley, recommended merger of the nation's railroads into 19 great systems, capable of maintaining railroad competition while achieving greater efficiency.[74] Although not acted on in this era, the plan was a recognition that the railroad system was overextended. It presaged the waves of mergers which would transform Indiana's railroads four decades later.

5

The Era of Transition: 1930–1960

FOR INDIANA RAILROADS the years from 1930 to 1960 were ones of organizational stability but abrupt technological change. With the exception of the Pere Marquette–C&O merger in 1947, railroad names and networks were largely unchanged throughout the period. Railroads weathered the Great Depression and World War II with relatively small impact on their overall operations. All around them, however, the state was changing, and forces were building up which would radically reshape the Indiana rail network after 1960.

The transition years witnessed the final evolution and then the disappearance of steam locomotives in Indiana, the birth and evolution of the diesels which replaced them, and the exciting but ephemeral appearance of the streamlined passenger train. World War II gave the railroads a challenge, and the optimistic postwar years saw the railroads investing in diesels and buying fleets of streamlined passenger cars. In 1949 the last steam locomotives were delivered, and by 1960 dieselization was complete, but signs of trouble also appeared. Jetliners and interstate highways eroded the passenger market, mail service was diverted, and passenger trains became a liability. Truck competition, aided by the interstates, destroyed the railroad less-than-carload (LCL) market and made inroads on carload business. By 1960 local passenger and freight service was largely gone, and railroad employment was shrinking fast. Trying to operate as they had before, the railroads were in fact drifting into a crisis.

NEW CONSTRUCTION

Although no new lines were built during this period, Indiana railroads completed several major improvements in the postwar years. In 1947 the C&EI completed its Nicholson cutoff between Decker and Alice, south of Vincennes. The 2.1

miles of new line eliminated four curves in the C&EI main line. In 1948 the Monon relocated its line around Cedar Lake. The new four-mile line bypassed the town and lake of that name, and replaced the 963-foot Paisley Trestle, itself part of an earlier relocation.[1] Monon president John Barriger proposed a series of other relocations to eliminate street running in four cities and reduce grades near the Wabash River, but finances limited improvements to a new bridge across the Wabash at Delphi.[2]

The Nickel Plate removed its Fort Wayne branch from a downtown Muncie street in 1953, replacing it with a longer circuitous route that crossed the White River three times within city limits. In Fort Wayne the Nickel Plate elevated almost two miles of track in 1955 to eliminate grade crossing hazards, carrying out the work within a narrow existing right-of-way without disrupting train traffic. The elevation included a new station platform downtown.

The postwar years saw the reconstruction of a major railroad yard at Elkhart, and the construction of a large new one at Avon, west of Indianapolis. Both were part of a program to improve the flow of freight on the New York Central. The Elkhart yard, rebuilt in 1957, replaced existing hump yards at Elkhart and at Niles, Michigan. Massive in size, it was over four miles long, up to one mile wide, and contained 72 classification tracks.[3] In place of brakemen riding each car off the hump, car speed was controlled by computerized car retarders, with photocells to fix the location of cars and radar units to calculate speed. The technology surpassed anything previously installed on the NYC. Elkhart brought together the traffic flows of the New York Central main line and the former Michigan Central and organized them into solid trains for delivery to western railroad connections, reducing expensive and time-consuming switching in Chicago. This improved service through the Chicago gateway, and substantially reduced the Indiana Harbor Belt's bill for switching westbound traffic at Gibson Yard in East Chicago.[4]

The 55-track Big Four yard, at Avon, just west of Indianapolis, provided similar improvements for the St. Louis line. Opened in September 1960, Avon replaced Brightwood yard, on the Indianapolis east side, and reduced two more Indianapolis yards, Hill and Westside, to local industrial switching. (After the Penn Central merger both would be replaced altogether by the Pennsylvania's former Hawthorne yard). In place of their obsolete rider humps was a modern retarder hump, whose computer controls even surpassed Elkhart in the accuracy of its distance-to-coupling input.[5] Avon also replaced an extremely inefficient terminal at Bellefontaine, Ohio.[6]

The Big Four yard was the most efficient plant of its type on the NYC system.[7] Like Elkhart, it classified cars for delivery to western connections. Solid trains were made up for two railroads and traffic was blocked for delivery to others in St. Louis, virtually eliminating classification work in East St. Louis and substantially reducing payments to terminal lines in St. Louis.[8] Both the Elkhart and Big Four (now simply Avon) yards remain as the key classification points on Conrail's western lines.

Other yards were rebuilt or updated, besides the universal replacement or conversion of steam locomotive facilities to handle the new diesels. In 1951 the NKP moved from its old roundhouse in Fort Wayne to an entirely new set of facilities at East Wayne yard.[9] In 1950–52 the EJ&E rebuilt its 1908 Kirk yard in Gary into a 58-track hump yard with automatic retarder control and switching.[10]

TECHNOLOGY AND INNOVATION

Steam "Superpower"

The 1930s and 1940s saw the final evolution of steam locomotives in Indiana, generally following the "superpower" precepts introduced by Lima in 1925. Characterized by high horsepower and large driving wheels, these late design steam engines had a versatile combination of speed and power. Most had four-wheel trailing trucks to support large fireboxes.

Most characteristic of the superpower-era locomotives were the 2–8–4 Berkshire and 2–10–4 Texas types derived from Lima's 1925 prototype for the Boston and Albany. The Erie had a successful fleet of 2–8–4s by 1930, though these would not appear on the Erie's Indiana line until displaced by diesels farther east in 1944. In the 1930s three Van Sweringen–controlled roads (C&O, NKP, and PM) developed a common Berkshire design drawn from the Erie 2–8–4s. Because of track limitations the C&O could not operate its 2–8–4s in Indiana, but the Berkshire became the hallmark of fast freight service on the Nickel Plate and Pere Marquette. From 1934 to 1949 the Nickel Plate bought 112 Berkshires, the mainstay of its postwar emergence as a fast freight line. From 1937 to 1944 the Pere Marquette bought 39 nearly identical Berkshires for Detroit-Chicago freight service. NKP Berkshire 765, restored by the Fort Wayne Railway Historical Society, has operated frequently in Indiana since 1980.

Larger cousin to the 2–8–4s were the 2–10–4 Texas locomotives, used in Indiana only by the Pennsylvania. During World War II 125 J1 2–10–4s were built by Altoona shops, based on a C&O design of 1930. At 288 tons, the J1s were massive and fast, but required heavy track. J1s operated on the Fort Wayne Division and on the St. Louis line through Indianapolis until 1954.

Also representative of superpower concepts were the modern 4–8–2s and the 4–8–4s used in Indiana by NYC, Wabash, and GTW. The Wabash bought 25 4–8–2 Mountains and 25 4–8–4 Northerns in 1930–31. With identical cylinders and driver size, both classes were used to speed up fast "manifest" freights between Detroit and St. Louis.[11] The Grand Trunk Western, with five modern 4–8–2s from 1925, bought successive groups of 4–8–4s from 1927 until 1944.[12] Though U.S. built, all were based on parent Canadian National designs, including enclosed cabs. Originally built for passenger service, many were used in fast freight service between Chicago and Detroit. They included six streamlined 4–8–4s built in 1938, which handled the Maple Leaf and other passenger trains until the mid–1950s.

On the Pennsylvania, the New York Central, and the B&O, fast freight traveled behind dual purpose 4–8–2 Mountain or Mohawk engines ("Mountains" to everyone else, NYC 4–8–2s were named for the Mohawk River, a pointed reminder of the NYC's Water Level Route). Augmenting earlier NYC Mohawks were 65 improved class L–3s built from 1940 to 1942, and 48 class L–4s. Primarily used for freight, 24 of them were fitted with roller bearings for passenger service. Mohawk No. 3001, built in

1940, survives today at the New York Central Museum in Elkhart. The Pennsylvania's class M1 Mountains, built starting in 1923, were joined in 1930 by 100 class M1a's, almost half of which went into freight service on the Panhandle and St. Louis divisions.[13] On the B&O, Class T–2 4–8–2s, first built in 1930, became the model for moving symbol freight across level terrain. Successive classes were built, including 13 class T4a in 1947.[14] They remained in service on the B&O Chicago line through Indiana into early 1958.[15]

The New York Central's famous J1 Hudsons, delivered from 1927 to 1932, were followed in 1937–38 by 50 J3s, 20% more powerful than the J1s.[16] The successive Hudson classes reduced running time for the Twentieth Century Limited from 20 hours to 18, and finally to 16, hours between New York and Chicago, almost three hours faster than 1996 Amtrak schedules.[17] The Wabash also assigned their best passenger trains to Hudsons, with seven engines rebuilt from older 2–8–2s in 1943–47.[18]

The ultimate New York Central steam engines were 27 Niagara class 4–8–4s built in 1945. Designed for 6,000 hp, 30% more power than the Hudsons, they could make the entire 928-mile run from Harmon to Chicago on a daily basis. Redesigned water scoops permitted taking water from track pans at speeds as high as 80 mph. Although as powerful as a three-unit diesel, and slightly cheaper to buy and run, the Niagaras were simply too powerful for most NYC passenger trains.[19] They lasted in Indianapolis until 1956, but none was preserved.

Least conventional of the new locomotives were the Pennsylvania's "duplexes," featuring four cylinders driving two separate sets of non-articulated drivers. The divided cylinders reduced the weight of the reciprocating rods, but added complexity plus a long rigid wheelbase.

Best known of these experiments was the "Locomotive of Tomorrow," S–1 6100, the centerpiece of the Railroads on Parade exhibit at the New York World's Fair of 1939. The only one of its class, the 6100 had a 6–4–4–6 wheel arrangement and weighed 304 tons, while engine and tender together weighed 1 million pounds and stretched 140 feet. Following two seasons at the fair, the 6100 entered regular service in 1940 on the Fort Wayne Division, where it could easily pull 1,200-ton trains at 100 mph. It handled the Broadway and other limiteds, and was liked by its crews, but it was simply too much engine. Too inflexible for the railroad's needs, it was cut up in 1949.

A lighter and more practical version of the S–1 was the T–1, introduced between 1942 and 1946 to eliminate frequent double heading of K–4s on fast passenger runs. The T–1 was a non-articulated 4–4–4–4: essentially a 4–8–4 with an extra set of cylinders to divide and reduce the stresses of the side rods. Weighing 476 tons with tender, the 52 T–1s saw service on the Fort Wayne Division main line, on the St. Louis line through Indianapolis, and sometimes on secondary lines. With a distinctive streamlined knife nose, the T–1s' day on the fast limiteds was cut short by dieselization. Fast but slippery, they were mostly out of service by the end of 1949.

The Pennsylvania also experimented with duplex drive locomotives for freight service, including a sole Q1 4–6–4–4 in 1942 and 26 Q2 4–4–6–4s in 1944–45. With an even longer rigid wheelbase than the S1 and the T1s, they were also assigned to the Fort Wayne Division. The Q2s weighed slightly more than the World's Fair engine, and were the largest and most powerful ten-drivered engines ever built, producing almost 8,000 hp.

The final Pennsylvania steam experiment was the S2 class 6–8–6. Built in 1944, the S2 was powered not by reciprocating pistons but by a 6,900-hp steam turbine. Weighing almost 300 tons, it ran well on fast passenger and freight, pulling the Broadway Limited on occasion. It was economical in fuel and steam use at high speeds, but inefficient at starting. A solitary example in life, it was duplicated thousands of times by Lionel in miniature, long after it was removed from service in 1949. The Pennsylvania's experiments were magnificent failures. Almost all were out of service by the end of 1949, while older designs continued working well into the 1950s.

Streamlining

The most dramatic popular innovation on railroads in the 1930s was the sudden appearance of "streamlining." In 1934 Hoosiers first glimpsed this new image of railroading as a three-car stainless steel diesel-powered "streamliner," the Burlington Zephyr, made its delivery journey from Philadelphia to Chicago along the PRR's Fort Wayne line.[20] On May 24, 1934, the Zephyr grabbed newsreel attention with a dawn-to-dusk run between Denver and Chicago—1,054 miles nonstop at an overall average of 77 mph, with bursts of speed up to 112. The Zephyr and its cousin, the Union Pacific's aluminum-bodied M–10000, spent the summer of

Streamlining was applied to existing equipment to enhance its market image. The James Whitcomb Riley was assembled in 1941 using older engines and cars rebuilt at the Beech Grove shops. The Cincinnati-Chicago coach streamliner is seen climbing the hill at West Lafayette in 1946.   *Jay Williams collection*

1934 side by side at the Chicago Century of Progress Exposition and barnstormed the country introducing millions to the new image.

Streamlining emerged from the new field of industrial design, and was as much a marketing device as a technical innovation. It was made possible by reliable internal combustion power, by air-conditioning and sealed windows, and by new materials and construction methods, like the Budd Company's "shot-weld" process for building stainless steel bodies without the thousands of rivets of the heavyweight era. It was given form by industrial designers like Henry Dreyfus, Raymond Loewy, and Otto Kuhler, who put their stamp on everything from locomotive shrouds to dining-car china. Part

technical innovation, part image-building, the streamliners marketed speed, comfort, and design. Bright hues and fluted stainless exteriors hinted at a new level of comfort inside, and gave the railroads a dramatic though short-lived tool to rebuild a shrinking railroad passenger market.

Streamlining was widely applied to steam power before diesels became competitive. In November 1934 the New York Central unveiled the first U.S. streamlined steam engine, a 4–6–4 Hudson wrapped in a gun-metal grey shroud. Named the Commodore Vanderbilt, it was assigned to the Twentieth Century Limited between Toledo and Chicago.[21] In 1936 a complete steam-hauled streamlined train, the Mercury, designed by Henry

Dreyfus, was built at Beech Grove shops in Indianapolis using a 1926 Pacific type engine and seven remodeled coaches. The C&EI and the L&N each streamlined older steam engines to match the stainless-steel cars of the 1940 Dixie Flagler. For the C&EI, a 1911 Baldwin Pacific was the unlikely recipient of a streamlined stainless-steel shroud. As on most such engines, the shrouding was later removed and the engine finished its career minus the extra weight and glamour. The GTW bought new streamlined 4–8–4s in 1938, identical to engines of its parent Canadian National, and the Wabash painted blue and partially "streamstyled" their rebuilt 4–6–4s in 1945.

By 1938 the New York Central and the Pennsylvania were buying streamlined equipment to upgrade their premier services to Chicago and St. Louis. The New York Central streamlined the Twentieth Century Limited in 1938 with lightweight cars from Pullman-Standard Car Co. and new streamlined Hudsons, all styled in two-tone grey by Henry Dreyfus. His locomotive styling, with its dramatic vertical fin on the nose, is considered one of the most successful streamline designs ever applied to steam engines. The Pennsylvania responded with a streamlined Broadway Limited designed by Raymond Loewy, with gold pinstriping and accents to augment its conservative Tuscan red. Existing K4 Pacifics were streamlined by Loewy to match.

Dreyfus and Loewy, and their respective clients,

In 1938 the Twentieth Century Limited was totally reequipped with streamlined cars and a new J3 Hudson with streamlining by Henry Dreyfus. The new equipment is seen June 18, 1938, at Englewood, just across the state line on the way from Indiana into Chicago.   *Robert H. Kennedy—Jay Williams collection*

went head to head at the New York World's Fair of 1939. The huge steam 6100, styled by Loewy, was exhibited with steam up and revolving drivers, the centerpiece of the quarter-mile-long Court of Railroads.[22] An outdoor amphitheatre presented the pageant "Railroads on Parade," with working locomotives, a chorus of 250 actors and dancers, and music by Kurt Weill. The pageant culminated as two streamlined steam locomotives slowly emerged to face each other: Henry Dreyfus's silver-grey Hudson and Raymond Loewy's Tuscan-red K4. "No one could doubt," as one author notes, "that these beautiful aerodynamic forms were synonymous with progress."[23] Loewy was later responsible for the knife-nose streamlining of the 4-4-4-4 T1s built from 1942 to 1946.

Other trains received the streamlined treatment before World War II cut short equipment purchases. The New York Central introduced the coach-only streamlined Pacemaker between New York and Chicago in 1939, and bought lightweight cars in 1939 for the premier St. Louis train, the Southwestern Limited. The Pennsylvania applied streamlined equipment to the Washington-Chicago Liberty Limited and the Spirit of St. Louis. For all trains the intention was, in the words of the New York Central's publicists, to design the train as "one long metallic tube" rather than a string of discrete cars. Some roads, unable to afford new equipment, restyled older equipment to give a sleeker "streamline" look. The Baltimore and Ohio rebuilt heavyweight cars for the Washington-Chicago Capitol Limited in 1938 and for the Washington–St. Louis National Limited in 1940. Interiors were refurbished, new sealed windows installed, and fairing added to give a streamlined external appearance, but there was no weight reduction involved.

World War II halted passenger car construction, but wartime crowds made railroads optimistic about postwar passenger traffic. The first postwar passenger car was delivered to the New York Central in February 1946, part of a huge order for 720 streamlined cars. General Motors promoted streamlining with its four-car domeliner Train of Tomorrow, powered by an EMD diesel. Following a demonstration trip from Chicago to French Lick in May 1947, the domeliner toured the East during 1947, bringing a million people to trackside.[24]

The Twentieth Century, dieselized in 1945, received a second streamlining in 1948, followed by the Broadway in 1949. By 1951 the Central was operating seven different streamline services

World War II required peak effort by Indiana railroads. Eight engines are visible on the ready tracks at Frankfort in 1943, with coaling in progress in the foreground.
Photo by William Rittase—Jay Williams collection

through Indiana, including the Century, New England States, Commodore Vanderbilt, Pacemaker, Chicago Mercury, Twilight Limited, and James Whitcomb Riley. The PRR was operating nine, the Broadway, General, Trail Blazer, Liberty Limited, Spirit of St. Louis, Jeffersonian, Penn Texas, South Wind, and Golden Triangle.[25] The B&O operated the Capitol Limited, National Limited, and Columbian, though the last was composed of restyled older equipment rather than new streamliners. The Capitol Limited, with new streamlined equipment in 1949, included a "strata dome coach," among the few such cars to regularly operate through Indiana. One of the C&O-Pere Marquette fleet, initiated between Chicago and Grand Rapids in 1948, briefly carried a vista-dome observation car, and the Pennsylvania operated a Chicago-Miami vista-dome sleeper in the 1950s. The C&EI introduced the streamlined Whippoorwill between Evansville and Chicago in 1946, and added the streamlined Chicago-Atlanta Georgian to its existing streamlined Dixie Flagler in 1948.[26] The Whippoorwill's blue-and-orange-striped coaches were named for Indiana counties, but it was not a commercial success and was gone by the early 1950s.

Less passenger-conscious roads like the Nickel Plate and Erie made do with modernized older equipment augmented by small orders of new streamlined cars. The Nickel Plate in 1947 ordered 25 new stainless-steel coaches and sleepers from Pullman-Standard. Because of the backlog of streamlined car orders they were not delivered until 1950.[27] The Monon, whose passenger service during World War II had been reduced to one daily train each way on most of the system, embarked on an ambitious campaign after 1946 to upgrade passenger service. Unable to afford the expense or the wait for new streamlined cars, President John Barriger found 28 war surplus army hospital cars, retained Raymond Loewy to style them and the Lafayette shops to rebuild them for the 1947 Chicago-Indianapolis Tippecanoe and Hoosier and the Chicago-Louisville Thoroughbred and Bluegrass. Pulled by Loewy-styled red and grey diesels, they were streamliners in appearance if not in underlying construction.

Diesels Arrive

Dieselization began in Indiana in the late 1930s, but was not completed until the late 1950s. Railroads dieselized at different rates depending on the nature of service, the age of the railroad's existing steam engines, the terrain and track capacity, and the railroad's financial condition. Yard switching jobs and premier passenger trains typically were dieselized first, followed by freight and secondary passenger trains.

Early road diesels were streamlined, with enclosed bodies, rounded or stylized noses, and automotive-style windshields on the "A" units. Each builder also provided "B" or booster units, mechanically identical but lacking the cabs of the "A" units to which they would be coupled. With multiple-unit (MU) controls, sets of three or four units could be coupled to match the horsepower of the largest steam locomotives. With flexibility, high availability, and high starting power, diesels could outperform steam engines even though costing roughly twice as much per horsepower.[28]

The most successful early road diesels were the E series passenger diesels introduced by the Electro-Motive Corporation (EMC), later simply the Electro-Motive Division of General Motors (EMD). In 1938, only four years after the inaugural run of the first diesel-powered Zephyr, the Baltimore and Ohio introduced EMC passenger diesels on the Capitol Limited to Chicago, Indiana's first passenger diesels. By 1941 both the National Limited and the Diplomat on the St. Louis run were dieselized with EMD power. The New York Central and the Pennsylvania, with their fleets of modern steam power, waited until after World War II to dieselize. In 1945, however, NYC acquired EMD passenger diesels to power the Twentieth Century Limited, followed later the same year by the Pennsylvania's first E unit.[29] The small Pere Marquette dieselized its whole passenger fleet in 1946, again with EMD E units.[30] The E series locomotives, with streamlined automotive styling, six-wheel trucks, and twin V–12 diesels, were produced until 1963, with horsepower gradually increasing from 2,000 to 2,400 in succes-

sive models. The bulk of production was over by 1954, by which time E units powered Indiana passenger trains for NYC, PRR, B&O, Erie, Wabash, C&EI, L&N, and PM.

The freight equivalent of the E unit was the four-axle EMD F unit, whose prototype A-B-B-A set barnstormed the nation's railroads in 1939. Each unit produced 1,350 hp (later increased to 1,500 and then 1,750) from a single V–16 diesel, and sets of two to four units were semi-permanently assembled to produce power equivalent to the largest steam locomotives. The B&O received its first six sets of four-unit diesel freight locomotives in 1942 and 1943. Three sets were placed in through freight service between Washington, Indiana, and Cumberland, Maryland. The railroad's 1945 annual report noted that these engines "operated daily, 1944 and 1945, without missing a trip—averaging 138,000 miles per locomotive per annum."[31] EMD F units were used by most Indiana roads, including NYC, PRR, B&O, Erie, Wabash, C&EI, Southern, L&N, C&O, GTW, and Monon. With streamlined styling identical to the E units, Fs were intended primarily for freight but could be geared for passenger service. The Monon, for example, dieselized most of its main-line road service in 1946–47 with A-B sets of passenger Fs and A-B-A sets of freight Fs.[32] NYC, PRR, B&O, C&EI, and Erie all had some F units in passenger service as well, and GTW would add them later.

Diesels, unlike steam locomotives, were designed by manufacturers rather than by railroad engineering departments. EMD, subsidiary of an automotive giant, followed automobile standardization practice rigorously, leaving only the paint scheme and minor options to the railroad's whim. EMD could also provide builder financing, at a time when railroads were finding it increasingly hard to raise money on their own. When New York Central bought 114 diesels from EMD in 1953, they arranged to pay for them in 40 quarter-annual installments, with financing arranged in part by the General Motors Acceptance Corporation.[33]

While EMD dominated, Indiana roads also bought streamlined road diesels from Alco, Baldwin, and Fairbanks-Morse during the late 1940s. Alco, a steam builder turned diesel, had success with diesel switchers and an early streamlined passenger unit before the war, and set out in 1946 to capture a market share with its ruggedly handsome PA passenger units and FA freight units, with corresponding booster units. The 16-cylinder, 2,000-hp

After World War II, steam power culminated in the largest and most powerful steam engines ever operated regularly in Indiana. Weighing 500 tons with tender, Pennsylvania Railroad Q2 4–4–6–4 duplex 6190 pounds westbound across the NKP diamond at Plymouth.   *Photo by Joe Collias*

PAs, with their long six-wheel trucks and broad noses, resembled sports models when compared with the more conservative contours of their EMD competition. In Indiana the NYC, PRR, Erie, and Wabash all used PAs in relatively small numbers. The Nickel Plate, however, when it dieselized its principal passenger runs in 1947 and 1948, relied entirely on PAs, the only streamlined diesels it ever bought. Alco's streamlined freight offering was the 1,500-hp 12-cylinder FA (later upgraded to 1,600-hp), with four-wheel trucks and a foreshortened version of the PA nose styling. They appeared in Indiana on the NYC, PRR, B&O, Erie, and Wabash.

Baldwin, another traditional steam engine builder, produced several streamlined designs, including pug-nosed versions of EMD designs. Inclined to experiment rather than standardize, in 1947 Baldwin produced for the Pennsylvania 24 gigantic passenger diesels, nicknamed "centipedes"

for their 4–8–8–4 wheel arrangement. Producing 3,000 hp each from twin prime movers, the engines were semi-permanently coupled in 6,000-hp pairs. They operated on New York–Chicago passenger trains for a few years, and occasionally on St. Louis trains through Indianapolis.[34] More successful were Baldwin's 2,000-hp twin-engined passenger units built in 1948 for the Pennsylvania, with tapered upper side panels and dramatic jutting noses designed by Raymond Loewy, stylistically reminiscent of his earlier design for the PRR T–1 duplexes. Nicknamed "sharknoses," they operated on the main line and later on Chicago-Louisville trains. More numerous were the four-axle, 1,500- and 1,600-hp freight "sharknoses," built from 1949 to 1952 for Pennsylvania, NYC, B&O, and EJ&E. Despite their rakish profiles, they were good at slow speed tonnage, and NYC based theirs at Beech Grove to haul coal out of southern Indiana.[35]

Early dieselization featured streamlined units by a number of builders. Baldwin and Fairbanks-Morse passenger diesels bring this westbound New York Central passenger run past the Muncie depot.   *Photo by Herb Harnish*

Fairbanks-Morse, the Beloit, Wisconsin, builder of a unique opposed-piston diesel engine, also entered the streamline diesel field between 1945 and 1949. Its 2,000-hp six-axle locomotives were used in limited numbers in Indiana by NYC and PRR. Styled by the ubiquitous Raymond Loewy, the F-M diesels had a wedge-shaped nose and were unusually tall to accommodate the large opposed-piston engine block. Assembled by General Electric at its Erie, Pennsylvania, plant, the F-M streamliners were the precursors to GE's own later entry into the road diesel field.

Through the 1950s the thrust of dieselization changed. Production shifted from streamlined units to more utilitarian designs. Diesel utilization changed as well, with semi-permanent sets giving way to changing combinations of units from different builders. Baldwin, whose multiple unit controls were incompatible with other builders, disappeared

from the locomotive field, and Alco and F-M increasingly took a back seat to EMD.

Most new production followed the "road-switcher" model, with access walks and end steps like those on a switch engine. A long hood housed the diesel and generator, while a short hood provided space for accessories and protection for the cab and its occupants. Streamlined "A" and "B" units disappeared, giving way to uniform units which could be coupled in any order.

The road switcher, first introduced in 1940 by Alco, was originally intended as a light-duty or branchline engine. In 1949, following an awkward attempt to design a semi-streamlined "BL" (Branch Line) diesel, EMD introduced their highly successful GP "general purpose" road switcher, with 1,500-hp engines identical to those in the F units. Mass production of the GPs lasted from 1950 to 1959, and outsold all competing road switcher designs

An early Centralized Traffic Control (CTC) installation controlled the NKP Sandusky Division between Frankfort and Arcadia, Ohio. Levers and buttons on this section of CTC board controlled switches and signals between Celina, Ohio, and Elwood.
Richard S. Simons collection

In the 1950s streamlined road diesels gave way to versatile road switchers, used for everything from switching to passenger service. EMD GP7s replaced steam on the Nickel Plate Indianapolis Division in 1951. Newly arrived 402 sits on the Indianapolis turntable in March 1951. The 1918 roundhouse had just been rebuilt to service diesels. J. D. Burger—Jay Williams collection

combined by over two to one.[36] Alco was second with their RS series, replacing the original 1,000-hp design with the 1,600-hp RS 3 in 1950. Fairbanks-Morse, Baldwin, and Lima-Hamilton also built road switchers in smaller numbers.

The flexibility of the "Geeps" set the standard for subsequent dieselization. They could run singly or in multiple, and handle both freight and passenger. When the Peoria and Eastern dieselized in 1951, it was entirely with GP units for road service, including two with steam heat boilers for use on the Indianapolis-Peoria passenger trains. Parent NYC also used GP units for a number of secondary passenger trains. The GTW, having bought streamlined Fs for freight service, dieselized their Chicago passenger trains in the mid–1950s with steam boiler–equipped GPs.[37] The NKP, dieselizing late, bought nothing but road switchers for freight service. The Michigan City line was dieselized entirely with GP–7s, and the Nickel Plate replaced streamlined PA–1s in passenger service with steam boiler–equipped road switchers in 1955–56. The IC dieselized largely with GPs.

By the late 1950s, higher horsepower six-axle diesels were replacing the typical 1,500-hp freight units of the first diesel era. EMD introduced a six-axle "Special Duty" or SD version of the GP in 1952, with extra motors for slow speed hauling. Two of these, specially equipped, took over from steam engines on the famous Madison hill.[38] Alco followed with a six-motor RSD in 1954, and Fairbanks-Morse introduced its six-axle 2,400-hp "Train Master" in 1953.[39] The Train Masters were the first locomotives producing over 2,000 hp from a single diesel engine. They were used in Indiana by Wabash and PRR, including a stint on the PRR Valparaiso commuter. EMD introduced higher horsepower GP20 and SD24 units in 1959, with 2,000 and 2,400 hp respectively, setting the stage for horsepower increases that would follow.

The End of Steam

Nothing affected the Indiana railroad scene more in the 1950s than the total replacement of steam with diesel power. In 1949 the first major railroad in Indiana, the Monon, became completely dieselized, while the Nickel Plate Railroad was still buying the last of its magnificent Berkshires. By 1955 the ranks of steam engines were thinning on all roads in Indiana, and by 1960 the transition was complete, carrying with it not only the romance of the steam engine itself, but most of the vast infrastructure of water tanks, coaling towers, round-houses, and repair shops which supported steam, together with large numbers of railroad jobs directly related to the maintenance and repair of steam.

Roads with the oldest steam power were candidates for early dieselization. The Monon and EJ&E dieselized in 1949, followed by NYC subsidiaries P&E and IHB by 1952. The Southern, limited by cramped tunnels and light loaded trestles on its line across southern Indiana, could use only light 2–8–0 consolidations on its freights from Louisville to St. Louis. It was a natural for dieselization, and four-unit EMD freight diesels were handling most through freights by 1949, although light Pacifics handled the passenger runs until they were discontinued in 1953. The C&EI, whose newest steam engines were built in 1923, was seriously dieselizing its freight and passenger operations by 1934. The C&O, although owning modern steam engines, could not use them on the relatively light bridges across Indiana and made do with older steam until dieselization in the early 1950s. Diesels could pull the fast through freight trains without requiring expensive track and bridge updates which would have been necessary for modern steam.

Once the commitment to dieselize was made, the process was remarkably rapid. The Wabash, having begun serious dieselization only in 1949, retired its last steam locomotive in August 1955.[40] The L&N, which had bought new steam as late as 1949, dropped all steam from the roster in 1956.

Steam lasted longest for those roads with large fleets of modern steam. By 1953 all New York Central territory east of Cleveland and Detroit was dieselized, but steam was still concentrated in midwestern system locations like Indianapolis. 4–6–4 Hudsons, 4–8–2 Mohawks, and occasional 4–8–4 Niagaras handled traffic on the former Big Four as well as NYC, aided by 2–8–2 Mikados in local and helper service. By late 1956 all Niagaras had been scrapped, some with only five years of actual operation. Steam lasted on the New York Central in Indiana until 1957, and steam operation system-wide ended in May of that same year.[41]

By 1950 most of the Pennsylvania's exotic super-power experiments were out of service. The J1 2–10–4s lasted until 1954 west of Indianapolis on the St. Louis line.[42] The Pennsylvania operated its last steam engine, a World War I–vintage 2–10–0, in November 1957.[43]

The B&O, despite its early start on dieselization, was among the last to drop steam. In 1949 diesels were moving 19% of B&O freight, carrying 38% of the passengers, and doing 45% of the switching, although still outnumbered almost five to one by steam engines on the roster.[44] In 1953, for the first time, diesels on the B&O outnumbered the steam engines, but passenger connections on the North Vernon to Louisville line remained in steam until 1956. Fast freight 4–8–2 types operated in northern Indiana into early 1958. The Baltimore and Ohio's annual report for 1958 noted that the railroad had been completely dieselized since March 1, 1958, although some steam engines remained on the roster into 1959.[45]

The Nickel Plate, with its fleet of fast freight 2–8–4 Berkshires, kept the steam flag flying until late in the 1950s. It was not until 1951 that NKP began receiving diesels for road freight service. The Michigan City–Indianapolis Division of the NKP, dieselized in 1951, was the first of the NKP lines to go, but the Berkshires continued in fast freight service on the east-west lines. The LE&W district was entirely dieselized by 1957. In 1958 the Nickel Plate operated its last Berkshires on the main line across northern Indiana, and in 1960 the last steamers left the NKP roster.

The Grand Trunk Western, influenced by its Canadian National parent, kept Chicago passenger trains in the hands of streamlined Northern type 4–8–4s until the mid–1950s, after freight service had already been dieselized, and steam served on passenger specials and freight in Indiana at least into 1957.[46] GTW Northerns, Pacifics, and Mikados lasted on Detroit area commuter service until March 1960, the last stand of main-line steam in the Midwest.[47]

Dieselization changed more than the power at the head of the train. The diesel made redundant the entire infrastructure of water tanks and coaling towers which once dominated the railroad land-scape. The costly and dramatic track pans on the PRR and NYC disappeared, as did the need for large numbers of roundhouses and turntables. The seven-stall LE&W roundhouse in Indianapolis, built in 1918, was converted to a diesel maintenance and repair facility in 1951.[48] Many roundhouses were razed, since the diesel typically operated longer distances between servicings. Passenger diesels on the Erie completed an entire New York–Chicago round trip before being serviced, replacing the relays of steam which once characterized railroad service.

The transition from steam to diesel contributed substantially to a drop in rail employment. Between 1947 and 1958, railroad employment nationally dropped 38%, from 1,350,000 to 846,000. From 1945 to 1959, employment on the Pennsylvania system alone dropped 51%.[49] Older diesels were traded in rather than receive the periodic heavy repairs of steam engines, so most steam-era shops in Indiana were closed or converted to other uses. Railroad division point towns like Garrett, Fort Wayne, Huntington, Peru, Lafayette, Logansport, Richmond, Washington, and Princeton lost substantial parts of their railroad shop employment.

Signals and CTC

Improvements in signaling gained higher productivity from existing lines, especially with the introduction of Centralized Traffic Control in the 1930s. Centralized Traffic Control, or CTC, was a system of power-controlled signals and switches, operated by electric impulse from a remote dispatcher's console. Instead of delivering train orders by telegraph to a lineside depot, for hand transmission to the train crew, the dispatcher set signal indications and track switch positions to operate the railroad directly. Time was saved, and railroad capacity increased. The NKP estimated that CTC boosted single-track capacity to about 75% that of double track with automatic signals.[50]

CTC was first installed on the New York Central at Fostoria, Ohio, in 1927, and by the Pere Marquette in Michigan in 1928.[51] The first Indiana application was at Limedale on the Pennsylvania in 1930.[52] After the war CTC was expanded from local installations to entire lines. The C&EI installed CTC on its heavily traveled single-track line between Clinton and Evansville in 1946. The C&O installed CTC east of Porter on the former Pere Marquette in 1949, and between Peru and Cincinnati in 1953, a line handling 5–8 trains each way daily.[53] By 1950 CTC was in place on the eastern half of the NKP main line across northern Indiana, and on the NKP line through Muncie to Frankfort.[54] CTC was also in place by 1950 on the PRR between Indianapolis and Terre Haute, on the Wabash east of Fort Wayne and west of Delphi, and on the entire length of the C&EI from Chicago to Evansville.[55]

In 1940 the Erie installed teletype machines to expedite the movement of perishables.[56] By 1950 the Erie boasted that 85% of its main line between New York and Chicago was equipped with VHF radio communication between trains and dispatcher. In the 1950s radio communication became widespread, setting the stage for direct contact between trains and dispatchers. Coupled with the decline of local passenger and freight business, radio made redundant the small-town depot with its train-order semaphore and operator. Still seen until recently, however, was the High Speed Delivery Fork, invented by Chester G. Shepherd, a retired train dispatcher, and manufactured in Shelbyville, probably starting in the 1930s. A light, tough wooden fork, it held a twine-held written order between its prongs for the passing trainman to scoop up. It replaced the old bent-wood order hoop, and could be picked up safely at higher speeds.[57]

PASSENGER SERVICE

Between 1930 and 1960 most branch-line passenger service in Indiana disappeared. Service on the main lines, stimulated by streamlined equipment and the huge World War II boom, continued strong into the early 1950s but then began an inexorable slide into unprofitability and abandonment. The 1930s saw the last passenger service to Madison, the last between Indianapolis and Michigan City, between Cincinnati and Connersville, on the Vandalia south of Logansport, and on many other lightly used lines. The 1940s saw the disappearance of trains from Logansport to South Bend, from the old Clover Leaf east of Frankfort, from the NYC north out of Fort Wayne, and from the C&O between Chicago and Cincinnati, among other discontinuances. The density of main-line passenger service, however, remained high through these decades.

In 1938, stimulated by the public enthusiasm for streamlining, the NYC and the Pennsylvania upgraded their competing flagships. The reequipped

Twentieth Century and Broadway each featured new dining and lounge accommodations, barber shops, and all-room sleeping space to replace the former open-section Pullmans, and round-end observation cars including master bedrooms and showers.

Augmenting the first-class overnight trains in the late 1930s was a new passenger train concept, the high-speed all-coach train linking major markets. When combined with the appeal of streamliners, this was a way to win back passengers weary of the traditional daycoach but unable to afford Pullman space for overnight trips. The NYC inaugurated the all-coach Pacemaker between New York and Chicago in 1939, followed by the Pennsylvania's New York–Chicago Trail Blazer and New York–St. Louis Jeffersonian by 1941. B&O added the all-coach Washington-Chicago Columbian in 1942. The New York Central introduced the Cincinnati-Indianapolis-Chicago James Whitcomb Riley in 1941, using equipment originally assigned to the Mercury plus new stainless steel coaches. All these trains, while streamlined, were steam powered until after World War II.

In 1940 nine railroads announced joint plans to operate coordinated coach streamliner service via three routes between Chicago and Miami in the winter season of 1940–41. Each route would operate every third day, but advertising and tickets were joint for all three.[58] Three seven-car all-coach streamliners were built. Two operated on routes through Indiana; the C&EI/L&N Dixie Flagler through Evansville and the PRR/L&N South Wind through Louisville. The Dixie Flagler, in shining stainless steel, was hauled by specially assigned streamlined Pacific steam engines on both the C&EI and the L&N, changing engines in Evansville. The South Wind, also stainless steel but painted in Pennsylvania Tuscan red, was assigned streamlined K4 Pacifics. The seasonal service was so popular that it was continued in the summer of 1941.[59]

World War II, with gas rationing and major military movements, saw passenger services stretched to their absolute limit, and postwar optimism led to massive investment in new or restyled passenger equipment. The Monon's John Barriger, seeing a market for passenger service, doubled service frequency after the war and restored previous cuts, and the C&EI introduced its new streamlined Whippoorwill between Chicago and Evansville at the same time. Unfortunately the market was not there. By 1949 the Monon's out-of-pocket passenger train losses were running about $85,000 per month.[60] The Monon dropped overnight Louisville-Chicago trains, and their French Lick connections in 1949. The C&EI dropped the Whippoorwill in the early 1950s, and the Southern dropped all passenger service across Indiana in 1953.

Major passenger carriers like the NYC, PRR, and B&O whittled their long distance fleets back one train at a time. The Baltimore and Ohio operated 185 passenger trains system wide in 1948, but had cut this to 98 trains daily by 1956, with trains losing $13 million in 1955.[61] In 1960 the Diplomat was discontinued, the B&O's number-two train on the St. Louis run and the first of the big-name East Coast–Midwest trains to go. Rising losses in the late 1950s led the Monon to discontinue all Indianapolis-Chicago trains in 1959, the same year the Nickel Plate ended service across Indiana to St. Louis.[62]

In 1951 *Railway Age* noted with concern that airline passenger traffic had increased 18% in a year, and already totaled 45% of the first-class travel market.[63] With the construction of the interstate highway system after 1956, and the availability of all-weather jet airliners, the railroad share of intercity passenger traffic plummeted. From 1950 to 1960, the railroad's share of the intercity passenger traffic market fell from 47% to 29%, a harbinger of things to come.

FREIGHT SERVICE

Freight service, after declining during the Depression, boomed with war production in the 1940s. Solid trainloads of oil and gasoline, diverted inland from the submarine-infested waters off the East Coast, clogged Indiana railroads. During 6½ months of 1943, the NYC moved 124,193 carloads of oil—up to 30 trains each way each day—from a pipeline in southern Illinois, east across Indiana on the Big Four or the B&O, with some interchanged to the Pennsylvania at Indianapolis.[64] Even after the pipeline was extended east, oil trains continued. An eastbound oil train on the NKP had a fiery collision with an NYC train at Alexandria, Indiana, on June 3, 1944.[65]

Following the war, railroads introduced expedited freight service in an attempt to counteract the speed advantage of trucks for high value small shipments. Second morning delivery of merchandise was inaugurated by the principal lines between New York and Chicago in 1950, including trains such as the Erie's Flying Saucer.[66] The NYC Pacemaker freight service, begun between New York and Buffalo in 1946, was extended to Chicago and other points in 1950, and was renamed "Early Bird" service in 1954.[67] Roads like the Nickel Plate and Wabash competed with fast freight service; manifest freights on the Wabash frequently averaged 35 mph from terminal to terminal, including intermediate stops.[68] Remarkable by railroad freight standards, such speeds were insufficient as long stretches of interstate became available in the 1950s.

Trailer-on-flatcar or "Piggyback" service became an important trend in the 1950s. As early as 1936 the Chicago Great Western had begun regularly hauling loaded motor trucks, but railroads had been slow to adopt the practice for fear of "giving aid and comfort to the enemy."[69] By 1956, however, highway trailers began riding piggyback from coast to coast, and railroads by 1958 owned some 4,000 flatcars and 3,000 trailers, with the number growing rapidly.[70] Piggyback operated according to several rate plans, depending whether the railroad provided its own door-to-door service with its own trailers (Plan II) or simply provided the line haul service for trailers owned by truckers or other customers (Plans III and IV). The rationale behind all plans was to let the truck mode replace the costly local switching and delivery of boxcars, while railroads continued to handle the efficient long haul. In 1955 the Pennsylvania created the Trailer Train Company, eventually joined by 39 other railroads, to pool the investment in new longer flatcars.[71] In 1958 the NYC introduced its alternative "Flexi-Van" service, with containers which could be switched from highway bogies to specially equipped flatcars. It was another attempt to save business and recapture traffic lost to the highways.[72]

6

Railroads Reconfigured: 1960 to the Present

The last third of the twentieth century has seen the greatest changes in Indiana's railroad network in a century. Railroads that were household names for 100 years have been replaced with a limited number of "super-systems"—all new since 1976—supported by a second tier of new short lines and regionals. Major portions of the state's rail network have been abandoned, leaving a slim core of through lines augmented by stub-ended feeders. Passenger service by individual railroads has been replaced since 1971 by a skeleton Amtrak service. Freight traffic has been transformed from a network serving small shippers and receivers throughout the state to one handling primarily bulk shipments between a few major terminals. Indiana railroads are tightly integrated parts of a national system, and locomotives from western railroads are a common sight on coast-to-coast trains of containers, chemicals, and agricultural products.

With this reconfiguration has come abandonment of much of railroads' once-familiar infrastructure. Depots, freight houses, interlocking towers, coal and water towers, engine terminals have all but vanished. Even the sidings which once served local railroad customers are largely vanished, and once-busy freight yards are often grassy fields. This loss has given rise to a growing railroad preservation movement, including museums, depot restorations, and operation of individual lines by dedicated volunteers.

New short lines, primarily emerging since 1976, have preserved service on fragments of the former trunk lines. These include purely local operators, sometimes serving only a single customer, as well as lines hundreds of miles long, operated by a constantly shifting array of companies, often with brightly painted locomotives and locally flavored railroad names.

Indiana railroads in the 1990s are both leaner and more productive than they were 30 years ago.

Following decades of decline, railroads are approaching the millennium in a surge of cautious optimism. In 1994, for the eighth consecutive year, American railroads broke records for the most freight tonnage moved in a single year.[1] The new volume of freight on Indiana rails was evident in investment to boost capacity on key routes through the state. The modern rail industry is economically stronger than it has been for decades, paradoxically at the same time that it is also less visible to the average Hoosier. The modern railroad has become a long-distance pipeline for wholesale transportation, abandoning the retail role which once made it so central to the lives of Indiana communities.

Although the years since 1960 have been noted more for track removals than track additions, there have been local examples of new track construction to solve specific bottlenecks or serve new traffic sources. Examples include new passing sidings and connections between lines, a 1973 L&N bypass north of Evansville, a 1992 South Shore extension to South Bend Airport, and the 1994 Lafayette Railroad Relocation project. The Lafayette project, under way for years, has removed CSX (former Monon) tracks from downtown 5th Street, and will soon eliminate an NS (former Wabash) line cutting diagonally across the city. In November 1994, the former NYC-LE&W depot was moved three blocks north to a riverside site on the new line to become an Amtrak station and local transit center.

THE 1960s:
THE DISAPPEARING RAILROAD BLUES

In 1958 a report prepared for the ICC predicted that parlor and sleeping car service would disappear by 1965, and coach service by 1970. Controversial at a time when railroads still promoted their flagship trains, the report proved prophetic. The

TTX 85' flatcar exemplified the first generation of "Piggyback" cars introduced by Trailer Train Company after 1955. Bridge plates between cars indicate that these Nickel Plate trailers have been loaded from a ramp, typical of early piggyback.   *Jay Williams collection*

Transportation Act of 1958 made their exit from the passenger train business easier for railroads, and by 1970 those that remained faced staggering losses. In 1967 the post office removed almost all first class and storage mail from the railroads, followed soon after by the announcement from REA (the former Railway Express Agency) that they were ending operations on passenger trains.[2] By the end of the 1960s the deficit for U.S. passenger service was around $500 million annually.[3] Passenger losses crippled already weak railroad finances. Deteriorating tracks, schedules, and equipment compounded an existing downward spiral.

The year 1960 saw discontinuance of the Diplomat, the B&O's number-two train on the St. Louis run and the first of the big name trains to go. All B&O service to Louisville ended the following year with the last overnight Detroit-Louisville train through North Vernon. Nickel Plate passenger service was gone by 1964: the Monon's last passenger trains ran in September 1967; and the Erie's last train to Chicago ran in early January 1970. One by one, the proudest names of Indiana railroading passed into the night. On December 3, 1967, the Twentieth Century Limited, emblematic of premier passenger service since 1902, passed westbound through Indiana for the last time. It was in a snowstorm, and running nine hours late.[4]

The 1960s also saw a steady erosion of the railroad freight base. Despite diesels, railroad freight service was still too slow to match competition in the form of ever larger trucks on parallel interstate highways. Railroad management blamed labor for inefficiencies, labor blamed management for its failure to invest and maintain the network, freight customers fumed and left, and railroad morale generally reached a nadir during this period.

One of the predicated solutions was that of merger, either end-to-end to provide one-system service to additional destinations, or parallel mergers to permit pruning of redundant competitive facilities. Merger may have promised more than it delivered in the decade of the 1960s, but it radically altered the railroad map of Indiana. First up was the Erie Lackawanna merger in 1960, with little immediate effect on the Erie's single main line across Indiana. In 1963 the Chesapeake and Ohio acquired the historic but weak Baltimore and Ohio, although the two systems continued as independent names until 1987. Of much greater impact was the absorption of the Wabash and the Nickel Plate by the Norfolk and Western in 1964, adding a new name to the Indiana railroad map in place of two historic names. The Chicago and Eastern Illinois line to Evansville, the route of the great "Dixie" fleet of Florida and Gulf Coast trains, disappeared into the Louisville and Nashville in 1969, followed by the Monon, that most Hoosier of railroads, in 1971.

These mergers were dwarfed by the blockbuster Penn Central merger of 1968. On February 1, 1968, the New York Central and the Pennsylvania, archrivals for over a century, merged in a doomed effort to achieve financial success through coordination, eliminating overlap and competition. The two systems together reached 76 Indiana counties, and ranked first and second in total Indiana mileage by a wide margin.

The Penn Central merger, driven in part by fear of the C&O and N&W expansions, combined two once mighty carriers now burdened by expensive facilities and a declining traffic base. Throwing together two vast and formerly hostile systems, with only the most rudimentary planning, resulted in horror stories of failed communications and lost cars. Cars of fresh cantaloupes, intended for Kroger Supermarkets in Indianapolis, mistakenly went to Pittsburgh instead, finally arriving rotten and a total loss. Cars of fresh fruit from California, intended for Stokely–Van Camp in Indianapolis, were misclassified as empties and sent back to California, again a total loss. A carload of frozen animal glands from Davenport, Iowa, routed to Eli Lilly in Indianapolis, arrived 27 days late and thawed—an "unholy mess."[5]

With incompatibilities in everything from computers to marketing philosophies, with inadequate management and plummeting performance, the Penn Central debacle was the nadir of railroading in the Northeast. Morale disappeared as the once-proud standardbearers of the industry struggled to find the anticipated benefits of merger, while corporate energies were dissipated in investments totally unrelated to railroading. After two years, Penn Central declared bankruptcy in June 1970, the largest corporate failure in U.S. history. It was time to start over.

THE 1970s: RAIL REORGANIZATION, AMTRAK, AND CONRAIL

The Penn Central bankruptcy, combined with the imminent or actual bankruptcies of other northeastern carriers, raised fears of a domino effect on the rest of the nation's railroads. From this crisis came the demand for public intervention in the railroad industry on a scale unmatched since government control in World War I, and requests for public assistance larger than anything in this century. The two major responses were Amtrak, which took over the nation's railroad passenger service in 1971, and Conrail, which succeeded Penn Central and six other failed railroads in the Northeast and Midwest in 1976.

Amtrak

By 1970 the railroad share of intercity passenger service had fallen to 7%, amid predictions that the intercity passenger train was nearing extinction.[6] Concerned voices on Capitol Hill and in the states called for a national policy to ensure survival of the passenger train. Among them was that of Senator Vance Hartke of Indiana, whose $435 million subsidy bill led eventually to the creation in May 1970 of the National Railroad Passenger Corporation, or Amtrak.

Amtrak was a semi-public corporation, with federal funding. In return for an entrance fee, Amtrak

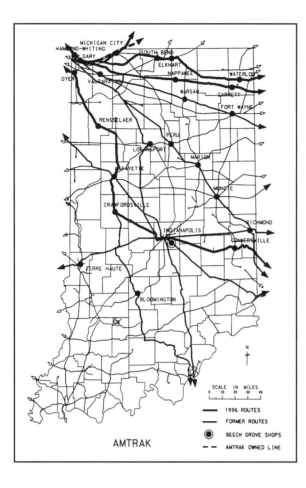

AMTRAK

1996 ROUTES
FORMER ROUTES
BEECH GROVE SHOPS
AMTRAK OWNED LINE

SCALE IN MILES
0 10 20 30 40

would take over intercity passenger trains from those railroads who elected to join, freeing them from any further financial responsibility for passenger service. Amtrak would designate a "basic system" of routes linking important city pairs, and participating railroads would then operate the routes on a contractual basis.

The basic system as presented to Congress in January 1971 included 21 city pairs. Half the routes terminated in Chicago, guaranteeing that Indiana would share in at least some routes. Four railroads opted to continue long distance passenger service outside Amtrak, including the South Shore Railroad, whose longer runs to South Bend would have qualified for Amtrak. Commuter service was also unaffected by Amtrak, and included the shorter South Shore runs to Gary and Michigan City as well as the Valparaiso commuter trains operated by Penn Central.

The "basic system" that began May 1, 1971, was truly a skeleton. Of 23 trains still serving Indiana on April 30, only six remained under Amtrak: the Broadway Limited (Chicago–New York), the James Whitcomb Riley (Chicago-Cincinnati), the Spirit of St. Louis (New York–St. Louis), the South Wind (Chicago-Miami), and two Chicago-Detroit trains. Gone for good were the George Washington and Wabash Cannon Ball to St. Louis, the Admiral and Pennsylvania Limited to New York, the Maple Leaf to Toronto, and nine pairs of unnamed Penn Central trains, themselves the remnants of once-famous midwestern services.[7] Gone temporarily was the Capitol Limited and all service on the former NYC main line to Chicago.

Amtrak's story since 1971 has been one of constant political struggle and frequent service changes. As a publicly subsidized corporation, it has been a constant target for critics of government action. As a guest on private rights-of-way, it has encountered problems with poor track conditions, forcing frequent rerouting. Indianapolis fared well initially with three separate Amtrak routes, but by 1976 deteriorated Penn Central track had forced two routes away from the city, which now has only alternate day service in each direction. Amtrak only owns its own track in the busy Boston-Washington corridor, and in one midwestern corridor, where 97 miles of line between Porter, Indiana, and Kalamazoo, Michigan, were purchased from Conrail in 1976.

Of the initial 1971 Amtrak trains through Indiana, only the Chicago-Detroit trains remain on their original route. The others have been canceled, rerouted, renamed, or added in a constantly shifting network (see Table 1).

Amtrak began service with the best of the remaining passenger cars and locomotives from the participating railroads. Passenger cars built between 1937 and 1964 were refurbished and remained in service on some trains into the mid–1990s. Primarily stainless-steel streamliners, these included dome-liners briefly on the early Amtrak South Wind, Floridian, and George Washington, and again on the Lake Shore and Capitol in the early 1990s.[8]

In 1973 Amtrak began placing orders for 492 standardized "Amfleet" cars, based on the Metroliner design introduced in the late 1960s on the Northeast Corridor. With interchangeable interiors and a standard shell, the cars became the backbone of Amtrak's eastern and midwestern routes, augmented by the aging "heritage fleet" cars. For the long distance western trains, Amtrak placed orders starting in 1975 for 284 Superliner cars— double-decked coaches, sleepers, lounge cars, and

Train	City Pairs	Route through Indiana	Dates of Operation
Broadway Limited	NYC-Chicago	PRR thru Fort Wayne	1971–1990
		B&O thru Garrett	1990–1995 canceled fall 1995
Capitol Limited	Chicago-Washington	PRR thru Fort Wayne	late 1981–1990
		NYC thru Elkhart	spring 1990-present
Lake Shore Limited	NYC-Chicago	NYC thru Elkhart	late 1971; 1974-present
James Whitcomb Riley/George Washington (renamed Cardinal in 1977)			
	Chicago-Cincinnati-Washington	NYC thru Ipls	1971–1973
		PRR thru Logansport, Ipls	1973–1974
		C&O thru Muncie, Peru	1974–1986
		B&O, P&E, Monon thru Ipls, Lafayette	1986-present
South Wind (renamed Floridian in November 1971)			
	Chicago-Miami	NYC to Ipls, PRR to Louisville	1971–1975
		Monon to Louisville	1975–1979
Spirit of St. Louis (renamed National Limited)			
	NYC-St. Louis	PRR to Ipls, NYC to Terre Haute	1971–1979 canceled fall 1979
Pere Marquette	Chicago-Grand Rapids	C&O thru Michigan City	1984-present
Hoosier State	Chicago-Ipls	P&E, Monon thru Lafayette	1980–1995 canceled Fall 1995
Wolverine, The Lake Cities, and The Twilight Limited			
	Chicago-Detroit	MC thru Michigan City	1971-present
Blue Water Limited	Chicago-Port Huron	MC thru Michigan City	1974–1982
International	Chicago-Port Huron-Toronto	MC thru Michigan City	1982-present
Calumet	Chicago-Valparaiso	PRR to Valparaiso	taken over from Conrail canceled 1991

diners built by Pullman-Standard in Hammond, Indiana. Confronted by cost problems and strikes, Pullman-Standard exited the passenger business upon completing this order in 1981, apparently the last private passenger car builder in Indiana, and almost the last in the U.S. Amtrak has subsequently assembled cars at Beech Grove using components manufactured elsewhere.

Because of clearance problems in the East, the Indiana-built Superliners did not serve Indiana trains until the 1990s. In 1989 Amtrak began receiving 106 single-level Horizon passenger cars, some of which entered service on midwestern corridor trains. These were followed in the 1990s by single-level Viewliners for eastern service, and more double-level Superliners built by Bombardier Corporation of Montreal. In 1994 the Capitol Limited became the first double-level Amtrak train in eastern service. In 1995 the Cardinal through Indiana was reequipped, followed by the International.

Amtrak began service in Indiana with aging but

dependable EMD E-units, later replaced by 3,000-hp EMD F40PH diesels built between 1976 and 1988. GE P30CH diesels have also served Indiana routes, and gas-turbine trainsets have been used between Detroit-Chicago and Chicago-Port Huron. In 1993 Amtrak received 44 strikingly different Genesis 1 diesels from GE. With 4,000 hp and a 103-mph rated top speed, the slant-nosed engines marked the first U.S. diesels since the 1950s to be designed initially as passenger units. Genesis diesels appeared by 1995 on Amtrak's Capitol Limited through Indiana.

Amtrak facilities in Indiana include a new passenger station serving Hammond-Whiting, opened in 1982, and a new station in Indianapolis in 1985. Opened when the old Indianapolis Union Station was renovated, the Amtrak facility is unfortunately isolated both from the renovated structure and from the downtown side of the tracks. In smaller Indiana communities Amtrak has provided modest waiting shelters and platform improvements, and has shared use of older historic depots such as the one in Elkhart and the relocated Lafayette NYC depot.

Amtrak's crown jewel in Indiana, however, is not a depot but a shop. In 1975 Amtrak purchased, for $3.8 million, the Penn Central repair shops at Beech Grove in southeastern Indianapolis, originally built as locomotive and car shops for the Big Four system between 1908 and 1914. Following a $29 million upgrade, and with 13 acres under roof, Beech Grove is now the central passenger car repair and rebuilding facility for the entire Amtrak system. It has also repaired Amtrak diesels, and has done contract work for commuter lines. As of 1995 Amtrak employed 850 there.[10] The presence of Beech Grove in Indianapolis has helped to maintain Amtrak service to Chicago, as a way of delivering rebuilt cars to Amtrak's Chicago hub.

After years of annual budget battles and fights for survival, Amtrak is still struggling toward a viable future. Amtrak has ordered new 150-mph American Flyer trains, based on French TGV prototypes, to enter northeast corridor service in 1999.[11] In the Midwest Amtrak has spent $150 million to upgrade its Indiana-Michigan line for 79-mph speed, and in 1995 began a $21.7 million project to upgrade 71 miles of the line in Michigan to 110-mph speeds.[12]

On the other hand, deep cuts in Amtrak service in 1995 led to the loss of the once-premier Broadway Limited, and put a halt to discussion about reinstating Chicago-Florida service through Indianapolis or Evansville. For Indiana, as for much of the country, Amtrak remains a skeleton service. From the standpoint of where service was headed before 1971, however, it is a wonder that the long distance passenger train exists at all.

Conrail

The Regional Rail Reorganization Act of 1973 responded to the collapse of Penn Central and other carriers, and addressed the issue of preserving essential rail freight services. The act provided for the identification of a rail service system in the Midwest and Northeast adequate to meet regional and national needs, and called for the reorganization of railroads in this region into an economically viable system capable of providing adequate and efficient rail service in the region. To accomplish this the act created the United States Railway Association (USRA) to plan the proposed system, the Consolidated Rail Corporation (Conrail) to oper-

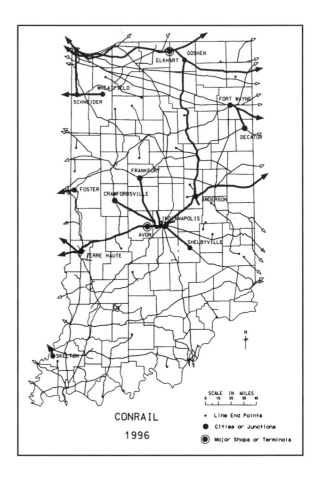

CONRAIL
1996

SCALE IN MILES
0   10   20   30   40

• Line End Points
● Cities or Junctions
◉ Major Shops or Terminals

ate a viable core system, and a short term subsidy program to assist areas which might otherwise lose rail service. The USRA took over from the ICC the power to determine which lines could be abandoned, which should become part of Conrail, and which would be available to other carriers to preserve service. The USRA Final System Plan, sent to Congress in 1975, became the basis for the Conrail system which emerged in 1976, including selected lines of the former Penn Central, Erie Lackawanna, and other bankrupt eastern carriers. Conrail began operations on April 1, 1976, backed by massive federal loan guarantees.

THE 1980s: ABANDONMENT, SPINOFFS, AND RESTRUCTURING

The mergers of the 1960s and the Conrail restructuring of the 1970s set the stage for further structural changes in Indiana's railroads in the 1980s. These included mergers, greatly accelerated line abandonments, the emergence of a new crop of short-line railroads, and the redesigning of rail service to address new target markets, particularly in auto related traffic and intermodal transportation.

A major impetus was the 1980 rail deregulation act, or Staggers Act, sponsored by Representative Harley O. Staggers of West Virginia. The Staggers Act eased the federal oversight on railroad rate-making, and also eased the barriers to rail abandonment by larger lines. The Staggers Act also gave railroads freedom to raise or lower rates, to refuse unprofitable cargo, to enter into contracts, and otherwise to control their economic destiny.[13] The stage was set for the disappearance of the ICC itself, replaced at the end of 1995 by the Surface Transportation Board. The reforms also favored the creation of new short lines. The railroad industry became increasingly bifurcated, with a basic core of high intensity long distance lines controlled by a few Class I railroads, fed by a larger number of low density regional and short line railroads.

By the late 1980s, Indiana was down to three basic big systems: Conrail, Norfolk Southern, and CSX.

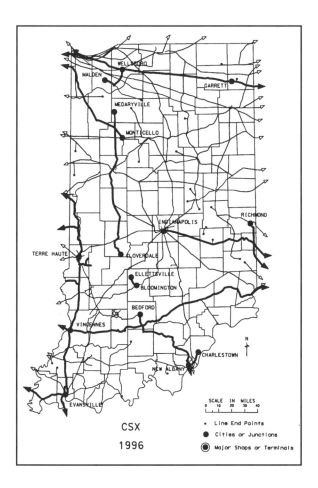

CSX

1996

SCALE IN MILES
0 10 20 30 40

• Line End Points
● Cities or Junctions
◉ Major Shops or Terminals

On June 1, 1982, Norfolk and Western and the Southern Railway became operating units of a new Norfolk Southern (NS). In 1986 the Chessie System, created by the merger of the B&O and C&O in 1963, merged with the L&N and its partners in the Family Lines to form CSX. On March 26, 1987, the U.S. government sold its 85% interest in Conrail to the public. Conrail by now was a lean and profitable entity, with two high-density lines across Indiana joined by a line between Anderson and Goshen, linking the major yards at Avon and Elkhart.

Most of the lines controlled by the three big systems can trace their corporate ancestry directly back to their pre-merger predecessors. Notable exceptions are two of the heavy-duty lines now operated by Norfolk Southern. In one case Norfolk Southern acquired a former Pennsylvania Railroad line between New Castle and Richmond, integrated it with a former lightweight Nickel Plate line between Fort Wayne and New Castle, and created a new heavy-duty main line between the Midwest and Southeast. In 1994 and 1995 Norfolk Southern also acquired from Conrail the former Pennsylvania Railroad main line across northern Indiana, in order to augment the capacity of its own closely parallel line between Fort Wayne and Chicago.

Mergers may go still further. Through the early 1990s Norfolk Southern and Conrail appeared to be exploring a merger, and offered integrated RoadRailer service between the Midwest and East Coast. Speculation on this had cooled by October 1996 when Conrail and CSX unexpectedly announced plans to merge, already approved by both boards of directors.[14] One week later Norfolk Southern announced a higher counter-offer for Conrail.

On April 8, 1997, following intensive negotiations, CSX and Norfolk Southern jointly announced a plan by which they would divide the routes and assets of Conrail, reducing the Northeast to two major systems so arranged as to maintain competition in major markets. In Indiana, NS would take over the Conrail main line from Cleveland to Chicago, including the major yard at Elkhart and the line from Elkhart north to Kalamazoo, Michigan. CSX would take over the Conrail main line from Cleveland to St. Louis through Indianapolis, including the Avon yard. CSX would also operate the former Conrail (previously PRR) line from Crestline, Ohio, to Chicago through Fort Wayne. Portions of this line west of Fort Wayne were acquired by NS as recently as 1994–95, but would be

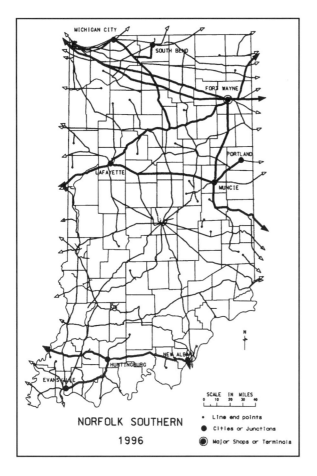

NORFOLK SOUTHERN
1996

• Line end points
● Cities or Junctions
◉ Major Shops or Terminals

SCALE IN MILES
0 10 20 30 40

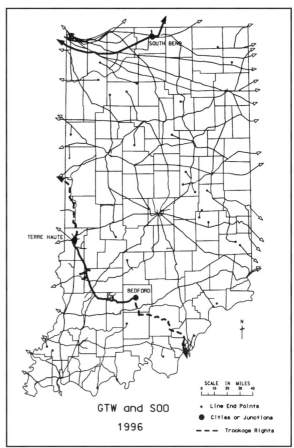

GTW and SOO
1996

• Line End Points
● Cities or Junctions
– – – Trackage Rights

SCALE IN MILES
0 10 20 30 40

traded to CSX to maintain balance on the Chicago route.

Conrail secondary lines would also be divided between the two new super-systems. NS would acquire the Conrail line linking Goshen and Anderson, the Marion-Redkey branch, the Adams-Decatur branch, the northwest Indiana branch from Highland south to Schneider, east to Tefft, and west into Illinois. CSX would operate present Conrail branches from Indianapolis to Crawfordsville, Frankfort, and Shelbyville, and from Terre Haute to Danville, Illinois. NS and CSX would share access to certain lines in the immediate Indianapolis area.[15]

The proposed division of Conrail, while still to receive federal approval, would leave Indiana with two major rail systems rather than three. There is every likelihood that these two eastern systems will in turn pair up in some way with the two recently merged major western systems created by the 1995 merger of the Santa Fe and Burlington Northern, and the September 1996 merger of Union Pacific and Southern Pacific, thus creating two major trans-

continental systems traversing Indiana. Augmenting these big two in Indiana will be offshoots of the two Canadian transcontinental systems, in the form of the Grand Trunk Western and the Soo Line. The Soo Line, a component of the Canadian Pacific, made its appearance in southern Indiana after purchasing the Milwaukee Road in 1986. The Grand Trunk Western, now fully integrated into parent Canadian National, continues its operations across northern Indiana into Chicago.

Abandonment

Railroad mergers have greatly accelerated the pace of rail abandonments. During the first century of Indiana railroad history, abandonments totaled 922 miles, or less than ten miles a year. Most of these were short spurs which served extractive industries that had ceased to operate. Until the 1960s, abandonments affected mostly branch lines of light traffic and marginal importance. By the mid–1960s, with railroad mergers gathering momentum in In-

Penn Central train No. 66 (Chicago-Cincinnati), led by a tattered former PRR E unit, waits at Logansport on October 23, 1970, for its northbound counterpart, train No. 65. The foreshortened trains would last till the 1971 advent of Amtrak. *Photo by Jeff Strombeck*

diana, abandonments began affecting main lines as well. During the 1970s abandonments totaled 983 miles, more than the total for the first 100 years.

The emergence of Conrail in 1976 drastically accelerated Indiana abandonments. Between 1982 and 1986 103 abandonment petitions were filed under Conrail.[16] The former Erie main line went first, followed in the 1980s by the former Panhandle line from Ohio through Terre Haute. In 1981–82 Conrail rerouted its Chicago traffic off the former Pennsylvania main line through Fort Wayne. Reduced to single track, it would be sold in 1994 and 1995 to NS, which had already acquired the former

Pennsylvania line from New Castle through Richmond. The former NYC main line from Cincinnati to Chicago was mostly abandoned or sold to short line operators, and many former Pennsylvania and NYC secondary lines were abandoned.

Other mergers also generated abandonments. Louisville and Nashville and its successor CSX abandoned former Monon lines to French Lick, Michigan City, Indianapolis, and the southern Indiana coal fields in the 1980s, followed by breaks in the former Monon main line starting in 1993. Former C&EI branches were also abandoned. Former B&O lines to Louisville and from Indianapolis west were severed, followed by most of the C&O's former Indiana main line in 1993. Starting in 1982 Norfolk Southern abandoned most of the former Wabash across northern Indiana, and in 1987–88 abandoned the entire former Clover Leaf west of Frankfort. Abandonments are described in more detail in chapter 12.

Short-Line Spinoffs

An unexpected side effect of major system restructuring was the emergence of short lines created to maintain service to specific customers or on specific links of the former major systems. There was little precedent for this. For a century the trend had been just the opposite—for smaller railroads to be swallowed by larger railroads. One of the few exceptions in Indiana, the Chicago, Attica and Southern, had been formed in 1921 to operate an unwanted Chicago and Eastern Illinois line, but its last rails had been taken up in 1946, hardly a model for success.

The development of a new crop of short lines was hardly anticipated on the eve of Conrail. The Indiana State Rail Plan, submitted to the Federal Railroad Administration in 1975, examined each rail segment deemed nonessential by the United States Railway Association, estimated the amount of subsidy which would be needed to maintain operations, and posited the state's interest with respect to continuing service on that line. The 1975 state rail plan was pessimistic with regard to short lines: "There are one or two line segments in Indiana which may have the connectivity and traffic to merit consideration as a short line. However, ConRail's attitude toward short lines . . . is not encouraging; and it is probably not a very feasible alternative unless other carriers are willing to negotiate reasonable divisions."[17]

Nevertheless, there was provision in the USRA planning for "designated operator" lines, to maintain service on Penn Central lines not absorbed by Conrail. These lines, which could include other main-line carriers or new entities, would be designated by the states to maintain service on specific segments, and would be eligible under the Regional Rail Reorganization Act of 1973 for no more than two years of federal operating subsidies. These were often envisaged simply as a transitional device to give former rail customers lead time to relocate or make other transportation plans.

On April 1, 1976, the day of the Conrail takeover,

the first "designated operator" line in the country commenced operations in Michigan and Indiana.[18] The Hillsdale County, incorporated in Michigan in January 1976 by shippers and local investors, was designated to maintain service on former NYC lines in southeastern Michigan and across the state line to Angola, Indiana. It bought secondhand equipment and set out enthusiastically to operate a railroad rather than phase it out.

Following the Hillsdale County, other short lines emerged to operate fragments of other former New York Central, Pennsylvania, and Erie lines unwanted by Conrail, all spun off by the USRA Final System plan. Although the initial two-year subsidy for designated operator lines no longer applies, the short line model itself came to be accepted by the major roads. Conrail itself has subsequently made more lines available as it continues to pare its system to an irreducible minimum of long distance heavy-volume through lines.

A second impetus to short line formation was the 1980 rail deregulation act. Although not a subsidy act, the Staggers Act created marketing freedoms and favored the creation of new short lines. Under its guidance the ICC decided not to require wage continuation for workers displaced when an established railroad sold a line to a new entrant in the business.[19] From 1984 to 1993, 225 new regionals and short lines went into operation nationwide.[20]

By 1995, before the BNSF and UP-SP mergers, the Association of American Railroads reckoned that there were 12 Class I railroads in the country.[21] In Indiana these included Conrail, Norfolk Southern, and CSX, plus the Canadian-owned Soo Line and Canadian National (former Grand Trunk Western). Nationally there were more than 500 other railroads, categorized by the ICC as Class II and Class III. The railroad industry characterized these lines in a different way, as "regionals" (sometimes described as having line hauls of 200 miles or more) or "short lines" (everything under 200 miles). Altogether, these 500 other railroads accounted for 26% of all the miles of road operated in the U.S., 11% of railroad employment, and 9% of all freight revenues.[22]

First to take advantage of the 1980 Staggers Act was Indiana Hi-Rail Corporation, incorporated in 1980 to take over operation of 5.7 miles of isolated Conrail switching track in Connersville. The line was physically isolated from other Conrail properties since the connecting Whitewater Valley line, of which it had been a part, had been abandoned by

Amtrak's Cardinal stops at Marion during its run between New York and Chicago via Washington and Cincinnati. After using this "temporary" route for 12 years, it now travels through Indianapolis and Lafayette. *Photo by Harold A. Miller*

Penn Central. It was the type of operation for which local control made more sense than remote control from Conrail headquarters. Indiana Hi-Rail ultimately became one of the most active short line operators in the Midwest, at various times operating 509 miles on 16 different lines in Indiana, Illinois, Kentucky, and Ohio. Equipment was transferred as needed between lines.[23]

As the short line phenomenon took hold, major railroads not only accepted but encouraged the idea, an example being the Norfolk Southern's Thoroughbred Short Line Program. Shedding un-

wanted branches permitted the major railroads to focus on what they felt was their best investment—the movement of long distance freight, while permitting the short lines to handle the costly gathering of freight one carload at a time. Being typically non-union, the short lines had lower labor costs and more flexible work rules, permitting them to survive where the big roads could not. In a previous era this would have been anathema to the rail unions, but they accepted a de facto union/non-union distinction between the Class I railroads and the smaller lines. Individual workers sometimes found that employment on the short lines offered a scheduling certainty and work conditions which made up for the higher wages on the Class I lines.

By the 1990s a new pattern of Indiana railroads had emerged. A core of lines controlled by the three big systems—Conrail, Norfolk Southern and CSX—crossed the state primarily from east to west, with each of the three having a supplemental north-south connecting line somewhere in the state. The Soo Line, via its own track and trackage rights, crossed southwestern Indiana to reach Louisville, and the Canadian National, as the former Grand Trunk Western, crossed northwestern Indiana to enter Chicago. Everything else was regional or short lines. A few of these—specifically Indiana Rail Road, Indiana Southern, Louisville and Indiana, and Toledo, Peoria and Western—provided long hauls, but everything else was disconnected fragments of line, feeding traffic to one or more of the major lines.

CHANGING TECHNOLOGY

Diesels: Horsepower and Innovation

By the 1960s steam was gone from Indiana rails, and the production of the early streamlined diesel units had all but ceased. Smaller diesel builders Baldwin and Fairbanks-Morse were gone or about to go, and in 1968 Alco, the last of the former steam locomotive builders, dropped from the scene. General Electric emerged in 1959 as a new competitor in the large locomotive field, and after 1982 moved ahead of rival EMD in diesel sales. From then until the present GE and EMD have divided the U.S. diesel field between them.

The 1960s saw the introduction of "second generation" diesels—high speed, high horsepower four- and six-axle units for freight service. EMD introduced its 2,250-hp GP30 in 1961, followed by the 2,500-hp GP35 in 1963. Alco introduced its Century series with the 2,000-hp C–420 in 1963, and the new entrant, General Electric, produced its Universal series starting with 2,500-hp U25B demonstrators in 1959. By the late 1960s EMD was producing 3,000- and 3,600-hp units based on a new engine block. EMD and GE competed with units in this power range through the 1970s, adding more sophisticated electronic controls for fuel economy and better adhesion.

A further horsepower escalation began in 1987, when GE introduced its C40–8, the first single-engine unit to break the 4,000-hp barrier. EMD followed with its 4,000-hp SD70 in 1992, and GE followed with a 4,400-hp C44–8W in 1993. Both builders then followed with alternating current versions of their newest high-horsepower units. In early 1996 Conrail began receiving EMD SD80-MACs, each with 5,000 hp and AC traction motors. Each unit was the equivalent of three first-generation diesels. Operated in multiple, they are applying horsepower on a scale never before seen on Indiana railroads.

The 1990s saw a visible design change, the first since the ubiquitous road-switchers replaced streamlined diesels in the 1950s. The wide-nosed "North American Cab," first introduced to the U.S. in 1989, rapidly became the new standard for high-horsepower road diesels. Also called "comfort" cabs, the wide-nosed design offered more protection for the crew but retained the open side walkways behind the cab for easy engine access. Wide nose models with "W" suffixes (GE) or "M" suffixes (EMD) were a common sight on Conrail and CSX lines in Indiana by 1996, with some units also appearing on Norfolk Southern.

Railroad Freight: The Changing Scene

The typical Indiana freight train in 1960 was pulled by first-generation streamlined diesels or road-switchers, with a preponderance of 70-ton-capacity boxcars, hoppers, gondolas, refrigerator cars, tank cars, and a smattering of new extra-long piggyback flats. The train ended with a caboose—lettered, like the locomotives, for the home railroad on which it stayed—and it was manned by a crew of five. On trains of 70 or more cars, Indiana's full crew law required six trainmen.

By 1996 the same train was pulled by high-horsepower modern units, sometimes mixed with engines from western connections or competing Indiana roads. The preponderance of cars might be 100-ton-capacity covered hoppers and elongated tank cars, mixed with "Hi-Cube" extra-length boxcars carrying auto parts and tri-level "Auto Racks" carrying finished autos. Increasing numbers of trains carried only intermodal, with articulated platforms for outsized trailers and double-stacked containers. Some trains might be dedicated to a single customer, such as a power utility, with all cars belonging to the customer rather than the railroad. Most trains now operate with only an engineer and a conductor. Indiana's full crew law, while nominally still on the books, was effectively preempted

Fort Wayne is the hub of Norfolk Southern's Triple Crown Service, operating between the Midwest, East, and Southeast. Wabash National of Lafayette manufactures the unique RoadRailer trailers, which can travel on rails or highways.   *Photo by Harold A. Miller*

under terms of the Federal Regional Rail Reorganization Act of 1973, and by the 1990s most Class I railroads had reached labor agreement permitting operation of through trains with only two men.[24] Both men rode the engine, while the rear of the train carried an automated end-of-train device (EOT, also called Flashing Rear End Device, or FRED) to monitor air brake pressure and transmit it by radio to the engine.

The changing freight trains reflected changes in the railroads' marketing and positioning. Traffic moves increasingly in multi-car blocks or unit trains, while sidings for single-car shippers have largely disappeared along with railroad freight houses for less-than-carload shipments. Rate deregulation favors 50- or 100-car grain movements, so larger grain elevators drive out individual small-town ones. The location of large grain elevators often explains the reason for retention of stub-ended rail fragments in northern Indiana, preserved to serve a single customer. The elevators themselves may own the massive covered hoppers, whose cargoes can be unloaded with the aid of vacuum or air pressure.

Coal, a traditional railroad commodity, continues to move from Southern Indiana and Illinois, as well as from western connections. The local coal dealer, once a common customer, is almost extinct, and most coal moves in solid blocks or trainloads bound for large utility power stations. Some utilities own their own fleet of cars, and the railroad provides only the locomotive. Hoosier Energy REC, Inc., in Bloomington, owns 112 cars, which cycle 13 trips a month to nearby coal mines. Indianapolis Power and Light Co. in Indianapolis owns 576 cars, making 1 to 4 trips per week, while Northern Indiana Public Service Co., with 300 cars, sends them on longer trips, cycling 3 to 6 times per month.[25]

The general-purpose boxcar fleet, the mainstay of traditional railroading, decreased by half between 1961 and 1977. Boxcar tonnage fell 36% during roughly the same period.[26] Railroad inability to borrow money for new equipment during the bleak 1960s led to periodic car shortages which only compounded the flight of former customers. Railbox, a subsidiary of Trailer Train Corporation, was formed in 1974 to finance a pool of "free-running" boxcars available to any participating railroad.[27] The bright yellow Railbox cars, with a vivid slogan proclaiming, "next load—any road," became a common sight on Indiana rails, but by the early '80s part of its fleet was sold back to individual railroads.

The same problem generated a brief but colorful flowering of boxcars lettered for unfamiliar short line railroads. Per-diem rates for car use were adjusted upward in 1973 to encourage investment in new equipment. The rates favored railroads which were increasing the size of their car fleets, so many short lines, having no car fleets to begin with, found themselves being cultivated by equipment financiers looking for a place to put their money.[28] The short line itself put up no money, but provided a home for the cars, and put them in play through an outbound shipment. It was hoped that the cars would then float freely, providing a stream of revenue but seldom returning to their home road. Unfamiliar railroad names suddenly appeared on passing freight trains, including the grandly named New Jersey, Indiana and Illinois in South Bend and the historic Ferdinand Railroad and Louisville, New Albany and Corydon in southern Indiana. The latter two, both owned during this period by an Illinois car builder and lessor, suddenly had so many boxcars that they could not physically have held them all. A recession in the late '70s put the brakes on this exuberant short-line boxcar movement, and

roads had to search for locations to store the surplus cars.

Indiana's auto-related economy has driven one of railroading's success stories, the movement of autos and auto parts. Indiana rail traffic includes many "Hi-Cube" auto parts cars, up to 86' long and often dedicated to a single customer. Before 1960 new automobiles were delivered in boxcars, and railroads had lost all but 10% of the business.[29] Starting in 1959 and 1960, railroads added multi-level racks to long piggyback flatcars. Bi-level or tri-level racks, loaded from the end like a highway auto carrier, could hold 15 or more autos. The cars were a powerful tool with which to compete for auto delivery traffic once given up as lost. After 1974 most new rack cars were totally enclosed, with a roof, side panels, and locking end doors. Railroad clearances were raised in places like the B&O's Willow Valley Tunnel in southern Indiana to handle the new cars, 19 feet tall and over 89 feet long.[30]

In 1994 railroads shipped almost 70% of new automobiles in the U.S., the first time in four decades that the share had gone above 50%. The new GM truck assembly plant at Roanoke and the Subaru-Isuzu plant at Lafayette each fill 60 autorack cars per day, and swell the automotive related traffic on the NS's former Wabash line across Indiana.[31] Autoracks move in solid blocks or unit trains from factories to distributors. Like grain shipment, auto racks support a centralized pattern of traffic, in which branch lines or single-car railroading have little role to play.

Intermodal

Intermodal traffic, including TOFC ("trailer-on-flatcar") and COFC ("container-on-flatcar"), has become an increasing share of rail traffic since 1960. By the 1960s the Pennsylvania advertised "Tructrain" terminals at Fort Wayne, Marion, Indianapolis, and Jeffersonville. The New York Central advertised "Super Van" service to Indianapolis, the B&O offered "Trailer Jets" on both the Chicago and St. Louis lines, and the Norfolk and Western advertised piggyback service at South Bend, Fort Wayne, Kokomo, Lafayette, Marion, Muncie, and Indianapolis.[32] Trailer Train Company, formed in 1955, had 40 participating railroads by 1964, and had introduced the 89' piggyback flatcar, capable of carrying two of the newly legalized 40' trailers.[33] Piggyback use tripled in 10 years, but by 1967 was still only 4% of all railroad carloadings.[34]

Autos and auto parts feature heavily in modern Indiana railroading. Conrail units pull a string of triple-deck auto cars.   *Photo by Jonathan Bremer*

Railroad containers for LCL freight had been put in service on the NYC between Chicago and Cleveland back in 1921.[35] In 1958 the New York Central introduced "Flexi-Vans"—highway trailers with demountable wheels, which could be loaded onto special flatcars from the side and locked in position for the rail trip. By 1965 almost 4,000 Flexi-Vans and 787 flatcars were in service, and 11 special Super Van trains served NYC's major terminals, including Indianapolis. Flexi-Vans contributed 15% of New York Central's net income in 1965, but were phased out in favor of conventional TOFC after the Penn Central merger in 1968.[36]

Containers and container ships for international freight had been introduced in 1956, and TOFC cars were soon equipped with tiedown devices to handle either containers or highway trailers. American railroads provided a "land-bridge" connecting Asia and Europe. Five-unit articulated double-stack cars were introduced in 1981, and starting in 1984 American President Lines, an international container company, introduced a nationwide network of "stack" trains, utilizing both Conrail and NS. Sea-Land, which was acquired by CSX, followed suit.[37] Containers and stack trains doubled the intermodal volume during the 1980s, and by 1992 container loadings exceeded trailers for the first time.[38] The excess height of the stack trains has prompted railroads to increase tunnel and bridge clearances, and stimulated the construction of a completely new international tunnel under the St. Clair River between Port Huron, Michigan, and Sarnia, Ontario. Opened in spring 1995, the tunnel eliminated a bottleneck between Canada and the U.S. and was expected to generate increased train traffic through northern Indiana to Chicago.

Whereas trailers could be driven onto flatcars from a ramp, containers required overhead cranes or massive forklift tractors to load and unload. The massive investment encouraged centralization of container loading at major terminals, rather than at individual ramps. With its centralized facilities, intermodal traffic is largely a prerogative of the major carriers. On Conrail, the Avon yards provide intermodal service for Indianapolis. A few smaller roads participate, notably the TP&W, with its large "Hoosier Lift" terminal at Remington, Indiana. The Hoosier Lift collects containers and trailers from Indiana via I–65 and dispatches blocks of intermodal cars direct to the West Coast. Containers handle an increasing variety of freight. From the East Coast, "WastePacker" cars of environmental cleanup companies shuttle across Indiana carrying sewage sludge bound for disposal sites on the Plains.[39] The short, heavy containers are loaded on two-platform articulated cars, distributing the weight.

By the mid–1990s a substantial number of dedicated intermodal trains are scheduled around the needs of customers like U.S. Mail and UPS. By 1992 major truckload carrier J. B. Hunt and Conrail introduced "seamless transcontinental intermodal service," and Hunt's routes now include Conrail, NS, and CN through Indiana.[40] Truckload competitor Schneider National moved about 25% of its business by rail in 1994. Following a teamsters strike in 1994, unionized LTL truckers in 1994 secured a labor agreement permitting up to 28% of their traffic to go by rail.[41] Container and trailer loadings exceeded 8 million in 1994 and 1995, more than double that in 1979.[42]

RoadRailer

An intermodal offshoot has been the RoadRailer, a concept in which highway trailers themselves are linked to become a train. In 1955 the C&O introduced Railvans—highway trailers with supplemen-

tary railroad wheels—and hauled mail in them behind Pere Marquette streamliners between Detroit and Chicago. Although technically successful, they were set aside when the passenger trains were eliminated in 1971.[43] The concept was revived by a new company in 1977. Testing at speeds up to 110 mph, followed by a Congressional Act in 1980 to waive conventional requirements for freight car safety appliances, cleared the way for the new equipment, now termed RoadRailers.

Beginning in 1980, experimental RoadRailer service began on ICG, Conrail, and BN. In 1986 Norfolk Southern inaugurated a daily RoadRailer train between Detroit and St. Louis on the former Wabash main line across Indiana. A Chicago-Atlanta train was added in 1987, and a Fort Wayne–Buffalo train in 1988. A Norfolk Southern subsidiary, Triple Crown Services, based in Fort Wayne, markets the service, and arranges for highway pickup and delivery with the customers. The railroad serves simply as a wholesaler of transportation, hauling fast scheduled trains between major terminals. The service is centered on Fort Wayne, originally at the Hugo Yard in southwest Fort Wayne and later at the former PRR Piqua yard.

RoadRailers are manufactured in Lafayette by RoadRailer Division of Wabash National. Early units, using retractable rail wheels on each trailer, were supplanted in 1994 by designs using separate rail wheels, eliminating dead weight and allowing increased highway payloads. Originally limited to 75 trailers, Triple Crown trains now permit up to 100 trailers and may require two engines to make their fast schedules. Triple Crown Service, jointly controlled by NS and Conrail in 1996, has spread to Alexandria, Va., Jacksonville, Fla., Harrisburg, Pa., and to the New York area in 1994. Intended to compete with highway trucks for distances over 400 miles, the Triple Crown trains are the hottest schedules on the NS. Carrying auto parts, mail, and other priority freight, the trains are both a marketing and a technological breakthrough in intermodal service.

APPROACHING A NEW CENTURY

Consistent with the new philosophy of concentrated long distance hauls have been changes in operating procedures. Trains move as units or as blocks of cars for distant destinations, avoiding switching and carrying power through from one railroad to another. Locomotives from western rail-

Bulk commodities like grain move in solid trainloads. CSX units here are tied up at grain facility in Linden on former Monon route.   *Photo by Francis H. Parker*

roads are commonly seen in Indiana. Trains stay out of yards and crews are changed wherever convenient. An incidental sight in 1990s railroading is a taxi or crew van at a remote crossing, delivering a new crew in place of one whose 12-hour service limit has expired. Whether the enormous cost in taxi bills is really a mark of efficiency is up for discussion, but the operation is far more fluid than the traditional one based on division points.

Even the terminology of railroad organization is different. The basic unit of traditional railroading was the division, set at approximately 100 miles by steam engine servicing needs. Just as railroads

themselves have merged, so have divisions become larger, so that now the subdivision, or "sub" in railroad parlance, is the common reference to individual lines. In place of main lines and branches railroaders refer to specific running tracks. With the almost universal adoption of Centralized Traffic Control on the major lines, the dispatching center is farther removed from the actual railroad than ever before. CSX train dispatching for Indiana is done from Jacksonville, Florida. Individual freight car and locomotive locations are monitored electronically by radio transponders on each unit, activated by signals from trackside readers. Required by the AAR since 1994, this AEI (Automatic Equipment Identification) system replaces an earlier ACI (Automatic Car Identification) system using optical scanners in the late '60s and '70s.[44]

High-Speed Rail?

Is there a high-speed rail passenger line in Indiana's future? In 1996 the Indiana-based USA Rail Passenger and Light Freight Systems, Inc. announced plans to build a high-speed rail line from Pittsburgh though Indianapolis to St. Louis for an estimated $3.5 billion.[45] Their sources of funding were not identified, and other high-speed rail advocates were doubtful that the proposed project would happen. In other states, however, after years of expectation and disappointment, high-speed rail was finally making headway. Florida in 1996 committed state funding for the 220-mph Florida Overland Express, to serve Miami, Orlando, and Tampa by 2004. Ohio was pursuing conventional service between Cleveland, Columbus, and Cincinnati, as a precursor to a high-speed system. Indianapolis-Chicago has been identified as a possible mid-distance corridor in which high-speed rail would be competitive with air and highway service.

Indiana's first exposure to high-speed rail, ironically, will come thanks to the Michigan Department of Transportation! In 1992 the Detroit-Chicago corridor was designated by the U.S. Department of Transportation as one of five priority high-speed rail corridors, with funding available through the High Speed Rail Development Act of 1993 for incremental improvements to permit higher speeds. The 279-mile Chicago-Detroit corridor, including 97 miles already owned by Amtrak, now has top speeds of 79 mph. A project was begun in fall 1995, with funding from Amtrak and from the Michigan Department of Transportation, to install a High Speed Positive Train Control System on 71 miles of line starting at the Indiana state line. Costing $21.7 million, the project uses computers and advanced communication techniques to activate crossing signals ahead of high-speed trains, and to constantly monitor and report permissible top speeds to the engineer. With expected completion of the test section in 1997, the project could be extended to the entire 280-mile corridor for an estimated $40-$45 million, plus $160-$180 million in track improvements. The goal is to reduce travel time between Chicago and Detroit from the present $5\frac{1}{2}$

hours to $3\frac{1}{2}$ hours.[46] Indiana would share the benefits through existing station stops at Hammond/Whiting and Michigan City, and it would be reasonable for Indiana to share a part of the cost.

Indiana Railroads—Busy but Invisible

Indiana's railroad system is moving more freight than ever before. In 1994, for the eighth consecutive year, American railroads broke records for the most total freight moved in a single year. Continuing a streak which began in 1987, traffic increased steadily from 943 billion ton miles (breaking a previous record of 921 billion set in 1984), to 1 trillion ton miles in 1989, 1.1 trillion in 1993, and a projected 1.2 trillion by the end of 1994.[47] More trailers and containers were moved by rail in 1994 than ever before, the 13th record year in a row, and the share of new automobiles moved by rail climbed above 50% for the first time in any recent decade. Within Indiana, east-west lines saw an increasing parade of traffic, and new passing sidings were being added to break the gridlock on the north-south line between Fort Wayne and Cincinnati. After years of corporate downsizing, railroad industry leaders were commenting on the need to build capacity again.

The paradox of modern railroading is that while trains move more traffic than ever, they seem to have become all but invisible. The explanation for the paradox is that while the railroads are indeed busy, they now occupy a very specialized transportation niche, and one that is not apparent to the average citizen or to the press. The railroad has become a specialized transporter of bulk commodities over long distances. Railroad traffic passes in long trainloads bound for distant destinations. It is a part of the national industrial pipeline, as it always was, but it is no longer in the retail business of local freight and passenger service.

As Indiana railroads approach the twenty-first century, they are at once more efficient than their predecessors but also more remote from the daily lives of the communities they traverse. A train in Indiana today is apt to be simply passing through from one major gateway to another, or even one coast to the other. Communications flow from remote control centers through radio and microwave transmissions rather than through paper orders handed up by an operator at trackside. Local freight is unusual except for large bulk shippers like grain elevators, and in many communities the railroad no longer even has a siding on which to leave local cars. Depots and interlocking towers, the traditional local contact points for railroad watchers, are almost extinct. Railroad employment, once basic to the Indiana work force, has fallen until few people even know someone who works for the railroad. The trains of yesterday are themselves now museum pieces, either on display or in special operation, lovingly tended by volunteers and retired former railroaders. But the trains of today still roll. In the midnights of small Indiana towns the air horns still shatter the silence, and the thunder of passing grain cars, autoracks, and stack cars announces that the railroad is still alive and working in Indiana, as it has been ever since 1838.

Typical of informal tourist railway operation, Whitewater Valley No. 6 takes water at Laurel, Indiana, c. 1975 with the aid of a volunteer fire company.   *Photo by Cornelius Hauck*

┼┼┼┼┼┼┼┼┼┼┼┼┼ 7 ┼┼┼┼┼┼┼┼┼┼┼┼┼

Railroad Preservation

RAILROAD PRESERVATION in Indiana dates to 1901, when Purdue University initiated plans for a railroad collection in conjunction with its railroad engineering program.[1] The collection, which eventually included five historic locomotives plus an interurban car, was seen as an adjunct of the Purdue railroad engineering program rather than as a museum. The collection was eventually disbanded. Most went to the National Museum of Transport in St. Louis. The Reuben Wells was returned to the Pennsylvania Railroad, which later donated it to the Children's Museum in Indianapolis.

Organized interest in railroad history began with the Railway & Locomotive Historical Society in 1921, which established a journal and organized railroad excursions. A 1936 R&LHS excursion from Chicago covered the Pennsylvania's Eel River branch, the Fort Wayne engine terminal, and the Fort Wayne Division main line back to Chicago, pulled by two separate pairs of double-headed Pacifics.[2] The National Railway Historical Society, organized in 1935, now has 173 chapters nationally, including one in Indianapolis and one in the Marion-Muncie area.

Excursions were run to celebrate the waning days of steam, including a 1949 excursion from South Bend behind a Wabash 2–6–0, and a 1952 visit to the Ferdinand Railroad in southern Indiana.[3] Among the last trips behind in-service steam was an April 1961 trip from Chicago to South Bend, the last run of Grand Trunk Western 4–8–4 No. 6322.[4] As railroads dieselized, steam locomotives were donated for display in parks or museums in Evansville, Fort Wayne, Gary, Hammond, and Indianapolis.

In 1966, long after dieselization, the Southern Railway initiated a new series of steam excursions by leasing a former Southern 2–8–2 once used in Indiana. Over the next 28 years the Southern and its successor, Norfolk Southern, operated steam

excursions with nine different steam locomotives, covering the former Southern line across Indiana and a number of the former Nickel Plate lines, before the program was abruptly canceled in October 1994.

The 1960s saw the beginnings of ambitious volunteer efforts to preserve and even operate historic railroad equipment. The Indiana Museum of Transport and Communication (IMOTAC, later Indiana Transportation Museum) was organized in 1960 to build a museum in Noblesville focusing on Indiana interurbans, with a short display operation. The Indiana Railway Museum, organized the following year, sought a location where restored steam trains could be operated over an actual railroad line, and moved successively from Westport to Greensburg to its present location in French Lick.

The two groups represented different wings of the emerging railroad preservation movement, epitomized by the formation of separate national groups: the Association of Railway Museums (ARM) and the Tourist Railway Association, Inc. (TRAIN). While the lines between the groups have blurred in recent years, a philosophical division remains between those who emphasize museum goals of restoration and interpretation and those who provide a train ride either for profit or as a volunteer activity.

Preservation remains an activity financed primarily by enthusiasts themselves, often with painfully slow progress and heartbreaking setbacks. IMOTAC sought to reerect the 1904 Indianapolis Traction Terminal train shed in Forest Park, Noblesville. The vast train shed was dismantled and moved, but the cost of reconstruction was beyond the means of the fledgling museum. Other valuable exhibits, including the 1948 streamlined observation car Sandy Creek from the New York Central's Twentieth Century Limited were later lost due to financial setbacks. For those museums and tourist railroads with operating trains, the goals of preservation must also be balanced with the need to meet current Federal Railway Administration standards, first applied to tourist railroads in the 1990s.

Railroad preservation in the late 1990s is a growing field, with its own national organizations, conferences, and magazine. It is maturing slowly from its early beginnings as a hobby activity, and is seeing increasing emphasis on documentation, authentic restoration, and historical interpretion. Funding, however, remains a critical problem for most organizations. The following railway museums and tourist railways indicate the diversity of railroad preservation activity in Indiana as of 1997.

Indiana Railway Museum, Inc.

Despite its name, IRM is primarily a volunteer operated tourist railway, the oldest one in Indiana. After several false starts IRM has operated since 1978 over 16 miles of former Southern Railway track between French Lick and Dubois, and is headquartered in the historic 1907 French Lick passenger station. The trip includes a 2,217-foot tunnel and scenic right-of-way through the Hoosier National Forest. Operations were steam powered from 1980 to 1989, with diesels used more recently. In 1984 a short electric trolley ride was added between French Lick and West Baden, using an imported trolley car similar to one that connected those towns between 1903 and 1919. A number of streamlined and heavyweight passenger cars are also on display.

Carthage, Knightstown and Shirley Railroad

The CK&S is a privately owned railroad operating a five-mile portion of the former CCC&StL (Big Four) Railroad, Michigan Division. In April 1987 the road purchased 20.5 miles of Big Four track between Emporia and Carthage, formerly run by the Indiana Eastern and Indiana Midland railroads. Diesel passenger excursions operated from the 1903 Big Four depot in Shirley, and freight service was operated, primarily to a paper products plant in Carthage. By 1990 the CK&S abandoned track north of Knightstown, and now provides tourist train operation on the isolated five miles from Knightstown to Carthage.

Whitewater Valley Railroad

The Whitewater Valley Railroad, a not-for-profit volunteer organization, operates 19 miles of the former CCC&StL Whitewater branch between Connersville and Metamora. The group was incorporated in 1972, and in 1974 first ran weekend tourist trains 24 miles between Connersville and Brookville. After the first season, service was cut back to Metamora and the section between Metamora and Brookville was torn out. The railroad purchased the remaining 18 miles from Penn Central in 1984, and later purchased an additional mile of track in Connersville from Indiana Hi-Rail Corporation.

The railroad is built primarily on the towpath of the 1845 Whitewater canal, paralleling and crossing the Whitewater River. Trains were steam powered until 1990, and the railroad hopes to resume steam operations in the future, operating in 1997 with diesels. A new depot, based on an original in Cambridge City, was under construction in Connersville in 1997.

Logansport Iron Horse Festival

The Logansport Iron Horse Festival is an annual one-weekend event in July, started in 1980. In 1984 the Festival association acquired a 2–8–0 steam locomotive, originally from West Virginia. Relettered Logansport and Eel River No. 1, the engine pulled festival excursions on several routes before being moved to Ohio in 1993. For 1996, excursions were run over the TP&W line using a C&O Berkshire restored by the Fort Wayne Railway Historical Society.

Corydon Scenic Railroad

Unique in Indiana, the century-old Louisville, New Albany and Corydon continues to offer passenger service over its own line. Starting in 1991, the Corydon offers weekend (weekday in summer) trips from Corydon eight miles over the steep grades of this historic short line to Corydon Junction, the interchange point with Norfolk Southern.

Volunteers replace boiler tubes during restoration of Nickel Plate 587 at Beech Grove shops. The 1918 USRA Mikado, a designated national historic landmark, was returned to excursion service by Indiana Transportation Museum in 1988.   *Photo by James Vawter*

New Haven and Lake Erie
Narrow Gauge Steam Railroad

The NH&LE is a private tourist railroad located on Edgerton Road, northeast of New Haven, Indiana. In operation since 1988, it is 2' gauge, and features a ten-ton German 0–4–0T locomotive. The railroad includes the 1879 Clover Leaf depot from Craigville, moved 40 miles, restored, and placed on the National Register of Historic Places. It operates on selected weekends in summer and fall.

Indiana Transportation Museum

Begun in 1960 as the Indiana Museum of Transport and Communication, the name was changed in 1980 to Indiana Transportation Museum. It has been located since 1965 in Forest Park, Noblesville, where the former NKP Hobbs depot was moved in 1966. The initial focus was on interurbans, and several Indiana interurban car bodies have been recovered. Demonstration rides are provided using cars from outside Indiana. A large collection of railroad passenger and freight equipment is displayed, ranging from wooden to streamlined stainless-steel equipment. An exceptional exhibit is Florida East Coast private car No. 90, built for tycoon Henry Flagler in 1898, later used on the Central Indiana Railroad, and still later owned and restored by Mr. and Mrs. Anton (Tony) Hulman, Jr.

In 1983 the museum acquired F-unit diesels and streamlined coaches and began "Fairtrain" service

Restored F7 diesels pull Indiana Transportation Museum streamlined passenger cars through Liberty en route to the Cincinnati "Tall Stacks Festival" in 1988. The former B&O depot has since been restored. *Photo by Dick Acton, Sr.—Jay Williams collection*

between Carmel and the Indiana State Fairgrounds. Painted in Monon red and grey, the equipment has also offered occasional excursions to Bloomington, Spencer, and Cincinnati. In 1988 former LE&W-NKP steam locomotive 587 was moved from Broad Ripple Park, Indianapolis, and restored to operating condition in a five-year volunteer effort. In 1984 it was designated a national historic landmark, the first steam locomotive in the United States to win that honor.

Weekend excursions and Fairtrains are offered now on portions of the 39-mile Indianapolis-Tipton line, with which the museum connects. Owned by the Hoosier Heritage Port Authority, the line connects a number of potential tourist sites, and has the potential of being rebuilt for service into the Indianapolis Union Station.

Railway Heritage Network

Based in Linden, Indiana, the Railway Heritage Network promotes, funds, researches, and displays railroad history through a variety of programs. They have participated with the Linden-Madison Township Historical Society in restoring the 1905 Junction depot once used by the Clover Leaf and the Monon Railroad. The museum also includes a restored Nickel Plate Railroad caboose and a model railroad display.

Evansville Museum of Arts and Science

The museum displays a replica railroad depot and a full-size train, including Milwaukee Road 0–6–0 No. 12, built by Milwaukee Road shops in 1908, a Louisville and Nashville tavern-lounge car, and a Louisville and Nashville caboose.

Fort Wayne Railway Historical Society

The Fort Wayne Railway Historical Society restored Nickel Plate 2–8–4 No. 765, formerly on display in Fort Wayne, and operated it for the first time in May 1980. The locomotive has subsequently operated throughout much of the East. It has been joined by a similar 2–8–4, C&O No. 2716, which the society operated for the first time at the Logansport Iron Horse Festival in 1996. The group is also restoring former Wabash 0–6–0 No. 534 at its shop facilities in Casad Industrial Park, New Haven, Indiana.

Garrett Railroad Museum

Housed in the relocated Garrett B&O freight depot (built c. 1880), the museum houses railroad artifacts and a model train club. A B&O semi-streamlined passenger car is displayed outside, along with smaller artifacts.

National New York Central Museum

The National New York Central Museum, opened in 1987, is owned by the city of Elkhart, and located in a former NYC freight house across from the former NYC depot now used by Amtrak. New York Central equipment on display includes L3 Mohawk 4–8–2 No. 3001, built by Alco in 1940, an E–8 passenger diesel, a 1920 steam wrecking crane from Harmon, N.Y., and a wood caboose. Equipment from other railroads is also on display, and a restaurant on the site is housed in streamlined passenger cars painted in NYC colors. The museum has hosted visiting exhibits, including "Women in Railroading," and the Michigan "Art Train."

Hesston Steam Museum

Established as a traction engine museum in 1957, the museum added its first steam locomotive in 1964. Several rare narrow-gauge engines are restored or operated, including 2' gauge locomotives from Germany, Czechoslovakia, and the Darjeeling Himalayan Railway in India, plus a 3' gauge Shay geared locomotive from Oregon. The museum operates weekends over a $2\frac{1}{4}$-mile loop of track, and features an annual four-day Labor Day weekend steam show.

Hoosier Valley Railroad Museum, Inc.

Originally known as the Miami County Steam Locomotive Association, the HVRM was established in 1961 to restore C&O steam locomotive 2789, then on display in a park in Peru. The engine was moved to a new site in North Judson in 1988, and the new name was adopted in January 1992. The museum is located at the once-busy crossing point of four railroads—the Erie, C&O, PRR, and NYC. The museum is currently working to restore No. 2789 to working condition. Short excursion rides are pulled by a 1946 Whitcomb 44-ton diesel switcher, formerly used at the Port of Indiana. Passenger and freight cars, cabooses, and a railroad crane are also on display. As of 1996 the museum was negotiating for possible acquisition and movement of the 1883 Erie Railroad depot from Leiters Ford, currently owned by the Fulton County Historical Society.

A French Lick, West Baden and Southern tourist train emerges from a 2,217-foot tunnel southwest of French Lick. Built by the Southern Railway, it was part of the road's 1907 extension to French Lick.
French Lick, West Baden and Southern Railway

Three Rivers Railroad Heritage Council

Three Rivers Railroad Heritage Council, Inc. was formed in Fort Wayne in 1994 with the intention of establishing a railroad museum in the former Fort Wayne and Jackson (NYC) freight station north of downtown, accompanied by electric trolley operation on an adjacent spur track to the Fort Wayne water treatment plant. Still in its early stages, the organization sponsored a NS steam excursion in July 1994 and has salvaged the body of the last Fort Wayne streetcar. Monthly meetings are held at the Allen County Public Library in Fort Wayne.

The Children's Museum

The Children's Museum in Indianapolis has an interpretive exhibit devoted to railroading. The pride of the exhibit is the locomotive Reuben Wells, named for the master mechanic of the JM&I who designed and built it in 1868, for service on the Madison incline. Rebuilt as an 0–8–0T in 1886, it was retired in 1905 and placed at Purdue University. Retrieved by the Pennsylvania Railroad in 1940, the Reuben Wells was restored at Altoona Works to its original 0–10–0T design and appearance. It was donated to The Children's Museum in 1968. An 1888 Pennsylvania Railroad wrecking train caboose is also on exhibit, along with the nation's largest collection of pre–World War II toy trains.

American-European Express

Since 1989 Indiana has enjoyed sporadic visits of a privately operated luxury passenger service. Dressed in a blue, white, and gold livery emulating the European Orient Express, the American-Euro-

Former Nickel Plate (LE&W) depot at Spiceland, which became a restaurant, typified non-railroad uses after discontinuance of passenger trains. Like many other depots, it has now disappeared. *Photo by Richard S. Simons*

pean Express is a luxury cruise train, featuring plush accommodations, gourmet dining, and upscale prices. The train began operation in fall 1989 as a five-car section attached to Amtrak's Capitol Limited, and was later expanded to a separate train following the Cardinal route with stops in Indianapolis, Cincinnati, and the Greenbrier Hotel in West Virginia. Refurbished equipment included a former Twentieth Century Limited observation car. Scheduled service was disrupted by a June 21, 1991, derailment near Monon, Indiana, and ended after the 1991 season, but the train returned in 1995 with an itinerary of coast-to-coast cruises passing through Indiana. For 1996 the train was scheduled on a more southerly route, but may return to Indiana in the future.[5]

National Railway Historical Society

The National Railway Historical Society, organized in 1935 and incorporated in 1937, has stimulated enthusiasm through the development of 173 local chapters. Chapters sponsor railroad talks and excursions, promote consciousness of railroad history, and cooperate with active railroads in the "Operation Lifesaver" program. Indiana has two NRHS chapters, the Indianapolis chapter and the Hoosierland chapter in the Marion-Muncie area.

Former Tourist Railways

With erratic funding and reliance on a shifting railroad network, it is not surprising that some tourist railroad operations have dropped out. A steam-powered tourist train based in Middlebury ran briefly on a former NYC branch until the equipment was moved to Logansport in 1984. Diesel-powered trains were briefly operated out of Brazil and out of Monterey, both on short lines established for freight service. Between 1975 and 1993 the Little River Railroad operated steam excursions in Steuben County, operating out of Pleasant Lake over the tracks of the Hillsdale County Railway (former LS&MS). In 1994 the operation was moved 30 miles north to Coldwater, Michigan.

The Indiana Dinner Train began operations in 1990 over the tracks of the new Indiana Rail Road between Indianapolis and Bargersville, with occasional operations to Bloomington and beyond. With stainless steel cars pulled by a streamlined diesel E unit, the train offered gourmet dining and entertainment. Although successful, most of the equipment was sold and the train discontinued by 1995.

Other Preserved Equipment

Besides railroad equipment in museums, other equipment is displayed at individual sites. This includes Elgin, Joliet and Eastern 2–8–2 No. 765, on display at Lake Front Park, Gary, and NKP 2–8–2 No. 624, on display in Hammond. Cabooses are widely distributed. A 1995 inventory counted 47 cabooses at Indiana tourist railroads or museums, plus another 76 at local museums, parks, or in private hands.[6]

Depots and Preservation

Indiana railroad depots, while rapidly disappearing, have also been targets for preservation in recent years. Of almost 1,500 steam road depots existing in Indiana in 1914, fewer than 250 remained by 1989.[7] Ninety depots had disappeared in the previous ten years alone. Only 69 depots remained in railroad uses; 10 were museums; and 87 had found new uses in a variety of public and private functions. While 8 depots were under restoration, 51 stood vacant, subject to decay, arson, and neglect.

Remaining depots, while still threatened, are more likely today to be recognized and the subject of some form of preservation. Twelve Indiana depots have been listed individually in the National Register of Historic Places, and at least ten more included in designated historic districts. National Register listing per se, while important, cannot guarantee survival, however. The 1851 New Albany terminal depot and train shed of the New Albany and Salem, the oldest and most unique of Indiana's depots, was destroyed in 1995 despite its National Register status. At least 21 of the depots identified in 1989 have been lost by 1995, but others of those once threatened or vacant have found caretakers or new uses.[8]

Preeminent among the surviving depots is the Indianapolis Union Depot. On the site of the original 1853 Union Depot, the present complex includes the brick 1888 Romanesque headhouse by architect Thomas Rodd and the 1922 concrete train sheds. After an abortive 1974 renovation effort, the city of Indianapolis became owner of the structure and spent $12 million for basic repairs, and private developers reopened the complex as a festival marketplace, hotel, and Amtrak station in April 1986. Progress since then has been erratic, and in 1997 the facility was scheduled to close unless a new developer could be found to invest in and reposition it.

The 1914 Fort Wayne PRR station was rehabbed in 1996 for use by an architectural firm, while the Gary NYC/B&O station and the Richmond PRR depot, both publicly owned, have yet to find new uses. The success rate has been higher for smaller depots scattered around the state, where manageable restoration costs combine with greater ease of finding new uses. While relatively scarce, and frequently still endangered, enough depots survive around Indiana to suggest their prevalence and the important role they once played in local communities.

Major Railroads in Indiana

THE FOLLOWING PAGES include line-by-line descriptions of the 15 major rail systems which operated in Indiana during the mid–1940s, before the era of megamergers and reduction of trackage to that of three major systems. They are listed in in-state mileage order from largest to smallest.

Each includes a family tree which shows corporations operated in Indiana. In most instances it does not include out-of-state predecessor corporations, short-lived transition corporations, out-of-state merger partners, or non-operating companies. The charts, however, show the relationships and acquisitions among parts of each system.

NEW YORK CENTRAL

The New York Central Railroad, which ranked first in Indiana in mileage operated, evolved by merger, acquisition, and lease from three earlier systems: Lake Shore and Michigan Southern, which was the first to come under the control of the original New York Central; Cleveland, Cincinnati, Chicago and St. Louis (Big Four); and Michigan Central. Peak system mileage in Indiana, exclusive of terminal and switching roads, was 1,629, which accounted for approximately 22% of the state total.[1]

Of the system's three components, the Big Four was by far the largest presence in Indiana with 1,103 miles or 68%, followed by the New York Central with 453 miles or 28%. The small balance of 73 miles or 4% was Michigan Central trackage.[2]

Two eventual New York Central lines were the first to connect the East with Chicago, and by the early 1850s components of the system had established a strong presence in Indiana with routes that would connect Chicago and St. Louis with Cleveland and the East, plus lines to Cincinnati, Indianapolis, Lafayette, and other points. With a single exception, these were Indiana's earliest trunk lines.

The Lake Shore Route

What is now Conrail's main New York–Chicago line had its western beginnings on March 20, 1837, when the State of Michigan established the southern line in its internal improvements program.[3] Encountering financial problems reminiscent of those in Indiana's internal improvements program, the state sold its interest to a private company, the Michigan Southern, on December 28, 1846.[4] Racing the Michigan Central, likewise a castoff of the state's internal improvements program, the Michigan Southern reached Chicago in February 1852, a few weeks ahead of the Michigan Central. Its route lay across southern Michigan through Hillsdale and Sturgis to Elkhart, Indiana.[5] Meanwhile the Northern Indiana Railroad had been established in 1850 to build eastward from La Porte to a junction with the Michigan Southern.[6] In 1855 the Michigan Southern and the Northern Indiana merged to form the Michigan Southern and Northern Indiana, a 243-mile Toledo-Chicago line that became known as the "Old Road."[7] Of the total, approximately 117 miles were in Indiana.[8]

While these developments were taking place in the West, even more important ones were occurring in the East. In 1853, 12 small roads, including the pioneer Mohawk and Hudson Rail Road, which dated from 1831, merged to form the New York Central, a continuous through line between Albany and Buffalo.[9] As the railroad marched westward it consolidated with the Lake Shore, which began as the Cleveland, Painesville and Ashtabula Railroad between Cleveland and Erie, Pennsylvania, in 1852. This in turn merged with the Michigan Southern and Northern Indiana to become the Lake Shore and Michigan Southern Railroad.[10]

Not pleased with the existing circuitous route, the MS&NI built directly west from Toledo in 1858, joining the Old Road at Elkhart. This shaved nine

NYC Hudson, running fast with postwar James Whitcomb Riley at Zionsville, typified New York Central passenger service.   *Jay Williams collection*

miles from the distance between Toledo and Elkhart, and included what was then the longest tangent track in the United States, 68.49 absolutely straight miles stretching eastward from Butler, Indiana. Today it remains the third longest tangent in the country.[11]

In 1869 "Commodore" Cornelius Vanderbilt became the principal player on the New York Central scene when he began to acquire stock control of small roads and merge them into an ocean-to-Great Lakes system. Although controlling both the New York Central and Hudson River and the Lake Shore and Michigan Southern, he was content with nothing less than a monopoly, and so he also bought

heavily into Michigan Central.[12] This too became part of his New York Central system, which was established April 29, 1914. On February 1, 1930, after many years of control through stock ownership, New York Central leased the Michigan Central.[13]

The Lake Shore routes from the beginning were heavily traveled. In 1868, when the first *Official Guide of the Railways* was published, four passenger trains were operated daily each way between Chicago and Toledo with a fifth pair being added east of Elkhart. Three of these continued to operate over the slower, circuitous "Old Road," rather than the new "Air Line."[14]

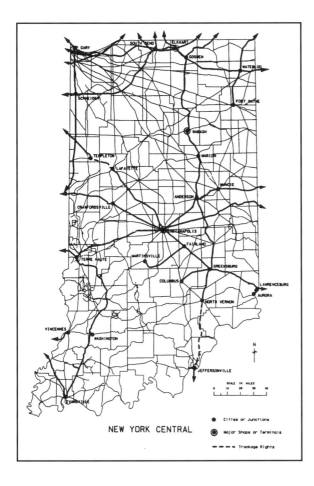

NEW YORK CENTRAL

● Cities or Junctions
◎ Major Shops or Terminals
- - - - Trackage Rights

SCALE IN MILES
0   10   20   30   40

N

On September 14, 1875, the New York Central and the LS&MS put in operation the Fast Mail, the first regular, fast, through service between New York and Chicago, with a 26-hour schedule westbound.[15] On June 15, 1902, the New York Central's ultimate flagship, the Twentieth Century Limited, began her much publicized career.[16]

By 1916—the high-water mark in U.S. rail mileage—most trains had shifted to the fast Air Line, which carried 26 movements daily, including the Twentieth Century Limited, on a 20-hour schedule from New York to Chicago. Meanwhile the Old Road traffic grew more slowly to four trains each way, one of which was a through run between New York and Chicago.[17]

Successive generations of steam engines powered these trains, culminating in the famous Hudson or 4–6–4 design introduced in 1927. Dieselization permitted further speedups. By 1947, the peak of the post–World War II travel boom, 36 trains daily sped over the Air Line route, including the Twentieth Century Limited, which by now had cut its run to a minimum time of 15½ hours but lasted

only until 1967.[18] Mistakenly foreseeing a boom in rail travel, New York Central scheduled through Los Angeles and San Francisco cars to and from New York City and invested $56,000,000 in 720 new cars.[19]

Amtrak now routes two passenger trains a day each way over the former Air Line, but it carries a vast amount of freight. Conrail schedules 88 freights daily (1993), or an average of one every 16 minutes, in or out of the electronic Elkhart Yard toward Chicago or the East. Trains made up here are sent directly to other railroads, relieving congestion in Chicago, long known as the graveyard of freight cars.[20]

In addition to its main line, the historical New York Central operated six other Indiana routes.

"Old Road" Main Line

The original line between Toledo and Chicago, the Michigan Southern and Northern Indiana, continued to carry a surprising amount of traffic for years after the Air Line was built, but gradually lost out as a through route. By the end of World War II, passenger service was down to four trains daily, including one Chicago–New York run.[21] In 1964 a 10-mile section between Osseo and Hudson, Michigan, was abandoned, thus ending the Old Road as a through route. The Indiana portion exists today as part of Conrail's main freight route between Chicago and Detroit via Kalamazoo.[22]

Fort Wayne and Jackson

One of the Lake Shore's earlier acquisitions was the 100-mile Fort Wayne, Jackson and Saginaw Railroad, which began construction March 20, 1869, to connect Fort Wayne and Jackson, Michigan. The first train operated in 1870 to the Michigan State Fair at Jackson. In 1879 the railroad was reorganized as the Fort Wayne and Jackson Railroad, which the Lake Shore leased effective September 1, 1882.[23] The line passed through Auburn, Waterloo, and Angola before entering Michigan where it traveled through Hillsdale and Jonesville amid a thicket of NYC lines before reaching Jackson. During its peak it carried six daily passenger trains, but these were gone by the end of World War II, after service had been eliminated north of Hillsdale about 1939.[24]

As a Penn Central line, much of it was abandoned piecemeal in 1973 and 1976.[25] All that remains in

NEW YORK CENTRAL

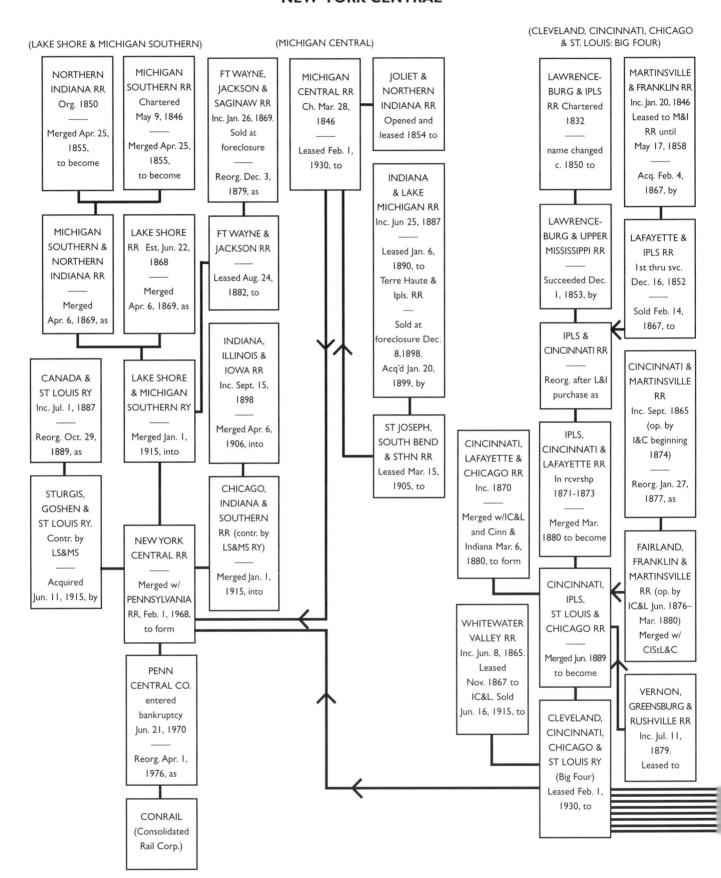

(LAKE SHORE & MICHIGAN SOUTHERN)

(MICHIGAN CENTRAL)

(CLEVELAND, CINCINNATI, CHICAGO & ST. LOUIS: BIG FOUR)

NORTHERN INDIANA RR
Org. 1850
———
Merged Apr. 25, 1855, to become

MICHIGAN SOUTHERN RR
Chartered May 9, 1846
———
Merged Apr. 25, 1855, to become

FT WAYNE, JACKSON & SAGINAW RR
Inc. Jan. 26, 1869. Sold at foreclosure
———
Reorg. Dec. 3, 1879, as

MICHIGAN CENTRAL RR
Ch. Mar. 28, 1846
———
Leased Feb. 1, 1930, to

JOLIET & NORTHERN INDIANA RR
Opened and leased 1854 to

LAWRENCE-BURG & IPLS RR Chartered 1832
———
name changed c. 1850 to

MARTINSVILLE & FRANKLIN RR
Inc. Jan. 20, 1846
Leased to M&I RR until May 17, 1858
———
Acq. Feb. 4, 1867, by

MICHIGAN SOUTHERN & NORTHERN INDIANA RR
———
Merged Apr. 6, 1869, as

LAKE SHORE RR Est. Jun. 22, 1868
———
Merged Apr. 6, 1869, as

FT WAYNE & JACKSON RR
———
Leased Aug. 24, 1882, to

INDIANA & LAKE MICHIGAN RR
Inc. Jun 25, 1887
———
Leased Jan. 6, 1890, to Terre Haute & Ipls. RR
———
Sold at foreclosure Dec. 8,1898. Acq'd Jan. 20, 1899, by

LAWRENCE-BURG & UPPER MISSISSIPPI RR
———
Succeeded Dec. 1, 1853, by

LAFAYETTE & IPLS RR
1st thru svc. Dec. 16, 1852
———
Sold Feb. 14, 1867, to

CANADA & ST LOUIS RY
Inc. Jul. 1, 1887
———
Reorg. Oct. 29, 1889, as

LAKE SHORE & MICHIGAN SOUTHERN RY
———
Merged Jan. 1, 1915, into

INDIANA, ILLINOIS & IOWA RR
Inc. Sept. 15, 1898
———
Merged Apr. 6, 1906, into

IPLS & CINCINNATI RR
———
Reorg. after L&I purchase as

CINCINNATI & MARTINSVILLE RR
Inc. Sept. 1865 (op. by I&C beginning 1874)
———
Reorg. Jan. 27, 1877, as

ST JOSEPH, SOUTH BEND & STHN RR
Leased Mar. 15, 1905, to

CINCINNATI, LAFAYETTE & CHICAGO RR
Inc. 1870
———
Merged w/IC&L and Cinn & Indiana Mar. 6, 1880, to form

IPLS, CINCINNATI & LAFAYETTE RR
In rcvrshp 1871-1873
———
Merged Mar. 1880 to become

STURGIS, GOSHEN & ST LOUIS RY.
Contr. by LS&MS
———
Acquired Jun. 11, 1915, by

NEW YORK CENTRAL RR
———
Merged w/ PENNSYLVANIA RR, Feb. 1, 1968, to form

CHICAGO, INDIANA & SOUTHERN RR (contr. by LS&MS RY)
———
Merged Jan. 1, 1915, into

FAIRLAND, FRANKLIN & MARTINSVILLE RR (op. by IC&L Jun. 1876–Mar. 1880)
Merged w/ CIStL&C

CINCINNATI, IPLS, ST LOUIS & CHICAGO RR
———
Merged Jun. 1889 to become

PENN CENTRAL CO.
entered bankruptcy Jun. 21, 1970
———
Reorg. Apr. 1, 1976, as

WHITEWATER VALLEY RR
Inc. Jun. 8, 1865.
Leased Nov. 1867 to IC&L. Sold Jun. 16, 1915, to

VERNON, GREENSBURG & RUSHVILLE RR
Inc. Jul. 11, 1879.
Leased to

CLEVELAND, CINCINNATI, CHICAGO & ST LOUIS RY (Big Four)
Leased Feb. 1, 1930, to

CONRAIL
(Consolidated Rail Corp.)

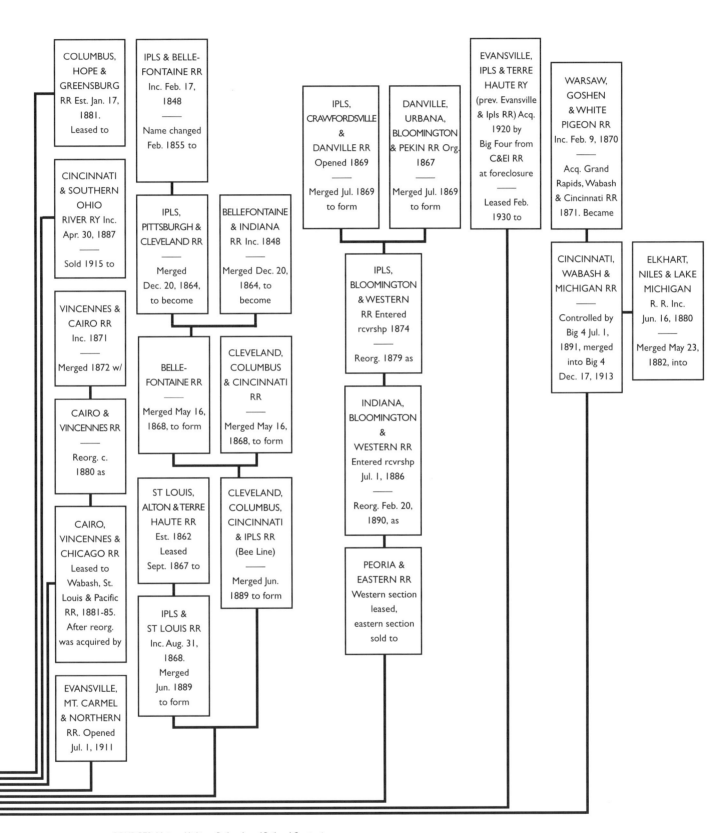

COLUMBUS, HOPE & GREENSBURG RR Est. Jan. 17, 1881. Leased to

IPLS & BELLE-FONTAINE RR Inc. Feb. 17, 1848

Name changed Feb. 1855 to

IPLS, CRAWFORDSVILLE & DANVILLE RR Opened 1869

Merged Jul. 1869 to form

DANVILLE, URBANA, BLOOMINGTON & PEKIN RR Org. 1867

Merged Jul. 1869 to form

EVANSVILLE, IPLS & TERRE HAUTE RY (prev. Evansville & Ipls RR) Acq. 1920 by Big Four from C&EI RR at foreclosure

Leased Feb. 1930 to

WARSAW, GOSHEN & WHITE PIGEON RR Inc. Feb. 9, 1870

Acq. Grand Rapids, Wabash & Cincinnati RR 1871. Became

CINCINNATI & SOUTHERN OHIO RIVER RY Inc. Apr. 30, 1887

Sold 1915 to

IPLS, PITTSBURGH & CLEVELAND RR

Merged Dec. 20, 1864, to become

BELLEFONTAINE & INDIANA RR Inc. 1848

Merged Dec. 20, 1864, to become

IPLS, BLOOMINGTON & WESTERN RR Entered rcvrshp 1874

Reorg. 1879 as

CINCINNATI, WABASH & MICHIGAN RR

Controlled by Big 4 Jul. 1, 1891, merged into Big 4 Dec. 17, 1913

ELKHART, NILES & LAKE MICHIGAN R. R. Inc. Jun. 16, 1880

Merged May 23, 1882, into

VINCENNES & CAIRO RR Inc. 1871

Merged 1872 w/

BELLE-FONTAINE RR

Merged May 16, 1868, to form

CLEVELAND, COLUMBUS & CINCINNATI RR

Merged May 16, 1868, to form

INDIANA, BLOOMINGTON & WESTERN RR Entered rcvrshp Jul. 1, 1886

Reorg. Feb. 20, 1890, as

CAIRO & VINCENNES RR

Reorg. c. 1880 as

CAIRO, VINCENNES & CHICAGO RR Leased to Wabash, St. Louis & Pacific RR, 1881-85. After reorg. was acquired by

ST LOUIS, ALTON & TERRE HAUTE RR Est. 1862 Leased Sept. 1867 to

CLEVELAND, COLUMBUS, CINCINNATI & IPLS RR (Bee Line)

Merged Jun. 1889 to form

PEORIA & EASTERN RR Western section leased, eastern section sold to

EVANSVILLE, MT. CARMEL & NORTHERN RR. Opened Jul. 1, 1911

IPLS & ST LOUIS RR Inc. Aug. 31, 1868. Merged Jun. 1889 to form

SOURCES: Meints, *Michigan Railroads and Railroad Companies*; Drury, *Historical Guide to North American Railroads*; Harlow, *The Road of the Century*; Poor, *Manual of the Railroads of the United States*; Edson, *Railroad Names*

Indiana in 1996, besides the 1.7-mile Auburn Port Authority Railroad, is the line north of Steubenville to the Hillsdale, Michigan, area.[26] In 1976 the Hillsdale County Railway, an independent short line, was organized to acquire the remaining route. In 1992, following a merger, it became the Indiana Northeastern Railroad.[27] Until 1993 the tourist-hauling Little River Railroad operated a steam engine over parts of the line south of Angola.[28]

Indiana, Illinois and Iowa

The 200-mile Indiana, Illinois and Iowa Railroad, known as the "Three I," was chartered December 27, 1881, and connected Zearing, in the Illinois coal fields, with South Bend, Indiana, via Streator and Kankakee, Illinois. It was opened between Streator and Momence, Illinois, on July 1, 1882, completed to North Judson in December 1886, and reached South Bend in November 1894. Early directors were all from Iowa and Illinois, and the railroad was one of the few in Indiana to be built from west to east.[29]

Unofficially called the Kankakee Belt, it was controlled jointly by the LS&MS and the Michigan Central, but later officially became part of the New York Central.[30] It was promoted as an early bypass route to avoid Chicago freight yard congestion, and in 1993 operated run-through service with the Santa Fe via Streator, Illinois.[31] Passenger traffic was never heavy and at the 1916 peak consisted of two daily round trips between South Bend and Streator. By 1939 this had been reduced to one mixed (passenger and freight) train daily, and by 1940 it too was gone. Until the 1920s there was also a daily passenger train from Indianapolis to South Bend, which used the 19.6 miles of the Kankakee Belt between Walkerton and South Bend after switching off the Lake Erie and Western (now Norfolk Southern) Michigan City line at Walkerton.[32] The Kankakee Belt track east of Wheatfield was abandoned in 1982 and run-through freight trains are routed via other lines east of Schneider.[33]

Sturgis, Goshen and St. Louis

This 29-mile branch was opened December 20, 1888, by the Canada and St. Louis Railway and was acquired by the Sturgis, Goshen and St. Louis Railway for the LS&MS after a foreclosure sale August 17, 1889. The LS&MS operated it under lease until it was consolidated into NYC in 1915.[34] A seven-mile branch to Findley, Michigan, was added to connect with the Michigan Central and provide a through service to Battle Creek. Two round trips operated daily during the World War I peak, but regular passenger trains were replaced by mixed trains by the late 1920s.[35] It was known locally as the Pumpkin Vine. New York Central abandoned most of the line north of Shipshewana in 1960. Its successor, Indiana Interstate, abandoned the balance in 1980.[36] A steam tourist train operated briefly out of Middlebury, Indiana.

Chicago, Indiana and Southern

A latecomer to the New York Central system, the 109-mile Chicago, Indiana and Southern was completed in 1906 to form part of a through New York Central route between southern Illinois coal fields and heavy industries of the Calumet region. It connected with the main line of the LS&MS at Indiana Harbor, and extended south through Schneider and Kentland, just inside the state line, finally curving west to Danville, Illinois. There it connected with a Big Four line built north from Cairo and the Harrisburg, Illinois, coal fields. It was controlled by the LS&MS and by 1915 was fully merged into the NYC.[37] The combined line, which was operated as a single unit, totaled 370 miles.

Never a heavy passenger carrier, during peak travel years it operated a curious schedule with only a northbound train between Cairo and Chicago, depending on connecting trains, which lacked same day service, for southbound passengers. By the mid–1940s this was down to an overnight trip in each direction between Harrisburg, Illinois, and Chicago. The line also carried traffic from Evansville over a branch that joined at Mt. Carmel, Illinois.[38] The entire line is mostly abandoned except for the Conrail segment north of Schneider and two short sections in Benton and Warren counties owned by the Bee Line and the Kankakee, Beaverville and Southern Railroads.[39]

Cleveland, Cincinnati, Chicago and St. Louis (Big Four)

The core of New York Central's Indiana operations, the Big Four's trackage in Indiana was more than double that of the other NYC components combined. Contrasted with the LS&MS and Michigan Central lines, which were mostly in the north, the Big Four covered the central and southern parts

The most modern of the NYC's steam locomotives, this 1945 Niagara takes water from the track pan at Lydick in 1953. It would be gone in four years. *Photo by Leo Witucki—Victor A. Baird collection*

of the state. Its rails radiated in six directions from Indianapolis, and during the peak years it dominated passenger travel by operating 50 trains daily, as well as nearly 60 trains in other parts of the state.[40]

Indianapolis and Bellefontaine (Bee Line)

With a charter going back to 1848, the Indianapolis and Bellefontaine Railroad was projected between Indianapolis and Union City, 85 miles away, where it would connect with the Bellefontaine and Indiana Railroad from Galion, Ohio, and with

the Dayton and Union Railroad to provide a through route to Dayton. The first train ran from Indianapolis to Pendleton on December 11, 1850, and by January 24, 1853, the entire line was open.[41] On December 20, 1864, the Indianapolis and Bellefontaine and the Bellefontaine and Indiana combined as the Bellefontaine Railway. In 1868 the Bellefontaine merged with the Cleveland, Columbus and Cincinnati to form the Cleveland, Columbus, Cincinnati and Indianapolis Railroad. A further merger in 1889 formed the Cleveland, Cincinnati, Chicago and St. Louis, the second Big Four.[42] The New York Central Railroad gradually gained stock control and on February 1, 1930, formally leased the Big Four.[43]

Always a heavy passenger carrier, the route, combined with its extension from Indianapolis to St. Louis, carried 21 passenger trains a day in the peak years, and still carried 18 in the post–World War II period. Some carried through cars between New York City and Texas, Oklahoma, and Mexico.[44] Today it is part of Conrail's St. Louis–New York main line. Doubletracked and well maintained, it was selected by Conrail for retention in place of the rival Pennsylvania main line from Richmond through Indianapolis. It carries heavy freight traffic, including run-throughs from Western roads.[45]

Indianapolis and St. Louis

Extension westward to St. Louis was a logical step for the Bellefontaine. Two earlier roads had been completed, the Terre Haute and Richmond between Terre Haute and Indianapolis in 1852 and the St. Louis, Alton and Terre Haute to St. Louis in 1856. But other roads were unable to effect a satisfactory traffic agreement, so the Bellefontaine, along with five roads which ultimately became parts either of the New York Central or the rival Pennsylvania system, built the 72-mile Indianapolis and St. Louis, a competing line between Indianapolis and Terre Haute. It opened on July 4, 1870. To complete an alternate route to St. Louis, it leased the St. Louis, Alton and Terre Haute.[46] It participated in a merger in June 1889 with the CCC&I that formed the "modern" Big Four.

The route is now Conrail's main line west of Indianapolis. Doubletracked to Terre Haute, it has replaced the abandoned former rival Pennsylvania line. West of Terre Haute it is largely abandoned across Illinois in favor of the St. Louis, Vandalia and Terre Haute (later Pennsylvania) line.[47] The large electronic hump yard at Avon, just west of Indianapolis, classifies traffic between St. Louis and the East. It handled 40 scheduled freight trains a day (1993), or one every 36 minutes.[48]

Indianapolis, Cincinnati and Lafayette

New York Central's 303-mile Cincinnati-Indianapolis-Chicago line has roots going back to 1832, when the state chartered the Lawrenceburg and Indianapolis Railroad and a second road to connect Indianapolis and Lafayette. By 1834 the Lawrenceburg and Indianapolis built a 1¼-mile horse-

powered demonstration railroad on the east side of Shelbyville. Short-lived, it was the first railroad in Indiana.[49]

After a succession of reorganizations, the road emerged as the Indianapolis and Cincinnati Railroad. The first train operated from Indianapolis to Lawrenceburg on November 1, 1853, with continued travel to Cincinnati by Ohio River steamer.[50] In 1856 it opened an extension along the riverbank into Cincinnati over the tracks of the Ohio and Mississippi, by laying a third rail between the O&M's broad-gauge rails. This was replaced in 1863 by the railroad's own line.[51]

At the north end of the line, the Lafayette and Indianapolis, divorced in 1848 from its initial connection with the Madison Road, completed its track and operated the first through train on December 16, 1852.[52] Henry C. Lord, president of the Indianapolis and Cincinnati, acquired the Lafayette line after he threatened to build a competing road by way of Crawfordsville. The Lafayette owners capitulated and Lord merged the two roads as the Indianapolis, Cincinnati and Lafayette Railroad on February 14, 1867.[53] The IC&L also controlled the White Water Valley Railroad and its extension, the Harrison Branch Railroad, as well as the Cincinnati and Martinsville Railroad and the Cincinnati and Indiana Railroad, all of which were to become parts of the Big Four. It was a part owner of the Indianapolis and Vincennes, which ultimately became a Pennsylvania system component.[54]

The logical extension to Chicago came with the incorporation of the Cincinnati, Lafayette and Chicago Railroad in 1870. It began operating August 25, 1872, using 19 miles of trackage rights between Lafayette and Templeton over the Lake Erie and Western (later NKP), 56 miles of its own track between Templeton and Kankakee, Illinois, and trackage rights over 54 miles of the Illinois Central between Kankakee and Chicago.[55] Always a heavy passenger carrier, this line operated 17 trains in the 1916 peak year and still carried 13 after the end of World War II, including the flagship day train, the James Whitcomb Riley. It also carried through Florida cars.[56]

The line was abandoned between Indianapolis and Lafayette in 1976, 1985, and 1987. The Shelbyville-Cincinnati segment was sold to the new Central Railroad of Indiana, and the Lafayette-Kankakee line became the Kankakee, Beaverville and Southern Railroad, leaving only Indianapolis-Shelbyville still in Conrail hands.[57]

NYC coal train, led by 4–8–2 Mohawk, climbs West Lafayette hill with a helper engine pushing on the rear. White flags denote an "extra" train.   *Photo by William Swartz—M. D. McCarter collection*

White Water Valley

The first Indiana railroad to supplant a canal, the White Water Valley Railroad opened between Harrison, Ohio, and Hagerstown, Indiana, 62 miles, on July 21, 1868, connecting with the Harrison Branch Railroad from Valley Junction (near Cincinnati). It had purchased the Whitewater Canal for use as a right-of-way. The Indianapolis, Cincinnati and Lafayette operated the road until 1871, when it became independent until 1875. The Big Four assumed operation in 1890 and purchased it on June 16, 1915.[58]

Passenger service in the early years included through cars to Indianapolis and to Chicago via connections in Cambridge City and Hagerstown.[59] Later a joint service was operated briefly with the Lake Erie and Western through Connersville to Muncie and Fort Wayne, with through parlor cars between Cincinnati and Fort Wayne. During the World War I peak there were 12 passenger trains daily, but the last disappeared in 1933.[60] The track between Hagerstown and Beesons (north of Connersville) was abandoned in 1931. Freight service was discontinued by Penn Central in 1972, leaving an isolated Penn Central (later Conrail) switching operation between Connersville and Beesons, which was taken over by Indiana Hi-Rail.[61] Nineteen miles from Connersville to south of Metamora have been operated for tourist service since 1974 by the Whitewater Valley Railroad, while the 26 miles from Brookville to Valley Junction, Ohio, are operated by the Indiana and Ohio Railroad, which acquired the track from Penn Central in 1979.[62]

Cincinnati, Wabash and Michigan

What became the Big Four's Michigan Division was the longest New York Central line in Indiana, running the length of the state to connect Benton Harbor, Michigan, and Louisville, Kentucky, 303 miles. The first segment was opened August 15, 1870, between Goshen and Warsaw. Following a consolidation in 1871 to form the Cincinnati, Wabash and Michigan Railroad, the line was extended south to Anderson in 1876, and north to Benton Harbor in 1882.[63]

Meanwhile the Vernon, Greensburg and Rushville Railroad completed a route between North Vernon and Rushville in July 1881, and in 1891 the Cincinnati, Wabash and Michigan Railroad closed the gap by building between Anderson and Rushville.[64] The Big Four operated the entire line by lease or acquisition after 1892, and on December 17, 1913, merged it into its own system.[65] With its eye on Louisville, the Big Four attempted to obtain trackage rights over the Ohio and Mississippi from North Vernon to Jeffersonville. When that road refused, the Big Four began a parallel survey. The O&M then capitulated and granted trackage rights to Jeffersonville, where the Big Four later owned an Ohio River bridge to which it owned no connecting tracks, while the O&M, which owned connecting trackage, used a different bridge.[66]

During the passenger traffic peak, the Michigan Division operated 12 trains daily, running solid consists both to Louisville and Indianapolis. It also operated through cars between Louisville and Chicago, via Greensburg and Indianapolis. Passenger service south of Anderson was abandoned by 1942, but continued between Anderson and Elkhart until about 1950. Twenty scheduled freight trains operated daily in 1930.[67] The line was abandoned north of Goshen in 1942 and south of Emporia beginning in 1973. Conrail operates most of the balance as a bridge route connecting its St. Louis and Chicago lines. A succession of short lines operated between Emporia and Carthage but only the isolated Knightstown-Carthage segment remains, operated as a tourist line by the Carthage, Knightstown and Shirley Railroad.[68]

Columbus, Hope and Greensburg

This 26-mile line connecting its namesake cities was opened May 5, 1884, and operated by the Big Four. The first ten miles west of Greensburg had been partly completed in 1871 by the Cincinnati

and Terre Haute Railroad, which failed.[69] During the peak passenger years, it operated six trains daily, but by the early 1930s this had been reduced to two mixed trains.[70] The line was abandoned in 1973.[71]

Fairland, Franklin and Martinsville

Opened on May 17, 1853, as the 25.5-mile Martinsville and Franklin, this line connected the two cities in its name, and was operated by the Madison and Indianapolis, Indiana's first steam railroad, under a lease that expired May 17, 1858. The road was then abandoned, but after seven years was conveyed to General Ambrose E. Burnside, Civil War commander of the Army of the Potomac, and rebuilt as the Cincinnati and Martinsville Railroad. On June 14, 1866, it was completed to a junction with the Indianapolis and Cincinnati at Fairland, making the total length 38 miles.[72] In 1876 the name was changed to Fairland, Franklin and Martinsville Railroad. During the peak passenger years, it operated six daily trains, but by the mid–1930s this had been reduced to a tri-weekly mixed train each way.[73] It was abandoned west of Trafalgar in 1942, and east to Franklin in 1961. The balance survived until the early 1970s.[74]

Cincinnati and Southern Ohio River

The seven-mile Cincinnati and Southern Ohio River Railway was incorporated April 30, 1887, to connect Aurora with Lawrenceburg Junction on the Big Four's Cincinnati-Indianapolis line. It was operated by the Big Four and was sold to it in 1915.[75]

Cairo and Vincennes

Built as part of a projected line to Cairo, this 10-mile spur, opened in 1872, connected Vincennes at St. Francisville, Illinois, with what became the Danville, Illinois-Cairo line of the Big Four. In 1906 it was extended from Danville to the Calumet region.[76] Twelve trains operated daily during the peak passenger years as shuttles to serve Vincennes. The road was abandoned in 1968 and the Wabash River bridge was privately purchased and converted to highway use.[77]

Evansville, Mt. Carmel and Northern

One of the last Indiana roads built, this Big Four branch was opened July 1, 1911, as a connection northward from Evansville.[78] It joined the Cairo line at Mt. Carmel, Illinois, 35 miles away, and operated through trains to Chicago which carried sleeping cars.[79] Most of the line was abandoned in 1976.[80]

Evansville, Indianapolis and Terre Haute

This 138-mile line, which connected Evansville and Terre Haute, survived a complex corporate history as the successor to numerous failed attempts to construct rail lines. It became part of the Chicago and Eastern Illinois, was separated from it during a receivership, and ended as part of the New York Central Lines in 1920. At least 19 corporations participated in constructing or operating the railroad.[81]

Occupying 60 miles of the Wabash and Erie Canal right-of-way, the line utilized the partially completed grade of the Cincinnati and Terre Haute Railroad for the first 26 miles, swinging in a long arc southeast from Terre Haute, through Worthington and Washington, that made it 29 miles longer between Terre Haute and Evansville than its parent Chicago and Eastern Illinois. A 1916 receivership wiped out the parent's interest and it was acquired in 1920 by the Big Four.[82] Successor Penn Central abandoned most of the line north of Worthington in 1981 and the southern portion was sold to a new short line, Indiana Southern, in 1992. Its principal business is delivering coal from on-line mines to power plants located at Martinsville, Indianapolis, and other points.[83]

Two short branches were built to serve coal mines. The three-mile Lancaster line in Clay and Owen counties was built by predecessor Terre Haute and Southeastern Railroad in 1880 and abandoned by 1919. The seven-mile Somerville branch in Gibson County was built in 1924 and abandoned in 1936.[84]

Peoria and Eastern

Numerous mergers beginning in the Civil War era resulted in the Indiana, Bloomington and Western Railroad, which connected Indianapolis and Peoria. East of Indianapolis, a line to Springfield, Ohio, also consolidated with IB&W and began operation in 1882 as part of a through Indianapolis-Columbus, Ohio, route. The system unraveled in an 1886 receivership and was reorganized as separate companies east and west of Indianapolis. Although separate corporations were set up in each state they were quickly merged to become the Ohio, Indiana and Western Railroad. Further financial woes brought about a foreclosure sale in 1890 in which the Big Four purchased the eastern section of 139 miles and the new Peoria and Eastern acquired the 202-mile western line, which had reached Danville, Illinois, in 1867, and leased it to the Big Four.[85]

The eastern section, from Indianapolis through New Castle and Lynn, carried four daily passenger trains during the peak years, two of which traveled between Columbus, Ohio, and Chicago via Indianapolis. Most of this line was abandoned in 1976–77.[86] The western section, from Indianapolis through Crawfordsville to Peoria, carried eight passenger trains during the peak years, and still operated one pair in 1957. Amtrak now uses the line for its Chicago-Cincinnati-Washington service. For years the P&E also operated an intensive commuter service one day a year—Memorial Day—to serve 500-Mile Race fans in Indianapolis.[87] Most of the former P&E west of Crawfordsville was abandoned in 1982.[88]

Michigan Central

The Michigan Central Railroad had the least Indiana mileage of the New York Central's three constituent companies. Like its competitor, the Michigan Southern, it was a product of Michigan's internal improvements program and was chartered in 1846 to assume control of the state's central route from Detroit westward. Heading for Chicago, it entered Jackson, Kalamazoo, and Niles before making a long arc around the foot of Lake Michigan. On October 30, 1850, the first train entered Michigan City from the East, and in May 1852 the line was completed to Chicago, several weeks after its competitor, the Lake Shore and Michigan Southern. In 1869 Cornelius Vanderbilt, newly in control of the Lake Shore and Michigan Southern, also bought heavily into Michigan Central. On February 1, 1930, after many years of control through stock ownership, New York Central leased the Michigan Central.[89]

A heavy traffic artery from the beginning, it operated 28 passenger trains daily in the peak period, many originating in Buffalo and traveling through Canada. Twenty trains survived after World War II.[90] Amtrak purchased the segment from Porter, Indiana, to Kalamazoo, Michigan, in 1976, to maintain service when Penn Central rerouted its Detroit-

Chicago freight traffic south from Kalamazoo to Elkhart. The only line Amtrak owns outside the Northeast corridor, it carries eight trains daily east of Porter. West of Porter the line is freight only.[91]

The Joliet cutoff, incorporated as the Joliet and Northern Indiana Railroad, was completed in 1854 from the Michigan Central at what is now East Gary 45 miles to a connection with the Chicago, Rock Island and Pacific Railroad at Joliet, Illinois. It was leased to the Michigan Central in September 1854, forming one of the earliest of numerous bypass lines around Chicago.[92] Twelve miles from East Gary through Griffith to Hartsdale were abandoned in 1976.[93]

St. Joseph, South Bend and Southern

A 37-mile line between South Bend and St. Joseph, Michigan, the St. Joseph, South Bend and Southern Railroad opened August 4, 1890, and was immediately leased to a Pennsylvania Railroad affiliate, the Terre Haute and Indianapolis, as part of a Terre Haute–St. Joseph route. Following a foreclosure sale in 1898, it was acquired by the New York Central system and leased to its Indiana, Illinois and Iowa Railroad in 1900. In 1905 the lease was transferred to the Michigan Central, which itself was leased by the New York Central in 1930.[94] Passenger traffic was carried on three round trips daily in 1910, but by 1924 through service had been discontinued. In 1942, 21 miles of track were abandoned between South Bend and Baroda, Michigan.[95]

Michigan Air Line

The Michigan Air Line Railroad was opened in 1871 between Jackson and Niles, Michigan, with Michigan Central assistance, forming a more direct "air line" compared with the main Michigan Central route through Kalamazoo. Michigan Central leased it shortly after completion.[96] A Niles–South Bend branch carried four trains daily during the peak passenger years.[97] The 11-mile South Bend branch was abandoned in 1984.

PENNSYLVANIA RAILROAD

Four constituent systems gradually merged into what became the Pennsylvania Railroad in Indiana. With a peak of 1,556 miles of line, or 21% of the state's total, it narrowly trailed only the New York Central. The railroads ranged from the heavy-duty

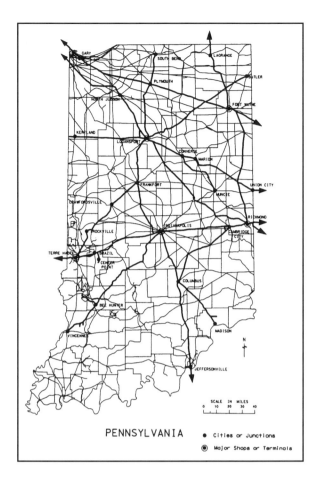

PENNSYLVANIA • Cities or Junctions ⊙ Major Shops or Terminals

doubletrack lines across northern and central Indiana to obscure coal mine branches in the south.[98] Indiana's first steam railroad became part of the Pennsylvania system and the state's first abandonment likewise was from the Pennsylvania family.[99] Systems which evolved into the Pennsylvania, in order of total mileage in Indiana, were the Pittsburgh, Cincinnati, Chicago and St. Louis Railroad (Panhandle), the Vandalia Railroad, the Pittsburgh, Fort Wayne and Chicago Railway; and the Grand Rapids and Indiana Railway. The Panhandle, by far the largest, consisted of 878 route miles, mostly on the east side of the state, or 56% of the system total in Indiana; the Vandalia, which essentially consisted of lines west of Indianapolis, included 471 miles or 30%; the 153-mile Fort Wayne line across northern Indiana had 10% of the total, and the Grand Rapids and Indiana, stretching north from Fort Wayne, had the remaining 53 miles or 3.5% of the system.[100]

The parent Pennsylvania Railroad Company had been chartered in Pennsylvania in 1847, to connect Philadelphia and Pittsburgh. By the early 1850s, however, the management was looking westward, and in 1869 moved to a policy of leasing connecting roads.[101]

PITTSBURGH, FORT WAYNE AND CHICAGO

The Pennsylvania's 468-mile Chicago line began as a combination of three smaller roads which the Pennsylvania assisted. Seeking relief from financial difficulties, they merged as the Pittsburgh, Fort Wayne and Chicago in 1856. One company, the Ohio and Indiana Railroad, had reached Fort Wayne from Crestline, Ohio, in 1854. The PFW&C

reached Chicago in 1858. Level and straight, the 153-mile Indiana section was known as a race track.[102]

By the World War I passenger traffic peak, the line carried 26 through passenger trains daily. After World War II, contrary to national trends, it increased to 32 daily.[103] Following the Penn Central merger, through freight was rerouted via Elkhart on the former New York Central main; one track was removed; and only local freights, and Amtrak until 1990, used the line. Plans called for abandonment. In 1994–95, however, the Norfolk Southern, whose former Nickel Plate line paralleled the Penn-

Vandalia Railroad (PRR) No. 349 is southbound at Culver with patriotic decorations on August 3, 1907. The lawn slopes down to Lake Maxinkuckee. The Vandalia standard depot shown burned in January 1920, to be replaced five years later by one now used as a community center.   *Hoosier Valley Railroad Museum Collection*

PENNSYLVANIA

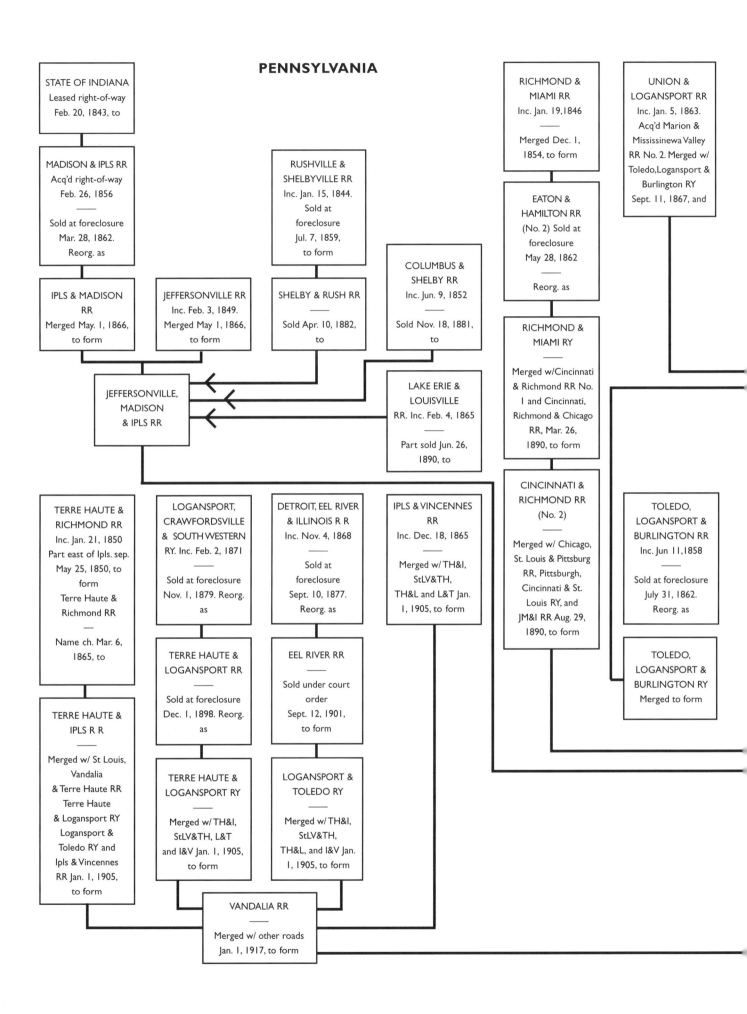

STATE OF INDIANA
Leased right-of-way
Feb. 20, 1843, to

MADISON & IPLS RR
Acq'd right-of-way
Feb. 26, 1856
———
Sold at foreclosure
Mar. 28, 1862.
Reorg. as

IPLS & MADISON RR
Merged May. 1, 1866,
to form

JEFFERSONVILLE RR
Inc. Feb. 3, 1849.
Merged May 1, 1866,
to form

RUSHVILLE & SHELBYVILLE RR
Inc. Jan. 15, 1844.
Sold at foreclosure
Jul. 7, 1859,
to form

SHELBY & RUSH RR
———
Sold Apr. 10, 1882,
to

COLUMBUS & SHELBY RR
Inc. Jun. 9, 1852
———
Sold Nov. 18, 1881,
to

RICHMOND & MIAMI RR
Inc. Jan. 19,1846
———
Merged Dec. 1,
1854, to form

UNION & LOGANSPORT RR
Inc. Jan. 5, 1863.
Acq'd Marion &
Mississinewa Valley
RR No. 2. Merged w/
Toledo,Logansport &
Burlington RY
Sept. 11, 1867, and

EATON & HAMILTON RR
(No. 2) Sold at
foreclosure
May 28, 1862
———
Reorg. as

JEFFERSONVILLE, MADISON & IPLS RR

LAKE ERIE & LOUISVILLE
RR. Inc. Feb. 4, 1865
———
Part sold Jun. 26,
1890, to

RICHMOND & MIAMI RY
———
Merged w/Cincinnati
& Richmond RR No.
1 and Cincinnati,
Richmond & Chicago
RR, Mar. 26,
1890, to form

CINCINNATI & RICHMOND RR
(No. 2)
———
Merged w/ Chicago,
St. Louis & Pittsburg
RR, Pittsburgh,
Cincinnati & St.
Louis RY, and
JM&I RR Aug. 29,
1890, to form

TERRE HAUTE & RICHMOND RR
Inc. Jan. 21, 1850
Part east of Ipls. sep.
May 25, 1850, to
form
Terre Haute &
Richmond RR
—
Name ch. Mar. 6,
1865, to

LOGANSPORT, CRAWFORDSVILLE & SOUTH WESTERN
RY. Inc. Feb. 2, 1871
———
Sold at foreclosure
Nov. 1, 1879. Reorg.
as

DETROIT, EEL RIVER & ILLINOIS R R
Inc. Nov. 4, 1868
———
Sold at
foreclosure
Sept. 10, 1877.
Reorg. as

IPLS & VINCENNES RR
Inc. Dec. 18, 1865
———
Merged w/TH&I,
StLV&TH,
TH&L and L&T Jan.
1, 1905, to form

TOLEDO, LOGANSPORT & BURLINGTON RR
Inc. Jun 11,1858
———
Sold at foreclosure
July 31, 1862.
Reorg. as

TERRE HAUTE & LOGANSPORT RR
———
Sold at foreclosure
Dec. 1, 1898. Reorg.
as

EEL RIVER RR
———
Sold under court
order
Sept. 12, 1901,
to form

TOLEDO, LOGANSPORT & BURLINGTON RY
Merged to form

TERRE HAUTE & IPLS R R
———
Merged w/ St Louis,
Vandalia
& Terre Haute RR
Terre Haute
& Logansport RY
Logansport &
Toledo RY and
Ipls & Vincennes
RR Jan. 1, 1905,
to form

TERRE HAUTE & LOGANSPORT RY
———
Merged w/ TH&I,
StLV&TH, L&T
and I&V Jan. 1, 1905,
to form

LOGANSPORT & TOLEDO RY
———
Merged w/ TH&I,
StLV&TH,
TH&L, and I&V Jan.
1, 1905, to form

VANDALIA RR
———
Merged w/ other roads
Jan. 1, 1917, to form

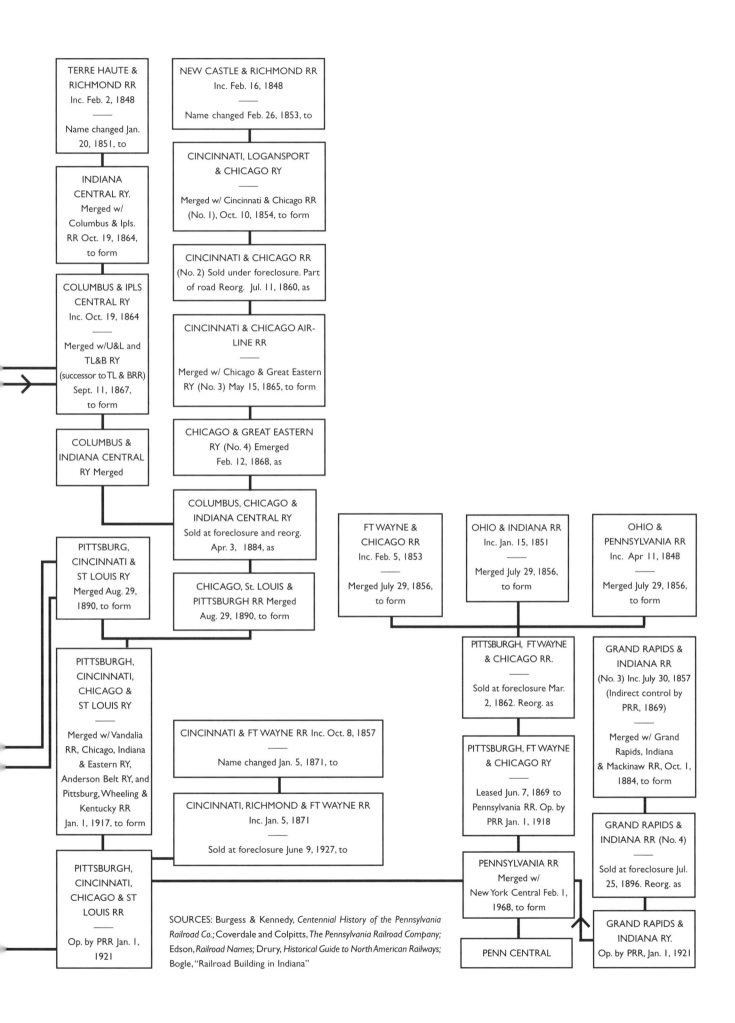

TERRE HAUTE &
RICHMOND RR
Inc. Feb. 2, 1848
——
Name changed Jan.
20, 1851, to

INDIANA
CENTRAL RY.
Merged w/
Columbus & Ipls.
RR Oct. 19, 1864,
to form

COLUMBUS & IPLS
CENTRAL RY
Inc. Oct. 19, 1864
——
Merged w/U&L and
TL&B RY
(successor to TL & BRR)
Sept. 11, 1867,
to form

COLUMBUS &
INDIANA CENTRAL
RY Merged

PITTSBURG,
CINCINNATI &
ST LOUIS RY
Merged Aug. 29,
1890, to form

PITTSBURGH,
CINCINNATI,
CHICAGO &
ST LOUIS RY
——
Merged w/ Vandalia
RR, Chicago, Indiana
& Eastern RY,
Anderson Belt RY, and
Pittsburg, Wheeling &
Kentucky RR
Jan. 1, 1917, to form

PITTSBURGH,
CINCINNATI,
CHICAGO & ST
LOUIS RR
——
Op. by PRR Jan. 1,
1921

NEW CASTLE & RICHMOND RR
Inc. Feb. 16, 1848
——
Name changed Feb. 26, 1853, to

CINCINNATI, LOGANSPORT
& CHICAGO RY
——
Merged w/ Cincinnati & Chicago RR
(No. 1), Oct. 10, 1854, to form

CINCINNATI & CHICAGO RR
(No. 2) Sold under foreclosure. Part
of road Reorg. Jul. 11, 1860, as

CINCINNATI & CHICAGO AIR-
LINE RR
——
Merged w/ Chicago & Great Eastern
RY "(No. 3) May 15, 1865, to form

CHICAGO & GREAT EASTERN
RY (No. 4) Emerged
Feb. 12, 1868, as

COLUMBUS, CHICAGO &
INDIANA CENTRAL RY
Sold at foreclosure and reorg.
Apr. 3, 1884, as

CHICAGO, St. LOUIS &
PITTSBURGH RR Merged
Aug. 29, 1890, to form

CINCINNATI & FT WAYNE RR Inc. Oct. 8, 1857
——
Name changed Jan. 5, 1871, to

CINCINNATI, RICHMOND & FT WAYNE RR
Inc. Jan. 5, 1871
——
Sold at foreclosure June 9, 1927, to

FT WAYNE &
CHICAGO RR
Inc. Feb. 5, 1853
——
Merged July 29, 1856,
to form

OHIO & INDIANA RR
Inc. Jan. 15, 1851
——
Merged July 29, 1856,
to form

OHIO &
PENNSYLVANIA RR
Inc. Apr 11, 1848
——
Merged July 29, 1856,
to form

PITTSBURGH, FT WAYNE
& CHICAGO RR.
——
Sold at foreclosure Mar.
2, 1862. Reorg. as

PITTSBURGH, FT WAYNE
& CHICAGO RY
——
Leased Jun. 7, 1869 to
Pennsylvania RR. Op. by
PRR Jan. 1, 1918

GRAND RAPIDS &
INDIANA RR
(No. 3) Inc. July 30, 1857
(Indirect control by
PRR, 1869)
——
Merged w/ Grand
Rapids, Indiana
& Mackinaw RR, Oct. 1,
1884, to form

GRAND RAPIDS &
INDIANA RR (No. 4)
——
Sold at foreclosure Jul.
25, 1896. Reorg. as

PENNSYLVANIA RR
Merged w/
New York Central Feb. 1,
1968, to form

PENN CENTRAL

GRAND RAPIDS &
INDIANA RY.
Op. by PRR, Jan. 1, 1921

SOURCES: Burgess & Kennedy, *Centennial History of the Pennsylvania
Railroad Co.*; Coverdale and Colpitts, *The Pennsylvania Railroad Company*;
Edson, *Railroad Names*; Drury, *Historical Guide to North American Railways*;
Bogle, "Railroad Building in Indiana"

sylvania, bought most of the line as an alternate route between Chicago and Fort Wayne, increasing its own capacity.[104]

Grand Rapids and Indiana

Originally projected to connect Hartford City and Grand Rapids, Michigan, the southern terminal was switched to Fort Wayne before construction began. The 53-mile Indiana section was completed in 1870 through Kendallville and Lagrange, but only after it placed a majority of its stock in trust for the Pennsylvania-controlled Fort Wayne line, which had helped it over serious financial hurdles. The road ultimately was extended to Mackinaw City and became part of the Pennsylvania Railroad. It was the only line in Indiana that received a federal land grant, although it was one for the Michigan segment.[105] In return the railroad, like other land grant roads, gave the government half rate haulage for freight and passengers until the law was repealed in 1946.[106]

Using the slogan "The Fishing Line" because it served the northern Michigan resort area, it was a heavy passenger carrier. Cars from Chicago were switched onto the GR&I in Fort Wayne. In addition to the 9 regular trains it carried during the peak passenger years there were numerous seasonal runs. The line in Indiana was abandoned between 1979 and 1982.[107]

Pittsburgh, Cincinnati, Chicago and St. Louis

The Pittsburgh, Cincinnati, Chicago and St. Louis Railroad—"The Panhandle"—comprised lines from Pittsburgh to Indianapolis and St. Louis, and a network throughout Ohio and Indiana. The nickname came from an early constituent that crossed the narrow West Virginia "panhandle." It went many of the same places as the Vanderbilt-controlled CCC&StL (the Big Four), and the two competed heavily. The PCC&StL Railway Company was formed by a merger August 29, 1890, of the Pittsburg, Cincinnati and St. Louis Railway, the Cincinnati and Richmond Railroad, the Jeffersonville, Madison and Indianapolis Railroad, and the Chicago, St. Louis and Pittsburgh Railroad. These components had evolved from earlier roads, including Indiana's first, the Madison and Indianapolis. The PCC&StL Rail*way* was merged January 1, 1917, with the Vandalia and other Pennsylvania-controlled lines to form a new PCC&StL Rail*road*. On March 26, 1921, the Pennsylvania Railroad con-

solidated its operations by formally leasing the properties of the PCC&StL as well as the GR&I and other constituent roads.[108]

Indiana Central

The 74-mile Indiana Central Railway was completed from Indianapolis to Richmond and New Paris, Ohio, in 1853, a year after the connecting Terre Haute and Richmond Railroad was built between Terre Haute and Indianapolis. At New Paris a connection was made with another road, connecting eventually to Columbus, Ohio. In 1868, by now the Columbus, Chicago and Indiana Central Railway, it was leased by the newly organized Pittsburg, Cincinnati and St. Louis Railway and became a major segment of the Pennsylvania System's St. Louis–Pittsburgh–New York route. After merger in 1890, it became the Pittsburgh, Cincinnati, Chicago and St. Louis (Panhandle).[109] The road handled heavy passenger and freight traffic. In the peak passenger era it operated, in conjunction with the lines west of Indianapolis, 19 passenger trains, of which 17 passenger trains survived World War II. Two operated to Texas cities and some trains carried through cars to Mexico and Oklahoma. Most of the route was abandoned in 1981–82.[110]

Cincinnati and Chicago

Building from Cincinnati, the Cincinnati and Chicago Railroad reached New Castle, via Richmond, in 1853, and by 1857 was extended to Logansport. It reached La Crosse and continued to Valparaiso in 1861 to connect with the Pittsburgh, Fort Wayne and Chicago. In 1865 the 10.4 miles between La Crosse and Valparaiso were abandoned after the affiliated Chicago and Great Eastern Railway built its own line from La Crosse through Crown Point to Chicago. Many corporate maneuvers, mergers, leases, and reorganizations and no fewer than 24 corporations were involved, including four successive Chicago and Great Easterns and two each Cincinnati and Richmond, Eaton and Hamilton, and Cincinnati and Chicago railroads. In 1890 the 298-mile line became part of the Panhandle.[111]

The Chicago-Logansport road became a major secondary route feeding lines to Indiana, Ohio, and Kentucky and was eventually rebuilt for high-speed operation and doubletracked. Logansport was the hub, and Pennsylvania-controlled lines radiated in seven directions. The Panhandle shops here built locomotives. Twenty-three passenger trains were operated in the peak era, and this had fallen only slightly to 18 by the post–World War II period.[112] In 1982 and 1986 the Winamac-Schererville segment was abandoned, as well as most of the line from Kokomo to New Castle. Short sections became the Winamac Southern (later A&R), Indian Creek, and Honey Creek short lines. The section from New Castle through Richmond to Cincinnati was sold in the mid–1970s to the Norfolk and Western Railway, which rebuilt it into part of its busy Cincinnati-Chicago route through Fort Wayne.[113]

Columbus, Chicago and Indiana Central

The Columbus, Piqua and Indiana Railroad, which was built from Columbus, Ohio, to Union City, Indiana, in 1856 was extended to Anoka Junction, 89 miles, by the Columbus, Chicago and Indiana Central Railway and a successor in 1867–68, where it joined a line previously built by the Chicago and Great Eastern Railway.[114] This became a secondary main line between Chicago and New York via Columbus, Ohio, and was doubletracked around 1910 to accommodate increased coal traffic. During the peak passenger era it carried eight passenger trains daily, including two that ran through to or from New York. By the post–World War II period this had been reduced to four, although two additional trains between Cincinnati and Chicago were sometimes routed over part of the line.[115] Conrail abandoned most of the road between Marion and Logansport in 1984, and between Red Key and Union City in 1993. The Ohio segment has been abandoned, and the remaining section near Marion sees only local freight service.[116]

Madison and Indianapolis

Indiana's first intercity railroad, the 86-mile Madison and Indianapolis, reached Indianapolis via Columbus in 1847, 10 years after construction was started in Madison. It was designed to connect Ohio River navigation with the interior of the state and for eight months in 1854 was consolidated with the Peru and Indianapolis Rail Road, extending at that time from Indianapolis to Kokomo. The original property was acquired from the state of Indiana, which had included the route in its 1836 internal improvements program. Following a reorganiza-

tion, the road merged in May 1866 with the Jeffersonville Railroad to form the Jeffersonville, Madison and Indianapolis Railroad. In 1871 the JM&I was leased to the Pittsburg, Cincinnati and St. Louis Railway, with which it was formally merged in 1890 to create the Pittsburgh, Cincinnati, Chicago and St. Louis Railway.[117]

The Madison road is noted for the 5.89% grade which carries it 413 feet up from the Ohio riverfront in Madison, and which survives as the steepest common carrier standard-gauge line in the United States. After being operated for six years by horse power and for 21 years as a cogwheel system, the hill was converted to adhesion working in 1868 after the construction of the 0–10–0T locomotive Reuben Wells, at that time the heaviest locomotive in the country. The locomotive was named for its builder, master mechanic of the JM&I, and was built in the railroad shops in Jeffersonville. It survives on permanent display in the Children's Museum in Indianapolis.[118] An effort was made about 1852 to reroute the line and reduce the grade by tunneling through the valley wall, but this was never completed. Tunnel remains are visible in Clifty Falls State Park.[119]

The 17-mile section between Columbus and North Vernon was abandoned by Penn Central in 1976. The balance was acquired by the City of Madison Port Authority and remains in operation.[120]

Jeffersonville

The Jeffersonville Railroad was completed between Jeffersonville (opposite Louisville) and Columbus, 67 miles, in 1852, where it anticipated negotiating trackage rights to Indianapolis over the Madison and Indianapolis. When the roads could not agree, the Jeffersonville began building a parallel line, which proceeded 10 miles to Edinburg before an agreement was reached. The original M&I line in this parallel section was abandoned in 1864, and two years later the Jeffersonville and the M&I, now reorganized as the Madison and Indianapolis Railroad, merged to form the Jeffersonville, Madison and Indianapolis Railroad. The PC&StL leased the JM&I in 1871 and merged with it to form the PCC&StL in 1890.[121]

The line evolved into the important Indianapolis-Louisville route, which carried 12 daily passenger trains in the peak era, and 11 in the post–World War II period, including through Florida trains.[122]

Most modern of the PRR's passenger steam power were the T1s, built between 1942 and 1946. They featured a 4-4-4-4 "duplex" wheel arrangement and streamlining by Raymond Loewy. No. 6110 forwards a solid train of mail and express across Indiana ca. 1943.   *U.I.D.—Jay Williams collection*

The line continued in service under Conrail, but was sold in 1994 to a new short line, the Louisville and Indiana Railroad.[123]

Shelbyville Lateral Branch

Incorporated in 1845 to construct a feeder from Shelbyville to the Madison and Indianapolis at Edinburg, the 16-mile Shelbyville Lateral Branch was opened in 1849. In 1851, the Jeffersonville Railroad acquired it as part of a planned route to Indianapolis, but had no further use for it after trackage rights were obtained over the Madison and Indianapolis. The railroad was abandoned in 1855.[124]

Knightstown and Shelbyville

Serving, like the Shelbyville Lateral Branch, as a feeder for the Madison and Indianapolis, the 26-mile Knightstown and Shelbyville Railroad pushed Indiana's early railhead northeast to Knightstown on the National Road. Opened in 1850, it served only until 1854 when default of its mortgage caused it to close. It not only was Indiana's shortest-lived railroad line but also the first to be abandoned.[125]

Rushville and Shelbyville

The Rushville and Shelbyville Railroad completed an 18-mile line between the cities of its corporate title in 1850. In 1853 the Columbus and Shelby Railroad extended it 24 miles to Columbus. The Lake Erie and Louisville Railroad added 21 miles from Rushville to Cambridge City in 1867. The Jeffersonville, Madison and Indianapolis acquired most of the line in separate transactions in 1881, 1882, and 1890.[126]

This provided an Indianapolis bypass route between Louisville and the East, and both freight trains and a through passenger train with a New York sleeping car operated here. Four daily local passenger trains rode this line during the peak years, but by 1930 they had disappeared.[127] During World War II the line was restored to full freight service to relieve congestion through Indianapolis.[128] It was used for military traffic between the East and Camp Atterbury (itself named for a former Pennsylvania Railroad president), near Columbus. Total abandonment took place in segments between 1962 and 1976.[129]

Cincinnati, Richmond and Fort Wayne

Completed in 1871 between Richmond and Adams, a junction east of Fort Wayne, the 86-mile Cincinnati, Richmond and Fort Wayne Railroad served as a through route with the Grand Rapids and Indiana between Cincinnati and northern Michigan. The Panhandle acquired it at a foreclosure sale June 9, 1927.[130] During the nation's peak passenger period it operated six daily trains in addition to seasonal schedules, and by the post–World War II era had dropped only two of these.[131] The 69 miles between Decatur and Richmond were abandoned in 1976 and 1979.[132]

Toledo, Logansport and Burlington

The Toledo, Logansport and Burlington Railroad opened a 62-mile line between Logansport and Effner on the Indiana-Illinois state line in 1859. It formed part of a through route with a Toledo, Peoria and Western Railroad predecessor to Peoria and the Mississippi River. After numerous reorganizations, it merged with other companies in 1890 to form the Panhandle route.[133] Peak era passenger traffic totaled four daily trains.[134] After Conrail dropped the line in 1976 the Toledo, Peoria and Western purchased it for an eastern connection. The line is known today for "Hoosier Lift," an extensive rail-truck transfer terminal off Interstate 65 near Remington.[135]

Chicago, Indiana and Eastern

Born of the east central Indiana turn-of-the-century natural gas boom, the Chicago, Indiana and Eastern Railway was constructed in 1895 from the new promotional town of Matthews to the nearest railroad, which was the Big Four eight miles west at Fairmount. By 1900 it had been extended west to Converse and east to Muncie. The Pennsylvania Railroad purchased the line on May 1, 1907, and in 1917 merged it with other roads to create the Pittsburgh, Cincinnati, Chicago and St. Louis Railway.[136] At its peak it carried eight trains daily over its 43-mile route, including an overnight Chicago sleeping car that was carried to Converse, where it was attached to a Chicago train coming from Columbus, Ohio.

Matthews's boom days ended abruptly after the natural gas supply was exhausted between 1905 and 1910, and by World War I, when most other roads reached their peak, this line had cut its passenger schedules by half. The line was abandoned between Converse and Matthews in 1933 and the balance, from Matthews to Muncie, was discontinued in 1976.[137]

Vandalia

The fourth major component of the Pennsylvania System in Indiana, the Vandalia Railroad Company, was formed in 1905 by a merger of the St. Louis, Vandalia and Terre Haute Railroad with the Terre Haute and Logansport Railway, the Terre Haute and Indianapolis Railroad, the Logansport and Toledo Railway, and the Indianapolis and Vincennes Railroad. The consolidated Vandalia Railroad connected Indianapolis and St. Louis, with other lines stretching from Vincennes in the south to South Bend and Butler in the north. In 1917 the Vandalia was merged with the Pittsburgh, Cincinnati, Chicago and St. Louis Railway (Panhandle) and other roads to form the Pittsburgh, Cincinnati, Chicago and St. Louis Railroad, which was then formally leased by the Pennsylvania Railroad in 1921.[138]

Terre Haute and Richmond

Chartered in 1847, this company completed a 73-mile line between Terre Haute and Indianapolis in 1852, and on April 26, 1870, completed a short extension from Terre Haute to the Illinois state line to connect with the newly constructed St. Louis, Vandalia and Terre Haute. This formed a second Indianapolis–St. Louis route, competing with the Indianapolis and St. Louis/St. Louis, Alton and Terre Haute. After 1865 the road became the Terre Haute and Indianapolis, a name it retained until the 1905 merger into the Vandalia. With its connecting road east of Indianapolis, the line formed a major segment on the Pennsylvania's St. Louis–Pittsburgh–New York route.[139] Always a busy railroad, the joint line carried 19 daily passenger trains during the peak passenger era, and continued all but two into the post–World War II period. These included two through trains between New York and Texas cities. The line was abandoned by 1984 after Conrail elected to concentrate traffic on the parallel former Big Four between Indianapolis and Terre Haute. A 33-mile section west of Limedale became the Terre Haute, Brazil and Eastern Railroad short line, which abandoned service in 1992.[140]

The eight-mile Center Point branch was built in 1870 from Knightsville south to Center Point to serve coal mines, although it also carried four daily passenger trains by World War I. It was abandoned in 1967.[141]

Indianapolis and Vincennes

Conceived as a route to the Gulf of Mexico, the Indianapolis and Vincennes began construction in 1867 with the Indianapolis, Cincinnati and Lafayette Railroad (later part of the Big Four), guaranteeing financial obligations in return for a lease on the line. A year later two Pennsylvania Railroad companies were added as guarantors and the line was completed in 1869 between Indianapolis and Vincennes, 117 miles. One of its early promotors was General A. E. Burnside, Civil War commander of the Army of the Potomac and later a governor of Rhode Island, who also promoted the Big Four's Fairland, Franklin and Martinsville Railroad. The Pennsylvania Railroad obtained control in 1871.[142]

The Indianpolis and Vincennes never became the through route its promoters anticipated. During the nation's peak passenger era the line carried ten local trains. A through Indianapolis-French Lick service used the line from Indianapolis to Gosport, where it transferred to the Monon. Passenger service disappeared in 1941.[143]

Most of the line south of Sandborn was abandoned in 1976 and 1984, and the balance became part of the Indiana Southern Railroad, a new coal hauler serving southern Indiana mines. A one-mile section at Bicknell briefly became the Indiana Interstate Railway.[144]

The I&V built four coal branches between 1884 and 1923 in the Bicknell and Dugger areas and a limestone hauling branch near Gosport. They totaled approximately 22 miles. A miners' train once operated over the Dugger branch. The lines were abandoned between 1956 and 1973 as mines were worked out.[145]

Terre Haute and Logansport

The Terre Haute and Logansport Railroad initially built a line northeast from Rockville through Crawfordsville and Frankfort 93 miles to Clymers, six miles southwest of Logansport, in 1871. Four years later it built into Logansport in place of using trackage rights over a Wabash Railroad predecessor. In 1872 it leased the 23 miles from Terre Haute to Rockville from the Evansville and Crawfordsville Railroad, a corporate ancestor of the Chicago and Eastern Illinois Railroad, and purchased this segment outright in 1924 following the C&EI receivership. The entire line was leased to the Terre Haute and Indianpolis on completion.[146]

In 1884, the Terre Haute and Logansport completed a 69-mile extension from Logansport to South Bend, which it also leased to the Terre Haute and Indianapolis. In 1890, the Terre Haute and Indianapolis extended its route to St. Joseph, Michigan, by leasing the newly built Indiana and Lake Michigan Railway. After a foreclosure in 1898, that road was reorganized and the Michigan Central gained control.[147]

During the nation's peak passenger years, the entire Terre Haute–South Bend line was operated as a single unit and carried seven daily trains. By the late 1930s passenger service was gone west of Frankfort, and service to South Bend was discontinued about 1948.[148] The line was progressively abandoned from Terre Haute to Frankfort between 1972 and 1976, and from Logansport to South Bend between 1973 and 1979. A new short line, Winamac Southern, acquired a 20-mile segment south of Logansport in 1993. Trackage between Frankfort and Bringhurst has been abandoned.[149]

Detroit, Eel River and Illinois

Conceived as a farm-to-market road, this 93-mile line was completed in 1874 between Logansport and Butler, in the northeast corner of Indiana.[150] In 1879, the Wabash, St. Louis and Pacific leased it and immediately converted it into the middle link of an important St. Louis–East Coast line. After a bizarre and long-running legal battle, the lease was canceled. Reorganized as the Logansport and Toledo Railway, it became a Pennsylvania Railroad property in 1901. Passenger service, which had totaled 14 daily trains under the Wabash, including the Erie's joint Chicago-Detroit operation partly on this line, dwindled to four trains by the World War I era, and was gone altogether by 1930. The road's history is developed more fully in chapter 13.[151]

The road was abandoned piecemeal between 1954 and 1977, with end segments going first. The middle section, branching southwest from the Pennsylvania's Fort Wayne line at Columbia City, went last.[152]

Indianapolis and Frankfort

Incorporated in 1913 to build a 41-mile line from Frankfort through Lebanon to Indianapolis, the Indianapolis and Frankfort Railroad was built by the Pennsylvania primarily to carry southern Indiana coal to the Chicago area on the company's own line. It was opened June 16, 1918, and enabled the Pennsylvania to drop trackage rights over the Lake Erie and Western between Kokomo, on the Pennsylvania's Cincinnati line, and Indianapolis.[153] The new line joined the St. Louis Division of the PCC&StL at Ben Davis on the west side of Indianapolis. It carried through passenger trains between Chicago and Louisville and was also a route for such Chicago-Florida trains as the South Wind.[154]

NEW YORK, CHICAGO AND ST. LOUIS

The original New York, Chicago and St. Louis Railroad opened a line in 1882 between Buffalo and Chicago which Vanderbilt interests immediately acquired and operated as part of the future New York Central system. Main lines of the two roads ran parallel and often adjacent to each other.[155] After the government forced the New York Central to divest itself of the Nickel Plate in 1916, the Lake Erie and Western Railroad and the Toledo, St. Louis and Western (Clover Leaf) Railroad merged with the Nickel Plate in 1923.[156] In Indiana, the expanded system was the state's third largest

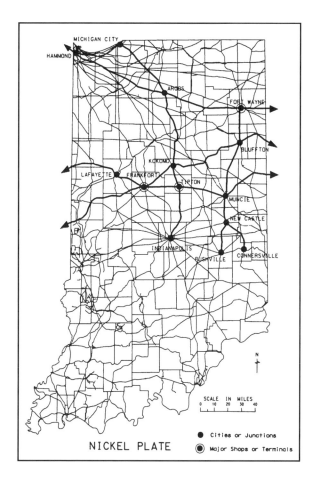

NICKEL PLATE

● Cities or Junctions
◉ Major Shops or Terminals

and totaled 773 miles or 10% of the state's peak trackage. Of this, the original line extended 151 miles and comprised 19% of the system's mileage in Indiana; the Lake Erie and Western totaled 451 miles or 58%; and the Clover Leaf operated 171 miles or 22%.[157]

In 1964 the Norfolk and Western Railway acquired the Nickel Plate and leased the Wabash Railroad.[158] On June 1, 1982, Norfolk and Western, along with the Southern Railway, became an operating unit of Norfolk Southern, which in early 1997 was one of three principal railroads east of the Mississippi River.[159]

New York, Chicago and St. Louis

The first train on this Buffalo-Chicago line arrived in Fort Wayne from the East on November 3, 1881.[160] The line was opened across Indiana through Argos, Knox, Valparaiso, and Hammond to Chicago on October 16, 1882. The nickname—the Nickel Plate Road—may have stemmed from a facetious remark that the railroad cost so much that

NEW YORK, CHICAGO & ST. LOUIS RAILROAD (NICKEL PLATE)

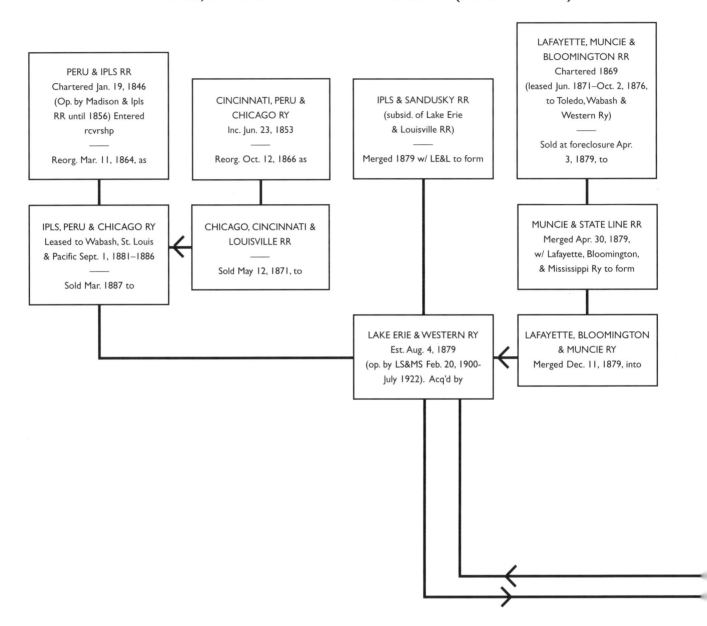

PERU & IPLS RR
Chartered Jan. 19, 1846
(Op. by Madison & Ipls
RR until 1856) Entered
rcvrshp
———
Reorg. Mar. 11, 1864, as

CINCINNATI, PERU &
CHICAGO RY
Inc. Jun. 23, 1853
———
Reorg. Oct. 12, 1866 as

IPLS & SANDUSKY RR
(subsid. of Lake Erie
& Louisville RR)
———
Merged 1879 w/ LE&L to form

LAFAYETTE, MUNCIE &
BLOOMINGTON RR
Chartered 1869
(leased Jun. 1871–Oct. 2, 1876,
to Toledo, Wabash &
Western Ry)
———
Sold at foreclosure Apr.
3, 1879, to

IPLS, PERU & CHICAGO RY
Leased to Wabash, St. Louis
& Pacific Sept. 1, 1881–1886
———
Sold Mar. 1887 to

CHICAGO, CINCINNATI &
LOUISVILLE RR
———
Sold May 12, 1871, to

MUNCIE & STATE LINE RR
Merged Apr. 30, 1879,
w/ Lafayette, Bloomington,
& Mississippi Ry to form

LAKE ERIE & WESTERN RY
Est. Aug. 4, 1879
(op. by LS&MS Feb. 20, 1900-
July 1922). Acq'd by

LAFAYETTE, BLOOMINGTON
& MUNCIE RY
Merged Dec. 11, 1879, into

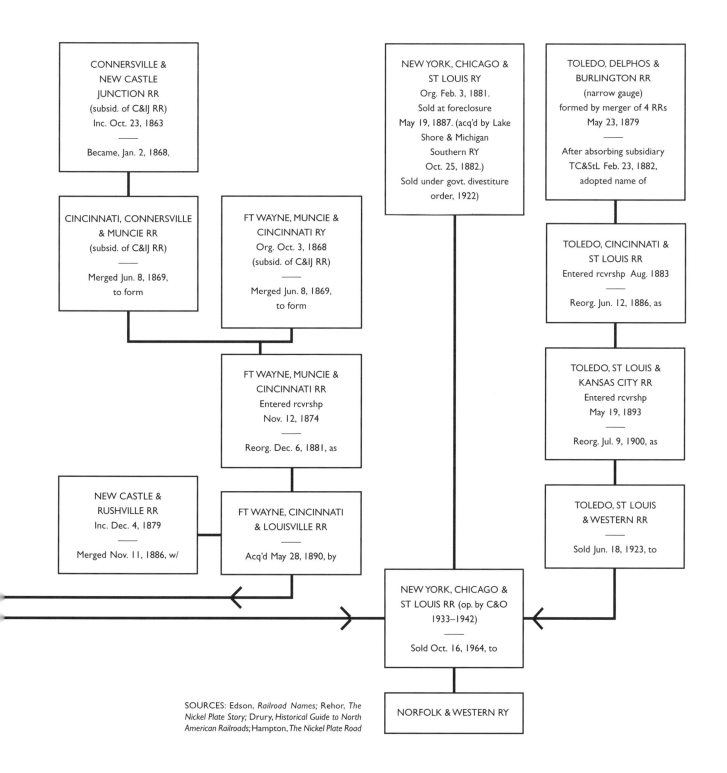

CONNERSVILLE &
NEW CASTLE
JUNCTION RR
(subsid. of C&IJ RR)
Inc. Oct. 23, 1863
———
Became, Jan. 2, 1868,

NEW YORK, CHICAGO &
ST LOUIS RY
Org. Feb. 3, 1881.
Sold at foreclosure
May 19, 1887. (acq'd by Lake
Shore & Michigan
Southern RY
Oct. 25, 1882.)
Sold under govt. divestiture
order, 1922)

TOLEDO, DELPHOS &
BURLINGTON RR
(narrow gauge)
formed by merger of 4 RRs
May 23, 1879
———
After absorbing subsidiary
TC&StL Feb. 23, 1882,
adopted name of

CINCINNATI, CONNERSVILLE
& MUNCIE RR
(subsid. of C&IJ RR)
Merged Jun. 8, 1869,
to form

FT WAYNE, MUNCIE &
CINCINNATI RY
Org. Oct. 3, 1868
(subsid. of C&IJ RR)
———
Merged Jun. 8, 1869,
to form

TOLEDO, CINCINNATI &
ST LOUIS RR
Entered rcvrshp Aug. 1883
———
Reorg. Jun. 12, 1886, as

FT WAYNE, MUNCIE &
CINCINNATI RR
Entered rcvrshp
Nov. 12, 1874
———
Reorg. Dec. 6, 1881, as

TOLEDO, ST LOUIS &
KANSAS CITY RR
Entered rcvrshp
May 19, 1893
———
Reorg. Jul. 9, 1900, as

NEW CASTLE &
RUSHVILLE RR
Inc. Dec. 4, 1879
———
Merged Nov. 11, 1886, w/

FT WAYNE, CINCINNATI
& LOUISVILLE RR
———
Acq'd May 28, 1890, by

TOLEDO, ST LOUIS
& WESTERN RR
———
Sold Jun. 18, 1923, to

NEW YORK, CHICAGO &
ST LOUIS RR (op. by C&O
1933–1942)
———
Sold Oct. 16, 1964, to

NORFOLK & WESTERN RY

SOURCES: Edson, *Railroad Names;* Rehor, *The
Nickel Plate Story;* Drury, *Historical Guide to North
American Railroads;* Hampton, *The Nickel Plate Road*

Mogul-type (2–6–0) locomotive was built in 1883 for the narrow-gauge Toledo, Cincinnati and St. Louis Railroad, which extended from Toledo, Ohio, through Marion, Kokomo, Frankfort, and Cayuga to St. Louis. *Richard S. Simons collection*

it might as well have been nickel plated (a popular finish for lamps and utensils at the time). Although never a major passenger carrier, the Nickel Plate operated six through trains and six locals during the peak passenger era, but this had been reduced to four trains during the post–World War II period.[161] The Nickel Plate was among the last major carriers to rely on steam locomotives, and it became famous for the power and efficiency of its Berkshire types.[162]

After the N&W and subsequent Norfolk Southern mergers, the Fort Wayne–Chicago segment became part of its route from the Southeast through Cincinnati to Chicago. The heavy traffic so strained its single-track capacity that in 1994 and 1995 Norfolk Southern bought from Conrail the parallel former Pennsylvania Railroad Chicago–New York main line between Gary and Fort Wayne.[163] This gave it in effect a doubletrack route. As much as 52

miles longer than the other three Cincinnati-Chicago routes, it is the only survivor.[164]

Lake Erie and Western

The Lake Erie and Western Railroad was created in 1879 by merging two isolated companies and a connecting link between them. The main line, envisioned by its promoters as part of a new Boston–Kansas City route, ultimately connected Sandusky, Ohio, and Peoria. In addition, it acquired branches from Michigan City to Indianapolis, Fort Wayne to Connersville, and New Castle to Rushville.[165] The main line west of Lafayette was opened in 1872, the middle section in 1876, and the segment east of Muncie in 1879.[166] Its history is marked by a bewildering succession of false starts, receiverships, foreclosures, reorganizations, mergers, leases, acquisitions, and outside control. Discovery of natural gas and oil along its routes in the late 1880s saved it from economic disaster, and it advertised itself for years as "The Natural Gas Route."

The east end began as the Fremont and Indiana Rail Road, incorporated in 1853. After three receiverships, its successors completed the road from Fremont, Ohio, to Muncie in 1879.[167] Meanwhile the Lafayette, Muncie and Bloomington completed a line in 1872 from Lafayette to Bloomington, Illinois. It leased this to a Wabash predecessor until 1876 as a feeder to start central Illinois grain on its way toward eastern markets.[168] A Muncie-Lafayette section was opened in February 1876.[169] The Lake Shore and Michigan Southern Railroad, a New York Central predecessor, acquired stock control in 1900 and operated the road until 1922.[170]

One of Indiana's earliest roads, the Indianapolis–Michigan City branch dated to an 1846 charter and had been opened as far north as Peru in 1854.[171] The Madison and Indianapolis, Indiana's first railroad, operated it briefly. Eventually it became part of a Wabash Railroad predeccessor, from which the Lake Erie and Western acquired it in 1887.[172] A succession of companies built roads on the north end which were completed to Peru in 1869. A Lake Erie and Western predecessor acquired them in 1871 to complete the 159-mile route.[173]

Norfolk Southern, successor to Nickel Plate and Norfolk and Western, leased the Indianapolis-Tipton section briefly to Indiana Rail Road under its Thoroughbred Short Line Program, but in 1995 sold the 38-mile road to the Hamilton County Port Authority. Noblesville and Fishers formed the authority, which was renamed Hoosier Heritage Port Authority after Indianapolis joined in 1996. The line carries Fairtrain and other excursions, as well as freight service.[174]

The first segment of the 109-mile Fort Wayne–Connersville branch was completed between Connersville and Cambridge City in 1865. It reached Muncie in 1869 and Fort Wayne in 1870 through a separate company with which it merged. A subsidiary, the New Castle and Rushville Railroad, opened a 23-mile line in 1881 between the cities of its corporate name, thus creating a Fort Wayne–Louisville route in connection with the Vernon, Greensburg and Rushville Railroad, which the Big Four eventually acquired.[175]

The Lake Erie and Western was a strong participant in joint passenger operations. Teaming up

Clover Leaf Consolidation (2–8–0) was built in 1904 for the Toledo, St. Louis and Western Railroad, which called itself the Lucky Way and adopted the clover leaf as its symbol after the natural gas boom of the 1890s gave it a last-minute reprieve from financial doom.   *John H. Keller collection*

Passes illustrate the confusing genealogy of what became the Nickel Plate Road's Toledo–St. Louis line. Reading upward, they designate various owners beginning with the narrow-gauge Toledo, Delphos and Burlington Railroad in 1880. *John H. Keller collection*

ally important narrow-gauge center, and connected Toledo with St. Louis. It first operated in 1877 and by 1882 was completed to East St. Louis, Illinois, as the Toledo, Cincinnati and St. Louis Railroad.[178] In time it became part of an ambitious scheme known as the Grand Narrow Gauge Trunk, which would have connected Toledo with the Mexican border. It nearly succeeded.[179]

Barely weathering successive financial crises, the road was standard gauged, beginning with an 11-hour conversion of 206 miles between Toledo and Frankfort in 1887.[180]

Although always a minor passenger train operator, it initiated the overnight "Commercial Traveler" between terminals in 1901 amid great fanfare. However, the road was known primarily for its fast manifest freights, which hauled heavy tonnage of meat, livestock, and perishables out of St. Louis.[181]

Hampered by its original narrow-gauge alignment, the TStL&W was downgraded in importance after its 1923 merger with the Nickel Plate, later Norfolk and Western and Norfolk Southern. The road was abandoned east of Douglas, Ohio, in the late 1970s and beginning in 1987 most of the line west of Frankfort disappeared. Central Railroad of Indianapolis now operates the segment west of Marion under a lease through the Norfolk Southern Thoroughbred Short Line program, and Indiana Hi-Rail operates east of Van Buren.[182] Further details will be found in chapter 13.

WABASH RAILROAD

Operating a 2,422-mile system across the heart of America,[183] the Wabash Railroad crossed northern Indiana with two separate lines, in addition to short branches in Steuben and Fountain counties plus six leased lines that it operated briefly beginning in the late 1870s.[184] Loyal to Indiana, it retained "Wabash" in its corporate title through nine receiverships, mergers, and name changes.[185]

The road had a stormy history and a feast-or-famine existence. Jay Gould, a master manipulator with unbridled ambition, had seized control by 1879 and used the road as the center link of his grand plan to create a truly transcontinental railroad. Gobbling up other roads by purchase or lease, he overexpanded until his house of cards collapsed in 1884.[186] Dismembered, then reunited in 1889, the road came under Pennsylvania Railroad control in 1928 and remained until 1964 when

with the Big Four, it operated through trains from Fort Wayne to both Indianapolis and Cincinnati. It also ran Indianapolis–South Bend trains in conjunction with the New York Central. Some consists carried parlor cars.[176]

Norfolk Southern operates the main line between Lafayette and Portland and the Michigan City branch north of Argos. Independent short lines run trains on the balance. NS rebuilt the Fort Wayne branch as far south as New Castle into a high-speed, heavy-duty link in its Chicago-Cincinnati-Southeast service. Indiana Hi-Rail, a short line, operates the Connersville branch south of New Castle. Most of the Rushville branch is abandoned, and a short line, the Honey Creek Railroad, operates the remaining segment north of Rushville.[177]

Toledo, St. Louis and Western (Clover Leaf)

The Toledo, St. Louis and Western Railroad originated at Delphos, Ohio, which briefly was a nation-

Nickel Plate Berkshires (2–8–4) were famous for fast freight duties. S class Berkshire No. 714, built in 1934, is turned on the Frankfort turntable in 1944.   *Photo by William Rittase—Jay Williams collection*

the Norfolk and Western Railway leased and later purchased it.[187] Total all-time ownership in Indiana was 361 miles plus 316 miles leased briefly under the Gould expansion, or 9.1% of the state's total.[188]

In 1855, during Indiana's first serious decade of railroad building, the Lake Erie, Wabash and St. Louis Railroad, a Wabash ancestor, pushed westward from Toledo through Fort Wayne, and continued in 1856 through Peru, Lafayette, and Attica toward Danville, Illinois. Here it merged with roads that eventually reached St. Louis, and it became the Toledo, Wabash and Western Railroad.[189] Indiana mileage totaled 168, most of it within sight of the

Wabash and Erie Canal.[190] This was the first railroad in Indiana to compete with an artificial waterway, and it presaged the end of the canal era.

Foreseeing that Detroit not only would succeed Toledo as his important eastern terminal but that it also could give him control of roads to the east, Gould on August 26, 1879, leased the Eel River Railroad, which had begun operating in 1871 on a segment from Logansport to Butler.[191] Linked shortly afterward with the Detroit, Butler and St. Louis, built in 1880 from Detroit, this became the Wabash main line. Further rerouting took place after the Wabash on December 1, 1890, leased and

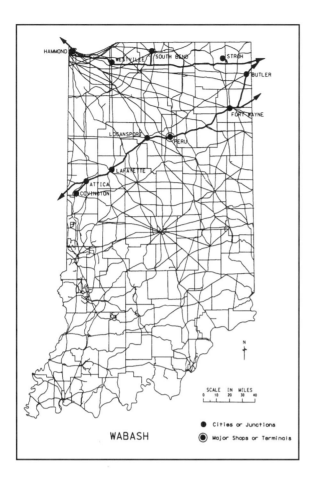

WABASH

● Cities or Junctions
◉ Major Shops or Terminals

SCALE IN MILES
0   10   20   30   40

parts, including Triple Crown RoadRailer trains, for which Fort Wayne is the systemwide hub.[195]

The famous Wabash Cannon Ball, whose name came from an earlier hobo ballad, traveled this route until Amtrak was established in 1971. It had descended directly from the glamorous Continental Limited, which was established in 1896 over the Eel River route to connect St. Louis and Weehawken, New Jersey, opposite New York City.[196] A 15-mile branch was built in 1881 to connect Covington with Attica, on the main line. In its peak period, it carried four daily passenger trains and survived until 1932.[197]

On May 4, 1893, the Wabash opened a 175-mile line between Chicago and Montpelier, Ohio, where it connected with the Detroit route.[198] During the peak passenger era, it had carried six trains, including four between Chicago and Buffalo, via southern Canada. Two carried South Bend–Detroit Pullmans, which the 11-mile New Jersey, Indiana and Illinois Railroad delivered to the Wabash.[199] Last passenger service on the Chicago line was a tri-weekly Gary-Montpelier mixed train, the last such service in Indiana. Indispensable to Amish farmers because of the implements and supplies delivered from its express car, it expired about 1959.[200] Most of the line was abandoned in 1982, 1984, and 1988.[201] A five-mile branch built in 1899 from Helmer to a cement mill at Stroh carried six passenger shuttles daily but was abandoned in 1945.[202]

In addition to the Eel River and the Peru and Detroit Railroads, the Wabash leased four other Indiana roads but lost them in the crash of the Gould empire. They were:

• Indianapolis, Peru and Chicago Railway, a 159-mile line that connected Indianapolis and Michigan City. It became the Norfolk and Western before being divided among three short lines.[203]

• Lafayette, Bloomington and Mississippi Railway, which became Norfolk and Western and is now the Kankakee, Beaverville and Southern Railroad. Thirty-six miles are in Indiana. It originally connected Lafayette with Bloomington, Illinois.[204]

• Havana, Rantoul and Eastern Railroad, which extended from Leroy, Illinois, to a junction with the Wabash at West Lebanon. Built as narrow gauge in 1878–79, it subsequently became a standard-gauge Illinois Central branch whose nine-mile Indiana segment was abandoned in 1937 and 1942.[205]

• A ten-mile branch that connected Vincennes with St. Francisville, Illinois, where it joined a line that became the New York Central's Chicago-Cairo,

later purchased the 9.6-mile Peru and Detroit Railway, which had been completed in 1889 between the original main line at Peru and the Eel River at Chili. This eliminated through traffic on the Eel River between Logansport and Chili.[192]

As a result, Eel River stockholders sued the Wabash and regained possession after a bizarre and long-running court battle. Stripped of its railroad, the Wabash built a 26-mile connection between New Haven, six miles east of Fort Wayne on its original line, and Butler. This line was opened in 1902 and at the same time the Peru and Detroit was abandoned, only to be sold to the Winona Interurban Railway in 1906 for use on its Goshen-Peru route.[193]

During the peak passenger era, 14 trains sped daily over the main line, but this had been reduced to eight by the post–World War II period, including four fast Chicago-Detroit trains operated via Fort Wayne jointly with the Pennsylvania Railroad.[194] The line is now a heavy carrier of automobiles and

WABASH RAILROAD

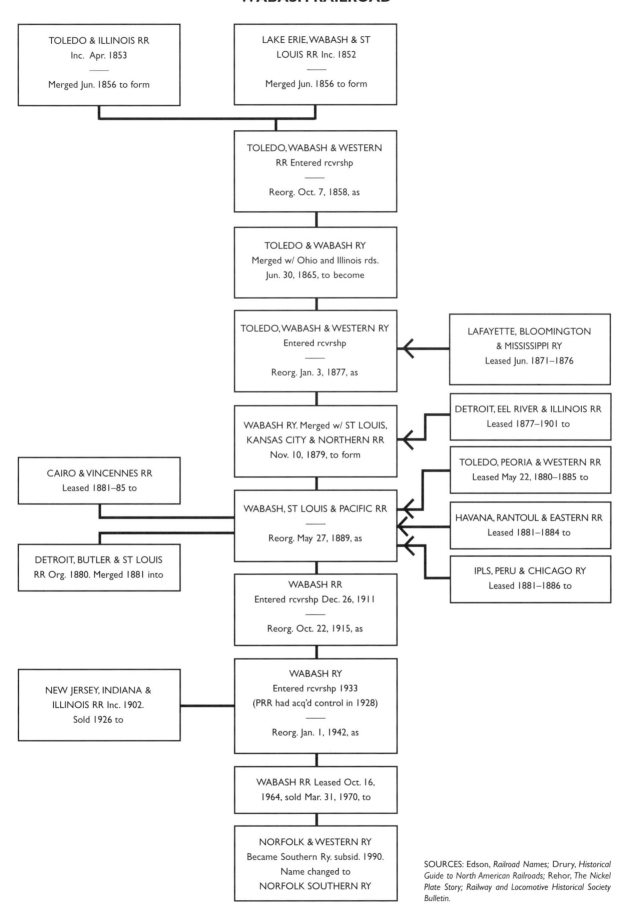

TOLEDO & ILLINOIS RR
Inc. Apr. 1853
———
Merged Jun. 1856 to form

LAKE ERIE, WABASH & ST
LOUIS RR Inc. 1852
———
Merged Jun. 1856 to form

TOLEDO, WABASH & WESTERN
RR Entered rcvrshp
———
Reorg. Oct. 7, 1858, as

TOLEDO & WABASH RY
Merged w/ Ohio and Illinois rds.
Jun. 30, 1865, to become

TOLEDO, WABASH & WESTERN RY
Entered rcvrshp
———
Reorg. Jan. 3, 1877, as

LAFAYETTE, BLOOMINGTON
& MISSISSIPPI RY
Leased Jun. 1871–1876

WABASH RY. Merged w/ ST LOUIS,
KANSAS CITY & NORTHERN RR
Nov. 10, 1879, to form

DETROIT, EEL RIVER & ILLINOIS RR
Leased 1877–1901 to

TOLEDO, PEORIA & WESTERN RR
Leased May 22, 1880–1885 to

CAIRO & VINCENNES RR
Leased 1881–85 to

WABASH, ST LOUIS & PACIFIC RR
———
Reorg. May 27, 1889, as

HAVANA, RANTOUL & EASTERN RR
Leased 1881–1884 to

DETROIT, BUTLER & ST LOUIS
RR Org. 1880. Merged 1881 into

IPLS, PERU & CHICAGO RY
Leased 1881–1886 to

WABASH RR
Entered rcvrshp Dec. 26, 1911
———
Reorg. Oct. 22, 1915, as

NEW JERSEY, INDIANA &
ILLINOIS RR Inc. 1902.
Sold 1926 to

WABASH RY
Entered rcvrshp 1933
(PRR had acq'd control in 1928)
———
Reorg. Jan. 1, 1942, as

WABASH RR Leased Oct. 16,
1964, sold Mar. 31, 1970, to

NORFOLK & WESTERN RY
Became Southern Ry. subsid. 1990.
Name changed to
NORFOLK SOUTHERN RY

SOURCES: Edson, *Railroad Names;* Drury, *Historical Guide to North American Railroads;* Rehor, *The Nickel Plate Story;* Railway and Locomotive Historical Society Bulletin.

The Wabash Cannon Ball, newly introduced in 1950, is seen here at Lafayette Junction July 25, 1953, with steam-era heavyweight coaches, diner, and parlor-observation, but modern diesel power.   *Jay Williams collection*

Built for Wabash fast freight service in 1930, 4–8–4 Northern-type No. 2900 pauses for coal at Lafayette, July 18, 1936.   *Photo by C. L. Harper—M. D. McCarter collection*

Illinois, route. It was projected as a line to the Gulf of Mexico but was abandoned in 1967.[206]

Prior to building its Chicago-Montpelier, Ohio, line, the Wabash operated Chicago-Detroit passenger trains on trackage rights over the Erie-controlled Chicago and Atlantic Railway as far east as Newton (Wabash County) and then to Detroit on the Eel River and its connections.[207]

MONON RAILWAY

Thoroughly Hoosier, the Monon (formally known as the Chicago, Indianapolis and Louisville Railway) at its peak totaled 603 miles or 8.1% of the state's total and was the fifth largest system in Indiana.[208] Intended to provide an Ohio river outlet for central Indiana farm products, it became instead principally a hauler of northbound coal and other commodities.[209] It operated in three states, yet it owned rails only in Indiana and entered its three principal cities over trackage rights.[210] It was the first railroad to connect the Ohio River and Lake Michigan, where its promoters saw Michigan City, rather than Chicago, as the most promising port.[211] It weathered four court supervisions but was unable to withstand acquisition by a larger road.[212]

The system consisted of its original 296-mile line between Louisville and Michigan City, a 183-mile Indianapolis-Chicago route, and several short branches. The main lines crossed at Monon, which gave the road its popular and later corporate name.[213] An important Hoosier institution for a century and a quarter, it was dismembered after the Louisville and Nashville Railroad acquired it in 1971.[214]

The Monon began as the New Albany and Salem Railroad, which the legislature chartered in 1847 as the successor to a defunct plan to connect New Albany and Crawfordsville by road under the state's Mammoth Internal Improvements Act. Completed to Salem on January 14, 1851, it reached Gosport via Bedford and Bloomington in January 1854. Meanwhile, in 1852, the NA&S had acquired the recently completed Crawfordsville and Wabash Railroad, which connected Crawfordsville with the important Wabash and Erie Canal town of Lafayette. The 56 miles between Gosport and Crawfordsville were completed in 1854.[215]

While this was taking place, construction was proceeding in the north, including a 65-mile tangent between Brookston and Westville, which be-

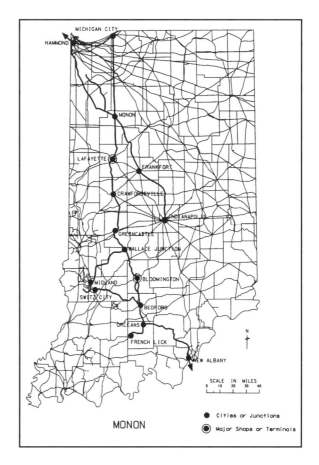

MONON

Cities or Junctions
Major Shops or Terminals

SCALE IN MILES
0 10 20 30 40

came the nation's fourth longest and at the time of construction may have been number one.[216] Starting at Michigan City, the rails reached Lafayette in 1853 to complete the entire line, but only after the NA&S had agreed to build on Fifth Street through downtown Lafayette. The city became famous for its colossal traffic tie-ups, which were not eliminated until 141 years later when the tracks were moved to the Wabash River bank in 1994. The last passenger train on the original line ran July 22.[217]

The northern extension was financed by the NA&S trading its charter rights to build toward Chicago to the Michigan Central Railroad in return for the purchase of $500,000 in stock.[218] It required 30 years to correct this lapse in judgment and then only by acquiring an Indianapolis-Chicago line then under construction.[219]

In 1859, the road was renamed the Louisville, New Albany and Chicago Railroad to reflect its newer, broader vision and to reaffirm that Chicago remained its goal. It achieved this in an unexpected way when it acquired the Indianapolis, Delphi and Chicago Railroad, which had opened in 1878 as a 3'

MONON

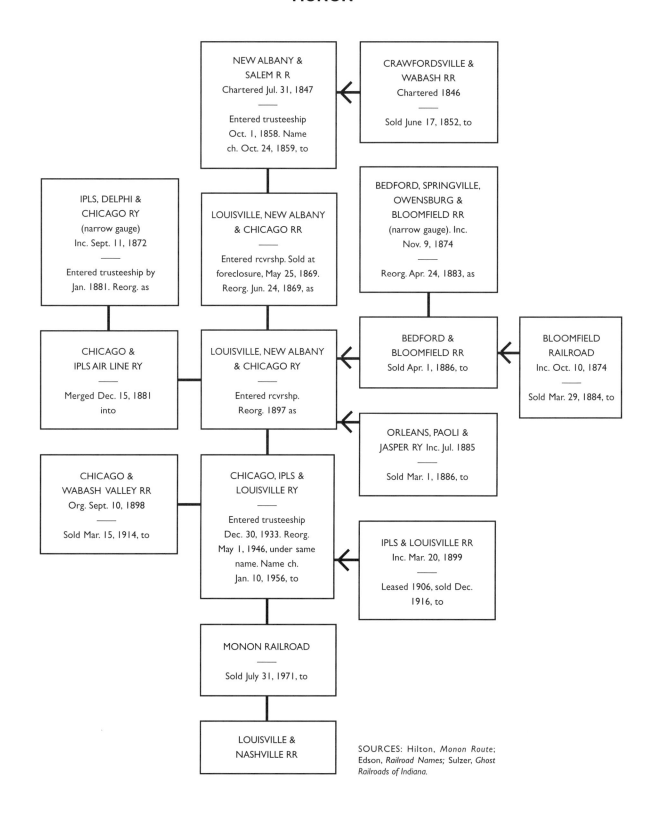

NEW ALBANY & SALEM R R
Chartered Jul. 31, 1847
———
Entered trusteeship Oct. 1, 1858. Name ch. Oct. 24, 1859, to

CRAWFORDSVILLE & WABASH RR
Chartered 1846
———
Sold June 17, 1852, to

IPLS, DELPHI & CHICAGO RY
(narrow gauge)
Inc. Sept. 11, 1872
———
Entered trusteeship by Jan. 1881. Reorg. as

LOUISVILLE, NEW ALBANY & CHICAGO RR
———
Entered rcvrshp. Sold at foreclosure, May 25, 1869. Reorg. Jun. 24, 1869, as

BEDFORD, SPRINGVILLE, OWENSBURG & BLOOMFIELD RR
(narrow gauge). Inc. Nov. 9, 1874
———
Reorg. Apr. 24, 1883, as

CHICAGO & IPLS AIR LINE RY
Merged Dec. 15, 1881 into

LOUISVILLE, NEW ALBANY & CHICAGO RY
———
Entered rcvrshp. Reorg. 1897 as

BEDFORD & BLOOMFIELD RR
Sold Apr. 1, 1886, to

BLOOMFIELD RAILROAD
Inc. Oct. 10, 1874
———
Sold Mar. 29, 1884, to

ORLEANS, PAOLI & JASPER RY Inc. Jul. 1885
———
Sold Mar. 1, 1886, to

CHICAGO & WABASH VALLEY RR
Org. Sept. 10, 1898
———
Sold Mar. 15, 1914, to

CHICAGO, IPLS & LOUISVILLE RY
———
Entered trusteeship Dec. 30, 1933. Reorg. May 1, 1946, under same name. Name ch. Jan. 10, 1956, to

IPLS & LOUISVILLE RR
Inc. Mar. 20, 1899
———
Leased 1906, sold Dec. 1916, to

MONON RAILROAD
———
Sold July 31, 1971, to

LOUISVILLE & NASHVILLE RR

SOURCES: Hilton, *Monon Route*; Edson, *Railroad Names*; Sulzer, *Ghost Railroads of Indiana.*

The Monon retained several original train barn depots until its 1971 merger into L&N. The 1854 Gosport depot, with its siding through the building, was on the Historic American Engineering record when it was torn down in the 1970s.   *Tom Douglas and* Spencer Evening World *collection*

narrow-gauge line connecting Rensselaer and Monon, which was then named Bradford.[220] Converted to standard gauge in 1881, shortly before the LNA&C acquired it, the line was extended to the Chicago area in 1881 and to Indianapolis in 1883. On entering Chicago, the company relegated its Michigan City road to branch status.[221]

Shortly afterward the road acquired its first two branches, one primarily for hauling coal and the other to serve passengers. On March 1, 1886, it purchased the newly organized 17.7-mile Orleans, Paoli and Jasper Railway, which became the Monon's French Lick branch.[222] Serving the twin spas of French Lick Springs and West Baden Springs, the railroad brought thousands of visitors to these nationally known resorts and at its peak operated 12 trains daily on the branch. Through sleeping cars arrived from Chicago and eastern cities, and into the 1930s, the Monon and Pennsylvania jointly operated through Indianapolis–French Lick service. Many special trains rode the branch, particularly on Kentucky Derby weekends when they arrived with surprising frequency.[223]

Only one month after acquiring the French Lick branch, the Monon purchased a narrow-gauge line that entered the Greene and Sullivan County coal fields from the southeast. Originally the Bedford, Springville, Owensburg and Bloomfield Railroad and later the Bedford and Bloomfield Railroad, it had been completed to Bloomfield in 1877 and later extended to Switz City. It covered 41 miles. Poorly constructed, it wound among the hills, through the Monon's only tunnel, and crossed White River on a wooden covered bridge. The line gained a modicum of local fame because of its lone, plodding passenger train, which was known affectionately as "Old Nellie." The line was standard gauged in 1895 and was abandoned in 1935.[224]

The Monon, most Hoosier of railroads, celebrated a rebirth in 1947 when it emerged from receivership. It promptly replaced its entire passenger car fleet and also became one of the nation's first 100% dieselized roads. *Indiana Historical Society Monon Collection, Neg. No. A84*

But the B&B was not the answer to the Monon's coal field development. Consequently in 1907 the Monon completed a 47-mile road from the northeast, which joined the main line at Wallace Junction. In 1920, it served 34 mines and, in addition to heavy coal traffic, carried two passenger trains. The line was abandoned in 1984 after mines were worked out.[225]

In northwestern Indiana, the Monon acquired the parallel 32-mile Chicago and Wabash Valley Railway in 1914 as part of a proposed doubletrack line but the plan did not materialize and the branch was abandoned in 1935. An agricultural hauler, it was known locally as the "Onion Belt." It carried passengers in daily mixed trains.[226]

During the peak passenger era, the Monon operated 45 trains daily, including six between Chicago and Cincinnati jointly with the Cincinnati, Indianapolis and Western Railroad, a Baltimore and Ohio predecessor.[227] Despite the Monon's inconsistent financial performance, it attracted the rich and famous. John Jacob Astor, the fur king, who was said to have been America's wealthiest man in his day, once controlled the road and was succeeded by banker J. Pierpont Morgan. President Franklin D. Roosevelt's father, James, served as president in 1883–1884 and his uncle, Frederic A. Delano, was president in 1913–1914.[228]

After the Monon emerged from a third court supervision in 1897, the Southern and Louisville and Nashville jointly acquired control, which they retained until another bankruptcy in 1933.[229] Following reorganization in 1946, the officers named as president John W. Barriger, who had solid credentials as a practical railroader, financial and marketing expert, and transportation visionary, and, as it turned out, was also a public relations wizard.[230]

With bold, imaginative moves he quickly captured the attention of the industry and the public alike as he rebuilt the road with new rolling stock, structures, and alignment, and reestablished service reliability and faster schedules. Seizing on the Monon's centennial as a theme, he sent performers up and down the road with song and pageant and created an entire new streamlined passenger car fleet from surplus U.S. army hospital cars. With these he restored double daily service to both Indianapolis and Louisville and at the same time he restored the French Lick Pullman.[231]

He replaced the antiquated Wabash River bridge at Delphi by a novel construction method and at Cedar Lake he built an entirely new railroad to bypass a "bottomless" bog. He didn't hesitate to experiment with innovation in schedules or equipment and under his direction the Monon became one of the nation's first roads to dieselize completely. He talked constantly about the industry's great potential and his vision of a super railroad toward which the Monon would lead the way.[232]

Although the new Monon was relatively prosperous, it soon became apparent that its salvation lay in a merger, particularly after the Interstate Commerce Commission refused permission to build coal loading facilities on the Ohio River and Lake Michigan. All passenger service ended to Indianapolis in 1959, to Louisville in 1967. The road, *Railway Age,* the industry publication, had once said, was "an unnecessary railroad."[233]

On July 31, 1971, the L&N purchased the Monon and subsequently became part of CSX. A systematic dismemberment soon began. First to go were most of the French Lick branch in 1976, followed by the Michigan City branch north of Medaryville in 1980 and the coal fields line in 1984. The once-busy Indianapolis branch is now gone south of Monticello and most of the main line between Cloverdale

and Bedford is abandoned. South of Bedford, the Soo Line, which operated to Louisville on trackage rights, is the principal user. Amtrak uses the road between Chicago and Crawfordsville.[234]

The Monon no longer connects any important terminals. What once was a busy 603-mile system has shrunk to 301 miles of dead end spurs and taken with it a friendly railroad that was dear to the hearts of Hoosiers.[235]

BALTIMORE AND OHIO RAILROAD

Indiana's sixth largest system, the Baltimore and Ohio, at its peak operated three cross-state lines and five branches that totaled 585 miles or 7.8% of Indiana's largest total. Like its competitors, Pennsylvania and New York Central, it linked Chicago and St. Louis with the East. Constituent companies were the Baltimore, Pittsburgh and Chicago Rail-

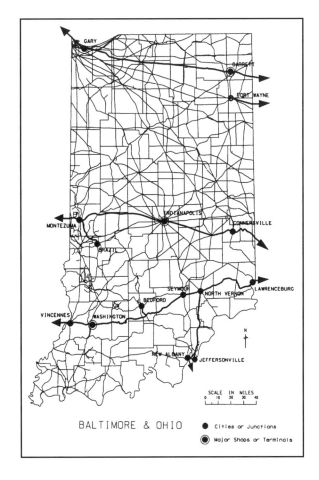

BALTIMORE & OHIO ● Cities or Junctions ◉ Major Shops or Terminals

BALTIMORE & OHIO

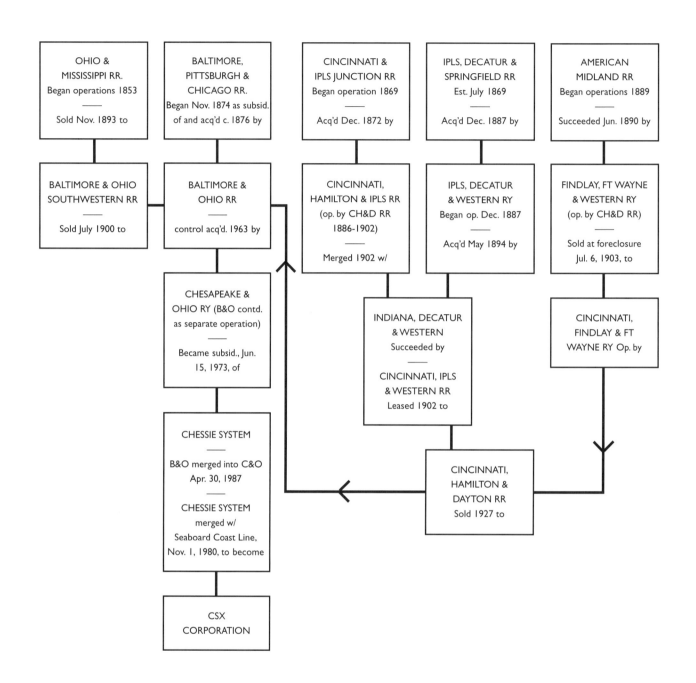

SOURCES: Edson, *Railroad Names;* Stover, *History of the Baltimore and Ohio Railroad;* Sulzer, *Ghost Railroads of Indiana;* Drury, *The Historical Guide to North American Railroads;* Bogle, "Railroad Building in Indiana"

North Vernon was a busy junction on the Baltimore and Ohio Railroad. In 1954 a passenger train off the Louisville branch meets a premier Washington, D.C.–St. Louis train before continuing to Cincinnati. *Photo by Richard S. Simons*

road, which connected the three cities of its corporate title; the Ohio and Mississippi Railroad, which became its St. Louis line, and the Cincinnati, Hamilton and Dayton, which controlled lines through Indianapolis, as well as the long-defunct Cincinnati, Findlay and Fort Wayne Railway.[236]

The parent B&O goes back to July 4, 1828, and was built to keep Baltimore competitive after the Erie Canal opened a new interior outlet to New York City.[237] The Chesapeake and Ohio Railway acquired control of the B&O in 1963, and merged with it on April 30, 1987. As of early 1997, both are part of CSX, one of the East's "Big Three."[238]

Ohio and Mississippi

The 339-mile Ohio and Mississippi Railroad, connecting Cincinnati and St. Louis, stretched 169 miles across Indiana. Completed in 1857, it was the earliest B&O-controlled line in Indiana and was the only railroad in the state built to the 6' broad gauge. Originally it was seen as a connection to other broad-gauge lines tributary to the Erie Railroad, rather than as a continuation of the standard-gauge B&O, but in 1871 both the main line and the Louisville branch were narrowed to 4'9".[239] Washington, Indiana, became the principal shop town in

A Baltimore and Ohio Mikado (2–8–2), pulling a westbound coal train, pauses for water at Syracuse on a summer Sunday afternoon in 1951.   *W. W. Spurgeon*

1888, succeeding Vincennes and Cochrane, near Aurora, and it also became the division point. In 1893, the Baltimore and Ohio Southwestern absorbed the O&M and in 1900 it became part of the parent B&O.[240]

Extensive rebuilding in 1899–1901 brought major relocations near Osgood, North Vernon, and Shoals. In addition, one tunnel was rebuilt, another added, and one converted into an open cut.[241] During the peak passenger years 25 trains traveled all or sections of the line but this had been reduced to 15 by the post–World War II period.[242]

In 1869 the O&M opened a 54-mile branch from North Vernon to Jeffersonville from which, in 1870, it ran trains into Louisville over a new Ohio River bridge. In 1887, however, it added an eight-mile extension from Watson to New Albany to enable it to use the new Kentucky and Indiana Railroad Company bridge which the O&M partly owned.[243] During the peak passenger era, 11 trains operated daily over the branch, compared to 10 following World War II. Most continued to Cincinnati and some to Detroit. The branch was abandoned between North Vernon and Charlestown beginning in 1980.[244]

In September 1893 the road opened an 11-mile

branch from Rivervale to Bedford to serve lime-stone quarries, but abandoned it in 1924. It carried four daily passenger trains during the peak period.[245]

Baltimore, Pittsburgh and Chicago

Aware that its destiny was tied to entering the burgeoning rail hub of Chicago, the Baltimore and Ohio established a subsidiary, the Baltimore, Pittsburgh and Chicago Railroad, to extend its eastern lines to the nation's principal rail gateway. Although projected to link Pittsburgh with Chicago, the line began at Chicago Junction, now Willard, Ohio, on the B&O's Sandusky-Newark, Ohio, branch, which connected indirectly to Pittsburgh. The new 263-mile line, which included 143 miles across northern Indiana, went into service November 23, 1874. The direct Pittsburgh road was not completed until 1891.[246]

The Indiana segment of the Chicago line was straight and level and included all told 240 miles of tangent track. Most grades were less than .5%. Swamps, however, were difficult to cross, and con-struction in De Kalb County was particularly challenging.[247]

Seeking a division point location, the railroad established the town of Garrett, three miles west of Auburn, and named it for John W. Garrett, the road's president. Truly a company town, it occupied more than 600 acres, which were divided into lots and sold. The railroad built extensive yards, a roundhouse, and shops with capability to produce both locomotives and cars.[248]

Always a heavy traffic line, the road carried 16 passenger trains during the peak era and retained 12 of these into the post–World War II period including the all-Pullman Capitol Limited. Today it is the CSX main line to the East.[249]

Cincinnati, Hamilton and Dayton

This 321-mile line which extended from Hamilton, Ohio, to Springfield, Illinois, through Indianapolis survived a confusing series of reorganizations, leases, spinoffs, mergers, and name changes, often involving B&O-influenced roads,

The B&O passenger station at Syracuse is lighted for the pre-dawn arrival of the Washington-Chicago Express in 1967. Passenger service continued on this line until 1971, and was later revived under Amtrak. *W. W. Spurgeon*

B&O Mountain-type locomotives (4–8–2) double-head a coal train westbound out of the Garrett yard in February 1957. Steam had only one year remaining on the Chicago main line. *William Swartz—M. D. McCarter collection*

before the B&O purchased it in 1927. Indiana mileage totaled 182.[250]

The earliest component was the Cincinnati and Indianapolis Junction (usually called the Junction), which completed its line to Indianapolis in 1869. In 1872 it became part of the Cincinnati, Hamilton and Indianapolis, which became part of the CH&D in 1886. In 1892 it again became the Cincinnati, Hamilton and Indianapolis, which through a 1902 merger with the western segment became the Cincinnati, Indianapolis and Western Railroad. The CH&D operated the merged road until 1906. Another reorganization took place in 1915 and the

new company, like its predecessor, remained under CH&D control. From 1910 to 1918, the B&O controlled the CH&D.[251]

The line west of Indianapolis was partially opened by 1875 and reached Indianapolis in 1880. It was successively the Indianapolis, Decatur and Springfield, from 1887 to 1894 the Indianapolis, Decatur and Western, and from 1894 to 1902 the Indiana, Decatur and Western. After the 1902 merger it became the Cincinnati, Indianapolis and Western.[252]

The eastern segment was part of a through Chicago-Cincinnati passenger route with the Monon, and during the peak passenger period operated six trains daily in addition to four between Indianapolis and Hamilton or Cincinnati. Although the B&O abandoned passenger service in 1950, it returned when Amtrak rerouted the Cardinal in 1986.[253]

The western segment, always a light carrier of both freight and passengers, operated four daily passenger trains during the peak period.[254] Most trackage was abandoned beginning in 1988. A 26-mile branch purchased from the Chicago and Eastern Illinois Railway in 1922 extended from West Melcher to Brazil, but was abandoned in 1965.[255]

Cincinnati, Findlay and Fort Wayne

A natural gas boom in the mid–1880s at Findlay, Ohio, generated demand for a railroad to the west, and the result was the American Midland, which was established in 1889. The Findlay, Fort Wayne and Western Railway succeeded it in 1890 and completed the road in 1895. In 1901 an operating agreement was made with the Cincinnati, Hamilton and Dayton Railway, but the FFW&W failed in 1903 and was reorganized as the Cincinnati, Findlay and Fort Wayne. The CH&D again leased the road, but it entered a second receivership in 1914.[256]

About 1900 the CF&FW operated a Findlay-Chicago Pullman car, which it turned over to the Pennsylvania Railroad at Fort Wayne. The service lasted only briefly, however, and by 1915 the road operated only four local trains daily, two of which were advertised for "adult male passengers only." The railroad, which was 78 miles long, was remarkably straight and ran due west from Findlay for 65 miles before it made a slight curve toward Fort Wayne. The Indiana portion totaled 18 miles. Operating through a thinly populated territory, the road was abandoned in 1919.[257]

CHICAGO AND EASTERN ILLINOIS

The Chicago and Eastern Illinois Railroad and numerous predecessors built a series of lines that ran 287 miles from Evansville to Chicago via Terre Haute and Danville, Illinois. It also operated a parallel road from Evansville to La Crosse through Brazil and Attica with a branch to the main line at Momence, Illinois.[258] The alternate road's south segment became the Big Four's Evansville, Indianapolis and Terre Haute Railway in 1920 and most of the north section became the locally owned

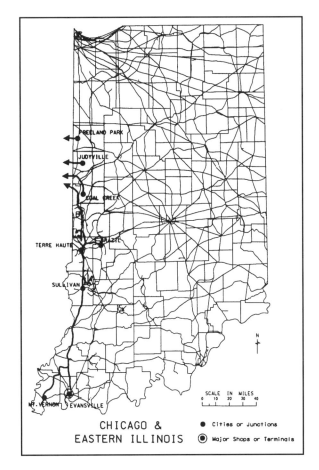

CHICAGO & EASTERN ILLINOIS

● Cities or Junctions
◉ Major Shops or Terminals

Chicago, Attica and Southern Railroad short line in 1922.[259] The main line developed into a through Florida route in conjunction with the Louisville and Nashville Railroad and others and carried heavy seasonal passenger traffic.[260] The L&N purchased the Evansville line on June 6, 1969, and subsequently both became part of CSX.[261] All-time total mileage was 580 or 7.8% of the state's total.

The Evansville and Crawfordsville Railroad, an early component, began service in 1854 between Evansville and Terre Haute and in 1860 was extended to Rockville. The Logansport, Crawfordsville and South Western Railway leased the Terre Haute–Rockville line in 1872 and a successor company, part of the Pennsylvania Railroad, purchased it in 1924.[262]

On October 26, 1871, the Evansville, Terre Haute and Chicago Railroad began service between Terre Haute and Danville, Illinois, and in November 1871 the Chicago, Danville and Vincennes Railroad opened service between Chicago and Danville. Together with the E&C, they inaugurated an Evans-

CHICAGO & EASTERN ILLINOIS

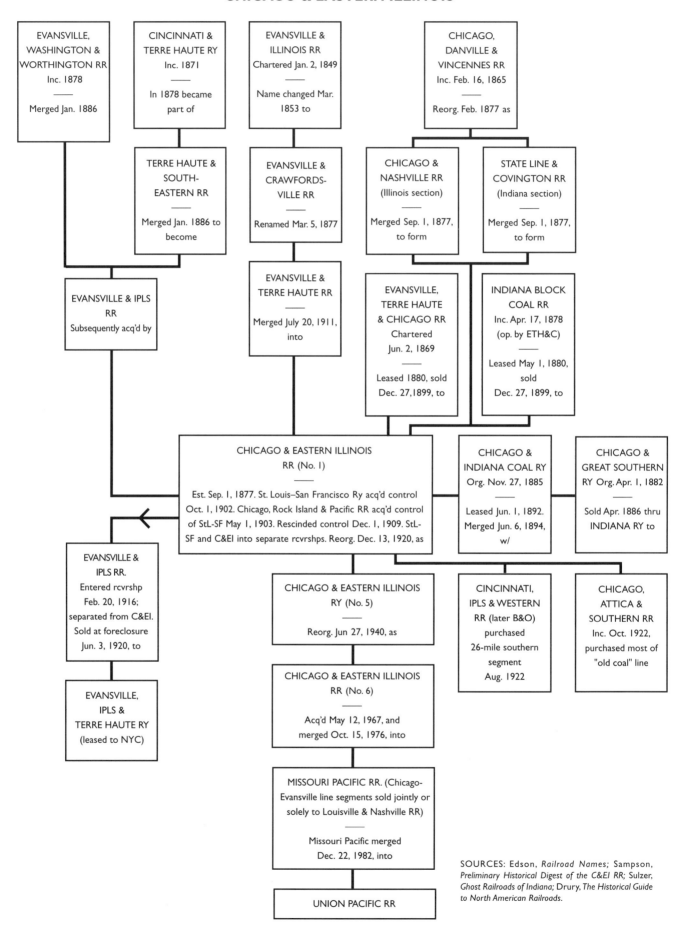

EVANSVILLE, WASHINGTON & WORTHINGTON RR
Inc. 1878
———
Merged Jan. 1886

CINCINNATI & TERRE HAUTE RY
Inc. 1871
———
In 1878 became part of

EVANSVILLE & ILLINOIS RR
Chartered Jan. 2, 1849
———
Name changed Mar. 1853 to

CHICAGO, DANVILLE & VINCENNES RR
Inc. Feb. 16, 1865
———
Reorg. Feb. 1877 as

TERRE HAUTE & SOUTH-EASTERN RR
———
Merged Jan. 1886 to become

EVANSVILLE & CRAWFORDS-VILLE RR
———
Renamed Mar. 5, 1877

CHICAGO & NASHVILLE RR
(Illinois section)
———
Merged Sep. 1, 1877, to form

STATE LINE & COVINGTON RR
(Indiana section)
———
Merged Sep. 1, 1877, to form

EVANSVILLE & IPLS RR
Subsequently acq'd by

EVANSVILLE & TERRE HAUTE RR
———
Merged July 20, 1911, into

EVANSVILLE, TERRE HAUTE & CHICAGO RR
Chartered Jun. 2, 1869
———
Leased 1880, sold Dec. 27, 1899, to

INDIANA BLOCK COAL RR
Inc. Apr. 17, 1878
(op. by ETH&C)
———
Leased May 1, 1880, sold Dec. 27, 1899, to

CHICAGO & EASTERN ILLINOIS RR (No. 1)
———
Est. Sep. 1, 1877. St. Louis–San Francisco Ry acq'd control Oct. 1, 1902. Chicago, Rock Island & Pacific RR acq'd control of StL-SF May 1, 1903. Rescinded control Dec. 1, 1909. StL-SF and C&EI into separate rcvrshps. Reorg. Dec. 13, 1920, as

CHICAGO & INDIANA COAL RY
Org. Nov. 27, 1885
———
Leased Jun. 1, 1892.
Merged Jun. 6, 1894, w/

CHICAGO & GREAT SOUTHERN RY Org. Apr. 1, 1882
———
Sold Apr. 1886 thru INDIANA RY to

EVANSVILLE & IPLS RR.
Entered rcvrshp Feb. 20, 1916; separated from C&EI. Sold at foreclosure Jun. 3, 1920, to

CHICAGO & EASTERN ILLINOIS RY (No. 5)
———
Reorg. Jun 27, 1940, as

CINCINNATI, IPLS & WESTERN RR (later B&O) purchased 26-mile southern segment Aug. 1922

CHICAGO, ATTICA & SOUTHERN RR
Inc. Oct. 1922, purchased most of "old coal" line

EVANSVILLE, IPLS & TERRE HAUTE RY
(leased to NYC)

CHICAGO & EASTERN ILLINOIS RR (No. 6)
———
Acq'd May 12, 1967, and merged Oct. 15, 1976, into

MISSOURI PACIFIC RR. (Chicago-Evansville line segments sold jointly or solely to Louisville & Nashville RR)
———
Missouri Pacific merged Dec. 22, 1982, into

UNION PACIFIC RR

SOURCES: Edson, *Railroad Names;* Sampson, *Preliminary Historical Digest of the C&EI RR;* Sulzer, *Ghost Railroads of Indiana;* Drury, *The Historical Guide to North American Railroads.*

An Evansville-bound Chicago and Eastern Illinois Railroad passenger train stands beside Terre Haute's Union Station in 1951, at the crossing of C&EI and Pennsylvania main lines. A 150-foot tower crowned the now-demolished building.   *Photo by Richard S. Simons*

ville-Chicago passenger service in January 1872.[263] On September 1, 1877, a merger created the Chicago and Eastern Illinois Railroad, the first of six corporations known as the C&EI.[264] In 1880, the C&EI leased the 43-mile ETH&C and in 1894 purchased it, as well as the parallel Indiana Coal Railway and the Indiana Block Coal Railway.[265]

The St. Louis–San Francisco (Frisco) Railway acquired the C&EI in 1902 and in turn was acquired by the Chicago, Rock Island and Pacific Railway, which held it until 1909. In 1913 the C&EI entered receivership and was separated from the Frisco, which also had failed.[266]

Although the C&EI operated 11 passenger trains during the World War I peak, it built on its Florida potential and increased this to 16 after World War II. Some operated to New Orleans. Most were part of the famous Dixie Fleet—Dixie Limited, Flyer, Mail, Express, Dixieland, and Dixie Flagler. Branch lines during the peak era carried 22 daily trains.[267]

In 1873 the CD&V opened a 24-mile branch from a point near Bismarck, Illinois, to mineral deposits along Coal Creek, south of Covington, Indiana. In 1879 the segment west of Covington was abandoned in favor of trackage rights over the Indiana, Bloomington and Western Railway (later Peoria and Eastern Railroad). The balance of the branch was abandoned in 1888.[268] A 38-mile line between Fort Branch and Mt. Vernon was opened in 1882 and remained intact for 100 years before abandonment began in 1982. The remaining segment became the Poseyville and Owensville Railroad, now Owensville Terminal. Daily mixed train service lasted until 1950.[269]

A 13-mile branch from Otter Creek Junction, north of Terre Haute, reached Brazil, the original destination of the Coal Creek branch, in 1879. It was abandoned in 1977.[270] An extensive network of coal mine branches, totaling consecutively more than 30 miles, covered the northeast quarter of Sullivan County between 1887 and 1955.[271] Numerous mine branches also were built in the Clinton area, mostly between 1903 and 1905. Nearly all were abandoned by 1994, although the initial discontinuance had occurred in 1893.[272] Two short grain hauling branches were built from the main line in Illinois to points in Warren and Benton counties. The 11-mile Milford, Illinois–Freeland Park line, of which two miles were in Indiana, was operated between 1901 and 1950. The 15-mile Rossville, Illinois-Judyville branch, with seven miles in Indiana, was built in 1903 and abandoned in the 1970s.[273]

Chicago and Indiana Coal

An abundant collection of railroads evolved into a line from Brazil to La Crosse with a branch to Momence, Illinois. Proposed to ship coal northward from the Brazil area, the Indiana North and South Railroad was opened between Attica and Veedersburg in 1874. A successor, Chicago and Block Coal Railroad, extended this 15-mile line seven miles south to Yeddo in 1882. A second successor, Chicago and Great Southern Railway, pushed the road northward 46 miles to Fair Oaks (Jasper County) in 1883, and a merger with the newly created Indiana Railway resulted in the Chicago and Indiana Coal Railway in 1886. In 1885 the line had been extended southward 42 miles to Brazil and in 1887 it reached its final northern terminus 27 miles away at La Crosse. The road did a brisk business carrying passengers to Mudlavia spa near Attica.[274]

Henry H. Porter of Chicago, who controlled the road, also acquired control of the C&EI and in 1888 added a 31-mile connection from Percy Junction, 2.5 miles north of Goodland, to Momence, on the main line. The C&EI leased and later acquired the C&IC between 1889 and 1894.[275] Six freight trains and eight passenger trains subsequently traveled daily between Brazil and Momence.[276]

The C&EI was sold at foreclosure in 1921 but the Brazil line was not included. The Interstate Commerce Commission authorized abandonment but a new corporation, the Chicago, Attica and Southern Railroad, emerged unexpectedly to operate all but the south 25 miles, which was sold to the Baltimore and Ohio. Following a receivership in 1931, the CA&S was progressively abandoned between 1945 and 1946. The B&O segment was abandoned in 1965.[277]

Evansville and Indianapolis

Beginning in 1853, a series of companies attempted to build northward from Evansville and southward from Terre Haute, although original intentions were not to connect the two cities. After numerous false starts, isolated segments were connected. The three owning roads were merged as the Evansville and Indianapolis Railroad, which began operation on January 1, 1886.[278] The Evansville and Terre Haute, a constituent of the C&EI, acquired the road and by leasing the 12-mile branch built in 1887 between Brazil and Saline City by the Terre

Haute and Indianapolis now had a continuous line from Evansville to Momence, and La Crosse. The Big Four acquired the Terre Haute–Evansville line following the C&EI's 1913 receivership.[279]

MILWAUKEE ROAD

Chartered as the Evansville and Richmond Railroad, this company built its center section, Elnora to Westport, in 1890. However, after an 1897 foreclosure it was renamed the Southern Indiana Railway, and the projected western terminus changed from Evansville to Terre Haute, where it arrived in 1900. It was extended to Humrick, Illinois, in 1903 and in 1907 to Chicago Heights.[280] Between 1900 and 1905 the road constructed a tight network of coal mine lines in Sullivan County, and followed this in 1911 and 1913 with coal branches in the Clinton area. Meanwhile, it also developed lines to serve the Lawrence County limestone quarries.[281] Approximately 236 miles were operated in Indiana.

Following a reorganization brought about by the

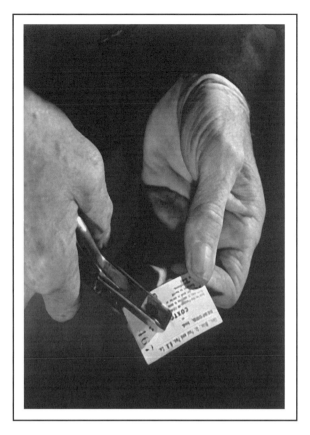

Conductor punches the last Milwaukee Road ticket sold at Bedford for the final passenger run in 1950. *Richard S. Simons collection*

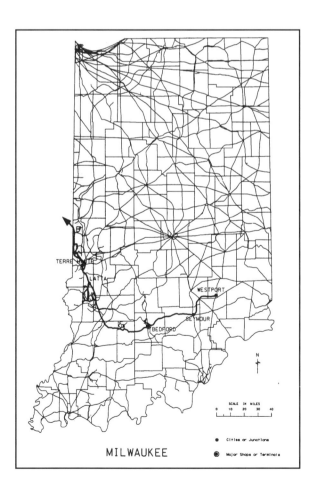

MILWAUKEE

· Cities or Junctions

◉ Major Shops or Terminals

SCALE IN MILES
0 10 20 30 40

N

failure of President John R. Walsh's Chicago banks, the new Chicago, Terre Haute and Southeastern Railway acquired the road, which it leased in 1921 to the Chicago, Milwaukee and St. Paul Railroad (Milwaukee Road). The Milwaukee purchased the road in 1948.[282]

Although an important mineral hauler, the road never developed a substantial passenger business and most runs were disconnected local hauls. Except for a few miners' trains, no passenger service was established north of Terre Haute. Indiana mileage totaled approximately 240.[283]

After the L&N acquired the Monon in 1971, the Milwaukee began service to Louisville on Monon trackage rights south of Bedford. After purchasing the Milwaukee Road in 1985, the Soo Line continued the arrangement. Major abandonments, however, began in 1961 and except for the 82 miles between Terre Haute and Bedford, trains operate over CSX (ex-C&EI and Monon) rails.[284]

Further details will be found in chapter 13.

MILWAUKEE ROAD

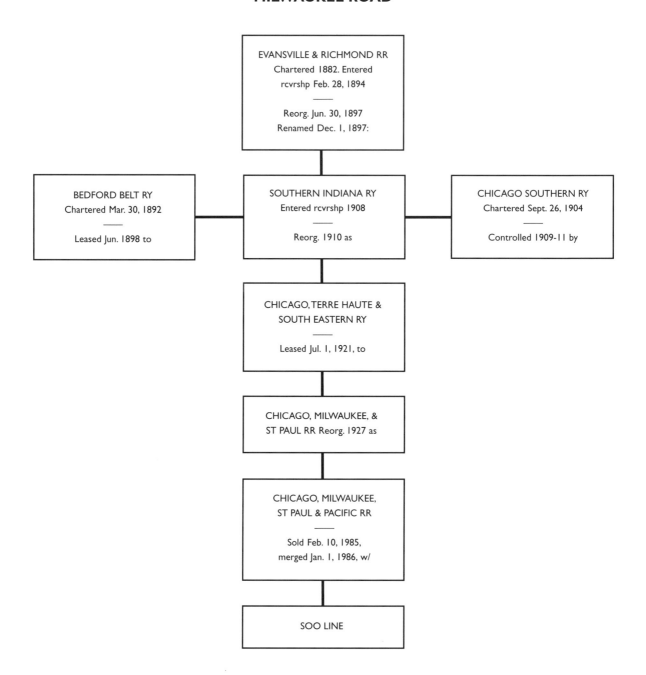

EVANSVILLE & RICHMOND RR
Chartered 1882. Entered
rcvrshp Feb. 28, 1894

———

Reorg. Jun. 30, 1897
Renamed Dec. 1, 1897:

BEDFORD BELT RY
Chartered Mar. 30, 1892

———

Leased Jun. 1898 to

SOUTHERN INDIANA RY
Entered rcvrshp 1908

———

Reorg. 1910 as

CHICAGO SOUTHERN RY
Chartered Sept. 26, 1904

———

Controlled 1909-11 by

**CHICAGO, TERRE HAUTE &
SOUTH EASTERN RY**

———

Leased Jul. 1, 1921, to

**CHICAGO, MILWAUKEE, &
ST PAUL RR** Reorg. 1927 as

**CHICAGO, MILWAUKEE,
ST PAUL & PACIFIC RR**

———

Sold Feb. 10, 1985,
merged Jan. 1, 1986, w/

SOO LINE

SOURCES: Edson, *Railroad Names*; Drury, *Historical Guide to North American Railroads*;
National Railway Historical Society, *National Railway Bulletin*; Johnson, *The Milwaukee
Road*

Mr. and Mrs Areli Jones of Bedford, who rode the first train on the line out of Bedford in 1890, buy tickets 60 years later for the final Milwaukee Road run.   *Photo by Richard S. Simons*

Milwaukee engineer H. E. Barnes takes a last look before departing Bedford July 15, 1950, on the next to last motor train to operate in Indiana. Built in 1928 by Pullman, the 69-ton car included Railway Post Office, baggage, and passenger sections.   *Photo by Richard S. Simons*

SOUTHERN RAILWAY

The Southern Railway's Louisville–St. Louis line (now Norfolk Southern) was built in disconnected sections by numerous companies during the 1870s and 1880s, and many bankruptcies, reorganizations, mergers, and name changes complicated its history before the Southern acquired it in 1900. In addition to the 263-mile main line, four branches that totaled 93 miles extended like fingers of a hand from Huntingburg.[285] The Indiana mileage totaled 234.

Early efforts go back to February 24, 1869, when the New Albany and St. Louis Air Line Railway was established. On July 1, 1870, the name was changed to Louisville, New Albany and St. Louis Air Line Railway and it began service in 1872 between Princeton, Indiana, and Albion, Illinois. After an 1875 bankruptcy, the road was split into separate corporations—the Louisville, New Albany and St. Louis Railway in Indiana and St. Louis, Mt. Carmel

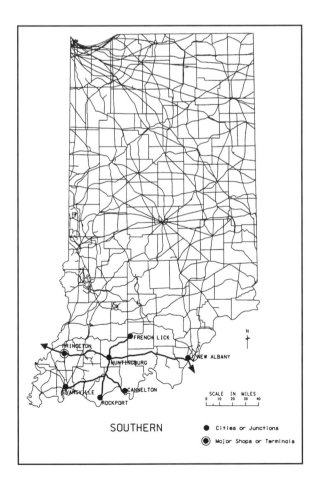

SOUTHERN

● Cities or Junctions
◉ Major Shops or Terminals

and New Albany Railroad in Illinois. They were reconsolidated in 1878 under the Indiana name.[286]

With a new infusion of capital, the line pushed eastward to Ingleton in 1880 and in 1882 it was extended both eastward to New Albany and westward to Mt. Vernon, Illinois. By this time, it had acquired railroads from Huntingburg to both Evansville and Rockport. In 1884 it again entered receivership and emerged as the Louisville, Evansville and St. Louis Railroad.[287]

In 1889 the LE&StL merged with three short Illinois railroads and one from Indiana to form the Louisville, Evansville and St. Louis Consolidated Railroad, and it constructed two missing links totaling 64 miles to complete the main line in 1890. The Kentucky and Indiana Railroad bridge, built in 1886, provided entrance into Louisville. In 1894 the road once again entered receivership and after reorganization was sold to the Southern Railway in 1900.[288]

Cutting across successive watersheds through some of Indiana's roughest terrain, the road was forced to drill eight tunnels, nearly half the state's total. One early company, attempting a difficult climb out of the Ohio River valley at New Albany, bored three successive tunnels but they were later abandoned as easier grades were sought. Although partly drifted shut, they are still accessible.[289]

During the peak passenger era, the road operated two St. Louis–Louisville round trips daily, in addition to Princeton-Mt. Vernon, Illinois, and Louisville-Huntingburg-Evansville round trips. By early 1953, all were gone.[290]

Following the Civil War, the Ohio River town of Rockport, which lacked rail service, began building northward toward Mitchell and a planned junction with the Ohio and Mississippi Railroad (later the Baltimore and Ohio and now CSX). As the Cincinnati, Rockport and Southwestern Railroad, subsequently the Evansville, Rockport and Eastern Railway, it reached Ferdinand Station, five miles west of that town, in 1874 and continued through Huntingburg to Jasper in 1878, a total of 38 miles.[291]

Here it stopped for nearly 30 years, and when it continued northward the goal was not a B&O connection but the brisk tourist traffic of that nationally famous spa, French Lick, and its sister resort, West Baden. The 25-mile extension, opened in 1907, carried a peak period of three daily round trips between Huntingburg and French Lick and a like number between Huntingburg and Rockport. All passenger service was gone by 1937. Hoosier

SOUTHERN

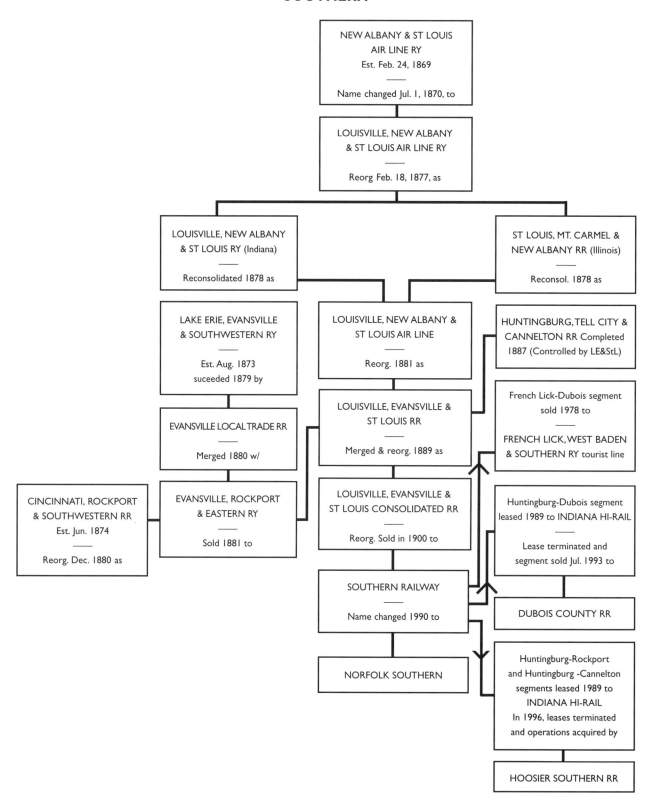

NEW ALBANY & ST LOUIS AIR LINE RY
Est. Feb. 24, 1869
Name changed Jul. 1, 1870, to

LOUISVILLE, NEW ALBANY & ST LOUIS AIR LINE RY
Reorg Feb. 18, 1877, as

LOUISVILLE, NEW ALBANY & ST LOUIS RY (Indiana)
Reconsolidated 1878 as

ST LOUIS, MT. CARMEL & NEW ALBANY RR (Illinois)
Reconsol. 1878 as

LAKE ERIE, EVANSVILLE & SOUTHWESTERN RY
Est. Aug. 1873
suceeded 1879 by

LOUISVILLE, NEW ALBANY & ST LOUIS AIR LINE
Reorg. 1881 as

HUNTINGBURG, TELL CITY & CANNELTON RR Completed 1887 (Controlled by LE&StL)

EVANSVILLE LOCAL TRADE RR
Merged 1880 w/

LOUISVILLE, EVANSVILLE & ST LOUIS RR
Merged & reorg. 1889 as

French Lick-Dubois segment sold 1978 to
FRENCH LICK, WEST BADEN & SOUTHERN RY tourist line

CINCINNATI, ROCKPORT & SOUTHWESTERN RR
Est. Jun. 1874
Reorg. Dec. 1880 as

EVANSVILLE, ROCKPORT & EASTERN RY
Sold 1881 to

LOUISVILLE, EVANSVILLE & ST LOUIS CONSOLIDATED RR
Reorg. Sold in 1900 to

Huntingburg-Dubois segment leased 1989 to **INDIANA HI-RAIL**
Lease terminated and segment sold Jul. 1993 to

SOUTHERN RAILWAY
Name changed 1990 to

DUBOIS COUNTY RR

NORFOLK SOUTHERN

Huntingburg-Rockport and Huntingburg -Cannelton segments leased 1989 to **INDIANA HI-RAIL**
In 1996, leases terminated and operations acquired by

HOOSIER SOUTHERN RR

SOURCES: Edson, *Railroad Names*; Harrison, *A History of the Legal Development of the Railroad System of the Southern Railway Company*; Drury, *Historical Guide to North American Railroads*; Prince, *Southern Railway System*

A Southern Railway train bound for Louisville and Danville, Ky., from St. Louis, makes its station stop at Huntingburg in 1948. The train made 69 stops and required 14 hours, 10 minutes to cover its 362 miles.   *Photo by Richard S. Simons*

Southern operates (1997) the branch south of Lincoln City and the Dubois County Railroad and its associate, French Lick, West Baden and Southern tourist line, operates north of Huntingburg.[292]

During the 1870s, the Lake Erie, Evansville and Southwestern Railway attempted to build east from Evansville but it sank into receivership in 1875 after completing 17 miles to Boonville. The more modestly named Evansville Local Trade Railroad succeeded it. After reaching the Rockport line near Gentryville, the two lines merged in 1880 to become the Evansville, Rockport and Eastern Railway. In 1881 this road was sold to the LNA&StL, which in 1889 was renamed the Louisville, Evansville and St.

Louis Consolidated Railroad.[293] Peak period passenger service on the Evansville branch consisted of three daily round trips, one of which continued to Louisville. By the mid–1930s, only the Evansville-Louisville train remained, and it was discontinued about 1939.[294]

A third link from the Ohio River reached Huntingburg in 1887 when the LE&StL-controlled Huntingburg, Tell City and Cannelton Railroad completed its line in 1887. It extended 23 miles from Cannelton to a junction with the Evansville and Rockport lines near Lincoln City.[295] Three daily round trips provided the peak period passenger service, but this was gone by 1937.[296]

Indiana Hi-Rail leased the branch from 1989 to 1991 under Norfolk Southern's Thoroughbred Short Line Program, but after three years of inactivity, the Perry County Port Authority acquired it and now operates it as the Hoosier Southern Railroad.[297]

CHESAPEAKE AND OHIO RAILWAY

Entering an already crowded field, the Cincinnati, Richmond and Muncie Railroad, and its successor, Chicago, Cincinnati and Louisville Railroad, completed a new Cincinnati-Chicago line in 1907. It was one of the last major railroads built in Indiana and at 285 miles was the shortest of four lines between its terminal cities. It advertised itself as "The Short Line."[298] Indiana mileage totaled 230.

Incorporated in 1900 as the Cincinnati, Richmond and Muncie Railroad, the company began construction at Cottage Grove, south of Richmond, and by mid–1902 had completed its line to North Judson via Muncie, Marion, and Peru.[299] Two additional corporations were formed to complete the road. The Chicago and Cincinnati Railroad was to build from North Judson to Chicago and the Cincinnati and Western Indiana Railroad would extend the line from Cottage Grove to Cincinnati. On June 1, 1903, the three companies were consolidated as the Chicago, Cincinnati and Louisville, which also planned, but never constructed, a road from Cincinnati to Louisville via Madison.[300]

The road reached Beatrice in western Porter County in 1903 but financial problems and inability to develop a satisfactory route into Chicago delayed it from extending the remaining 14 miles to Griffith until 1906. It later built a ten-mile line to Hammond adjacent to the Erie Railroad and operated by a paired track arrangement. Originally it entered Chicago via the Illinois Central but later used the Chicago and Western Indiana Railroad.[301]

The Cincinnati, Hamilton and Dayton Railway, which controlled the Pere Marquette Railroad, acquired the CC&L and it then came under PM control from 1905 to 1908.[302] This was to be part of "the Great Central Route" that the CH&D attempted to create through itself, the PM, and the CC&L. The plan collapsed when the two parent companies went bankrupt in 1905 and annulled the CC&L acquisition.[303]

However, the CC&L did enter receivership in February 1908, and after two years was sold to the Chesapeake and Ohio Railway, which operated it as the Chesapeake and Ohio of Indiana until 1934 when it consolidated with the parent company. This extended the C&O's East Coast–Cincinnati line to Chicago.[304]

Freight traffic, largely coal, increased and in 1930, for example, 31 trains were scheduled daily.[305] Passenger traffic, however, was light. Six trains were operated during the peak era but this dwindled to a pair of local runs between Cincinnati and Hammond following World War II.[306] Between 1911 and 1917, however, the C&O had operated the Old Dominion Limited between Old Point Comfort, Virginia, and Chicago.[307] Amtrak placed its Chicago-Cincinnati-Washington train on the C&O "temporarily" in 1974 but it remained for 12 years. After both the Chicago and Cincinnati ends were abandoned beginning about 1980, traffic was rerouted over connecting Baltimore and Ohio railroad tracks.[308]

By 1992 nearly all the balance had been abandoned. Heavy, welded rails were removed and relaid in Florida when the New Orleans–Jacksonville route was upgraded to accommodate extended Amtrak service. This was the route where the Sunset

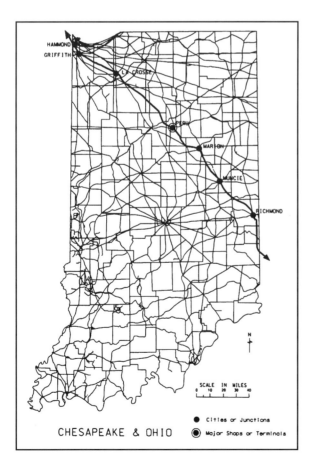

CHESAPEAKE & OHIO

● Cities or Junctions
◉ Major Shops or Terminals

SCALE IN MILES
0 10 20 30 40

CHESAPEAKE AND OHIO

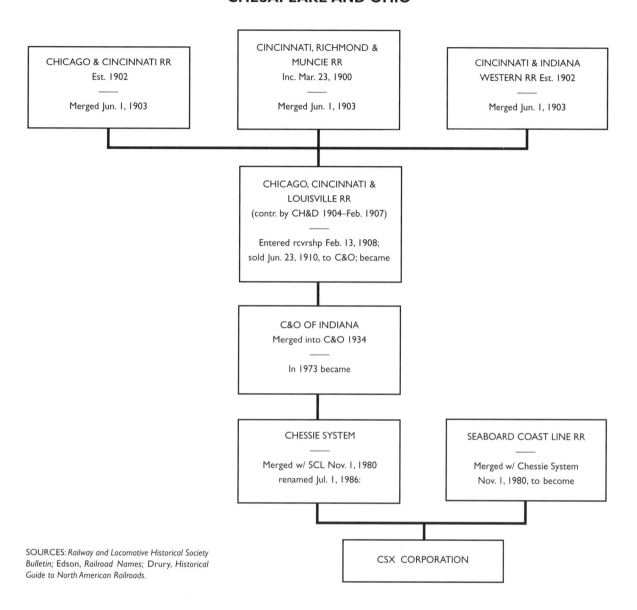

CHICAGO & CINCINNATI RR
Est. 1902
———
Merged Jun. 1, 1903

CINCINNATI, RICHMOND & MUNCIE RR
Inc. Mar. 23, 1900
———
Merged Jun. 1, 1903

CINCINNATI & INDIANA WESTERN RR Est. 1902
———
Merged Jun. 1, 1903

CHICAGO, CINCINNATI & LOUISVILLE RR
(contr. by CH&D 1904–Feb. 1907)
———
Entered rcvrshp Feb. 13, 1908;
sold Jun. 23, 1910, to C&O; became

C&O OF INDIANA
Merged into C&O 1934
———
In 1973 became

CHESSIE SYSTEM
———
Merged w/ SCL Nov. 1, 1980
renamed Jul. 1, 1986:

SEABOARD COAST LINE RR
———
Merged w/ Chessie System
Nov. 1, 1980, to become

CSX CORPORATION

SOURCES: *Railway and Locomotive Historical Society Bulletin;* Edson, *Railroad Names;* Drury, *Historical Guide to North American Railroads.*

The C&O's Chicago-bound train stands in front of the Marion station about 1920. Atlantic-type (4–4–2) locomotives still pulled this train in the late 1940s, among the last of the breed in the U.S.   *Harold A. Miller collection*

Limited plunged from a damaged bridge in 1993 in Amtrak's worst disaster.[309]

ILLINOIS CENTRAL RAILROAD

The Illinois Central Railroad, which completed a line between Chicago and Cairo, Illinois, in 1856, operated three branches into Indiana, including two of Indiana's early narrow-gauge lines.[310] The IC has abandoned or sold to short line operators all three. In addition, it built the Bloomington Southern Railroad to serve the limestone industry and operated a short branch to New Harmony.[311] It operated 175 miles in Indiana.

Havana, Rantoul and Eastern

First Illinois Central line in Indiana, the Havana, Rantoul and Eastern Railroad was completed in 1878 from Fisher, Illinois, to West Lebanon, but later was extended westward to Leroy, Illinois. Nine of the 75 miles were in Indiana.[312] Benjamin J. Gifford, a Rantoul, Illinois, attorney who later created the Chicago and Wabash Valley Railroad which

Coaling towers were a distinctive part of the steam era landscape. A C&O heavy Mikado (2–8–2) pauses at English Lake, halfway between the terminals at Peru and Hammond. *Van Dusen-Zillmer—M. D. McCarter collection*

became part of the Monon, promoted the line. Built to break the Illinois Central's stranglehold on eastern Illinois freight rates, it was ironic that the road eventually became IC property. Gifford was so mistrustful of the IC that he is said to have demanded all payments in gold.[313]

Built flimsily to a 3' narrow gauge, the road failed to prosper and in 1880 was acquired by the Wabash, St. Louis and Pacific Railway during the time that Jay Gould attempted to use it as the centerpiece for his proposed transcontinental railroad. After Gould's empire collapsed, the HR&E entered receivership and in 1886 was sold to the IC, which rebuilt and standard gauged it.[314] Always a light traffic branch, it carried six daily trains during the peak passenger era. The Indiana segment was abandoned in 1936 and most of the Illinois section also is now gone.[315]

Peoria, Decatur and Evansville

The Peoria, Decatur and Evansville Railway completed its 248-mile line to Evansville in 1881, but was in receivership by 1894. The Illinois Central bought the road in 1900 at a foreclosure sale and

later provided service from Mattoon, Illinois, on the main line, through Evansville to Hopkinsville, Kentucky. It used a car ferry to cross the Ohio River.[316] After the IC acquired trackage rights on the Louisville and Nashville Railroad's Ohio River bridge in 1904, it discontinued the ferry. In 1912 an Evansville and Ohio Valley Railway predecessor acquired trackage rights over 6.9 miles of Ohio River approach trackage for its interurban line and reestablished a ferry for Evansville-Henderson, Kentucky, use. This was one of two interurban ferries in the United States.[317]

Never a busy passenger line, the IC operated four daily trains during the peak era. Indiana Hi-Rail operated most of the 32-mile Indiana segment and a portion of the Illinois section until the Evansville Terminal Company acquired it in 1996.[318] A six-mile branch was built from Stewartsville to New Harmony after local residents voted a $16,000 subsidy in 1881. Six shuttle trains operated daily during the peak passenger era, but the line was abandoned in 1976.[319]

Indianapolis Southern

The original segment of the 177-mile line that connected Indianapolis with Effingham, Illinois, was a narrow-gauge railroad opened in 1880 between Effingham and Switz City. The company, Springfield, Effingham and Southeastern Railway, encountered severe financial problems, particularly after ice destroyed approaches to its Wabash River bridge, which was out of service for five years. Reorganized in 1886 as the Indiana and Illinois Southern Railway, it restored full service and the following year standard gauged the track. Illinois Central bought the road following foreclosure in 1900.[320]

In 1906 the Indianapolis Southern Railway inaugurated service on its 89-mile line between Indianapolis and Switz City with financial assistance of the IC, which assumed control in 1909. This created a single road between Indianapolis and Effingham.[321] The original survey ran under the north side of Bloomington through a tunnel, but this was changed so that the track went through Bloomington at grade and continued southwest instead of the originally planned south then west direction. The line penetrates rugged hill country and is famous for the 2,295-foot Tulip Trestle (Richland Creek Viaduct) in eastern Greene County. At 157 feet, it is the state's highest railroad bridge.[322]

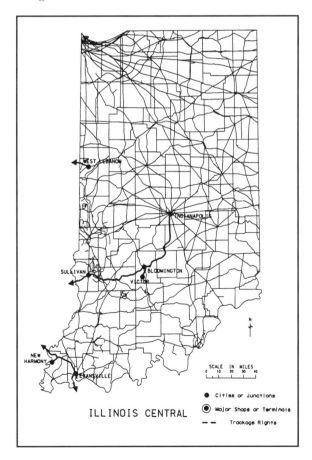

ILLINOIS CENTRAL

SCALE IN MILES
0 10 20 30 40

● Cities or Junctions
◉ Major Shops or Terminals
— — Trackage Rights

ILLINOIS CENTRAL

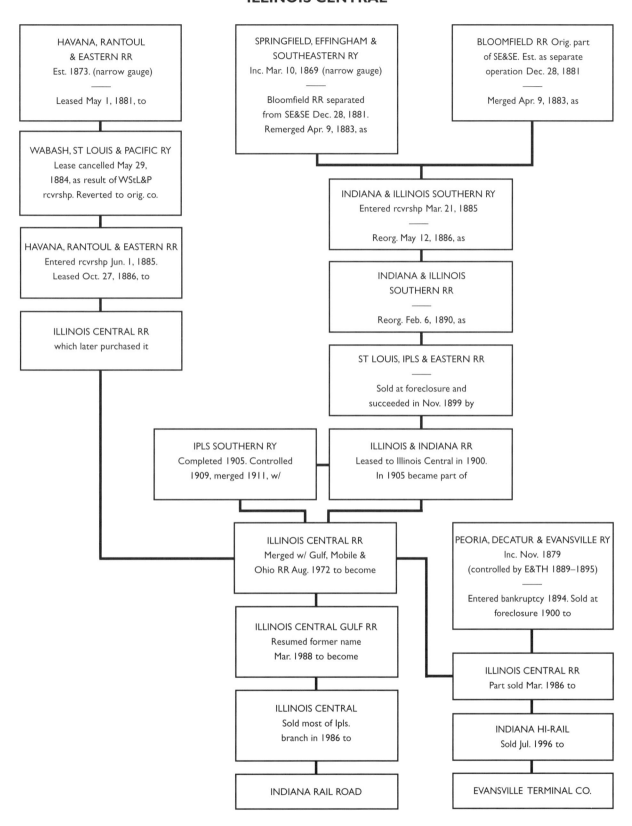

HAVANA, RANTOUL
& EASTERN RR
Est. 1873. (narrow gauge)
―――
Leased May 1, 1881, to

SPRINGFIELD, EFFINGHAM &
SOUTHEASTERN RY
Inc. Mar. 10, 1869 (narrow gauge)
―――
Bloomfield RR separated
from SE&SE Dec. 28, 1881.
Remerged Apr. 9, 1883, as

BLOOMFIELD RR Orig. part
of SE&SE. Est. as separate
operation Dec. 28, 1881
―――
Merged Apr. 9, 1883, as

WABASH, ST LOUIS & PACIFIC RY
Lease cancelled May 29,
1884, as result of WStL&P
rcvrshp. Reverted to orig. co.

INDIANA & ILLINOIS SOUTHERN RY
Entered rcvrshp Mar. 21, 1885
―――
Reorg. May 12, 1886, as

HAVANA, RANTOUL & EASTERN RR
Entered rcvrshp Jun. 1, 1885.
Leased Oct. 27, 1886, to

INDIANA & ILLINOIS
SOUTHERN RR
―――
Reorg. Feb. 6, 1890, as

ILLINOIS CENTRAL RR
which later purchased it

ST LOUIS, IPLS & EASTERN RR
―――
Sold at foreclosure and
succeeded in Nov. 1899 by

IPLS SOUTHERN RY
Completed 1905. Controlled
1909, merged 1911, w/

ILLINOIS & INDIANA RR
Leased to Illinois Central in 1900.
In 1905 became part of

ILLINOIS CENTRAL RR
Merged w/ Gulf, Mobile &
Ohio RR Aug. 1972 to become

PEORIA, DECATUR & EVANSVILLE RY
Inc. Nov. 1879
(controlled by E&TH 1889–1895)
―――
Entered bankruptcy 1894. Sold at
foreclosure 1900 to

ILLINOIS CENTRAL GULF RR
Resumed former name
Mar. 1988 to become

ILLINOIS CENTRAL RR
Part sold Mar. 1986 to

ILLINOIS CENTRAL
Sold most of Ipls.
branch in 1986 to

INDIANA HI-RAIL
Sold Jul. 1996 to

INDIANA RAIL ROAD

EVANSVILLE TERMINAL CO.

SOURCES: Edson, *Railroad Names;* Drury, *Historical Guide to North American Railroads;* Hilton, *American Narrow Gauge Railroads.*

Bound for Indianapolis, an Illinois Central freight crosses Tulip Trestle 8 miles northeast of Bloomfield. Measuring 2,295' at a maximum height of 157', it is the state's longest and highest railroad viaduct. *Richard S. Simons collection*

Although the line carried only four passenger trains during the peak era, it inaugurated a Pullman train, the Dixie Flyer, from Indianapolis to New Orleans in 1911.[323] After the Illinois Central Gulf, the IC's successor, made several unsuccessful abandonment attempts, it sold the road in 1986 to the new Indiana Rail Road, which has developed heavy traffic in coal, lumber, and other commodities. Most coal originates in southern Indiana mines and is shipped to Indianapolis-area power plants.[324]

Bloomington Southern

The nine-mile Bloomington Southern Railroad was completed in 1914 to serve limestone quarries and mills near Victor, south of Bloomington.[325] It was abandoned in 1988, although a short section, which includes a high 600-foot timber trestle, remains in use as a private quarry track.[326]

ERIE RAILROAD

The longest of five routes between New York and Chicago, the 999-mile Erie in 1851 became the first railroad to connect the Eastern Seaboard with the Great Lakes. At 447 miles, it was the world's longest railroad.[327]

Although built as a 6', broad-gauge line, it had adopted the standard 4'8½" measure by the time it reached Indiana; yet, ironically, in 1880 it ac-

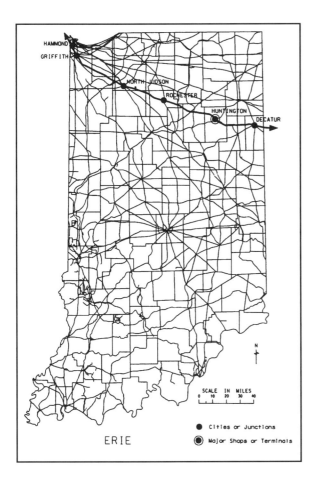

ERIE

● Cities or Junctions
◉ Major Shops or Terminals

quired a nine-mile 3', narrow-gauge segment between Huntington and Markle, which it soon standardized.[328] As the Chicago and Atlantic, an Erie-controlled road, it reached Chicago in 1883.[329] Indiana mileage was approximately 160.

Manipulated by Jay Gould and other early promoters, the Erie was perpetually poverty stricken and overwhelmingly debt ridden. Yet it survived five bankruptcies. Pushed to innovation to survive, it was an early user of telephone dispatching and a pioneer of diesel-electric locomotion.[330]

The superbly engineered line west of Marion, Ohio, was doubletracked about 1910 as a split level railroad. To relate grades to the flow of heaviest tonnage, the westbound track began to ascend near Laketon while then eastbound track rose from the opposite direction. The two grades, sometimes separated vertically by 20 to 30 feet, crossed near Disko.[331]

In 1887 the Wabash Railroad acquired trackage

rights over the Erie between Chicago and Newton (Wabash County), where it crossed the Eel River Railroad, then part of the Wabash's St. Louis–Detroit–Buffalo route. The Wabash operated two round trip Chicago-Detroit passenger trains as well as freights on the joint route until it built its direct line across northern Indiana in 1893.[332]

Shortly before it died in 1976, the Erie scheduled 21 daily freight trains over its 160 Indiana miles.[333] During the nation's peak passenger period, it operated 12 daily trains in Indiana; six survived into the World War II era.[334] Huntington was a principal shop town and for many years the railroad was the principal employer. At the end, its payroll stood at 400.[335]

Branch lines were conspicuously absent throughout the system and Indiana's only feeder was less than two miles long. Located in Starke County, it was built in 1898 to serve a resort on Bass Lake, carrying tourists in summer and ice in winter until 1928.[336]

In 1960 the Erie merged with the Delaware, Lackawanna and Western to become the Erie-Lackawanna Railroad.[337] From 1968 to 1975, Norfolk and Western Railway contolled it, but Conrail, which was formed in 1976 to take over ailing northeastern and midwestern roads, excluded it. Two successive short lines, Erie Western and Chicago and Indiana, attempted to operate the Indiana section, but they were unsuccessful, and the road was abandoned in 1980.[338] Sixteen miles remain as the J K Line, formerly Tippecanoe Railroad, between Monterey and North Judson. Ironically, the Laketon Refining Company at Laketon required rail service and after purchasing abandoned right-of-way built its own railroad 3.1 miles to a Conrail connection near North Manchester in 1991.[339]

PERE MARQUETTE RAILWAY

The next to last line to reach Chicago from the East, the Pere Marquette Railway was essentially a Michigan road and had only a minor presence in Indiana. Its main line connected Grand Rapids with Chicago, skirting Lake Michigan through Michigan City and Indiana Harbor. A short branch extended southward to the important junction of La Crosse.[340]

Created in 1899 by a merger of three Michigan regional companies, PM completed its line to Porter in 1903 but used trackage rights over the Lake

ERIE

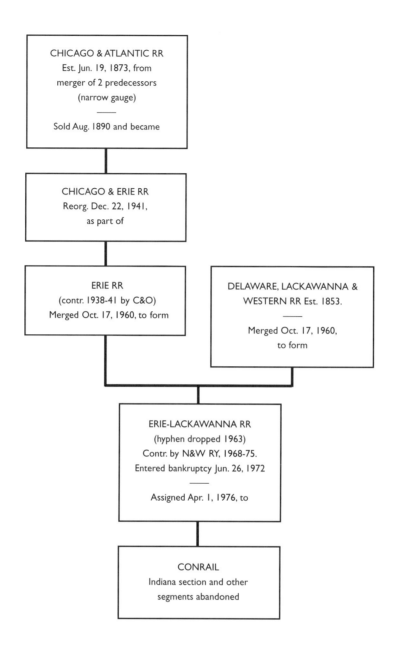

CHICAGO & ATLANTIC RR
Est. Jun. 19, 1873, from
merger of 2 predecessors
(narrow gauge)
———
Sold Aug. 1890 and became

CHICAGO & ERIE RR
Reorg. Dec. 22, 1941,
as part of

ERIE RR
(contr. 1938-41 by C&O)
Merged Oct. 17, 1960, to form

**DELAWARE, LACKAWANNA &
WESTERN RR** Est. 1853.
———
Merged Oct. 17, 1960,
to form

ERIE-LACKAWANNA RR
(hyphen dropped 1963)
Contr. by N&W RY, 1968-75.
Entered bankruptcy Jun. 26, 1972
———
Assigned Apr. 1, 1976, to

CONRAIL
Indiana section and other
segments abandoned

SOURCES: Hilton, *American Narrow Gauge Railroads*; Drury, *Historical Guide to North American Railroads*; Hungerford, *Men of Erie*; Edson, *Railroad Names*.

Shortly after the 1960 Erie-Lackawanna merger, former Erie Railroad EMD and Alco streamlined diesels idle at the Huntington depot and division office.   *Jay Williams collection*

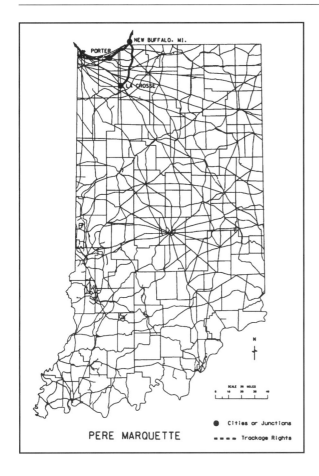

PERE MARQUETTE

● Cities or Junctions
■ ■ ■ Trackage Rights

Shore and Michigan Southern Railway (New York Central) and Baltimore and Ohio Railroad to enter Chicago. Approximately 48 of its 184 miles between Chicago and Grand Rapids are in Indiana.[341]

The Cincinnati, Hamilton and Dayton Railway acquired control of PM in 1907 but it was terminated by the PM's bankruptcy in 1912.[342] After 1910, the B&O had controlled PM as the parent of the CH&D.[343] The CH&D, along with PM and the recently purchased Chicago, Cincinnati and Louisville Railroad, attempted to create "the Great Central Route" but this failed following a 1905 bankruptcy.[344]

In 1929 the Chesapeake and Ohio Railway acquired PM control and merged it in 1947. Like the balance of the C&O, it is now part of CSX. Soo Line holds trackage rights over the Chicago–Grand Rapids–Detroit line to provide a connection with its parent company CP Rail.[345] During the peak passenger era, PM operated eight trains daily in addition to northern Michigan seasonal service. Amtrak operates two trains daily (in 1997) between Chicago and Grand Rapids.[346]

PERE MARQUETTE

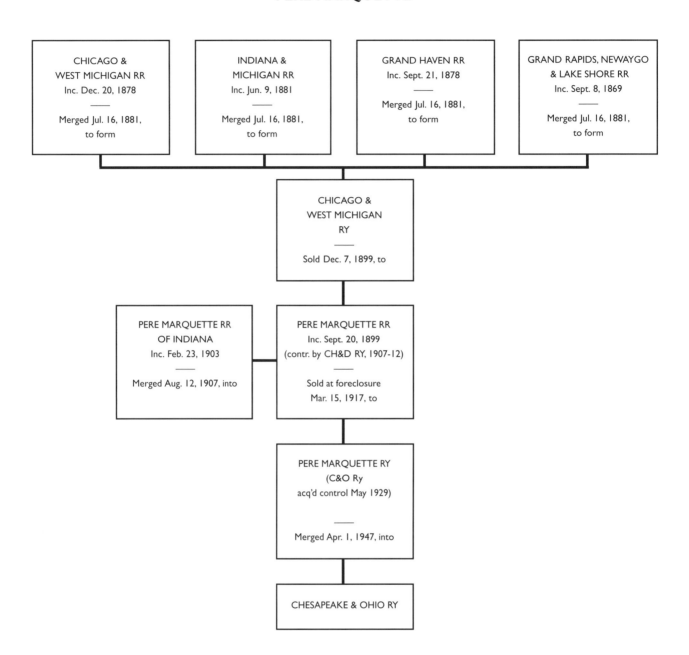

CHICAGO &
WEST MICHIGAN RR
Inc. Dec. 20, 1878
——
Merged Jul. 16, 1881,
to form

INDIANA &
MICHIGAN RR
Inc. Jun. 9, 1881
——
Merged Jul. 16, 1881,
to form

GRAND HAVEN RR
Inc. Sept. 21, 1878
——
Merged Jul. 16, 1881,
to form

GRAND RAPIDS, NEWAYGO
& LAKE SHORE RR
Inc. Sept. 8, 1869
——
Merged Jul. 16, 1881,
to form

CHICAGO &
WEST MICHIGAN
RY
——
Sold Dec. 7, 1899, to

PERE MARQUETTE RR
OF INDIANA
Inc. Feb. 23, 1903
——
Merged Aug. 12, 1907, into

PERE MARQUETTE RR
Inc. Sept. 20, 1899
(contr. by CH&D RY, 1907-12)
——
Sold at foreclosure
Mar. 15, 1917, to

PERE MARQUETTE RY
(C&O Ry
acq'd control May 1929)

——

Merged Apr. 1, 1947, into

CHESAPEAKE & OHIO RY

SOURCE: Meints, *Michigan Railroads and Railroad Companies*

An Erie-Lackawanna freight train races past Newton tower in northern Wabash County at the Pennsylvania Railroad's Eel River branch crossing. Interlocking towers once dotted the state but only a handful remain. *Photo by Harold A. Miller*

PM also operated a branch from New Buffalo, Michigan, on its main line, to La Crosse, an important junction once served by the Pennsylvania, C&O, Monon and Chicago, Attica and Southern railroads. In 1887, shortly after reaching La Crosse, the CA&S acquired trackage rights to New Buffalo. The Chicago and West Michigan Railway, a PM predecessor, had opened the 38-mile branch in 1882 as part of a 209-mile line to Pentwater, Michigan. The 89-mile midsection between New Buffalo and Holland, Michigan, became the PM main line.[347] During the peak passenger era, the line carried two daily passenger trains; but these were gone by 1931. All but three miles of the branch were in Indiana.[348]

After the C&O abandoned the Chicago end of its Cincinnati line in 1981, it sent all trains including Amtrak over the 15-mile La Crosse-Wellsboro segment, where they then utilized the B&O into Chicago. The remaining track through La Porte was abandoned in 1988.[349]

GRAND TRUNK WESTERN RAILROAD

Part of Canadian National Railways, now CN North America, the Grand Trunk Western Railroad

GTW streamlined 4–8–4 No. 6406 pulled the International Limited and other Chicago-bound trains until the mid–1950s. U.S. built in 1938, it was identical to engines built in Canada for parent Canadian National. *Jay Williams collection*

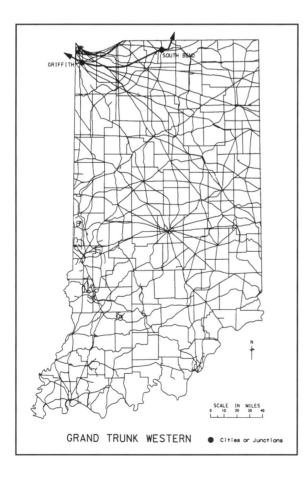

GRAND TRUNK WESTERN   ● Cities or Junctions

operates a 334-mile line from Port Huron, Michigan, where it connects with Canadian roads across the St. Clair River, to Chicago. Entering Indiana north of Mishawaka, it swings on a wide arc through South Bend and Valparaiso. Indiana mileage totals 81.[350]

Origins precede the Civil War. In 1860 the Grand Trunk Railway of Canada leased the Chicago, Detroit and Canada Grand Trunk Junction Rail Road, one of several roads that independently had built parts of what became the Grand Trunk Western. After two Indiana predecessors merged, construction began in 1868. It was completed to South Bend in fall 1872, and to Valparaiso on October 13, 1873, by the Peninsular Railway. Delayed in reaching Chicago, it arrived February 1, 1880, as the Chicago and Grand Trunk Railway, after successfully sparring with William Vanderbilt in one of the famous coups of the day.[351]

In 1900 the Port Huron and Indiana Railway and the Indiana and Illinois Railway were reorganized as the Grand Trunk Western Railway under control of the Grand Trunk Railway of Canada. On January 1, 1923, it became part of the new Canadian National Railway, whose first chairman and president was Sir Henry Thornton, a Logansport native.[352]

GRAND TRUNK WESTERN

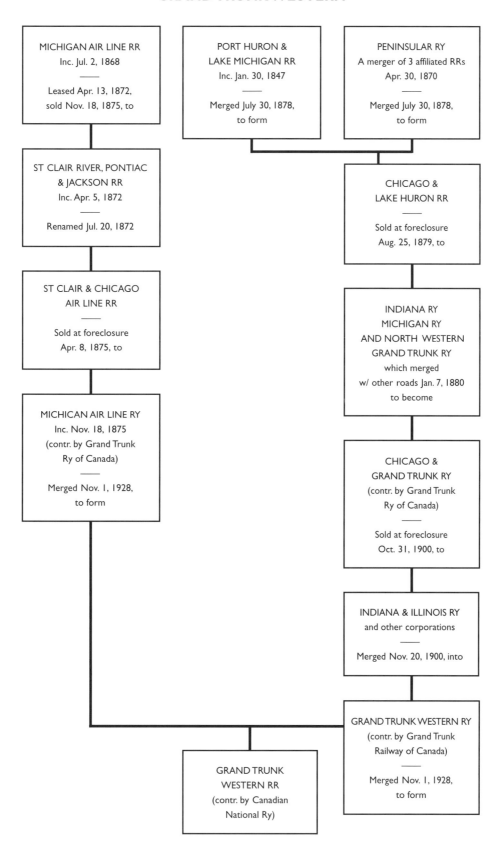

MICHIGAN AIR LINE RR
Inc. Jul. 2, 1868
——
Leased Apr. 13, 1872,
sold Nov. 18, 1875, to

PORT HURON &
LAKE MICHIGAN RR
Inc. Jan. 30, 1847
——
Merged July 30, 1878,
to form

PENINSULAR RY
A merger of 3 affiliated RRs
Apr. 30, 1870
——
Merged July 30, 1878,
to form

ST CLAIR RIVER, PONTIAC
& JACKSON RR
Inc. Apr. 5, 1872
——
Renamed Jul. 20, 1872

CHICAGO &
LAKE HURON RR
——
Sold at foreclosure
Aug. 25, 1879, to

ST CLAIR & CHICAGO
AIR LINE RR
——
Sold at foreclosure
Apr. 8, 1875, to

INDIANA RY
MICHIGAN RY
AND NORTH WESTERN
GRAND TRUNK RY
which merged
w/ other roads Jan. 7, 1880
to become

MICHICAN AIR LINE RY
Inc. Nov. 18, 1875
(contr. by Grand Trunk
Ry of Canada)
——
Merged Nov. 1, 1928,
to form

CHICAGO &
GRAND TRUNK RY
(contr. by Grand Trunk
Ry of Canada)
——
Sold at foreclosure
Oct. 31, 1900, to

INDIANA & ILLINOIS RY
and other corporations
——
Merged Nov. 20, 1900, into

GRAND TRUNK
WESTERN RR
(contr. by Canadian
National Ry)

GRAND TRUNK WESTERN RY
(contr. by Grand Trunk
Railway of Canada)
——
Merged Nov. 1, 1928,
to form

SOURCES: Edson, *Railroad Names;* Meints, *Michigan Railroads and Railroad Companies;* Drury, *Historical Guide to North American Railroads.*

The winter-only Dixieland, like other "Dixie" trains between Florida and Chicago, was handled by the Louisville and Nashville to Evansville, and the C&EI to Chicago. Seen here at Sullivan, Ind., northbound in 1946. *Paul Moffitt, Danville Junction Chapter collection.*

LOUISVILLE AND NASHVILLE

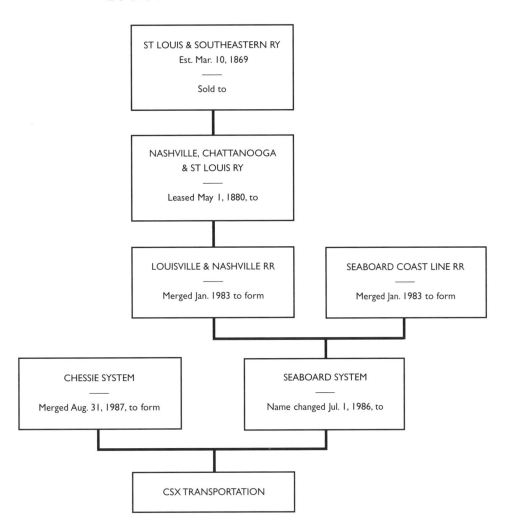

ST LOUIS & SOUTHEASTERN RY
Est. Mar. 10, 1869

———

Sold to

NASHVILLE, CHATTANOOGA
& ST LOUIS RY

———

Leased May 1, 1880, to

LOUISVILLE & NASHVILLE RR

———

Merged Jan. 1983 to form

SEABOARD COAST LINE RR

———

Merged Jan. 1983 to form

CHESSIE SYSTEM

———

Merged Aug. 31, 1987, to form

SEABOARD SYSTEM

———

Name changed Jul. 1, 1986, to

CSX TRANSPORTATION

SOURCES: Edson, *Railroad Names;* Drury, *Historical Guide to North American Railroads;* Herr, *Louisville & Nashville Railroad*

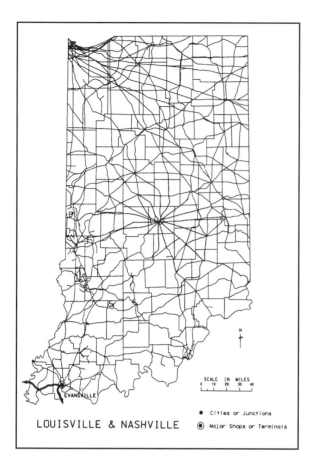

LOUISVILLE & NASHVILLE

● Cities or Junctions
◉ Major Shops or Terminals

SCALE IN MILES
0 10 20 30 40

and its predecessors had completed a 165-mile line between St. Louis and Evansville, which the L&N leased in 1880. Meanwhile the L&N had purchased in 1879 from the StL&SE its 146-mile line from Henderson, Kentucky, to Nashville, Tennessee. In 1905 it acquired the Louisville, Henderson and St. Louis Railway, which ran for 143 miles along the Kentucky side of the Ohio River and used L&N tracks to reach Evansville.[356]

The river created a bottleneck until 1885 when a bridge replaced the car ferries. A massive new structure nearly two and one-half miles long including approaches replaced it in 1932.[357] Originally built to the 5' southern gauge, L&N converted its tracks to 4'9" on May 30, 1886, and subsequently narrowed them an additional half-inch to conform to what came to be standard.[358]

An important line between St. Louis and the South, the L&N operated 12 passenger trains daily during the peak era, but, contrary to most roads, increased this to 16 following World War II. In the interim, it had developed a strong business to the South jointly with the Chicago and Eastern Illinois Railroad, which terminated at Evansville. The six daily peak period trains on the Louisville line remained after World War II.[359]

The Seaboard System absorbed the L&N in 1983 and in turn, following a further merger, became part of CSX in 1986.[360]

In 1890, the Grand Trunk opened a 6,028-foot tunnel under the St. Clair River between Port Huron and Sarnia, Ontario, and discontinued its car ferries. However, double-stack containers, auto racks, and other high loads eventually made the tunnel obsolete and on April 5, 1995, the GTW opened a new 6,130-foot tunnel with higher clearances parallel to the original one.[353]

During the peak passenger years, the Grand Trunk operated 12 trains daily, some featuring through service to New York City in conjunction with the Lehigh Valley Railroad. By the end of World War II, service had diminished to six trains.[354]

LOUISVILLE AND NASHVILLE RAILROAD

Chartered in 1850, the Louisville and Nashville Railroad was projected to connect the two cities of its corporate name. But as it expanded to a 5,000-mile system, it leased a line that extended for 38 miles across the extreme southwest corner of Indiana. Evansville was its principal terminal.[355]

By 1872 the St. Louis and Southeastern Railway

┼┼┼┼┼┼┼┼┼┼┼┼┼┼┼ **9** ┼┼┼┼┼┼┼┼┼┼┼┼┼┼┼

Historic Short Lines

Until the early twentieth century, all but the shortest travel and shipping moved by rail, and any bypassed community encountered serious problems. The more enterprising ones, such as Corydon and Ferdinand, built their own trunk line connections, and Peru, Elkhart, and South Bend, for other reasons, did the same. Three remain in operation today.

Other historic short lines were built to connect neighboring towns, but most were ill advised and short-lived. These include the Central Indiana Railway, whose abbreviated line now operates under a

different name; Chicago, Attica and Southern Railroad; Cincinnati, Bluffton and Chicago Railroad; Cincinnati, Findlay and Fort Wayne Railway, and the St. Joseph Valley Railway.

Some lines were built to serve coal, stone, or marl industries, or, in one case, to deliver coal to a consumer. These include the Algers, Winslow and Western Railway and the Yankeetown Dock Corporation, both coal carriers; the Bedford Stone Railway, Bedford and Wallner Railroad, and Bloomington Southern Railway in the Lawrence–Monroe County limestone belt; and the Fort Wayne, Terre Haute and Southwestern Railroad in the Parke County sandstone region. The Twin Branch Railroad delivered coal to a power plant, and the Syracuse and Milford Railway connected a marl pit with a cement mill.

Three lines, the Chicago, South Shore and South Bend Railroad, Southern Indiana Railway, and Winona Railroad, were converted electric interurban railroads. The Evansville, Suburban and Newburgh Railway and the Evansville and Ohio Valley Railway operated as steam and electric interurban roads simultaneously. The Department of Defense also operates a railroad in Indiana.

STONE RAILROADS

Three short lines, the Bedford and Wallner, Bedford Stone, and Bloomington Southern, were built early in this century to serve the oolitic limestone industry. They totaled approximately 15 miles and all are now abandoned. The ten-mile Fort Wayne, Terre Haute and Southwestern served the Mansfield sandstone region in southern Parke County.

Bedford and Wallner

The Bedford and Wallner Railroad began operating in 1907 to serve the newly opened quarry of its

HISTORIC SHORT LINES

owner, Bedford Stone and Construction Company. The line extended 2.79 miles northeast to the quarry and also served a stone mill. Investors were mostly Indianapolis businessmen headed by U.S. Senator Harry S. New.[1]

Failing to meet expectations, the quarry was closed about 1917. The Monon Railway bought the company in 1927 and continued operations until 1935, shortly after the mill had closed.[2]

Bedford Stone

The Bedford Stone Railway was opened in June 1901 to serve the American Quarries at Stonington, southeast of Bedford. The 2.96-mile line began at a junction with the Baltimore and Ohio Railroad at Rivervale and paralleled White River before ascending Fishing Creek Valley to the quarry and a nearby mill. Although the quarry was closed in 1903, the mill continued to operate until 1914. The railroad also hauled small quantities of lumber and merchandise and listed a daily round trip passenger train in the *Official Guide of the Railways*, although this may have been more nominal than actual.

The road was highly profitable during its early years, but after a B&O rate division contract expired in 1914, revenue and profits fell drastically. The line was abandoned in 1917.[3]

Bloomington Southern

An obscure stone-hauling branch of the Illinois Central Railroad and a predecessor, the Bloomington Southern Railroad extended 9.2 miles from Bloomington to quarries near Victor. Construction began in 1907 and continued until 1914 to serve a growing quarry region in which the Oliver plow manufacturing family of South Bend held significant interests. Much of it parallels the former Monon main line.[4]

In 1988 the new owner, Indiana Rail Road, abandoned most of the line, although a short disconnected section at the south end, which includes a high 600-foot timber trestle, continues to be used by the Victor Oolitic Stone Company.[5]

Fort Wayne, Terre Haute and Southwestern

Incorporated October 4, 1890, the Fort Wayne, Terre Haute and Southwestern Railroad was projected between Carbon in northern Clay County and a junction with the Monon at Bainbridge. Dr. William L. Breyfogle, president of the Monon, headed the group that promoted the road.[6]

Only a short segment on the west end was completed before Breyfogle was ousted from Monon control and the project died. Beginning in 1891, trains operated 5.29 miles between Bridgeton and Carbon and 4.5 miles between Bridgeton and Mansfield, an area rich in sandstone deposits. The Carbon line was sold to a Central Indiana Railway predecessor and became part of its Muncie-Brazil route. The Mansfield line was abandoned in 1899 after the quarry closed that supplied most of its traffic.[7]

CEMENT MILL RAILROAD

Syracuse and Milford

Built to serve a Sandusky Portland Cement Company mill, the Syracuse and Milford Railway extended from a junction with the Baltimore and Ohio Railroad (now CSX) at the east edge of Syracuse to marl deposits near Wabee Lake. The original road was completed in 1907 but later was extended a short distance to a junction with the Big Four Route (now Conrail) three-quarters of a mile south of Milford. Length was 6.82 miles.[8]

Although the line was built to haul raw material to the cement mill, it also was used for outbound shipments after the Big Four connection was completed. The road was dismantled in 1923.[9]

COMMUNITY SHORT LINES

Five short lines were built independently to give bypassed towns a connection with the nearest main line or to give shippers alternate routes. Two southern Indiana communities built connections to the Louisville, Evansville and St. Louis Railway or its successor (now Norfolk Southern), and three northern industrial cities built connections to existing trunk routes.

Elkhart and Western

The creation of H. E. Bucklen, a wealthy patent medicine manufacturer who also built the St. Joseph Valley Railway, the Elkhart and Western Railroad was opened September 26, 1893, between Elkhart and Mishawaka, 11.72 miles.[10] It connected at Elkhart with the Lake Shore and Michigan Southern Railroad (later New York Central and then Conrail), crossed to the north bank of the St. Joseph River, and continued westward to serve several industries before terminating at a connection with the Grand Trunk Western Railroad in Mishawaka.[11]

In 1898, Bucklen sold the road to the Lake Shore, whose successors continue to operate it.[12] As late as 1994, it served seven major industries and was known locally as the E&W industrial track to reflect its heritage.[13] In its early days, the road offered passenger service.[14] It is now a Michigan Southern Railroad line.

Ferdinand

Last of the state's general purpose short lines to be built, the Ferdinand Railroad was incorporated October 25, 1905, and began operation in 1909 as the Ferdinand Railway. Similar to the Louisville, New Albany and Corydon Railroad, it linked its home community to the Southern Railway (now Norfolk Southern), which had missed it by seven miles. Local residents financed it to meet a specific local need.[15]

The road ran 6.48 miles toward Huntingburg and acquired trackage rights over the Southern for the remaining .9 mile. It was built to serve local industries; its traffic consisted mainly of inbound raw materials for the furniture factories and limited finished products outbound. Initially, it also served a flour mill and carried milk to market from area farms.[16]

The Ferdinand operated mixed (freight and passenger) trains twice daily in each direction, trundling over the 56-lb. rails to connect with the Southern at Huntingburg.[17] Passengers rode in an 1880 combine until late years when the road purchased an interurban combine that had been operated between Indianapolis and Louisville. Passenger service stopped in 1953, when the Southern discontinued its Huntingburg connections.[18]

Most local residents were reported to have purchased stock to launch the road, but within two years it ran into financial difficulty and was reorganized as the Ferdinand Railroad.[19] In February 1966, Dolly Madison Industries, better known for producing baked goods, acquired the road to serve its local furniture factories.[20] After Dolly Madison encountered overexpansion problems, Evans Transportation Company acquired the road on December 10, 1983, and it was operated in conjunction with the Louisville, New Albany and Corydon Rail-

road. Like the Corydon, the Ferdinand entered the leasing business and operated an 897-car fleet that included 630 covered hopper and 136 refrigerator cars, in addition to smaller numbers of box and flatcars and gondolas.[21]

The Ferdinand Corporation acquired the road in September 1987, but abandoned it March 3, 1991. By this time the name had been changed to the Ferdinand and Huntingburg Railroad.[22]

Louisville, New Albany and Corydon

The oldest Indiana short line operating continuously under the same name, the Louisville, New Albany and Corydon Railway opened December 1, 1883, to connect Corydon, Indiana's first state capital, with the Louisville, New Albany and St. Louis Railway (now Norfolk Southern) at Corydon Junction, 7.7 miles north.[23]

The road was sold at foreclosure in February 1888, and was reorganized as the Louisville, New Albany and Corydon Railroad effective May 1, 1890.[24] The original gauge was 4'9", one-half inch wider than today's standard gauge.[25]

In 1889, the railroad built a three-mile extension eastward to serve the Corydon Stone Company's King's Cave quarry but abandoned most of it after the quarry closed in 1905.[26] The remainder, until it was removed about 1989, crossed Little Indian Creek through a ford.

Freight business, the railroad's lifeblood, sustained the early road, but during World War II, when most lines were pushed to their limits, the Corydon languished in the service of non-defense industries that initially produced wooden farm wagons and glass lamp chimneys.

As local shipping diminished, the road, then owned by the United States Railway Manufacturing Company, attempted to cash in on the car leasing bonanza that was enriching scattered short lines. It acquired 1,297 box and refrigerator cars, more than could be placed on the road at one time, and after the boom ended it stored many on line or at French Lick on the French Lick, West Baden and Southern Railway. Many cars, however, remain in service throughout the country.[27]

Until about 1953, when the Southern Railway discontinued its passenger service through Corydon Junction, the railroad operated a daily mixed (passenger and freight) train. Traditional frequency was three round trips daily.[28]

After the leasing business lost its bloom, the present owners, BPM Rail, concentrated on traffic flowing to and from the Corydon Industrial Park, which was established about 1980. This consists primarily of plastic pellets, sand, and fertilizer in-bound, popcorn outbound, and auto parts in both directions. Booming traffic forced the Corydon to increase its locomotive fleet from one, the Betty Sue, to four; it has increased employment and has begun converting nearly one-third of its line to 115-lb.-per-yard welded rail.[29]

Passenger service has come full circle since an affiliate, Corydon 1883 Scenic Railroad, began service in 1989. It operates weekend trips from May to November, much to the delight of passengers who crowd into two ex–Erie-Lackawanna commuter coaches that operated in New Jersey during their former lives. Heavy demand forced the Corydon to augment its fleet with three self-propelled diesel cars (RDCs) that had seen service on the Boston and Maine and New York, Susquehanna and Western Railroads. In true 1883 style, the road operates near its station in Corydon a stub switch. This is a type that disappeared from most railroads near the end of the Civil War.[30]

New Jersey, Indiana and Illinois

The New Jersey, Indiana and Illinois Railroad, with a name nearly 1,000 miles long, extended only 11.4 miles from South Bend to Pine, where it joined the Wabash Railroad's Chicago-Detroit line.[31] Operated by the Singer Manufacturing Company, which produced sewing machines at South Bend, it drew its name from the location of other Singer plants in New Jersey and Cairo, Illinois.[32]

The road began service in 1905.[33] During the World War I era, it offered two passenger round trips daily, one connecting with a Chicago-Detroit train. By the time the service was discontinued in the 1930s, it had been reduced to one daily round trip, which carried a South Bend–Detroit sleeping car.[34]

In 1926 the Wabash Railroad purchased the NJI&I but continued to operate it separately. Freight shipments, which had attracted the Wabash originally, consisted primarily of lucrative tonnage from Singer and new cars from Studebaker Corporation.[35] The road continued as a separate entity until August 1982, when the Norfolk Southern, which had acquired the Wabash, absorbed it.[36]

REGIONAL SHORT LINES

Near the turn of the century, when railroads dominated transportation, five Indiana companies perceived a need that neither trunk carriers nor short lines filled. Between 1875 and 1905, the five built regional roads but none lived up to expectations advanced by names or announced intentions. The lines, all in northern or central Indiana, ranged from 52 to 141 miles in length and averaged 93 miles. All but one was completely within the state. Of the aggregate 468 miles, only a 10.5-mile segment of one road remains.

Central Indiana

Throughout its checkered career, which began in 1875, the 127-mile Central Indiana Railway operated under a variety of corporate names. Three revealed grandiose interstate dreams that would have carried the road to three major Midwest cities: Chicago, St. Louis, or Cleveland. By contrast, two portrayed it more modestly as a strictly Hoosier line operated across the state's heartland. This was accurate because the road stretched only from Muncie to Brazil, but the regions it linked had little in common.[37]

For its first quarter century, the railroad operated independently, passing through frequent receiverships, reorganizations, and name changes. For the next three-quarters of a century, it was the vassal of those two rival giants, the Pennsylvania and New York Central systems. Admitting that they had made a mistake in buying it, they nevertheless held on despite a 19-mile duplicate service between Muncie and Anderson.[38] Perceived as a potential Indianapolis bypass route that never materialized, the road remained a consistent loser until a colorful, dollar-a-year president took command in 1951.[39]

Perhaps because of the disparate regions it served, the line never developed a viable end-to-end passenger service. Through trains operated over the middle 76 miles between Anderson and Waveland, but service on either end was not coordinated with the middle.[40]

The line was chartered in 1875 as the Anderson, Lebanon and St. Louis Railroad. But three years later it entered receivership and after a foreclosure sale emerged in 1882 as the Cleveland, Indiana and St. Louis Railway. Financial problems continued and in 1885 the road was reorganized as the Midland Railway Company. By now it extended from

American Locomotive Company turned out this 660-hp diesel unit for the grandly named 11-mile New Jersey, Indiana and Illinois Railroad, which served South Bend. *Richard S. Simons collection*

Anderson to Noblesville but the Midland pushed it westward to Waveland in Montgomery County.[41]

Although Paris, Illinois, had been the original destination, the company now saw greener pastures in the Brazil block coal fields and turned abruptly south. This required 9.4 miles of trackage rights over the Terre Haute and Logansport Railroad, later the Pennsylvania.[42]

Late in 1891 a Chicago attorney, Henry Crawford, acquired control and organized the Chicago and South Eastern Railway. This company built two unconnected segments, 10.7 miles from Sand Creek to Bridgeton and 5.7 miles from Carbon to Brazil. It joined the two by leasing 5.3 miles from the Fort Wayne, Terre Haute and Southwestern Railroad, a Monon affiliate, and later buying the line. In 1899 the road was extended 18.8 miles from Anderson to Muncie.[43]

Financial difficulty continued to be part of the road's daily diet and in 1902 the Pennsylvania and Big Four (later New York Central) jointly acquired control in a foreclosure sale. In 1903 they incorporated the road as the Central Indiana Railway and entered into a joint operating agreement, at the same time launching a program of physical improvements.[44]

Despite the efforts, the road remained a white elephant. A post-purchase marketing study concluded that it had no future and should be abandoned. But vigorous protests prevented removal until 1928, when the Anderson-Muncie segment and everything west of Ladoga were scrapped. The following year, the line was abandoned between Advance and Ladoga. In 1943 a further abandonment reduced trackage to Anderson-Lebanon.[45]

As maintenance problems piled up, service deteriorated to alternate days in each direction. Deficits ranged up to $249,000 annually. Then appeared Ike Duffey, a wealthy Anderson meat packer, who offered to buy the road, but compromised by becoming a $1 a year president.[46]

Tackling his new job with stunning enthusiasm, Duffey set out in 1951 to transform the moribund property. Turning first to the track structure, he worked shoulder to shoulder with his section crews to remove weeds, install new ties, replace unacceptable rails, and add new ballast. He called on every shipper, active and potential, urging all to use Central Indiana service. Improved track allowed the road to increase speed. This created better equipment utilization, which resulted in daily service in each direction. This impressed shippers and attracted new ones. By year's end, Duffey had converted a $37,000 mid-year deficit into an $8,900 profit. Further annual financial improvements followed.[47]

But the little Central Indiana did not fit into the larger railroad world created by Conrail and other mergers. It survived for ten years as part of Conrail but in 1986, after the line west of Lapel had been abandoned, the Anderson-Lapel segment began life anew as the Central Indiana and Western Railroad.[48]

Chicago, Attica and Southern

Snatched from authorized abandonment, the 141-mile Chicago, Attica and Southern Railroad was the reincarnation of the Chicago and Eastern Illinois Railway's Indiana Division, and because it paralleled the main line by as little as three miles, it was easily expendable. It was Indiana's longest short line and an early trunk line spinoff.

The road's roots went back to the vaguely titled Indiana North and South Railroad, which was opened between Attica and Veedersburg in 1874.[49] Successor companies pushed the line south into the Brazil coal fields and north to Fair Oaks (Jasper County), where it connected with the Monon's Chicago line. In 1887 it was extended to the important junction of La Crosse.[50]

In 1889 the successor road, Chicago and Indiana Coal Railway, was merged with the C&EI, which operated it until a 1920 reorganization set it adrift. Offered for sale separately, it attracted no bidders and operations halted on all but one tiny line segment. Abandonment was authorized May 10, 1922.[51]

Then out of nowhere came an intermediary who acquired the entire road for $15,000 and resold it within a year for $387,000! The south 26 miles went to the Baltimore and Ohio system for $137,500 and gave it entry into the rich Brazil coal fields and to local clay manufacturers. The remaining 141 miles were acquired by a new corporation, Chicago, Attica and Southern Railroad, for $250,000. It began operation on December 7, 1922.[52]

The road hoped to succeed solely as a freight carrier that would serve local industries and carry bridge traffic that would avoid Chicago's congested rail yards. It operated no passenger service. Assembling a dozen lightweight, secondhand steam locomotives, it depended on them throughout its life

and discontinued operations as the diesel age dawned. The road's herald was a swastika, which it adopted nearly a decade before Nazi Germany popularized it.[53]

Although its predecessors had been built primarily to haul coal, the mines were on the section that became the B&O. Not until 1939, when rail shipments began in Fountain County, did the road originate coal tonnage. It continued to ship coal every year except 1944, and, with one exception, tonnage increased annually. Ironically it set a record during its last year of operation when it hauled 87,434 tons.[54]

Meanwhile the company fought to operate on a shoestring. Track structure became deplorable and service deteriorated. Financially strapped, the road relied on ingenuity. Lacking a coal dock, it simply dumped fuel from hopper cars, moved it to trackside, and loaded it into tenders with a clamshell as needed. An early-model automobile with flanged wheels carried General Manager Charles F. Propst on his inspection trips. It was known popularly as the "Blue Goose."[55]

To save on locomotive expense, the road purchased an Auto-Railer, suitable for either rails or highways. Its body resembling an oversize van, it was used to carry less-than-carload freight. A second Auto-Railer, resembling a small automobile, could move up to ten freight cars on level track.[56]

On August 5, 1931, the CA&S fell into receivership. As track deteriorated and bridges grew weaker, crews were prohibited from double-heading engines. During the final days, a trainman would ride the locomotive footboard watching for track hazards as it inched slowly across the Wabash River north of Attica through a truss bridge. A fire in 1937 swept the road's shops and added to the financial woes.[57]

Continually shrinking income made liquidation inevitable. But, somehow, the road managed to stay intact until 1943, when it abandoned the 46.3 miles south of La Crosse, the 9.7 miles between Morocco and the Illinois state line, and the 23.9 miles south of Veedersburg. This left the road with less than half its original length.[58]

On January 1, 1943, receivership ended and new ownership and management moved into place.[59] The following year it applied for total abandonment but was refused because it served war industries. In 1945 it renewed the petition and the Interstate Commerce Commission granted it on April 12, 1946.[60]

The Louisville, New Albany and Corydon's No. 9 puffs impatiently while waiting for a Southern Railway connection at Corydon Junction. During the 1940s the train made three round trips daily over its 7.7-mile route. *Photo by Richard S. Simons*

Cincinnati, Bluffton and Chicago

The 52-mile Cincinnati, Bluffton and Chicago Railroad was the central section of a road purportedly built to connect the major terminals of its corporate title. A legend in its own time, it is still known from its initials as the Corned Beef and Cabbage line.

First operated in 1903, it connected Portland with Huntington via Bluffton. Misfortune dogged the line with bridge collapses, an unattended engine running through a grocery, and incredible financial problems and lawsuits. The road ceased operation in 1917 after only 14 years.

A detailed history will be found in chapter 13.

Cincinnati, Findlay and Fort Wayne

The 78-mile Cincinnati, Findlay and Fort Wayne Railway was opened in 1895 between the natural gas boom town of Findlay, Ohio, and Fort Wayne. Originally the Findlay, Fort Wayne and Western Railway, the line was operated by the Cincinnati, Hamilton and Dayton Railroad as part of a reorganization in 1901. The line was abandoned in 1919.

Further details will be found under the Baltimore and Ohio Railroad corporate history.

St. Joseph Valley

The St. Joseph Valley Railway and its affiliate, St. Joseph Valley Traction Company, extended across northeastern Indiana for 70 miles between Elkhart and Columbia, Ohio, a dot on the map just across the state line. Conceived as an electric line, it was electrified only for nine miles between Elkhart and Bristol, but the entire line also was operated by steam locomotives and a bewildering assortment of self-propelled passenger equipment.

The road began operation in 1905 but was abandoned in 1917, although 15 miles continued to operate for three years by a successor company.

A detailed history will be found in chapter 13.

COAL CARRIERS

Five short lines, one in the north and four in the south, were built to haul coal. In the south the Algers, Winslow and Western Railway and the Yankeetown Dock Corporation dispatch shipments from Pike and Warrick County mines. Two additional carriers also have operated. In the north, the Twin Branch Railroad received coal for Indiana and Michigan Electric Company's Twin Branch generating station. All were latecomers, built between 1927 and the 1970s.

Algers, Winslow and Western

One of the last three short lines to be built prior to the contemporary era of Class I spinoffs, the Algers, Winslow and Western Railway was incorporated September 7, 1927.[61] It became a common carrier in June 1931.[62]

Operating over a 16-mile wishbone-shaped route, the AW&W end points are southeast of Petersburg and near Spurgeon. The lines converge at Oakland City Junction, where they connect with Norfolk Southern (formerly Southern Railway) and Indiana Southern Railroad (formerly Conrail). The road carries coal from the Kindill No. 1 mine, southeast of Oakland City, and anticipates (as of March 1996) shipping from the Kindill No. 2 mine, northeast of Oakland City. These mines were Old Ben Nos. 1 and 2 until sold to the newly organized Kindill Company, whose name derives from a combination of Kentucky, Indiana, and Illinois.[63]

Norfolk Southern and Kindill jointly own the road. Previous coal company partners successively had been Enos, Amax, Ayrshire, and Old Ben. P. F. Goodrich, son of former Governor James P. Goodrich, was president during the early years, but after Southern Railway acquired a half-interest in 1973, W. Graham Claytor, Jr., Southern president and later president of Amtrak, headed the road. His successors included L. Stanley Crane, Southern president and later chairman of Conrail, and Harold H. Hall, also a Southern president. Subsequent presidents came from Norfolk Southern ranks.[64]

Built for heavy-duty haulage, AW&W operates (1996) four Electro-Motive diesel SD9 six-axle locomotives that move unit trains destined for Midwest power plants. All rail is welded and weighs 132 lbs. per yard. The road has moved as many as 35,000 cars a year in addition to cross ties processed from on-line timber.[65] Algers in the corporate title is said to be an accidental corruption of the nearby town of Algiers.[66]

Peabody Coal

Peabody Coal Railroad operated a private line between its Dugger Mine, southwest of Dugger, and the Miller preparation plant, about two miles south-

Louisville, New Albany and Corydon No. 9 and a mixed train leave Corydon on May 31, 1946. Passengers were accommodated in the caboose for the 40-minute trip to Corydon Junction. The Porter-built 4–4–0 would later serve the Ferdinand Railroad as the last operating American type on Indiana rails. *Photo by Richard J. Cook*

east of Jasonville. The line was estimated to be between 12 and 20 miles long. Two GP–7 locomotives provided motive power.

Dugger Mine was operated through the 1970s and early 1980s but was inactive by 1986. Operations probably began during the 1960s.[67]

Thunderbird Mine

Coal produced at the Thunderbird Mine, one mile north of Shelburn, Sullivan County, traveled over a private railroad to American Electric Power's Breed generating station on the Wabash River. The line was approximately 13 miles long and was built by Ayrshire Collieries Corporation, which owned the mine. It was active between 1958 and 1972.[68]

After the mine closed, the railroad continued to haul coal that originated at the Chinook Mine in Clay County. The Breed plant was closed during the middle 1990s, but the railroad in 1996 remained in place.[69]

Twin Branch

Less than two miles long, Twin Branch Railroad hauled coal to the Indiana and Michigan Electric Company's Twin Branch generating station on the St. Joseph River near the east edge of Mishawaka. It began operation in September 1927. Connected to the New York Central's Elkhart and Western branch, it also served a materials yard and was a common carrier.[70]

Two steam switch engines initially supplied motive power, but two storage battery locomotives replaced them during the 1930s. During World War II, catenary was strung and pantographs installed to reduce charging time. The locomotives, however, were not converted to electric operation.[71]

During the 1950s, diesel power replaced the electric locomotives.[72] The road was abandoned in June 1978, when the power plant was retired.[73]

Yankeetown Dock

The Yankeetown Dock railroad began service in 1954 to haul coal from Amax Coal Company's Ayrshire Mine and Peabody Coal Company's Lynnville Mine to a rotary dumper that loads Ohio River barges near Yankeetown. It is 22 miles long, laid with 120-lb. rail, and is entirely within Warrick County. In addition, Norfolk Southern and Squaw Creek Coal Company trains operate over parts of the line.[74]

A fleet of four locomotives, including a rare Fairbanks-Morse H12–44 diesel-electric, moves unit trains over the line. Yankeetown Dock initially could process 900 tons per hour, but this was increased to 2,200 tons or about 7,000,000 tons a year. The railroad, which is not a common carrier, is headquartered in Newburgh.[75]

CONVERTED INTERURBAN LINES

Five historic short lines originally had been electric interurbans built primarily to serve passengers. Two were located in the north, two radiated from Evansville, and one was near Jeffersonville.

The Chicago, South Shore and South Bend Railroad still carries heavy freight and passenger traffic in northwestern Indiana. The Winona Railroad, which connected Peru and Goshen, began as an interurban line but carried freight with internal combustion locomotives after passenger service was discontinued. The Evansville, Suburban and Newburgh Railway and the Evansville and Ohio Valley Railway both offered steam freight and electric passenger service simultaneously, and the Southern Indiana Railway is the surviving freight hauling remnant of an interurban line that connected Indianapolis and Louisville.[76]

Chicago, South Shore and South Bend

Sometimes described as America's last interurban, the Chicago, South Shore and South Bend

Romance of the rails gives way to nostalgia when a road makes its final run. G. R. Horrock, general manager of the Winona Railroad, rides the wreath-bedecked locomotive of the Winona funeral train prior to abandonment in 1952. *Photo by Richard S. Simons*

Railroad is more a heavy-duty electrified railroad than a traditional Midwest interurban. It began in 1903 as a streetcar line, the 3.4-mile Chicago and Indiana Air Line Railway. In 1904, the name was changed to Chicago, Lake Shore and South Bend Railway, and by 1908 it had been extended eastward from Hammond to South Bend. Well engineered, it was built for 75-mph maximum speeds.[77]

In 1909 the road reached Kensington, Illinois, on the Illinois Central Railroad where passengers could change trains for the Loop. Later a through service was inaugurated.[78]

After a 1925 foreclosure sale, it emerged as the Chicago, South Shore and South Bend Railroad and became part of the utility empire of Samuel Insull. He immediately totally rebuilt and re-equipped the line. By this time the city of Gary had sprung up and industrial cities stood shoulder to shoulder along the south shore of Lake Michigan. The dense population produced lucrative traffic for the railroad.[79] However, the road entered bankruptcy again in 1933, was reorganized in 1938, and came under Chesapeake and Ohio Railway control. In 1984, the Venango River Corporation acquired control, and after another bankruptcy, in 1989 the Northern Indiana Commuter Transportation District, a government-assisted agency, purchased it. It then leased trackage rights for freight to the newly formed Chicago SouthShore and South Bend Railroad, a private company.[80]

In 1983 the road replaced its entire 1926 fleet with 44 new passenger cars and in 1992 added another 17 with capacity of up to 133 persons. The same year it connected some freight branches to extend service to the Michiana Regional Airport terminal at South Bend, which is one of few such intermodal terminals in the country. The road operates (in late 1996) ten daily trains between Chicago and South Bend and 31 others, mostly between Chicago and Michigan City or other intermediate points. Trains cover the 89.7 miles in as little as two hours, 15 minutes, which is fast for a commuter line with frequent stops. The road carried 3,296,000 passengers in 1995.[81]

The freight company operates a 506-car fleet consisting mostly of gondolas and uses 11 diesel locomotives. Coal is the principal inbound commodity, and steel dominates outbound cargo. From 1949 to 1981, the South Shore was noted for its three "Little Joe" freight locomotives, originally built for use in the USSR. With a 4–8–8–4 wheel arrangement, and weighing 273 tons each, they were among the largest electric locomotives in the world. They survive in museums in Illinois, Ohio, and Pennsylvania.[82]

Evansville and Ohio Valley

The Evansville and Ohio Valley Railway was simultaneously a steam carrier and an electric interurban. It began operation on June 10, 1907, as the Evansville and Eastern Electric Railway, which connected Newburgh with Rockport, 21 miles east. The same year it built a 3.37-mile branch to Richland City from a point about six miles west of Rockport and in 1911 extended its main line east 6.25 miles to Grandview. All trains entered Evansville over the Evansville, Suburban and Newburgh Railway until disputes over division of revenue caused the E&EE to build its own 10.9-mile line along the Ohio River in 1908.[83]

Evansville Railways, which operated the city lines, also owned the E&EE, as well as electric lines to Mt. Vernon and Henderson, Kentucky. Following a 1919 reorganization, the three emerged as the Evansville and Ohio Valley.[84] The Henderson line, which operated over a leased Illinois Central Railroad branch, used one of two interurban ferries in the United States to cross the Ohio River. Both the Henderson and Mt. Vernon lines were abandoned in 1928.[85]

Passenger service continued to Grandview, however, until 1938. This line had offered a combination boat-interurban service on the Ohio River with connections at Rockport by fast motor boat to Owensboro, Kentucky, ten miles downstream, and from Grandview to communities upstream as far as Cannelton. The Crescent Navigation Company operated the boats until discontinuance in 1928.[86]

After discontinuing passenger service, the E&OV continued to haul freight, although it abandoned a total of 21 miles on both ends in 1941. After this, a coal mine and two moulding sand pits provided traffic.[87] The road was abandoned in late 1946. It hauled coal to the end and during the 1920s trans-ported more than 100,000 tons annually three times.[88]

Evansville, Suburban and Newburgh

Conceived as a coal hauler, the Evansville, Suburban and Newburgh Railway opened in 1889 as a ten-mile steam line connecting mines near Newburgh with Evansville. Heavy traffic so strained the line's capacity that it converted its passenger service to electricity in 1905.[89] In 1906 the road more than doubled its mileage by adding a 14.7-mile line from a junction four miles east of Evansville to Boonville, where coal mines also were located. This gave the ES&N the shape of a Y lying on its side. Passenger cars typically ran hourly to Boonville and every hour and 20 minutes to Newburgh.[90]

All passenger service was discontinued in 1930 and freight service to Newburgh ceased the same year, when the last mine closed. It continued until 1947 on the Boonville line when the mine that provided 98% of the road's revenue ceased operations. Official abandonment followed in 1948.[91]

During the post–World War I years, the ES&N hauled more than a quarter million tons of coal annually. In 1942, it carried a record 396,933 tons.[92]

A short section continued until 1956 to serve the F. W. Cook and Sons brewery in Evansville as the Cook Transit Company.[93]

Southern Indiana

The Southern Indiana Railway is a short segment of converted interurban line that continues to operate as one of the state's busiest railroads. Its sole purpose is to trudge back and forth on its 5.5-mile route with empty freight cars picked up from CSX's former Baltimore and Ohio branch at Watson Junction and return them loaded with cement from the huge Essroc Materials mill at Speed.[94]

The line reached Sellersburg, from Louisville 14 miles away, in 1907, a year after the short branch to Charlestown had been completed. By 1908 it was linked with a line coming from Indianapolis and through passenger service was inaugurated over the entire 117 miles. It became one of three interurbans in the United States to operate sleeping cars.[95] In 1912, the name was changed to Interstate Public Service Company, and in 1931 rail and power operations were separated. Successors became Indiana Railroad and Public Service Company of Indiana, later PSI Energy.[96]

The seven-mile Charlestown branch was abandoned on May 10, 1932, and most of the remaining Louisville line on October 31, 1939. But Interstate had promoted freight business vigorously and in 1934 had built the Watson Junction connection and in 1938 added two miles of new track from a point south of Sellersburg to the cement mill. After final abandonments, this left a cement mill–Watson Junction road.[97]

This road became the Southern Indiana on August 5, 1939, and its trains make up to five round trips daily utilizing a fleet of approximately 100 leased boxcars in addition to the covered hoppers that CSX supplies as needed. The road continued to use electric power until 1947, when it was dieselized. Three General Electric locomotives provide motive power. Rail varies between 75 and 132 lbs. to the yard and at the upper limits is equivalent to that used by some heavy-duty trunk lines.[98]

Winona

The Winona Railroad began operations in 1906 as an electric interurban but in 1938, after discontinuing passenger service, switched to a variety of internal combustion locomotives and continued until 1952 as a conventional freight carrier.[99]

It was unusual in several respects. It grew from a city streetcar system. It encountered serious financial difficulty because its strong Sabbatarian management refused to operate on Sundays. It was the only line that linked the northern and central Indiana traction systems. Hauling eggs was such an important factor that it operated a refrigerator car subsidiary. It acquired an abandoned steam road, converted it to electric operation, then reconverted to a traditional railroad. Its five locomotives represented four power types that operated on three different fuels.[100]

The road's forerunner was the Winona and Warsaw Railway, which began operation on May 1, 1903, but within a year, the Winona Assembly promoters, who controlled it, incorporated the Winona Interurban Railway to connect Goshen and Peru via Warsaw. Operations began on the north end May 1, 1903, and the first car ran the entire 68 miles on February 4, 1910, after the Winona had acquired the 9.6-mile Peru and Detroit Railway. With other interurban companies, the Winona in 1910 inaugurated a short-lived through service between Michigan City and Peru and until 1926 operated a through Goshen-Indianapolis car, which had succeeded a South Bend–Indianapolis service.[101]

Despite through passenger service and heavy freight promotion, the Winona slipped into receivership in 1916 and emerged in 1924 as the Winona Service Company, later renamed Winona Railroad. Passenger operation was discontinued September 1, 1934, and a total of 8.5 miles was abandoned at the two ends.[102]

Taking advantage of its location through one of the country's principal egg baskets, the Winona bought 39 secondhand refrigerator cars in 1934 and operated them to eastern markets in steam road interchange.[103]

The Winona de-electrified its line in 1938 and acquired a small direct drive propane-powered unit and a 65-ton propane-electric locomotive. A year later it added a direct drive gasoline engine and in 1944 expanded with two 44-ton diesel-electrics.[104]

In 1947 the Winona abandoned all but 18.5 miles between New Paris and Warsaw. Sand, which originated in a pit near Leesburg, and coal traffic were insufficient to support the road, and it ran its last train May 31, 1952.[105]

MILITARY ROAD

Naval Surface Warfare Center

Indiana's second greatest short line mileage is the Naval Surface Warfare Center Railroad, Crane Division, concentrated in a compact area in northern Martin County. Totaling 164 miles, it is operated by the Department of Defense on the installation that originally was named Crane Naval Ammunition Depot.[106]

A dense network that ties together production and storage areas, it moves ammunition and explosives both inbound and outbound to two connections with the Soo Line (former Milwaukee Road) that crosses the center. Nine sizes of rail from 60 to 115 lbs. are used. The road rosters 12 locomotives and a fleet of 372 cars, including gondolas, flats, a hopper, box and tank cars, and six coaches, in addition to two cranes. The railroad was built as part of the original base construction, which began in 1941.[107]

10

Modern Short Lines

APHENOMENON of successive waves of mergers that began in the 1960s is the proliferation of short lines spun off from the major carriers. In Indiana, 45 roads ranging from less than a mile to 175 miles have set up shop after the large roads threatened to eliminate the routes. All but three are spinoffs. It brings to full cycle the railroad era, which began with short local lines, progressed through mergers and acquisitions into national systems, and now sees the major roads spinning off light density branches or other lines that do not fit into their traffic patterns. Notwithstanding this, a reverse trend is beginning to manifest itself and some Class I roads are reacquiring castoffs. CSX has acquired stock control of Indiana Rail Road, which was a former Illinois Central Gulf line, although IRR will remain independent. RailTex, a short line conglomerate that includes Indiana Southern Railroad, recently acquired Indiana and Ohio Railroad. Outside the state, other spinoffs are being reacquired, which raises the question of the original trend's permanence.

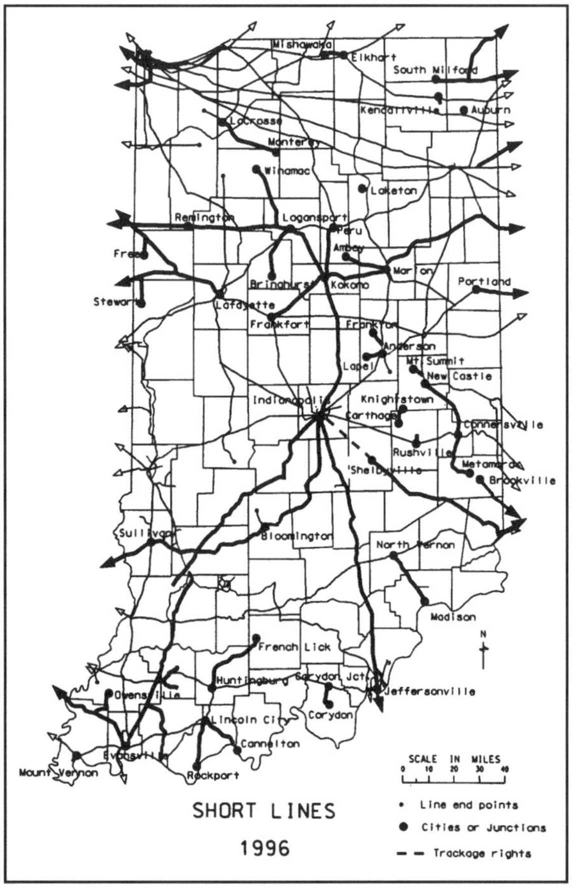

The railroad industry is both capital and manpower intensive. After years of marginal profits, roads began to concentrate on heavy tonnage that they can move at high speed on a limited number of lines. Many branches were greatly underutilized; some were in demand only seasonally and car utilization was poor. Maintenance that was deferred while dollars were diverted to main lines often set off a downward spiral that was difficult to control. The high cost of rail sometimes made it wise to re-lay the steel in locations of greater use.

Indiana's three principal systems—CSX, Norfolk Southern, and Conrail—used different approaches. CSX, with a single exception, moved to outright abandonment. Conrail, on the other hand, sought short line operators and found at least 30 eager to provide vital rail service to local industries. Norfolk Southern, however, ingeniously devised its Thoroughbred Short Line Program, which allowed 1,200 miles of light density track nationally to be leased. Traffic maintained at predetermined levels earns credits that are used to offset lease payments. Thus a short line may escape paying lease rentals altogether and divert the money to such essentials as traffic promotion or track improvements. The program preserves vital service for shippers, reduces short line operating costs, and retains rail traffic that otherwise would have been lost.[1]

SHORT LINES

1996

SCALE IN MILES
0   10   20   30   40

• Line end points
● Cities or Junctions
— — Trackage rights

More than 1,100 miles of Hoosier rails now are operated by short lines, in addition to approximately 350 miles that were operated briefly and either abandoned or turned over to successors. Of Indiana's 92 counties, 72 have short lines, reflecting the importance of rail service to local industries. Some have been financed with municipal, state, or federal assistance. A short line, by one definition, has annual revenue of less than $40 million or less than 350 miles of track.[2]

As major carriers merged, the number of redundant lines increased. N&W, for example, found itself with two redundant main lines after it absorbed the Wabash and the Nickel Plate in 1964. The Pennsylvania–New York Central merger of 1968 created single ownership of numerous parallel lines and CSX, at the cost of significant circuitry, found lines it considered excess.[3]

Motivation to establish short lines, as well as their success, varies greatly. The shorts range from busy companies such as Indiana Rail Road, Indiana Southern and Toledo, Peoria and Western, which each carried between 42,000 and 61,000 carloads in 1995, to roads of ten miles or less that intermittently serve a single industry, such as a grain elevator. In some instances, service is more essential to the customer than the sparse revenue is to the railroad.[4]

The need to invest capital and manpower where they would give the best return, coupled with restrictive labor agreements that escalated costs, drove Class I roads to shed marginal lines. A case in point was the 15-mile Pennsylvania branch that connected a large grain elevator at Matthews with Muncie. The line became disconnected from the balance of the system, so that crews had to be taxied to Muncie to begin their day's work. On a train that handled perhaps a half-dozen cars over a roadbed so deteriorated that speeds were held to as little as 5 mph, five crewmen were required. Obviously, costs were excessive and the line is now gone, forcing the elevator to use more expensive truck haulage.[5]

Some contemporary short lines, like coal carriers Indiana Rail Road and Indiana Southern, have expanded their business and increased employment. IRR in 1986 acquired a former Illinois Central Gulf branch that the ICG had attempted to abandon. It has steadily upgraded the line, won back shippers by improved service, and increased its employment from 17 initially to 75 in 1995. Indiana Southern's story is similar following its takeover of Conrail's former Indianapolis-Evansville line.[6]

At the other end of the spectrum, shippers, primarily grain elevators, snapped up short sections of endangered lines to preserve rail service. Sometimes they are the only customers. The J K Line at Monterey, Honey Creek near New Castle, Indian Creek near Anderson, and the Bee Line in Warren County are examples. The Central Indiana and Western Railroad near Anderson lives on traffic to a glass factory, although it has two additional seasonal shippers, and the Heritage Railroad was built new in 1991 on an abandoned Erie Lackawanna Railroad right-of-way in Wabash County to bring crude oil to a refinery. The Toledo, Peoria and Western Railway is essentially an intermodal carrier. Two lines were built new to serve state-operated Ohio River ports. The defunct Indiana Interstate Railroad served an aluminum industry, and its sole motive power was a trackmobile.

At least 14 Hoosier companies, including successors, have failed to survive. Two attempted to operate the Erie Lackawanna after Conrail dropped it, and two additional roads gave service on shorter segments. Three companies attempted to operate an ex-NYC branch between Emporia and Carthage, which is now a tourist line on a short segment. The Plymouth Short Line vainly tried to rescue 1.8 miles of Pennsylvania Railroad, and the Terre Haute, Brazil and Eastern Railroad discontinued operation after anticipated coal traffic failed to materialize.[7]

As through lines were chopped up and short traffic-producing segments were saved, strange bedfellows resulted. The ex–Nickel Plate (Norfolk Southern) Indianapolis–Michigan City branch and the ex-NYC Cairo, Illinois, branch each had four operators. Indiana Hi-Rail, an unusual group of unconnected lines, has operated 11 separate sections. Segments of the former Pennsylvania Railroad's Chicago-Cincinnati route survive as the Indian Creek, Honey Creek, A & R Line, and Winamac Southern railroads, in addition to 101 miles that N&W acquired and converted into an incredibly busy trunk line. The former NYC Chicago-Cincinnati line is now part Conrail, part Central Railroad of Indiana, and part Kankakee, Beaverville and Southern.[8]

Creation of short lines has resurrected some grand old names in new contexts. The new Toledo, Peoria and Western revives a name that goes back to 1885; the Indiana Rail Road duplicates the name of

Coal is the lifeblood of short lines
Indiana Rail Road, Indiana
Southern, and Algers, Winslow and
Western. Coal is being loaded
here for Indiana Southern at
Peabody Coal Company's Lynnville
Mine. Most Indiana coal goes to
electric generating stations.
Photo by Richard S. Simons

Grain is an essential part of the
commodity mix on many short lines;
some roads exist only to serve a
single customer. The 86-mile Central
Railroad of Indianapolis switches
cars at Ceres-Midland, Inc., in Sims,
Grant County.
Photo by Richard S. Simons

the one-time statewide interurban system and also a steam road of the 1880s, and the Central Railroad of Indianapolis originally was a World War I local switching road. The 11-mile Bee Line in northwestern Indiana recalls the original Bee Line, which operated eastward from Indianapolis as early as 1850.[9]

Roads listed below are alphabetized within northern, central, and southern geographical regions. The list includes both switching roads and true short lines because the distinction has blurred in recent years, and it also includes weight of rail per yard, which gives a rough index of the importance of the original line. Annual carloadings, unless otherwise attributed, are from *American Shortline Railway Guide*, 5th ed.

NORTHERN INDIANA

A & R Line

The 28-mile Winamac Southern segment between Winamac and Logansport became the A & R Line in 1995 following an ownership realignment. The line is agricultural, primarily moving outbound grain. Originally it was a high-speed, heavy-duty Pennsylvania Railroad secondary main between Chicago and Logansport and beyond. It is laid mostly with 130-lb. rail and moves 1,500 cars annually.

The name is the initials of Adam and Reed Frick, sons of the owner, Daniel R. Frick, whose J K Line is named for his two daughters, Jordyn and Katie.[10]

Auburn Port Authority

In 1976 Penn Central abandoned the last of its ex-NYC line through Auburn, leaving several local industries without rail service. The Baltimore and Ohio Railroad, which also serves Auburn, then provided switching service until deteriorating track threatened it.[11]

In 1981 the city established a port authority, which purchased 1.7 miles of track north from the B&O junction and leased it to the B&O. The line hauls coke, plastic, and metal inbound and manufactured goods outbound. Lightly built, rail varies between 85 and 100 lbs. per yard. It is not a common carrier.[12]

Bee Line

Established to assure rail service for the Stewart Grain Company in Stewart (Warren County), the Bee Line Railroad consists of 10.8 miles of former Conrail (ex-NYC) track. It extends from Stewart to the Kankakee, Beaverville and Southern Railroad (ex–Nickel Plate and Norfolk and Western) at Handy. First operation was on October 15, 1994.

Strictly an agricultural line, it carries outbound corn in unit trains as well as soybeans and wheat and receives fertilizer. Most cargo is outbound. Rail varies from 105 to 127 lbs. per yard. The company is not a common carrier.[13]

Benton Central

Benton Central Railroad was organized in September 1987 to protect rail service in anticipation of a Conrail abandonment. It acquired seven miles of CR's Chicago-Cincinnati line between Templeton and Swanington. In 1989, before it began operation, BC sold its track to the Kankakee, Beaverville and Southern Railroad, which had acquired lines extending from both ends.[14]

Chicago and Indiana

The Chicago and Indiana Railroad was the final attempt in Indiana to revive the Erie Lackawanna Railroad, a New York–Chicago trunk line that ran through Decatur, Huntington, Rochester, and Hammond. In addition, it operated 27 miles of former Pennsylvania Railroad between Decatur and Portland. It had been included in Conrail, but it did not fit into its long-range plans.[15]

The C&I began operating in June 1979 on approximately 150 miles between Wren, Ohio, two miles east of the Indiana line, Griffith, and, by trackage rights, to Chicago. Earlier a doubletrack line, it was built to high standards with heavy rail weighing 110 to 132 lbs. per yard. Headquarters was located in Huntington, which had been an EL division point. Most owners were on-line shippers. Operation ended in January 1980, six months after it started, and nearly the entire line was dismantled.[16]

Erie Western

Erie Western Railway was the first of two attempts in Indiana to revive the Erie Lackawanna Railway, a New York–Chicago trunk line that Conrail had abandoned. It extended 160 miles from Wren, Ohio, two miles east of the Indiana line, to Hammond and continued service to Chicago on Chicago and Western Indiana Railroad trackage rights. In addition it operated 27 miles of former Pennsylvania Railroad (later Penn Central) between Decatur and Portland. The main line had been a heavy-duty railroad laid with 110 to 132 lb. per yard rail and earlier had been doubletrack.[17]

EW began operation on September 25, 1977, and hauled grain, lumber, fertilizer, steel, food products, plastic, and manufactured goods. Owners were shippers and other investors, who established headquarters in Huntington, a former EL division point. The road ceased operation in June 1979 and was succeeded immediately by the Chicago and Indiana Railroad.[18]

Fulton County

Established to serve grain elevators on the abandoned Erie Lackawanna Railroad, the Fulton County Railroad operated during the 1980s as a connection to the Norfolk and Western (ex–Nickel Plate) at Rochester. Length was 16 miles. The road was an outlet for a grain operation in Monterey, which stands midway between a CSX connection at North Judson and the N&W at Rochester. Eventually the traffic was turned westward to CSX and the eastern section to Rochester was abandoned.[19] The line to North Judson was named Tippecanoe Railroad.

Heritage

Filling an urgent need for rail transportation, Laketon Refining Corporation in northern Wabash County built the 3.1-mile Heritage Railroad in 1991. It is a reincarnation of the Erie Lackawanna Railway, which was dismantled after a successor short line abandoned operations in 1980. Fortunately the right-of-way was available and the Eel River bridge at Laketon was intact; so the refinery built to a Conrail connection at Bolivar, two miles south of North Manchester. Rail is a sturdy 105 lbs. per yard.

The line carries inbound petroleum in leased tank cars for processing at the refinery. The road is not a common carrier.[20]

Hillsdale County

Operating over ex-NYC branches that Conrail deemed surplus, and the remnant of an ex–Wabash Railroad (later Norfolk and Western) line, Hillsdale County Railway began operation on April 1, 1976.

The route extended from Pleasant Lake, south of Angola, to Hillsdale and Quincy, Michigan, and via a seven-mile branch to Litchfield, Michigan. The system totaled 59.8 miles.

Threatened by Conrail's abandonment of its sole outside connection, at Quincy, Hillsdale County in April 1986 extended operations three miles from Pleasant Lake to Steubenville over unused ex-NYC rails and then acquired 25 miles from Norfolk and Western (ex-Wabash) to Montpelier, Ohio. This had once been part of an important Chicago-Detroit line. Hillsdale also leased six miles of Conrail (ex-NYC) between Quincy and Coldwater, Michigan. This increased mileage to 95.[21] Principal traffic included coal, grain, flour, sugar, food products, plastic, and fertilizer.[22] From 1975 to the early 1990s, the Little River Railroad operated what was believed to be the nation's smallest standard-gauge Pacific-type steam locomotive on excursions between Pleasant Lake and Steubenville.[23]

On-line shippers and local interests owned the road until 1992, when it became part of the newly formed Indiana Northeastern Railroad, which included the former Pigeon River Railroad.[24]

Indiana Interstate

Indiana Interstate Railway began operation in 1978 at Bicknell over one mile of the Pennsylvania Railroad's former Indianapolis-Vincennes line. Conrail, PRR's successor, had abandoned the balance of the route to Vincennes in 1976. Sole motive power was a trackmobile used to serve an aluminum products plant. Rail was a light 80 lbs. per yard. The line was abandoned in 1980.[25] In 1979, the company acquired 16 miles of an ex-NYC (later Penn Central) line between Goshen and Shipshewana but abandoned it in December 1980 after operating a tourist line briefly. The company went out of business after the abandonments.[26]

Indiana Northeastern

Owners of the 11-mile Pigeon River Railroad purchased the 95-mile Hillsdale County Railway, added their own road by lease, and formed the 104-mile Indiana Northeastern Railroad, which began service in December 1992. Headquartered in South Milford, it follows a Z-shaped route west from Montpelier, Ohio, to Steubenville and South Milford, north to Angola and Hillsdale, Michigan, and west to Coldwater, Michigan, and by a branch to

Litchfield, Michigan.[27] IN immediately launched a $1,500,000 rehabilitation program on the 16 miles between Pleasant Lake and Ray, Michigan, to allow higher speeds and longer trains.[28] Annual carloadings total 3,400.

Most shipments are outbound grain, some in unit trains. Flour, steel, plastics, and wheat move inbound. Rail varies from 80 to 112 lbs. per yard.[29]

The predecessor Hillsdale County Railway had begun operation in 1976 over ex-NYC lines and added 25 miles of an ex–Wabash Railroad line (later N&W) to Montpelier, Ohio, when Conrail closed its connection at Quincy, Michigan. The Pigeon River previously had acquired 14 miles of the Wabash line westward to Wolcottville. It was laid with 110-lb. rail.[30]

J K Line

The 16-mile J K Line operates a former Erie Lackawanna segment between Monterey and North Judson, where it connects with CSX (former Chesapeake and Ohio). It began operation in April 1990 after the present owner, Daniel R. Frick, purchased the Tippecanoe Railroad and renamed it for his two daughters, Jordyn and Katie. Principal traffic is outbound corn and soybeans in unit trains. Dry fertilizer moves inbound.[31] Carloadings total about 1,400 annually.

Built to main line standards, the road has 112- to 132-lb. rail and at one time was doubletracked. The line successively became Erie Lackawanna, Erie Western, and Chicago and Indiana. It is headquartered in Monterey.[32]

Kankakee, Beaverville and Southern

Beginning as a 30-mile eastern Illinois short line on December 1, 1977, the Kankakee, Beaverville and Southern Railroad has grown to a triangular 155-mile system. Approximately 62 miles are in Indiana. F. R. Orr, a Beaverville, Illinois, grain elevator and lumberyard owner, and others organized the company after Conrail (ex-NYC) abandoned part of its Chicago-Cincinnati line in 1976. Initially they leased 30 miles between Kankakee and Sheldon, Illinois, and in 1980 added 55 miles of ex–Milwaukee Road between Danville and Hooper, Illinois. It crossed the original line approximately six miles north of Sheldon.[33]

In 1980 KB&S bought the leased section and upgraded it two years later. In 1989 it acquired 22 miles of Norfolk Southern (ex-N&W and Nickel Plate) between Templeton and Cheneyville, Illinois, where it connected with the KB&S ex–Milwaukee Road line. It also purchased 25 miles of former Big Four (later NYC, Penn Central, and Conrail) between Lafayette and Swanington. In 1994 it acquired the 21-mile missing link between the end of its north section at Sheldon and its south section at Swanington, and in 1996 it acquired the six-mile segment between Free and its own line at Sheff, which Conrail had owned.[34]

The KB&S is an agricultural transporter. Outbound corn, soybeans, and wheat shipments, which include unit trains, predominate. Sunflower seed, millet, milo, and fertilizer move inbound. The road moves about 6,000 cars annually. Headquarters is in Beaverville, Illinois.[35]

Michigan Southern

Michigan Southern Railroad, which had begun operations in Michigan in 1989, added two leased ex-Conrail lines in Indiana in November 1996. The Elkhart and Western branch, formerly New York Central, extends 9.8 miles between Elkhart and Mishawaka on the north side of the St. Joseph River. Most traffic is inbound wood, paper, and corn syrup. The 1.1-mile Kendallville line was part of the Pennsylvania's Grand Rapids and Indiana Railway and its traffic is inbound syrup and sugar. Rail on both lines ranges from 105 to 120 lbs.[36]

Pigeon River

Acquiring a 14.3-mile segment of the former Wabash Railroad's Chicago-Detroit line, the Pigeon River Railroad began service in 1985 between Wolcottville and Ashley-Hudson. From here the road continued as Norfolk and Western Railway, which had acquired the Wabash in 1964. The Pigeon River was reduced to 10.5 miles when the Wolcottville–South Milford segment was abandoned in 1991.[37] Shipments are outbound grain, usually in unit trains.[38]

South Milford Grain, Inc., which had acquired the line from N&W, absorbed the Hillsdale County Railway and leased it to the Pigeon River in 1992. The combined road is now the Indiana Northeastern Railroad, a 104-mile system serving northeastern Indiana, northwestern Ohio, and southern Michigan. The Pigeon River is now a non-operating holding company.[39]

Plymouth Short Line

Operating over 1.8 miles of the Pennsylvania Railroad's South Bend–Logansport branch, the Plymouth Short Line served local industries. Traffic was foundry sand inbound and animal products outbound. Operation began in May 1985 after Penn Central had abandoned the track in 1973. It ceased operation in May 1990.[40]

Tippecanoe

Tippecanoe Railroad operated 16 miles of former Erie Lackawanna between Monterey and North Judson, where it connects with CSX (ex-C&O). It began operation in January 1980 after EL and two short line successors had discontinued service. The Buckeye Feed and Supply Company at Monterey and others owned the road.[41] Both the grain company and the railroad were sold to Frick Services, which began operation in April 1990. The road was renamed the J K Line.[42]

Winamac Southern

Winamac Southern Railway began operation on March 20, 1993, over 72 miles of former Pennsylvania Railroad (later Penn Central and Conrail) radiating from Logansport to Winamac, Kokomo, and Bringhurst. The owner is Frick Services of Monterey, which also owns J K Line. Central Properties, Inc., which also owns the Central Railroad of Indianapolis and the Central Railroad of Indiana, operates it. Traffic of about 2,400 cars annually is evenly balanced between outbound grain, usually in unit trains, and inbound chemicals, fertilizer, and freight cars bound for a repair facility.[43]

The 28-mile Winamac-Logansport segment is part of an earlier doubletrack, high-speed line from Chicago that funneled a large fleet of passenger trains to Logansport, where they were dispatched to destinations in Ohio, Kentucky, and Florida. Heavy freight traffic at that time included eastbound perishables and westbound coal.[44] In 1995 this segment was renamed the A & R Railroad following an ownership change.[45]

The 23-mile Kokomo segment was part of a heavy-duty line to Cincinnati, and the 20 miles to Bringhurst was part of the Chicago-Indianapolis-Louisville route, which carried through passenger trains to Florida. Rail on the three lines varies between 110 and 152 lbs. per yard.[46]

CENTRAL INDIANA

Borinstein

A. Borinstein, Inc., a scrap metal dealer, acquired a .4-mile ex-NYC siding to serve its business at the southeast edge of downtown Indianapolis. Operations began on May 23, 1985.[47] Scrap metal was moved in both directions but primarily outbound on rail that weighed 90–110 lbs. A trackmobile provided motive power. Operations halted in the early 1990s when the company discontinued business.[48]

Carthage, Knightstown and Shirley

The Carthage, Knightstown and Shirley Railroad was founded in April 1987 to operate 20.5 miles of former Big Four (later NYC and Penn Central) line, which originally connected Benton Harbor, Michigan, with North Vernon and Louisville. Penn Central abandoned most of the line south of Carthage in 1973 and the balance south of Emporia in 1989.[49] The Indiana Eastern Railroad and Transportation Company (Hoosier Connection) and the Indiana Midland previously had operated the Emporia-Carthage segment until the CK&S acquired it.[50]

Originally operating both freight and passenger excursions, the CK&S abandoned the 16 miles north of Knightstown, dropped freight service, and converted itself into a landlocked railroad. Since May 1988 it has operated only weekend excursions over the five miles between Knightstown and Carthage.[51]

Central Indiana and Western

First operated on November 4, 1986, the Central Indiana and Western Railroad acquired nine miles of the former Central Indiana Railway, which the NYC and Pennsylvania Railroads had operated jointly following a 1903 foreclosure purchase.[52] The original line had extended 127 miles between Muncie and Brazil, but it had been progressively abandoned west of Lapel. CI&W acquired it from Conrail, successor to the two parent companies.[53]

The road primarily carries inbound raw materials to the Owens-Brockway Glass Container plant at Lapel, but also transports outbound grain from two elevators. It connects with Conrail at Anderson. Traffic totals about 2,300 cars a year. Rail varies from 70 to 115 lbs. per yard. Headquarters is in Lapel.[54]

Central of Indianapolis

Operating over 86 miles of line leased from Norfolk Southern Railway under its Thoroughbred Short Line Program, Central Railroad of Indianapolis began service on August 14, 1989, on an 86-mile X-shaped system centered in Kokomo. The lines extend to Marion, Frankfort, Tipton, and Peru, plus a 36-mile Peru-Argos section subleased to Indiana Hi-Rail. The Peru-Rochester segment is being abandoned in 1997. The parent company is Central Properties, which operates three additional short lines.[55]

Auto parts and grain, which often moves in unit trains, are the principal outbound commodities and comprise slightly more than half the tonnage. Inbound movements consist primarily of sand and soda ash for Ball-Foster Glass Container Company, the state's largest, in Marion, and fertilizer. All traffic moves to Kokomo, where it is combined for forwarding to Frankfort and dispatched over connections.[56] The road moves 12,000 cars annually over 90 to 112-lb rail.

The original company was a switching line that the Big Four Railway operated in downtown Indianapolis during World War I. After it discontinued operation, the corporate title became vacant and the present Central Railroad acquired it. It also operates over the affiliated Kokomo Rail Company's 13-mile Marion-Amboy line, which had been part of Chesapeake and Ohio's Chicago-Cincinnati route.[57]

R. J. Corman

The R. J. Corman Railroad Company Western Ohio Line began service on August 21, 1993, over a route between Portland and Lima, Ohio, leased from Norfolk Southern. Originally only the 45 miles from Lima to a point near the Indiana boundary were to be operated, but 12 miles between Fort Recovery, Ohio, and Portland were added. Traffic on the Indiana portion is primarily grain and steel, both inbound and outbound.

The line is part of the former Nickel Plate (later N&W and NS) route between Peoria and Sandusky, Ohio. It is laid with 85 to 112 lb. rail and carries about 1,000 cars a year. The Corman Company operates other short lines in Kentucky, Tennessee, and Ohio.[58]

Honey Creek

Honey Creek Rail Road began operation on October 1, 1993, over two unconnected segments in Henry and Rush counties. The Sulphur Springs Division, which falls short of reaching Honey Creek by three miles, operates 6.6 miles between Sulphur Springs and a Norfolk Southern connection north of New Castle. The Rushville Division operates approximately seven miles north from Rushville to a point near Sexton. Both divisions haul outbound grain, some in unit trains up to 65 cars. Carloadings approach 500 annually. The road is not a common carrier. Morristown Grain Company is the parent company.[59]

The Sulphur Springs Division is part of the Pennsylvania Railroad (later Penn Central and Conrail) route between Chicago and Cincinnati. It was a heavy-duty line with rail ranging from 110 to 140 lbs. per yard. The Rushville Division, by contrast, was a 23-mile lightly built N&W (ex–Nickel Plate) branch that connected Rushville with New Castle. Rail ranged from 75 to 90 lbs. Indiana Hi-Rail acquired the line in 1983 but abandoned most of it in 1989.[60]

Indian Creek

Operating over 4.6 miles of the Pennsylvania Railroad's former Chicago-Cincinnati line, Indian Creek Railroad moves 2,000 cars annually of outbound corn in unit trains, as well as soybeans and wheat, and inbound fertilizer. The road, which is not a common carrier, began operation on July 20, 1980, and is controlled by Rydman and Fox, Inc., whose grain and fertilizer operations are located southeast of Frankton.[61]

Indiana Eastern

Indiana Eastern Railroad and Transportation Company, operating as the Hoosier Connection, began service in June 1979 over 22 miles of ex-NYC (later Penn Central) line. It extended from Carthage to Emporia, where it connected with Conrail, which operated the balance of the route to Anderson. Indiana Eastern operated it until December 1984, when Indiana Midland succeeded it.

The line originally was part of the Big Four's

Michigan Division, which connected Benton Harbor, Michigan, with Louisville. Rail weighs 90 lbs. per yard.[62]

Indiana Hi-Rail

Operating a group of unconnected short lines in Indiana, Ohio, Illinois, and Kentucky, Indiana Hi-Rail Corp. began service in December 1981 on a six-mile former New York Central (later Penn Central) branch between Connersville and a Norfolk and Western Railway connection at Beesons. As it expanded, adding and dropping lines, it operated more than 16 owned, leased, or shipper-controlled segments that at one time totaled 509 miles. At various times, approximately 275 miles of this was in Indiana.[63]

Although eight years elapsed before Hi-Rail extended its Connersville-Beesons line 20 miles to New Castle, it was busy in the interim. It first acquired N&W's ex–Nickel Plate companion line from New Castle to Rushville, 24 miles, but later abandoned all but the south seven miles. It was laid with lightweight 75-lb. rail.[64] Beginning in 1985, it briefly operated the former Monon segment between Sheridan and Indianapolis for a group of shippers before the line was abandoned.[65]

Successively Hi-Rail began to operate a 99-mile line between Henderson, Kentucky, Evansville, and Newton, Illinois, and two lines totaling 40 miles near Decatur, Illinois. All were former Illinois Central (later Illinois Central Gulf) lines with rail varying from 85 to 112 lbs. It also operated the Poseyville and Owensville Railroad in Posey County for the original owners, Merchants Management Corporation. This had been part of the Chicago and Eastern Illinois Railroad's Mt. Vernon branch. For a short time Hi-Rail also operated 52 miles of a former N&W (ex–Nickel Plate) line between Metcalf and Neoga, Illinois, for a shippers' group.[66]

In 1989 it leased five lines under Norfolk Southern's Thoroughbred Short Line Program. They were Woodburn–Liberty Center, Ohio (ex-Wabash), a lightweight 52-mile road laid with 80-lb. rail; Marion-Douglas, Ohio (ex-NKP) laid with 90- to 100-lb. rail; and the former Huntingburg cluster of ex–Southern Railway trackage to Cannelton, Dubois, and Rockport, which totals 55 miles. In addition it subleases from Central Railroad of Indianapolis 36 miles of ex-NKP track between Peru and Argos, although this is under abandonment proceedings (1996). It also operated a 26-mile former Pennsylvania Railroad segment between Tiffin and Woodville, Ohio, and the Spencerville and Elgin Railroad (ex-EL) between Lima and Glenmore, Ohio, 30 miles.[67]

The Connersville branch, Hi-Rail's first, carries outbound auto parts, supplemented by inbound fertilizer and lime. The Evansville line moved inbound coal and outbound grain in unit trains and chemicals, steel, and toys. The Woodburn branch carries grain in unit trains and cement outbound and food products, soda ash, and clinkers inbound. The Marion line has been shortened approximately seven miles on each end and is moving (1997) to abandon most operations east of Craigville (near Bluffton). Shipments now are largely grain in unit trains, popcorn to and from the Weaver Popcorn Company in Van Buren, and fertilizer. The Rockport branch, which was acquired in 1996 by Hoosier Southern Railroad, carries fly ash and particle board over 75-lb. rail, and the Rochester line is in service only northward to Argos, where it transports grain in unit trains and fertilizer over its 90-lb. rail.

Hi-Rail is under trusteeship (1996) and is being reorganized. Prior to this, it was split briefly into two corporations and operated as the Wabash and Erie and the Ohio and Erie Railroads. It has transferred to other operators the Evansville line, including the Poseyville and Owensville Railroad, which it operated for the owner, and the Rockport, Cannelton and Dubois branches. Hi-Rail no longer operates in Illinois or Kentucky and has dropped two lines in Ohio.[68] Carloadings total nearly 15,000 annually.

Indiana Midland

Successor on January 8, 1985, to the Indiana Eastern Railroad, Indiana Midland Railway operated from a Conrail connection at Emporia to Carthage, 22 miles, and also on a two-mile branch from Shirley to Wilkinson.[69] Both freight trains and passenger excursions traveled over the 90-lb. rail until the company discontinued business in April 1987.[70] The Carthage, Knightstown and Shirley Railroad immediately succeeded it. The route originally was part of a Benton Harbor, Michigan–Louisville line operated by New York Central and predecessors.[71]

Logansport and Eel River

The Logansport and Eel River Short Line operates over 2.2 miles of the Pennsylvania Railroad's former Eel River and South Bend branches.[72] A periodic steam tourist service initially used the line but a new corporation added freight service on July 1, 1989. It also continued occasional tourist trains. Traffic, approaching 25 carloads annually, is primarily coal and fertilizer inbound and lumber in both directions. Rail ranges from 100 to 130 lbs.[73]

Terre Haute, Brazil and Eastern

Incorporated on May 1, 1987, the Terre Haute, Brazil and Eastern Railroad began operation on October 15, 1987, over ex–Pennsylvania Railroad's St. Louis–Indianapolis–Pittsburgh line. THB&E used 30 miles between Terre Haute and Limedale plus a seven-mile branch to Amax Coal Company's Chinook Mine near Brazil.

Traffic was evenly balanced between inbound lumber, fertilizer, and plastic pellets and outbound grain, cement, and plastic pipe. The road also operated tourist excursion service. After anticipated coal traffic failed to materialize, the road entered bankruptcy. The last operation was on December 31, 1993, and the line, which had been built to unusually heavy standards with 135- to 145-lb. rail, was dismantled.[74]

Toledo, Peoria and Western

In 1860 the Toledo, Peoria and Western's predecessor, building eastward from Peoria, reached the Indiana state line at the tiny village of Effner and stopped there. More than a century later, it crossed the line and continued to Logansport by purchasing a Penn Central branch.[75] The contemporary TP&W extends from Fort Madison, Iowa, to Logansport, a total of 281 miles. It enters Fort Madison over 14 miles of Burlington Northern Santa Fe trackage rights.[76]

The road is known for its Hoosier Lift, a large intermodal facility near Remington that accommodates both double-stack containers and conventional intermodal shipments at the rate of approximately 50,000 carloads annually. Principal traffic is grain and chemicals, both inbound and outbound, in addition to auto parts inbound. Unit trains move fertilizer, grain, and coal. Heavily built, TP&W is laid with 100- to 136-lb. rail. Abandonment of Conrail (ex-Pennsylvania) lines at Logansport adversely affected interchange traffic, but connections with new short lines Winamac Southern and Central Railroad of Indianapolis have increased Indiana traffic.[77]

When Conrail was formed as Penn Central's successor in 1976, it omitted the Effner branch, which the TP&W bought to protect its eastern outlet.

The original TP&W has a long, turbulent history that includes the loss of 82 lives near Chatsworth, Illinois, in 1882 when an excursion train crashed through a fire-weakened trestle, and a 19-month strike in the mid–1940s, which resulted in the assassination of President George P. McNear Jr., and federal control.

The road has survived a confusing record of foreclosures, reorganizations, leases, mergers, sales, and repurchases. It has successively been an independent and the subsidiary of four Class I roads. A Wabash Railroad predecessor leased it in 1880 but lost it in a reorganization in 1885. In 1893 the Pennsylvania Railroad acquired control, intending to promote it as a Chicago bypass route, and sold a half-interest to the Chicago, Burlington and Quincy Railroad, which controlled it from 1911 to 1921. The road again went independent in 1926 following a reorganization, was reorganized a second time in 1947 and again in 1952.

In 1960 the Santa Fe Railway acquired the railroad and sold a half-interest to the Pennsylvania. In 1979 the Pennsylvania resold its interest to the Santa Fe, which abolished the company by merger in 1983. On February 1, 1989, Santa Fe sold the road to a group of investors, who in 1996 sold a 40% interest to the Delaware Otsego Corporation, which also operates the New York, Susquehanna and Western Railway and other eastern short lines.[78]

SOUTHERN INDIANA

Central of Indiana

Central Railroad of Indiana began service on December 31, 1991, over 85 miles of ex-NYC Cincinnati-Indianapolis-Chicago line between Cincinnati and Shelbyville and continues to Indianapolis on Conrail trackage rights. At the same time, it purchased a short branch to Lawrenceburg to serve the Seagram Distillery. It has since sold part of the line to a riverboat casino, which will use the right-of-way for a highway while the railroad will use trackage rights over CSX.[79]

Traffic, which is balanced evenly between inbound and outbound, consists primarily of inbound chemicals, nonmetallic minerals, lumber, and produce, and outbound fertilizer, scrap metal, and cullet. Grain, often in unit trains, moves in both directions.[80] The road moves about 10,000 cars a year.

Built to high standards, the line is laid with heavy rail that ranges from 112 to 127 lbs. per yard. One of four affiliated roads headquartered in Kokomo, Central is related to the Central Railroad of Indianapolis, Kokomo Rail Company, and by an operating agreement with Winamac Southern.[81]

Dubois County

Operating over a leased Norfolk Southern (ex–Southern Railway) branch, the Dubois County Railroad extends 16 miles from Huntingburg to Dubois. The line continues another 15 miles to French Lick but is used only for tourist excursions by Dubois County Railroad's parent company, the Indiana Railway Museum. The Southern Railway completed the road in 1907 to carry passengers to the resort at French Lick.[82]

Indiana Hi-Rail began service on June 30, 1989, under Norfolk Southern's Thoroughbred Short Line Program, but was succeeded by the newly formed Dubois County Railroad on July 15, 1993. Principal traffic is soybean meal inbound and particle board outbound at an anticipated rate of 500 cars a year. Rail varies from 75 to 85 lbs. per yard.[83]

Evansville Terminal

Evansville Terminal Company, a unit of RailAmerica, purchased Indiana Hi-Rail's Evansville-Browns, Illinois, line in July 1996. This earlier had been an Illinois Central branch. Indiana Hi-Rail also had operated the extended road from Browns to Newton, Illinois, but had abandoned this in 1996.

The 40-mile Evansville Terminal road, while under Hi-Rail operation, had moved outbound grain and inbound coal in unit trains, in addition to inbound chemicals, fertilizer, and steel. Rail weight varies between 85 and 112 lbs.[84]

Hoosier Southern

Hoosier Southern Railroad, established in 1994, operates approximately 20 miles of line between Cannelton, Tell City, and a junction with Norfolk Southern at Lincoln City, and in 1996 leased the 16-mile former Indiana Hi-Rail line to Rockport. The Perry County Port Authority purchased the dormant ex–Southern Railway branch after Indiana Hi-Rail discontinued service on it in 1991. Hi-Rail had operated under the Norfolk Southern Thor-

oughbred Short Line Program. Traffic of 300 cars a year on the Cannelton line is chemicals, lumber, and wood products, both inbound and outbound.[85]

Indiana and Ohio

The Indiana and Ohio Railroad began operation in June 1979 over a former New York Central branch between Brookville and Valley Junction, Ohio, 26 miles away. It connects with Central Railroad of Indiana, which acquired a portion of ex-NYC Indianapolis-Cincinnati line. Its principal traffic of 1,000 cars a year is inbound roofing granules and lumber. Rail weighs 90 to 100 lbs. per yard.[86]

I&O is the pioneer member of a group of short lines whose affiliated companies operate in southern Ohio. RailTex, a short line conglomerate, purchased I&O properties in 1996.[87]

Indiana Rail Road

Rescuing a threatened Illinois Central Gulf branch, Indiana Rail Road began service on March 18, 1986, between Indianapolis and Sullivan, 110 miles, and later extended it 43 miles to Newton, Illinois. Illinois Central, ICG's successor, retains the remaining 24 miles to its main line at Effingham, Illinois. It is one of Indiana's principal short lines and operates the third longest continuous railroad.[88]

The state's most spectacular short line, it is famous for the Tulip Trestle (Richland Creek Viaduct), which jumps 2,295 feet at a maximum 157-foot height across Richland Creek valley northeast of Bloomfield. East of Bloomington, the road bridges Shuffle Creek on an 880-foot-long, 80-foot-high structure and plunges through a 500-foot tunnel near Unionville.[89]

During the late 1970s, ICG unsuccessfully attempted to abandon the line between Indianapolis and Switz City. It was then ordered closed north of Bloomington because of safety hazards. Abandonment was forestalled, however, when ICG upgraded it with $3,000,000 of government assistance.

But by 1983, ICG, intent on downsizing itself to a core system, attempted to sell the road. Along came Thomas G. Hoback, experienced member of a railroading family, who had served as ICGs coal marketing director, and he saw potential in the mines along the route. Connections with numerous strong roads, particularly in Indianapolis, added to the appeal.

Indianapolis Terminal Corporation, a holding company, purchased the line for $5,300,000 or $48,624 a mile. In the first year it spent $1,000,000 on track improvements, which included seven miles of new rail, 13,000 ties, and 400 cars of ballast. Original rail ranged from 90 to 132 lbs. per yard. The company also leased briefly in 1990 Norfolk Southern's Indianapolis-Tipton line under the Norfolk Southern Thoroughbred Short Line Program.[90]

Coal is the backbone of Indiana Rail Road's business. Initially it accounted for 90%, but as the road developed traffic in other commodities, this dropped to about two-thirds. Approximately 1,200,000 tons annually go to IPALCO's E. W. Stout generating plant at Indianapolis. The road serves Black Beauty's Miller Creek and Triad's Switz City Mines in Greene County. Coal moves in unit trains.

As the road broadened its commodity base, it built a distribution center in Indianapolis for lumber and fertilizer storage. Coal, lumber, and chemicals are the principal inbound shipments and appliances, scrap metal, chemicals, and coal move outbound. Traffic is balanced among inbound, outbound, and local. IRR hauls approximately 60,000 cars (1995) annually and employs 75 persons.

At Bloomington, Indiana Rail Road has recaptured shipping from Thomson Consumer Electronics (former RCA) television plant and General Electric's refrigerator factory. Additional business developed unexpectedly after a washout closed CSX's ex-Monon line north of Bloomington following abandonment of its line to the south. Indiana Rail Road filled the gap by adding a Bloomington-Sullivan train to deliver traffic to CSX, former Chicago and Eastern Illinois Railroad, which connects Chicago and Evansville. Indiana Rail Road also operated a dinner train for a time and hosts occasional excursions between Indianapolis and Bloomington. Some continue to the spectacular Tulip Trestle, highest in the state.[91]

CSX purchased a controlling interest in Indiana Rail Road in 1995, but it will remain a separate operation. Headquarters is in Indianapolis.[92]

Indiana Southern

The longest short line operating entirely within the state, Indiana Southern Railroad connects Indianapolis and Evansville over a 175-mile former Conrail (ex-NYC, Pennsylvania and Penn Central) line. It is essentially a coal carrier.

RailTex Service Company, which operates more than 25 short lines in the United States, Canada, and Mexico, purchased the road over which it began service on April 11, 1992. Coal accounts for 95% of the 45,000 cars annually and moves both inbound and outbound, largely between on-line mines and power plants. Most traffic is in unit trains. Other shipments consist of plastics, steel, and brick inbound and grain outbound. IS also hauls expanded shale, fertilizer, aluminum, and lumber.

The road serves IPALCO's Petersburg Generating Station and the H. T. Pritchard Station near Martinsville, as well as the Perry-K Station in Indianapolis through a connection. Mines served are Peabody's Lynnville, the state's only 3,000,000-ton producer (1994), in Warrick County; and others in Greene, Knox, and Daviess counties.

A heavily built line, rails range from 105 to 132 lbs. per yard, including 55 miles, or nearly one-third of the mileage, in continuous welded rail. Headquarters is at Petersburg, where three of the five crews are based. Others operate from Worthington and Spencer.

IS abandoned 18 miles between Worthington and Elnora, including its White River bridge, in 1994. It replaced this with trackage rights over the Soo Line (ex–Milwaukee Road) from Elnora to Beehunter, where it joins its own branch to Worthington.[93]

Indiana Southern had been a Pennsylvania Railroad line north of Worthington and New York Central to the South. Penn Central (later Conrail) combined them into a through Indianapolis-Evansville route after abandoning major segments of both, although it retained 12 miles of ex-Pennsylvania southwest of Worthington to serve a coal mine. It also operates a six-mile former NYC branch to Lynnville to serve the state's most productive mine.[94]

Louisville and Indiana

Once a high-traffic Pennsylvania Railroad line, the Louisville and Indiana Railroad operates 111 miles between Louisville and Indianapolis plus several short switching branches. It began service on March 12, 1994. Anacostia and Pacific Company, which also operates the Chicago, SouthShore and South Bend freight service, is the owner. In addition to Indianapolis and Louisville metropolitan areas, the road serves industries in such cities as Seymour, Columbus, and Franklin. It crosses the Ohio River on the former Pennsylvania Railroad bridge, which it also purchased.

Most traffic is inbound or connecting, primarily plastics, steel, and chemicals. Auto parts, scrap metal, and grain, which may move in unit trains, are shipped out. Approximately 21,000 cars move annually. Largest customer is the Consolidated Grain and Barge Company, which operates the Clark Maritime Centre at Jeffersonville.

Trains run on heavy 130-lb. rail and are drawn by a fleet of ten locomotives. Headquarters is in Jeffersonville and operating terminals are there and at Columbus.[95]

Madison

The Madison Railroad operates the remaining segment of Indiana's first rail line, the Madison and Indianapolis Railroad, which dates to 1836 and reached Indianapolis in 1847. The present road extends 25.8 miles from Madison to North Vernon.[96]

Conrail, at its formation in 1976, dropped the line. The state then named a designated operator who managed it as the Madison Railway during 1977–78, when the city of Madison established a port authority to continue service. Original plan was to build an Ohio River mini-port to handle grain coming from the interior. However, this did not materialize so the road continues its historic function of serving local industries. Most activity, however, is switching service among North Vernon industries and CSX (ex-B&O). Line hauls are predominantly inbound polyethylene. In 1996, the road acquired land and trackage in the deactivated Jefferson Proving Ground, which would be available for an industrial park.[97]

The road climbs the country's steepest standard-gauge grade, 5.89%, as it leaves Madison. As local industry left the river bottoms for the upland behind the city, the incline was removed from service, but in 1992 it was rebuilt to accommodate heavy equipment being moved to a power plant at the foot of the hill. Although upgraded during World War II to serve the Jefferson Proving Ground, the line still uses rail ranging from 70 to 100 lbs. It moves about 500 cars a year. Headquartered in Madison, the road was the oldest in the Pennsylvania system west of Harrisburg, Pennsylvania.[98]

MG

A new line which began service in 1985, MG Rail serves the Clark Maritime Centre at Jeffersonville with 8.5 miles of track leased from the state of Indiana. It connects at Watson with CSX (ex-B&O) and Louisville and Indiana (ex-Conrail). The road moves annually about 4,000 cars. Grain products, grain, steel, and fertilizer provide the principal traffic, which is mostly inbound destined for Ohio River barges. Rail weighs 105 lbs. per yard.

Consolidated Grain and Barge Company became the operators in February 1991, succeeding Merchants Grain Company. Headquarters is in Covington, Louisiana.[99]

Owensville Terminal

The Owensville Terminal Company began service in June 1996 as successor to the former Poseyville and Owensville Railroad, which Indiana Hi-Rail had operated for its owner, Merchants Management Corporation of St. Louis. The line is part of RailAmerica, a short line conglomerate, which acquired it through bankruptcy proceedings. It moves agricultural products on an 11-mile line that originally had been part of the C&EI's Mt. Vernon branch.[100]

Poseyville and Owensville

The 11-mile Poseyville and Owensville Railroad, now Owensville Terminal, connected with a former Indiana Hi-Rail (ex–Illinois Central Gulf) line at Poseyville. It carried grain, some in unit trains, outbound and fertilizer inbound. Hi-Rail operated the line for its owner, Merchants Management Corporation of St. Louis, until July 22, 1996, when RailAmerica acquired it for operation as Owensville Terminal. Hi-Rail had begun service in May 1987. The road originally was part of the C&EI's Mt. Vernon branch. Rail is a light 90 to 100 lbs.[101]

Southwind Shortline

Beginning service in 1992, the Southwind Shortline Railroad serves the state's Southwind Maritime Centre near Mt. Vernon and connects it with CSX, formerly the Louisville and Nashville Railroad's Evansville–St. Louis line. The Indiana Port Commission owns the 6.2 miles of track and leases it to an operator. Traffic is predominantly inbound coal in unit trains, grain, and fertilizer, supplemented by outbound grain. The maze of sidings, loops, and storage tracks serve coal, grain, mineral pigment, and fertilizer shippers.[102]

Whitewater Valley

The Whitewater Valley Railroad is a nonprofit volunteer organization providing a variety of passenger excursions and limited freight service on 19 miles of track between Connersville and Metamora, connecting with Indiana Hi-Rail in Connersville. The line was part of the New York Central White-

water branch from Valley Junction, Ohio, through Connersville to Beesons. Passenger excursions began in the summer of 1974 over 24 miles of line from Connersville through Metamora to Brookville, leased from Penn Central. Service was cut back 6.3 miles the following year to a point two miles south of Metamora, and the remainder of the line to Brookville was abandoned by Penn Central.

On April 10, 1984, the Whitewater Valley purchased from Penn Central the remaining 17.9 miles, which it had been leasing. In February 1990 an additional 1.1 miles of track through Connersville were purchased from Indiana Hi-Rail.

A New York Central train reflects a transportation evolution as it pauses alongside a Whitewater Canal lock in Metamora. The branch line was the first in Indiana to supplant a canal. Whitewater Valley Tourist Railroad is the present owner. *Photo by Richard S. Simons*

++++++++++++++++++ II ++++++++++++++++

Belt Lines and Terminal Railroads

BELT AND TERMINAL RAILROADS served several distinct though often overlapping purposes, which included connecting different railroads, providing terminal facilities for them, and providing access to industries. The oldest example, the original Union Depot in Indianapolis, was a common terminal facility to be used by six railroads. Others, like the later Belt Railroad of Indianapolis, served both to connect railroads entering the city and to provide access to new commercial areas, specifically the Union Stockyards southwest of downtown on Kentucky Avenue. In the Hammond–East Chicago area, several roads served the function of terminal facilities for one or more railroads, while facilitating the interchange process. In Jeffersonville and New Albany, companies provided bridge facilities across the Ohio as well as access to them for one or more roads. Other belts served primarily for industrial access, being built either by a larger railroad to open up promising tracts of land, or by an industry to ensure competitive access to more than one railroad. With railroad restructuring, most belt railroads have been absorbed into the parent corporations.

CALUMET REGION

Baltimore and Ohio Chicago Terminal

One of three major Chicago-area switching roads to enter Indiana, the Baltimore and Ohio Chicago Terminal Railroad serves Hammond, Whiting, East Chicago, and Gary. In addition to serving the former parent Baltimore and Ohio Railroad and its on-line industry, it does intermediate switching between nonaffiliated road haul carriers.[1]

Its roots go back to the LaSalle and Chicago Railroad of 1867 and its successor, Chicago and Great Western Railroad (not the later Chicago Great Western), which had built a short terminal road in Chicago by 1885. Henry Villard, who had built the Northern Pacific Railway, acquired control in 1890, and his interests later added the Chicago and Calumet Terminal Railroad, which built a 29-mile connection between the Baltimore and Ohio Railroad at Whiting and the Atchison, Topeka and Santa Fe Railway at McCook, Illinois.[2]

Villard lost control in the Panic of 1893, and the road emerged as the Chicago Terminal Transfer Railroad. It acquired the Chicago and Calumet Terminal in 1898, and in 1910, following a bankruptcy, it was reorganized as the Baltimore and Ohio Chicago Terminal Railroad, which filled the B&O's need for a Chicago switching road.[3]

The railroad operates 78.2 miles of road, of which 18.6 miles are in Indiana. Extending in a large arc around the south and west sides of Chicago, the B&OCT interchanges traffic with all companies entering the city. The main line originally extended from Pine Junction in Gary to Chicago's Grand Central Station and provided the B&O's passenger route.[4]

Chicago, Hammond and Western

Chartered on April 21, 1896, the Chicago, Hammond and Western Railroad projected a 39-mile line from Whiting through Hammond to a connection with the Chicago, Milwaukee and St. Paul Railway in DuPage County, Illinois. George H. Hammond, who revolutionized the meat packing industry in 1869 when he pioneered the use of refrigerator cars, was a backer.

After Hammond's death in 1886, an English syndicate acquired the road along with the 14-mile Hammond and Blue Island Railroad. From Blue Island, Illinois, the CH&W in 1896 acquired trackage rights over the Chicago and Calumet Terminal Railroad to McCook, Illinois, and in return gave the

C&CT trackage rights over its own line to Franklin Park, Illinois. On January 1, 1898, the Chicago Junction Railway acquired the CH&W and it, in turn, was sold to the New York Central in 1922. It is now part of the Indiana Harbor Belt Railroad, a Conrail-controlled line.[5]

Chicago Junction

The Chicago Junction Railway was a switching road going back to the late nineteenth century, which served industries in Hammond, Whiting, and East Chicago. It also operated extensive trackage in Chicago's Union Stock Yards area. The road became part of the Chicago River and Indiana Railroad, which, like the CJ, was under New York Central control.[6]

Chicago Short Line

The Chicago Short Line Railway operates a switching and terminal road that serves industries in Indiana Harbor and at South Chicago and South Deering, Illinois. Operating 29 miles, of which six are in Indiana on trackage rights, it interchanges directly or indirectly with all railroads in the Chicago Switching District. Operations began in 1903. LTV Steel Company is the owner.[7]

East Chicago Belt

The East Chicago Belt Railroad was a switching road built in 1896 from the Chicago, Hammond and Western at the Illinois state line to a chemical plant in East Chicago, five miles away. Both came under control of the Chicago Junction Railway, which, in turn, was controlled by the New York Central. In 1907 the ECB's name was changed to Indiana Harbor Belt.[8]

Elgin, Joliet and Eastern

The Elgin, Joliet and Eastern Railroad describes a 130-mile arc around Chicago, from Waukegan, on the lake shore north of Chicago, to Joliet, Illinois, and then east as far as Porter, Indiana, plus branches from Griffith to Gary, Hammond, and Whiting, Indiana, and South Chicago, Illinois. A subsidiary of U.S. Steel from 1901 to 1988, the EJ&E serves both as a switching road and as the outermost of several belt lines around Chicago congestion. Connecting with every line-haul steam railroad serv-

ing Chicago, the line advertises itself as the "Chicago Outer Belt Line." Reflecting its concentration on freight service, the line operated no regular passenger trains after 1907.[9]

Separate EJ&E Railway Companies of Indiana and Illinois were formed in 1887, with backing by J. P. Morgan, to take over and extend an earlier line near a Joliet, Illinois, steel plant. Building east from the state line, the EJ&E of Indiana reached Griffith, Hobart, and McCool by late 1888 and was formally merged into the Illinois company on December 4, 1888. In 1893 it was extended from McCool to a connection with the Lake Shore and Michigan Southern in Porter.[10]

In 1897 the EJ&E purchased the Western Indiana Railroad, which operated one mile of track in Hammond, and extended it to East Chicago and Whiting, linked to its parent by trackage rights over the Monon. In 1898, as a result of a Morgan-backed merger, the EJ&E found itself part of a new Federal Steel Company, headed by Judge Elbert Gary. Also under Federal Steel was the Chicago, Lake Shore and Eastern Railway, completed April 1, 1896, between the state line and the LS&MS and Baltimore and Ohio at Clarke Junction, Indiana, serving a major steel plant in Chicago. These pieces were tied together when a new EJ&E subsidiary, the Griffith and Northern, built a line from Griffith north to Clarke Junction.

In 1901 Morgan merged several steel companies, creating United States Steel. Under Judge Gary's direction, the new company proceeded to lay out a steel mill at the new city of Gary, and the CLS&E served the site with a short extension in 1907 east from Clarke Junction, and the large Kirk Yard in 1908. In 1910 the full belt extended 130 miles from Waukegan, Illinois, to Porter, Indiana. Branches included Illinois state line–Whiting 7.1 miles; Griffith–Clarke Junction 7.5 miles; Cavanaugh-Shearson, Indiana 2.6 miles. Leased lines include South Chicago, Illinois–B&O Junction, Indiana 10.7 miles; Cavanaugh–Kirk Yard Junction 2.7 miles; Kirk Yard Junction–Gary 1.9 miles.[11]

The CLS&E, though operated by the EJ&E, remained separate on paper until December 30, 1938.[12] The line between Shearson and State Line tower in Hammond was replaced with Indiana Harbor Belt trackage rights in the 1930s. With its role as a belt line diminishing, the EJ&E abandoned 20 miles from Griffith to Porter in 1984, and short pieces in Hammond in 1987 and 1991. The EJ&E remains one of only two nineteenth-century railroads still operating in Indiana under its original name.[13]

Indiana Harbor Belt

Indiana Harbor Belt Railroad ranks as the nation's largest belt line carrier in track miles, number of locomotives, and revenue.[14]

The IHB originated in the 1890s with the Hammond and Blue Island Railroad, a 14-mile line between Whiting and Hammond and Blue Island, Illinois. The H&BI linked the new Standard Oil refinery in Whiting with the Michigan Central in Hammond and the Chicago, Rock Island and Pacific Railroad at Blue Island. The H&BI was soon acquired by the Chicago, Hammond and Western, chartered April 21, 1896, with backing from the Michigan Central, the Lake Shore and Michigan Southern, and G. H. Hammond and Company, the Hammond meat packing firm. The little H&BI became part of the CH&W's larger scheme to build a belt line around the southern and western sides of Chicago. With trackage rights and new construction, the CH&W was complete from Whiting to Franklin Park, Illinois, by 1897, creating a 40-mile arc around Chicago and connecting with all the western roads entering the city.

Also in 1896 the MC and LS&MS financed a smaller project, the East Chicago Belt, to build five miles from a CH&W connection at the state line to a chemical plant in Grasselli (East Chicago). In 1898 the CH&W and the ECB both came under control of the Chicago Junction Railway, an existing line with trackage primarily in the Stock Yards area on Chicago's southwest side. Chicago Junction's president was New York Central president Chauncey Depew, so the line remained under control of New York Central interests.

On June 29, 1907, the ECB's name was changed to Indiana Harbor Belt, and the new IHB purchased the CJ's interest in the CH&W. The NYC system reserved trackage rights over the entire IHB. The Central also leased to IHB the line of its subsidiary Chicago, Indiana and Southern between the lake front at Indiana Harbor and the Little Calumet River, crossing the former ECB at Grasselli. With trackage rights over lakefront lines acquired from the EJ&E, this opened up the new steel industry to the IHB. In 1913 the IHB acquired trackage rights over the MC from Calumet City, Illinois, to Gibson, Indiana. Gibson, where the MC crossed the CI&S, had shops, roundhouse, and a huge hump yard

along the east-west MC line. IHB trackage rights and new construction also reached 14 miles east from Gibson to serve Gary industries. Gibson yard became a major Chicago freight yard for the NYC. In 1924 one of Gibson's two humps received the world's first mechanical retarder system.[15] The air-actuated car retarders did away with brakemen manually controlling each car, reduced injuries and damage from rough coupling, and became the industry standard. This original installation now resides at the Smithsonian Institution in Washington.[16]

In 1911 two of the IHB's western connections—the Milwaukee Road and the Chicago and Northwestern—each acquired a major interest in the IHB, although operations and motive power remained closely tied to those of the NYC.[17] The IHB's original purpose was to gather, sort, and distribute the cars moving between its connecting railroads, while also keeping cars out of the congested center of Chicago. Changes in railroading have decreased this function as railroads now "pre-block" their trains, often hundreds of miles from the interchange point, and deliver solid trains directly to their connections. As a result, the IHB now serves more as a common-usage facility, with trains of many lines operating over it with their own locomotives. Run-through trains travel two or more different railroads, often with combinations of motive power from all participants.[18] Because of decreased need for switching, Gibson Yard, the former hub of the system, was shut down in 1982 but is operating again as a flat switching yard for automobile shipments.[19]

SOUTH BEND AREA

Chicago and South Bend

The Chicago and South Bend Railroad was a .9-mile switching line that opened on February 1, 1892, to serve the Studebaker Brothers Manufacturing Company in South Bend. It connected with the LS&MS (now Conrail) and other roads and continued in business until 1915.[20]

Indiana Northern

A two-mile connecting road at South Bend, the Indiana Northern Railway performed switching duties beginning in 1893. It served the nationally known Oliver Chilled Plow Company and became part of the New Jersey, Indiana and Illinois Railroad, which the Singer Manufacturing Company owned. The Wabash Railway acquired the NJI&I in 1926 but the Indiana Northern continued as a separate corporation until November 1959.[21]

FORT WAYNE AREA

Fort Wayne Union

Incorporated on October 11, 1922, and placed in operation on June 1, 1925, the Fort Wayne Union Railway was a 2.7-mile switching road near the east edge of Fort Wayne. It served an industrial complex that originally included Phelps-Dodge Copper Company and International Harvester.[22] Fort Wayne's four trunk railroads, Nickel Plate, Wabash, New York Central, and Pennsylvania, initially owned equal shares and used the road jointly for switching. After mergers in the 1960s reduced the four owners to two, the Norfolk and Western and Penn Central became its owners. In May 1989 the road became part of Norfolk and Western, later Norfolk Southern.[23]

Lake Erie and Fort Wayne

Organized on March 29, 1904, by the Fort Wayne Rolling Mill Company, the two-mile Lake Erie and Fort Wayne Railroad connected the mill with the Wabash Railroad at Hugo, a junction of the Lake Erie and Western (later Nickel Plate, Norfolk and Western, and Norfolk Southern) and the Wabash (also later N&W and NS). Located on Fort Wayne's west side, it paralleled the LE&W and gave the Wabash access to the mill, which successively became Joslyn Stainless Steels and Slater Steels Corporation.[24]

The Wabash acquired control in April 1929 and operated the road until September 1, 1966. By this time N&W had acquired both the Wabash and Nickel Plate, thus making the LE&FW redundant. The company was dissolved in 1982 and the road was later dismantled.[25]

CENTRAL INDIANA

Kokomo Belt

The Kokomo Belt Railroad, like similar roads in Elwood, Anderson, and Muncie, was built to serve industries attracted by central Indiana's natural gas boom, which began in the late 1880s. It was incorporated on November 22, 1888, began operation in 1889, and was acquired by the Chicago, St. Louis and Pittsburgh Railroad, a Pennsylvania system component, on January 27, 1890. The Lake Erie and Western Railroad, subsequently Nickel Plate, N&W, and NS, purchased a half-interest on July 18, 1902.[26]

The line connected the sprawling Continental Steel Corporation mill and other industries on the south side with two of Kokomo's three trunk lines and is now owned by the Central Railroad of Indianapolis.[27]

Lafayette Union

The Belt Railway Land and Improvement Company built a five-mile line on the east side of Lafayette to serve industries along what is now the U.S. 52 bypass. The group eventually included National Homes Corporation, Aluminum Company of America (ALCOA), Rostone Corporation, and Anheuser-Busch. Wabash National Corporation, builder of innovative RoadRailer trailers since 1991, now occupies the National Homes plant.[28]

Lafayette Union began operation on December 1, 1911, and was leased to the Wabash Railway, with which it connected, in 1924. The trackage is now part of Norfolk Southern, whose predecessor, Norfolk and Western Railway, acquired the Wabash in 1964.[29]

Elwood, Anderson and Lapel

The American Sheet and Tin Plate Company, which opened in Elwood in 1892 and was said to have been the country's largest tin plate producer, controlled the Elwood, Anderson and Lapel Railroad. This switching line was chartered on January 12, 1898, to connect the tin plate mill, which was located on the Pittsburgh, Cincinnati, Chicago and St. Louis Railway (Panhandle, a Pennsylvania Railroad component) with the Lake Erie and Western (subsequently the Nickel Plate, N&W, and NS) in Elwood. The line was 1.1 miles long and extended north from L Street between 25th and 27th Streets. The Nickel Plate purchased the road and later abandoned it in 1929.[30]

The "Lapel" in the title was spelled "Lapelle" in some early records, which evidently was a misspelling of the Madison County town of Lapel.

A few short lines and switching roads, like the recently abandoned Muncie and Western, operated their own car fleets. The 5-mile road, which belonged to the Ball Brothers Glass Manufacturing Company, operated 185 cars at its peak in 1953.   *Ball Corporation*

Anderson Belt

Central Indiana's natural gas boom of the 1890s abruptly converted many agricultural communities into industrialized cities. Anderson was among them. To serve these industries, the Anderson Belt Railway was opened in 1892 to connect the Anderson Wire Nail Works and other industries with the city's trunk lines.[31]

On January 1, 1917, its parent company, the Pennsylvania Railroad, merged it into the new Pittsburgh, Cincinnati, Chicago and St. Louis Railway and three other controlled lines to form the Pittsburgh, Cincinnati, Chicago and St. Louis Railroad.[32]

The Belt left the Pennsylvania Railroad (PCC&StL) near 18th Street and Columbus Avenue, went south to 25th Street, west to near Martindale Avenue, and north to a Big Four (New York Central) connection and to industries beyond. It was 2.2 miles long and was later abandoned.[33]

Muncie and Western

In 1888 Ball Brothers Glass Manufacturing Company relocated in Muncie after fire destroyed its Buffalo plant, and by 1902 was large enough to support its own railroad. This was the 4.9-mile Muncie and Western Railroad, a terminal line connecting with the city's trunk railroads.[34]

Although it leased motive power from the Muncie Belt Railway until 1926, it later owned seven locomotives that shuttled cars through the sprawling plant. The M&W initially leased boxcars from the Mather Humane Stock Transportation Company, using 185 cars at its peak in 1953, but it later acquired its own fleet. The cars were rolling billboards for the company. They were patented Mather models painted bright yellow with an oversize Ball jar emblazoned on the doors.[35] The road was busiest during the 1930s and 1940s and in 1946 moved a record 23,879 cars. It set separate one-day records of shipping 132 cars of finished products and receiving 200 cars of silica sand, zinc lids, rubber seals, and other materials.[36]

But the M&W lost its purpose in 1962 when the factory discontinued production. The road remained, although with decreasing trackage, to move plastic pellets into a plant that occupied a former Ball building, but in 1994 it was abandoned.[37]

Muncie Belt

The Muncie Belt Railway was built in the mid–1890s closely paralleling an existing Lake Erie and Western spur to the Ball Company Glass works and other new industries. The Belt's officers were executives from those industries. The Belt connected with the Big Four just west of its White River bridge and extended south and west to the LE&W line on Muncie's south side.[38]

In 1906 the Muncie Belt had 3.2 miles of line and two locomotives.[39] Between 1902 and 1911, the Muncie Belt took over parts of the former LE&W track, while parts of former Belt tracks became the Muncie and Western (1902). The Belt's first switch engine, built in 1895, was identical to a group built for the Big Four, and other engines were later bought or leased from the Big Four.[40]

INDIANAPOLIS AREA

Central of Indianapolis

Organized on December 5, 1899, the Central Railroad of Indianapolis was leased on February 7, 1917, to the Big Four (NYC), which continued to operate it at least into the mid–1950s. It consisted of 1.9 miles of yards and sidings concentrated in three blocks of Capitol Avenue between South and Norwood Streets.[41] The corporate name is now used by an unrelated north central Indiana short line that began operations in 1989.[42]

Indianapolis Union

The Indianapolis Union Railway operated two physically separate properties, including the Indianapolis Union Depot and its 1.7 miles of approaching line and the 14.2-mile Belt Railroad encircling three sides of the city. The Union Depot, the first of its kind in the nation, opened in 1853, while the Belt originated in 1876.

On August 15, 1849, a joint meeting of committees from the Madison, Peru, and Bellefontaine roads met and recommended construction of a "Union" railroad to connect their respective roads.[43] By the end of 1849 land had been purchased for the depot. Begun in 1850 and completed by 1853, the depot was a 120 x 420-foot structure, through which passed five tracks, used by the Madison, Terre Haute, Lawrenceburg, Central, Peru, and Bellefontaine roads. The depot attracted business and industry to the city's near south side, and also created a band of tracks blocking quality residential growth farther to the south. In 1866 the building was widened to 200 feet and an eating house added.[44]

In 1887 the original Union Depot was torn down, to be replaced by a majestic Romanesque "head house" and an arched iron train shed. By the turn of the century 200 trains steamed through Union Station daily and blocked grade crossings near the station. To reduce traffic conflicts, plans were made for an elevated and grade separated train shed. In 1913 construction began on the new train shed and its complex of elevated approach tracks. The first train to use the raised platforms arrived at the station in 1918, but completion of the train shed roof was delayed until 1922 because of material shortages during World War I. The new train shed was grafted on to the 1888 head house with its Grand Hall, and was built on the site of the two previous train sheds.

As early as 1849, in the midst of public debate preceding the Union Depot project, a proposal was advanced for a common track encircling Indianapolis on North, South, East, and West Streets:

the Depots could be located on or near these streets, and the cars from any road could traverse them at pleasure, thereby virtually making the depot for each road a common depot, as the business man would deliver and receive his goods at the depot nearest his house.[45]

With increasing traffic after the Civil War, the Union tracks were congested by transfer freight cars, and the idea of a belt line, permitting transfer of freight cars among connecting roads, was broached again in 1870. On June 28, 1873, the Indianapolis Belt Railway was incorporated to build a 12-mile road encircling the city from north Indianapolis in the northwest to Brightwood in the northeast, connecting with most of the roads entering the city. The road also would provide service to a proposed Union Stock Yard on the southwest side. After some false starts the line was reincorporated on August 29, 1876, as the Union Railroad Transfer and Stock Yard Company. Stimulated in part by high unemployment and threats of bread riots in the city following the Panic of 1873, the city pledged $500,000 of credit, and the project was completed as planned, followed by the addition in 1883 of two more miles from Brightwood to the LE&W tracks under a second corporation. Both Belt companies (excepting the stock yards) were leased on October 17, 1882, to the Indianapolis Union Railway for 999 years.

Incorporated on November 19, 1872, the Indianapolis Union Railway Company owned the original Union Depot and, after 1882, leased the Belt tracks. It had been formed by five railroads, three of which became parts of the Pennsylvania and two of the New York Central; thus 60% of the company was owned by the Pennsylvania and 40% by the New York Central. Eight other railroads were admitted as tenants, and owners and managers alike were represented on a Board of Managers established in 1883.[46] Originally member railroads were allowed to make interchanges via the belt line using their own power, but from 1891 the Indianapolis Union required the use of its own locomotives, adding costs for the member roads.[47] By the 1950s the Indianapolis Union was still owned 3/5 by the Pennsylvania and 2/5 by the New York Central, a fact which became moot with the Penn Central merger in 1968. The IUR still remains in service, now a part of Conrail.

White River

The meat packing firm of Kingan and Company built a half-mile road, the White River Railway Company, to serve its plant along White River in downtown Indianapolis. The city authorized Kingan to lay tracks in Senate Avenue on August 25, 1873.

Although described as little more than a switch, the railroad was operated as a separate company.[48] Originally the Kingan Railroad, .42-miles long, the name was changed to White River Valley in 1901 and later to White River.[49]

SOUTHERN INDIANA

Bedford Belt

Chartered on March 30, 1892, and opened on May 1, 1893, the Bedford Belt Railway extended 4.2 miles from limestone quarries northwest of Oolitic to a junction with the Southern Indiana Railway (now Soo Line) at Bedford. The Bedford Stone Quarries Company built the line in an effort to break the Monon Railway's grip on stone shipment rates and the Monon countered with litigation, which proved unsuccessful.[50]

John R. Walsh, a Chicago banker, acquired the Belt line after the parent company defaulted on a loan to finance its construction. He immediately moved to extend the Belt to the Evansville and Richmond Railroad, which he acquired after it was reorganized as the Southern Indiana in 1897. The additional traffic, which came from three quarries and ten mills, helped make the Evansville and Richmond the leading Bedford stone hauler by 1894.[51]

The Southern Indiana leased the Bedford Belt in June 1898. After Walsh's empire collapsed suddenly in 1905, the SI was reorganized as the Chicago, Terre Haute and Southeastern in 1910, was leased to the Milwaukee Road, which purchased it in 1921, and was acquired by the Soo Line in 1986.[52] The Milwaukee abandoned the Belt line trackage in 1984.[53]

FALLS CITIES AREA

Louisville and Jeffersonville

Formed under deed of consolidation dated April 25, 1890, under the name of Louisville and Jeffersonville Bridge Company—Kentucky and Indiana. This project was undertaken jointly by the Big Four and by Collis P. Huntington of the C&O, with which the Big Four had an alliance at the time. By 1891 the Big Four had assembled a north-south line from Benton Harbor, on Lake Michigan, to North Vernon, from which it acquired trackage rights to Jeffersonville over the O&M. The bridge project established a through route with the C&O through

Indianapolis Union Railway linked all the railroads entering Indianapolis. IU Ry 32, a heavy 0–8–0 switcher built in 1936, is on call at the Monon yards at 27th Street.   *Jay Williams collection*

Louisville, although a better route actually existed via Cincinnati.

Built in 1893 and rebuilt in 1929, it was the third railroad bridge completed from Louisville to Indiana and was shortly upstream of the Panhandle bridge. The Big Four owned two-thirds of the stock in the L&J bridge and the C&O owned one-third until 1927, when the Big Four purchased the C&O's interest.[54] The name was changed to Louisville and Jeffersonville Bridge and Railroad Company by amendment of charter on April 2, 1917. The company owned 2.7 miles of first main track from the bridge to a yard on the north edge of Jeffersonville and owned some terminal track in Louisville.[55] The Interstate Public Service Company electric interurban between Louisville and Indianapolis also used the bridge.

With the mergers and abandonments of the 1970s, Conrail consolidated traffic on the former

Panhandle bridge. The approaches to the the Big Four Louisville bridge were demolished but as of 1996 the bridge remains as a challenge for creative reuse.

Louisville

The Louisville Bridge Company was originally chartered in 1856, but no action was taken until after the Civil War, when the company was reorganized with the Jeffersonville, Madison and Indianapolis and the Louisville and Nashville Railroads as principal stockholders. Work began in 1867 and the bridge opened for traffic on February 24, 1870. In 1871[56] the Pittsburg, Cincinnati and St. Louis Railway (Pennsylvania Company) leased the JM&I, including interest in the bridge. As of 1873 the Pennsylvania Railroad owned 3,759 shares of stock in the Louisville Bridge Company, valued at $376,900.[57]

Elgin, Joliet and Eastern SD9 road-switcher 602 (built 1957), and caboose work in the smoky environment of the Gary steel mills. *Jay Williams collection*

In 1872 the two stockholder companies entered into an agreement with the Ohio and Mississippi, permitting its trains to use the bridge.[58] This continued until 1887 when the K&I bridge and the New Albany extension were completed, and the O&M shifted to that bridge.[59] In 1882 the Monon also contracted to use the bridge structure and tracks on the Kentucky side, and contracted with the Pennsylvania Railroad for five miles of trackage rights from New Albany to the Louisville bridge.[60] The Monon continued to use the bridge (by now the Louisville Bridge and Depot Company) until 1900, when the Kentucky and Indiana Bridge Company was reorganized and the Monon shifted to that bridge.[61]

Kentucky and Indiana Terminal

In 1886 the Kentucky and Indiana Terminal Railroad Company built a bridge over the Ohio from New Albany to Louisville. The O&M, which had been using an 1870 bridge from Jeffersonville into Louisville, built an eight-mile extension from Watson to New Albany to reach the K&IT bridge, in which the O&M had a financial interest.[62] The Louisville Southern, from Louisville to the CNO&TP, connected with the Kentucky and Indiana Bridge Company.[63]

The Kentucky and Indiana Bridge Company was reorganized in 1900 as the Kentucky and Indiana Bridge and Railroad Company. The reorganized line included the bridge, a ferry company, an electric suburban line, and the Louisville Belt Line. Stock in the new company was held one-third each by the B&O, the Southern, and the Monon. The Monon, which had been entering Louisville since 1882 over the Louisville Bridge and Depot Company via Pennsylvania rights to Jeffersonville, shifted to the K&I bridge.[64] Mileage in Indiana totaled .35.[65] In 1910 the company name was changed to the Kentucky and Indiana Terminal Railroad.[66] The original series of spindly trusses was replaced in 1911–1912 with heavier doubletrack trusses, providing longer spans and clearer river navigation.[67]

Motive power of the Monon, B&O, and Southern used the K&IT Youngtown Yard in Louisville as their terminal, along with the K&IT's own power.[68]

New Albany Belt and Terminal

The New Albany Belt and Terminal Railroad was chartered on April 5, 1890, and opened in 1891. It ran for two miles and was an extension of the Louisville, Evansville and St. Louis Consolidated Railroad.[69]

EVANSVILLE AREA

Evansville Belt

The 4.5-mile Evansville Belt Railway was incorporated on May 9, 1881, and was built by the Evansville and Terre Haute Railroad.[70] It ran north one mile from a junction with the Louisville and Nashville Railroad. In 1911 the Belt was consolidated with the C&EI, which was the successor to the E&TH.[71]

Henderson Bridge

Although a charter had been issued to the L&N-controlled Henderson Bridge Company on February 9, 1872, construction of an Ohio River span in the Evansville area did not begin until 1881. The first train crossed on July 13, 1885.[72]

The L&N found the bridge obsolete for modern traffic by 1931 and on December 31, 1932, opened a replacement 12,123 feet long, including approaches.[73]

L. B. Foster Co. crews dismantle the doubletrack Erie Lackawanna main line near Huntington. Such scenes were common during the 1970s and 1980s when more than 1,600 miles were abandoned.   *Photo by L. B. Foster Co.—Richard S. Simons collection*

╪╪╪╪╪╪╪╪╪╪╪╪╪╪ **12** ╪╪╪╪╪╪╪╪╪╪╪╪╪╪

Major Abandonments

Indiana's Initial Track abandonments closely followed completion in 1847 of the first railroad, which connected Madison and Indianapolis. Although occasional short abandonments took place during the first century, it was the mega-mergers that began in the 1960s that redrew the rail map. Occurring in an era when rails had lost their freight and passenger traffic monopolies, the industry not only found itself with excess capacity but discovered that many lines gradually had become marginal or suddenly had become redundant. This stimulated the abandonment pace, which soon raced ahead furiously. Discontinuances during the 1970s alone totaled 983 miles[1] compared to 825 miles during the entire first century of Indiana railroads.[2] This left a total of 4,503 miles in 1995, compared to the peak of 7,426, which occurred in 1920.[3]

Changing traffic patterns caused the earliest abandonments. Others followed because extractive industries had depleted their resources, a few unproductive branches required trimming, or companies that served little initial need had been dissolved.

First to go was the 26-mile Knightstown and Shelbyville Railroad, completed in 1850 between the two stations of its corporate name. At Shelbyville it connected with the Shelbyville Lateral Branch Railroad, which extended to Edinburg, where it connected with the Madison and Indianapolis. The Jeffersonville Railroad, heading north, purchased it as part of its proposed Indianapolis route after the M&I refused to grant trackage rights north of Columbus. Although intended as a feeder to the M&I, it served no purpose for either road after the M&I and the Jeffersonville reached a trackage rights agreement, and it was abandoned in 1854. The 16-mile SLB, which had been built in 1849, was abandoned in 1855.[4] In northern Indiana, the Chicago and Great Eastern Railway in 1865 dropped 10.4 miles between La Crosse and Valparaiso in favor of a new line it had built between La Crosse and Chicago.[5]

Until the waning days of World War II, the occasional abandonments were mine spurs, primarily in coal fields of Sullivan and nearby counties. However, three entire railroads disappeared in 1917–18: the 52-mile Cincinnati, Bluffton and Chicago Railroad between Huntington and Portland in 1917; and in 1918, the Cincinnati, Findlay and Fort Wayne Railway, 78 miles between Findlay, Ohio, and Fort Wayne, and most of the 70-mile St. Joseph Valley Railway between Elkhart and Columbia, Ohio.[6] No other significant abandonments took place until 1928 when the Central Indiana Railway dropped a total of 53.6 miles at each end of its Muncie-Brazil line.[7] Following this, the Monon abandoned three branches totaling 72.5 miles in 1935 and a cluster of electric interurban lines turned steam railroads disappeared from the Evansville and Warsaw areas during the 1940s and 1951.[8] In addition, the entire 141-mile Chicago, Attica and Southern Railroad was abandoned in the mid–1940s.[9]

Except for short segments of marginal branches, no abandonments took place in the 1960s, but by the 1970s the Penn Central merger of 1968, which united the state's two principal systems, New York Central and the Pennsylvania, abruptly changed the ball game. Suddenly many miles of heavy-duty, high-speed line became redundant. The previous companies had operated separate lines from both Chicago and St. Louis to New York City, between Chicago and both Cincinnati and Louisville, and from Indianapolis to Springfield, Ohio. Usually the Pennsylvania line, or sometimes both lines, were dropped. In addition, most of the New York Central's Fort Wayne–Jackson, Michigan, Anderson-Louisville, and Indianapolis-Peoria routes were abandoned.[10]

Even as its map changed, the railroad business

changed. It steadily became more a wholesale function, taking advantage of economies of scale, than a retail function, which once had depended on less than carload shippers, small country grain elevators, and retail coal yards. In its new world, the industry concentrated on large bulk commodity shippers, unit trains, double-stack containers, and truck trailers on flatcars. Coal shipments to power generating stations saved many a branch from extinction.

Conrail, which succeeded Penn Central, now consists in Indiana primarily of main lines from Chicago and St. Louis to New York City, a bridge route from Goshen to Anderson, and a few minor branches.[11] Conrail's largest single abandonment was the former Erie Lackawanna Railway. Included in Conrail at a late date, it was omitted when the final system was determined. After two short lines unsuccessfully attempted operation, most of the 160 miles in Indiana were abandoned in 1979.[12] By the mid–1980s most Conrail downsizing had taken place.[13]

But as the Conrail pace slackened, CSX abandonments speeded up. A combination in Indiana of Chesapeake and Ohio and Chicago and Eastern Illinois Railways and Baltimore and Ohio, Louisville and Nashville, and Monon railroads, the merged lines controlled so many routes that, obviously, many would have to go.[14]

The C&O, shortest route between Cincinnati and Chicago, dropped most of its line in the 1980s and the B&O abandoned most of its Indianapolis-Decatur, Illinois route in the late 1980s and mid–1990s, as well as most of its busy Louisville branch in 1980. CSX sent this traffic over alternate routes.[15]

But the merger was most cruel to the Monon. Advertising itself as the "Hoosier Line" and reflecting closely the state's character, the road underwent complete dismemberment during the 1980s and early 1990s until little more than disconnected parts of the Chicago-Louisville main line remain. Gone are most of the Indianapolis branch, which traditionally was a heavy passenger carrier, the 45 northernmost miles of the original main line to Michigan City, and the entire French Lick and coal field branches.[16]

Results of the 1964 Wabash–Nickel Plate merger into the Norfolk and Western Railway showed up only in the 1980s when two redundant lines were dropped. Most of the ex-Wabash Chicago-Montpelier, Ohio, line disappeared in the middle 1980s and much of the ex-Nickel Plate St. Louis–Toledo route followed in the 1980s. Some segments were turned over to newly created short lines.[17] The Milwaukee Road, now the Soo Line, dropped major sections between 1961 and 1980.[18]

Although major roads have largely trimmed to their core systems, further consolidations could lead to additional abandonments.

The following chart lists parent companies alphabetically, followed by an entire line abandonment listed by segments in chronological order, the petitioning rail corporation, year, mileage, and end points.

An asterisk indicates estimated mileage in Indiana and a double asterisk indicates that another railroad reactivated all or part of the line. (P) indicates a pending application.

Major Abandonments

Year	Mileage	Railroad	End Points
BALTIMORE & OHIO			
1918	17.5*	Cincinnati, Findlay & Ft Wayne	Ft Wayne–OH State Line
1966	24.0	Cincinnati, Ipls & Western	Brazil Junction–Brazil
1988	23.2	CSX	Hillsdale–Russellville
1989	26.7	CSX	Roachdale–Mitchellville
1990	9.7	CSX	Russellville–Roachdale
1980	28.2	B&O	North Vernon–Nabb
1985	11.9	CSX	Nabb–Charlestown
CHESAPEAKE & OHIO			
1981	29.7	C&O	Hammond–Malden

Major Abandonments (continued)

Year	Mileage	Railroad	End Points
CHESAPEAKE & OHIO (cont.)			
1987	20.2	CSX	Twelve Mile–Santa Fe
1988	38.6	CSX	North Judson–Twelve Mile
1989	71.3	CSX	Marion–Richmond
1988	17.4*	CSX	MI State Line–Wellsboro
CHICAGO & EASTERN ILLINOIS			
1880	10.0*	C&EI	Bismarck Jct., IL–Covington
1888	8.4	C&EI	Covington–Coal Creek
1943	9.7	Chicago, Attica & Southern	IL State Line–Morocco
1943	46.3	CA&S	La Crosse–Percy Junction
1943	23.9	CA&S	Veedersburg–West Melcher
1946	60.4	CA&S	Morocco–Veedersburg
1994	8.5	CSX	Clinton–Universal
1977	12.6	Louisville & Nashville	Terre Haute–Brazil
1982	22.5	L&N	Cynthiana–Mt. Vernon**
CHICAGO, MILWAUKEE, ST PAUL & PACIFIC			
1961	25.7	CMStP&P	Seymour–Westport
1978	37.5	CMStP&P	Bedford–Seymour
1980	23.6	CMStP&P	IL State Line–Fayette
CINCINNATI, BLUFFTON & CHICAGO			
1917	50.2	CB&C	Huntington–Portland
1917	2.0	CB&C	Pennville–Twin Hills
EVANSVILLE & OHIO VALLEY			
1941	28.1	E&OV	Evansville–Posey Station; Rockport–Grandview; Richland Jct.–Richland
1946	13.0	E&OV	Rockport–Posey Station
ELGIN, JOLIET & EASTERN			
1984	20.4	EJ&E	Griffith–Porter
ERIE LACKAWANNA			
1979	159.5	E L	Hammond–OH State Line
EVANSVILLE, SUBURBAN & NEWBURGH			
1941	5.5	ES&N	Evansville Jct.–Newburgh
1948	18.0	ES&N	Evansville–Boonville
FERDINAND			
1991	6.4	Ferdinand & Huntingburg	Ferdinand–Huntingburg
ILLINOIS CENTRAL			
1937	6.0	Illinois Central Gulf	West Lebanon-Hedrick
1976	6.3	Illinois Central Gulf	Stewartsville–New Harmony
1997	11.0*	Owensville Terminal	Poseyville–IL State Line (P)
MONON			
1935	35.9	Chicago, Ipls & Louisville (Chicago & Wabash Valley)	McCoysburg–north of Dinwiddie

MAJOR ABANDONMENTS ■ 207

Year	Mileage	Railroad	End Points
MONON (cont.)			
1935	33.8	CI&L	Avoca–Switz City
1943	4.2	CI&L	Dark Hollow–Avoca
1981	10.0	L&N	Bedford–Dark Hollow
1976	10.0	L&N	Paoli–French Lick
1981	7.8	L&N	Orleans–Paoli
1980	44.9	L&N	Medaryville–Michigan City
1993	22.5	CSX	Bedford–Bloomington
1994	13.1	CSX	Cloverdale–Gosport
1995	10.3	CSX	Gosport–Ellettsville
1997	4.3	CSX	Ellettsville–Hunter's (P)
1984	42.2	L&N	Wallace Jct.–Midland
1985	43.0	Seaboard	Frankfort–Ipls
1992	25.3	CSX	Delphi–Frankfort
1990	4.3	CSX	Hammond–Air Line Jct.
1993	14.2	CSX	Monticello–Delphi
MUNCIE & WESTERN			
1995	3.7	M&W—Entire line	within Muncie
NEW YORK CENTRAL			
1931	13.1	Cleveland, Cincinnati, Chicago & St Louis	Beesons–Hagerstown
1976	23.4	Lake Erie & Ft Wayne	Brookville–Connersville**
1942	19.5*	CCC&StL	Goshen–Niles, MI
1942	11.7*	St Joseph, South Bend & Southern	South Bend–Baroda, MI
1942	10.0	CCC&StL	Martinsville–Trafalgar
1961	6.9	CCC&StL	Trafalgar–Franklin
early '70s	12.5	—	Franklin–Fairland
1960	9.0	New York Central	Shipshewana–MI State Line
1980	17.0	Indiana Interstate	Goshen–Shipshewana
1968	7.3	CCC&StL	Vincennes–St Francisville, IL
1973	16.1	Penn Central	Ft Wayne–Auburn
1973	10.1	PC	Waterloo–Pleasant Lake**
1976	5.5	PC	Auburn Jct.–Waterloo**
1973	23.7	PC	Craig (Greensburg)–North Vernon
1973	27.8	PC	Greensburg–Carthage
1989	21.0	Carthage, Knightstown & Shirley	Carthage–Emporia**
1973	21.9	PC	Craig (Greensburg)–Columbus
1976	12.0	PC	East Gary–Hartsdale
1976	7.2	LE&FW	OH State Line–Lynn
1977	59.7	LE&FW	Lynn–Hunter (Ipls)
1976	22.0	PC	Skelton–Evansville
1976	11.6	PC	Zionsville–Lebanon
1984	2.0	Conrail	Ipls–Zionsville
1985	29.1	CR	Lebanon–Altamont
1981	27.6	PC	E of Riley–Worthington Jct.
1982	28.0	CR	Crawfordsville–Olin
1982	52.0	CR	Olivers (South Bend)–Wheatfield
1984	6.5	CR	Niles, MI–St Mary's College
1994	18.2	Indiana Southern	Worthington–Elnora
1996	57.7	CR	Schneider–Danville, IL**
NEW YORK, CHICAGO & ST LOUIS (NICKEL PLATE)			
1987	39.7	Norfolk & Western	IL State Line–Linden

Year	Mileage	Railroad	End Points

NEW YORK, CHICAGO & ST LOUIS (NICKEL PLATE) (cont.)

Year	Mileage	Railroad	End Points
1988	21.9	Norfolk Southern	Linden–Frankfort
1989	11.0	Indiana Hi–Rail	New Castle–Mays
1990	5.0	IHRC	Mays–Sexton
1997	17*	IHRC	Craigville–OH State Line (P)
1996	51.4	N&W/Central RR of Ipls	Rochester–Kokomo (P)
1997	21.5	N&W/NS	Michigan City–Dillon (P)

PENNSYLVANIA

Year	Mileage	Railroad	End Points
1854	26.0	Knightstown & Shelbyville	Shelbyville–Knightstown
1855	16.0	Shelbyville Lateral Branch	Edinburg–Shelbyville
1864	10.1	Ipls & Madison	Columbus–Edinburg
1865	10.4	Chicago & Great Eastern	La Crosse–Valparaiso
1910	5.8	PCC&StL	Bentonville–Cambridge City
1955	4.5	PCC&StL	Bentonville–Dublin Jct.
1962	12.3	Philadelphia, Baltimore & Washington	Rushville–Bentonville
1972	6.2	Penn Central	Flat Rock–Fenns
1976	22.2	PC	Fenns–North Rushville
1977	8.8	PC	Columbus–Flat Rock
1933	26.0	PCC&StL	Converse–Matthews
1976	13.8	LE&FW	Matthews–Muncie
1954	10.3	PCC&StL	Butler–Auburn
1961	7.8	PB&W	Columbia City–Churubusco
1968	13.7	PB&W	Logansport–Mexico
1973	14.1	PC	Churubusco–Auburn Jct.
1975	17.3	PC	North Manchester–Columbia City
1977	23.0	LE&FW	Mexico–North Manchester
1969	5.0	PC	Guion–Waveland
1972	11.3	PC	Rockville–Guion; Dewey–Otter Crk.
1973	17.0	PC	(Dewey)–Otter Creek–Rockville–(Guion)
1973	7.1	PC	Colfax–Frankfort
1976	34.0	PC	Waveland–Colfax
1973	25.6	PC	Nutwood (South Bend)–Culver
1976	3.0	LE&FW	South Bend–Nutwood
1979	32.7	PC	Culver–Logansport
1976	39.7	LE&FW	North Richmond–Portland
1979	25.4	PC	Kendallville–MI State Line
1979	28.7	PC	Portland–Decatur
1982	21.2	CR	North Ft Wayne–Kendallville**
1976	21.5	LE&FW	Kokomo–Frankton
1993	10.6	CR	Anderson–Honey Creek
1976	16.6	PC	Columbus–North Vernon
1976	15.4	PC	Bicknell–Vincennes
1984	10.5	CR	Sandborn–Bicknell
1973	13.2	PC	Bushrod–Linton Summit
1981	21.3	LE&FW	Cambridge City–Charlottesville
1982	26.5	CR	Charlottesville–Pine (Ipls)
1982	10.1	CR	Centerville–Cambridge City
1982	2.2	CR	OH State Line–Richmond
1992	5.2	CR	Richmond–Centerville
1982	48.8	CR	Crown Point–Winamac
1984	11.9	CR	IL State Line–Crown Point
1984	29.4	CR	Anoka–Sweetser
1993	19.5	CR	Redkey–Union City
1982	28.1	CR	Bridgeport–Greencastle
1984	5.3	CR	Greencastle–Limedale

Year	Mileage	Railroad	End Points
PENNSYLVANIA (cont.)			
1992	32.7	Terre Haute, Brazil & Eastern	Limedale–Terre Haute
1967	8.2	PB&W	Knightsville–Center Point
1916	7.5	Vandalia	N from Saline City
1945	2.0	PCC&StL	Saline City branch
1957	1.0	PB&W	Saline City branch
1993	13.8	CR	Bringhurst–Frankfort
1928	18.4	Central Indiana	Muncie–Anderson
1928	13.5	CI	Ladoga–Waveland Jct.
1928	21.7	CI	Sand Creek–Brazil
1929	11.7	CI	Advance–Ladoga
1943	8.3	CI	Lebanon–Advance
1976	13.8	CI	Westfield–Gadsden
1982	7.5	CR	Gadsden–Lebanon
1982	15.3	CR	Lapel–Westfield
ST JOSEPH VALLEY			
1918	31.6	StJV	Elkhart–Lagrange
1918	22.9	StJV	Orland–Columbia, OH
1920	15.0	Lagrange, Toledo & Eastern	Lagrange–Orland
SYRACUSE & MILFORD			
1923	6.8	Syracuse and Milford	Syracuse–Milford (entire line)
WABASH			
1932	14.8	Wabash	Attica–Covington
1945	4.8	Wabash	Helmer–Stroh
1982	46.4	N&W	Dillon–Clarke Jct. (Gary)
1984	33.5	N&W	Wolcottville–Wakarusa
1988	16.4	Norfolk Southern	Wakarusa–Pine
1991	5.0	Pigeon River	South Milford–Wolcottville
WINONA			
1947	39.6	Winona	Warsaw–Wabash Jct. (Peru)
1951	18.5	Winona	New Paris–Warsaw

SOURCE: Elmer G. Sulzer, *Ghost Railroads of Indiana;* INDOT, Railroad Division.

Case Histories in Railroad Promotion

RAILROADS EXPANDED RAPIDLY during the second half of the nineteenth century for many reasons and to fit varying circumstances. Some originated as short farm-to-market roads to enable agricultural regions to ship their produce out and to funnel manufactured products in. Some were built to move bulky products of extractive industries, such as coal or stone. Some were long-distance lines that passed through Indiana only incidentally as they connected major eastern cities with Chicago or St. Louis.

Unusual circumstances added drama to an already colorful industry and the five lines detailed below illustrate various forces that drove men to place their fortunes on the line to achieve an ideal. They illustrate, also, the absence of economic justification that some ignored, and, in one case, faith in an unproven technology that ultimately crumbled and disappeared. Determined wills and colossal egos were shared characteristics that inspired many promoters.

Legal battles characterized the early industry as companies fought each other toe to toe to monopolize a route or to prevent a competitor's success. The five railroads examined below illustrate the diverse factors that inspired railroad construction and determined their locations. The roads operated in 32 of Indiana's 92 counties.

THE EEL RIVER: LITIGATION UNLIMITED

Railroads, by the nature of their business, are no strangers to litigation. There are damage suits to defend, rate cases to decide, employee injuries to contend with, and problems with competing railroads that must be solved.

But few legal battles lasted as long as the marathon case between the Eel River Railroad and the Wabash, St. Louis and Pacific, which began its long-

running life in 1891 and continued for ten years. Along the way, it bounced through five courts, involved residents of at least three states, and pitted against each other communities that had been friendly neighbors for many years. It was a classic example of ingenious legal maneuvering within the rail industry and creative use of stalling tactics to win the war even while losing the battle.[1]

The Eel River Railroad, at that time the Detroit, Eel River and Illinois, began operation in 1871 over the initial segment of its 93-mile, strictly local line, which connected Logansport with Butler.[2] Although merely a secondary road, an odd succession of circumstances catapulted it into a vital nationally important interstate link. Then, just as dramatically, it fell into oblivion as a branch line to nowhere.

After bondholders had bought the road at foreclosure, they leased it to a Wabash Railroad predecessor in 1879 for 99 years.[3] Why the Wabash wanted the lightly built, backwoods line was a perplexing question—but not for long. Jay Gould, the master manipulator of his day, controlled the Wabash, and he had a plan. It began to unfold at Detroit. Gould's Detroit, Butler and St. Louis Railroad was taking shape, and there was no question about where it was headed. Its corporate name told the entire story.

Detroit and Butler were 115 miles apart and the Eel River would provide a link at Logansport with the Wabash main line, which extended from Toledo to St. Louis. Moreover, east of Detroit the Wabash, from 1898, extended through Ontario to Buffalo,[4] and under an agreement with the West Shore Railroad could send trains to Weehawken, New Jersey, opposite New York City. The route covered nearly 1,200 miles and without the little Eel River road it would have been impossible.[5]

Although the Wabash terminated at Toledo, Gould correctly saw Detroit as the city of the future. He concentrated on building Detroit traffic and within a short time the Eel River's four passenger trains a day grew to 14, plus countless freights. In 1898, the road inaugurated the glamorous Continental Limited, a luxury train of incomparable appointments that carried Pullmans, a diner, and vestibuled coaches. A passenger boarding at St. Louis could ride without change to Weehawken. The Wabash Cannon Ball, famed in song, became its direct successor.[6]

As part of the grand plan, a Peru group built a ten-mile connection to the Eel River at Chili, named it the Peru and Detroit, and leased it in 1890 to the Wabash for 999 years.[7]

Almost immediately the Wabash moved the Eel River shops to Peru, merging them with its own, and, for all practical purposes, abandoned the 22 miles between Logansport and Chili. All through trains now operated over the Peru and Detroit.[8]

This angered the people of Logansport, and they decided to fight. In 1891 Judge D. D. Dykeman, an Eel River stockholder, sued to revoke the charter and place the company in receivership. The Eel River, he charged, had forced its own destruction by leasing itself to the Wabash; only a pretense of service remained.[9]

At this point the lid blew off. Editorial wars raced up and down the Wabash Valley. Cities that had no connection whatever with the dispute jumped into the fray with both editorial feet. The editor of the *Peru Journal* took up his pen and charged that "the people of the old, dead town of Logansport are low, mean and envious and their remarks are idiotic." The feud he thus launched charged the atmosphere of the peaceful valleys for the next decade as gavels pounded and courts from Indiana to Massachusetts issued rulings.[10]

Editors being made of stern stuff in those days, the *Logansport Journal* could not let these insults pass unnoticed. "POUTING PERU. DRINKS MISSISSINEWA WATER AND REFUSES TO BE COMFORTED," retorted that paper's headline. "The Peru papers indicate that the citizens of that Indian village are as mad as wet hens."[11]

"A dog in the manger movement by the displeased people of Logansport," replied the Peru editor.[12]

"Now is the time to strike if the city is ever to recover what the Wabash lease euchered us out of," shouted the *Logansport Pharos*.[13]

"PERU STILL ANGRY," came back the *Journal* headline, "AND CHARGING LOGANSPORT WITH ENVY AND CUNNING." Then, feeling the

ground firmly beneath his feet, the editor swung wildly, raining invective on the people of Wabash, who had no connection with the feud. "It is amusing to see the exhibition of spleen by the people of the poor, old Wabash town in the Eel River Railway case. Although noted for piety, which is a natural result of her barren hills, she draws her sanctimonious robes about her in fiendish satisfaction at a bare prospect of the humility of Peru. Let her alone. It's about the only enjoyment she has."[14]

Not to be outdone by her sister cities, the *Huntington Herald,* a forerunner of the paper owned by former vice president Dan Quayle's family, leaped headlong into the battle: "If the litigation . . . shall result in the permanent transfer of the terminus of the Eel River from Peru to Logansport, we shall shed no tears."[15]

With the press having helped set the stage, the curtain opened on the legal drama, and for the next six years it was mostly a story of the railroads attempting to keep one jump ahead of the sheriff. This they managed with amazing agility.

Sheriffs in the eight counties through which the railroad operated at full throttle were unable to serve papers because the road's agents had disappeared as completely as if they had been swallowed alive by the parent company. Eventually two Eel River agents were located but their residence in Michigan and Massachusetts created complications.[16]

The railroads lost the next round, however, when they were forced to appoint a resident agent in Indiana and named William V. Troutman of Butler to this thankless position.[17]

Five years had now passed since Judge Dykeman had filed the original suit and the great railroad trial seemed about to get under way. But subsequent maneuvering sent the case bouncing like a yo-yo through four courts in Cass, Fulton, and Howard counties. Finally a judgment was handed down against the railroads, the Wabash lease was annulled, and a receiver appointed for the Eel River.[18]

But this was not the final chapter. The railroads appealed to the Indiana Supreme Court, which, after three years, denied a rehearing.[19] Faced with losing the middle link of its new main line, the Wabash rushed to completion a 26-mile connection between Butler and its original main line near Fort Wayne. The first train ran on January 1, 1902. On the same day, the Peru and Detroit line was abandoned and left to rust away.[20]

Abandoned by the Wabash, the Eel River was left to find its own way among the forest of railroads that had grown up about it. First it rebuilt the Chili-Logansport section so that through service once again operated over the entire line. Logansport regained its shops and terminal but it was a hollow victory.[21] Shortly after the Eel River left the protective arms of the Wabash, it sold itself to the Pennsylvania Railroad.[22] Its 14-train passenger fleet dwindled to four locals and by 1930 had ceased operating altogether.[23] Ironically,the abandoned Peru and Detroit was sold to the Winona Interurban whose passenger service between Goshen and Peru outlasted the Eel River's by four years.[24]

With traffic reduced to a steadily diminishing freight service, the Eel River was abandoned piecemeal beginning in 1954. By 1977 it had disappeared completely.[25]

THE CLOVER LEAF:
A DARING DREAM GONE WRONG

This country's great railroads were conceived and built by men who dared to dream. "Commodore" Cornelius Vanderbilt, James J. Hill, the "Empire Builder," and Collis P. Huntington were among them. So was Joseph W. Hunt.

Sometimes they succeeded; sometimes they failed. But all had vision and courage that sustained them whether the iron horse they bet on won or lost.

Hunt was not a railroadman, but a pharmacist in the solid, Germanic town of Delphos, Ohio. Yet his vision, when the country had not yet settled on the standard measure of 4'8½" between the rails, was that narrow-gauge tracks would blanket the nation. He stuck resolutely to his dream, compounding the basic prescription for a narrow-gauge empire that would extend nearly unbroken along a 1,642-mile route from Lake Erie to the Mexican border. Only 150 miles in Texas were left unbuilt. In addition, another 803 miles were projected in its Mexico City section. The 170 miles across Indiana was greater than mileage of the other five Hoosier narrow-gauge lines combined.[26]

Although Hunt and his associates incorporated the Toledo, Delphos and Indianapolis Railway in 1872, five years elapsed before they operated their first train on a five-mile section that eventually would reach Toledo.[27]

This success whetted the promoters' appetites and they decided to push rails to the Mississippi River under a new corporation, Toledo, Delphos and Burlington Railroad.[28] Convinced that narrow gauge was the wave of the future, the company bought the standard-gauge Frankfort and Kokomo Railroad, which connected the cities of its corporate title, and quickly converted it.[29]

In 1879 Hunt died—ironically, fatally injured in a railroad accident—but he had planted his dream, however misguided, so firmly that the eastern speculators who bought out his colleagues continued the narrow-gauge operation.[30]

By 1881 the Grand Narrow Gauge Trunk scheme was in the air and a year later the new Toledo, Cincinnati and St. Louis Railroad absorbed the earlier company. It became the longest narrow-gauge railroad east of the Mississippi and its rails also spread over southwestern Ohio, reaching the Ohio River at two points. Its promoters called their railroad the "Little Giant."[31]

Burlington, Iowa, remained the road's goal until Jay Gould, who controlled the Wabash, St. Louis and Pacific system, engineered a coup that foreclosed access. Forced elsewhere, the road fortunately turned to St. Louis, which was to become one of the nation's great rail centers.[32]

The new eastern owners infused the road with a massive dose of capital that brought it to East St. Louis in 1882, but it failed to cure the chronic financial woes. When a minor creditor petitioned for receivership in July 1882, the 1,500 employees had been unpaid for two months and 200 shopmen at Delphos were on strike. Although the system was valued at $1,500,000, it was mortgaged for $22,000,000. Foreclosure came late in 1883.[33]

Most lines were sold or abandoned under the reorganization. Only the Toledo–East St. Louis trunk remained, and the federal court soon ordered all service halted except for a single mixed train run.[34]

By now it was clear that the only hope of survival was to convert to standard gauge. This would require, it was estimated, $3 million for the 206-mile Toledo-Frankfort section alone, where 600,000 new ties, 119 miles of heavier rail, wider right-of-way, and new or strengthened bridges almost everywhere were needed. It was an impressive shopping list and the abrupt end of Hunt's dream. The road subsequently was sold under foreclosure for $1,501,000.[35]

But at the very moment the road struggled to

A balloon stacked 4–4–0 pulls a two-car Eel River Railroad train in the late 1870s. The 93-mile local road between Logansport and Butler for a time was a vital link in a projected transcontinental route. *Miami County Historical Society*

avoid abandonment, fortune smiled unexpectedly. Natural gas spewed out of a discovery well at Findlay, Ohio, in 1886, and within a short time the entire area blazed with wells that set off a fabulous economic boom.[36]

The moribund railroad suddenly took on a brilliant luster. Financiers saw a tempting pot of gold and snapped up securities enthusiastically. A $3 million bond issue was sold quickly, much of it to meat packing king Phil Armour and his brother, Herman.[37]

Happy with the turn of events, management adopted the three-leaf clover symbol to signify its good fortune and called itself the "Clover Leaf Line," although the new official name was Toledo, St. Louis and Kansas City Railroad.[38]

Immediately the road employed 600 men to replace the worn, light rail with new 61½-lb. iron,

which they spiked to fresh white oak ties. Extra spikes placed at the outer ends and new, wider bridges set the stage for what was to come swiftly on a June morning in 1887.[39]

On the 26th of that month, 2,000 men, divided into gangs of 40, began respiking the rails. Eleven hours later, the first train left Delphos over the new standard-gauge Clover Leaf Line. In a miracle of growth, the entire 206 miles east of Frankfort had been converted![40]

With the narrow-gauge cobwebs out of its head, the new management chose to meet competition head-on. It inaugurated both day and night passenger trains and scheduled fast new meat and livestock runs. In an expansive mood, the company extended service eastward to Buffalo in 1890 by leasing a pair of packets and establishing the Clover Leaf Steamboat Line. But despite the lucky clover

When the TStL&W (Clover Leaf) Railroad inaugurated a fast overnight train on its St. Louis–Toledo route in 1901, a contest was held to pick the name. The Commercial Traveler was chosen. Advanced for its day, it was fully vestibuled, lighted by Pintsch gas lights, and carried a sleeping car and dining space.   *Richard S. Simons collection*

emblem, ill fortune followed the line into the water. Fire severely damaged one boat on its maiden voyage, and the other sank with all hands aboard during a fierce autumn storm.[41]

Financial problems continued to snap at the heels of management, and in 1893 bankruptcy overtook it. The complicated receivership featured an all-star cast. Former president of the United States Benjamin Harrison represented the preferred stockholders, and future president William Howard Taft presided. In 1900 the road was sold at foreclosure to the bondholders for $12,200,000. The name was changed to Toledo, St. Louis and Western Railroad.[42]

Moving aggressively, the Clover Leaf seized on the Pan-American Exposition at Buffalo in 1901 as an opportunity to establish a new overnight run between St. Louis and Toledo. The train featured innovations that made heads turn. Four new Baldwin Ten-Wheelers equipped with the road's first carbon arc headlights provided motive power. Each pulled a five-car consist of two coaches, a 46-chair buffet car, an unusual 12-section observation–drawing room sleeper and a combination mail car. Pintsch gas lights, a vast improvement over the former system, illuminated the interiors. To illustrate its forward thinking, management named the sleepers "Advance" and "Progress," and opened the service with all the flair of a Hollywood premiere. It selected the name Commercial Traveler as the result of a public contest.[43]

By the early 1900s, the once penniless Little Giant felt a new strength generated by a heavy business in perishables augmented by coal traffic that originated in Illinois, and later at Indiana mines as well. The road expanded its herald to a four-leaf clover and adopted a new slogan, "The Lucky Way."[44]

But the good fortune was not to last. An ill-advised purchase of the Chicago and Alton Railroad in a debt-heavy transaction threw the parent company into receivership, where it languished for eight years. In the end, the Van Sweringen brothers of Cleveland bought it for $3,522,000 and merged it into the Nickel Plate as they set out to build a modern rail empire.[45]

In a 1964 merger, the Nickel Plate became part of the Norfolk and Western, which had acquired a better-built St. Louis-Toledo line from the Wabash in the same merger. East of a point near Delphos, the Clover Leaf line was abandoned, and west of that point it was turned over to two short lines, Indiana Hi-Rail and Central Railroad of Indianapolis. West of Frankfort, most of the line has been abandoned.[46]

Yet the Clover Leaf came close to its day of glory when it figured in speculation as a new independent trunk line to St. Louis during the Conrail formation days of the mid–1970s.

THE MILWAUKEE: AMBITION UNBRIDLED

If nothing else, John R. Walsh was an opportunist. A Chicago banker, he saw possibilities in a bankrupt southern Indiana railroad and acquired it to tie together the empires he would build in limestone, coal, and mineral springs.

Walsh typified the best and the worst in railroad building in his era. Like Jay Gould and other late nineteenth century manipulators, Walsh was driven by a relentless ambition. For eight whirlwind years, he built his empire, expanding opportunities for the region and the people who lived there. But in the end his transgressions caught up with him, and his empire collapsed with a mighty roar that was heard all the way to the Loop in Chicago.

The story began in 1886 when the Evansville and Richmond Railroad set out to connect the two Indiana cities of its corporate title. However, it reached neither destination and by 1890 controlled 102 uncertain, sparsely settled miles between Elnora and Westport. This was the central portion of the original project.[47]

Seven years, two devastating floods, and one receivership later, the E&R emerged as the Southern Indiana Railway with Walsh in complete control.

His plans were ambitious and brave and he quickly became the dashing, if controversial, hero of the entire area.[48]

Realizing that his road ran from nowhere to nowhere, Walsh quickly abandoned the original projected terminals and converted the east-west property into a north-south line headed for Chicago. Beginning at Elnora, he turned northward across the rich Sullivan County coal fields toward Terre Haute, where he battled his way into Union Station through the courts.[49]

On the east, he was content to leave the terminal at Westport since he saw little traffic east of the Bedford limestone quarries. It remained a sort of unconsolidated appendage to the main rail body, lacking through passenger service and hauling a different commodity mix. Bedford's importance, however, was reflected in the road's early "Bedford Route" slogan.

With one eye on the Bedford limestone quarries and the other on the coal fields, Walsh jumped into an amazing improvement program. He rebuilt the west end with heavier rail and better roadbed. He increased the locomotive roster more than 500% and added nearly 6,000 cars. At Seymour, he bought an expensive right-of-way and built into the center of town. He negotiated trackage rights over other roads that allowed him to run through passenger trains between Washington, Indiana, and Greensburg.[50]

To implement his grand scheme, he acquired four limestone quarries, which he merged into the Bedford Quarries Company, and developed the town of Oolitic to serve them.[51]

Often contentious, Walsh feuded with the Monon Railroad and apparently won his battle. As a result, the 4.2-mile Bedford Belt Railroad, serving three quarries and ten mills, became part of the SI organization and a principal traffic originator.[52]

Action must have been Walsh's middle name. Dissatisfied with local banks, he organized the Bedford National in 1899 and became its president. Unhappy with local hotels and unable to buy the site of the Greystone, he built accommodations near Oolitic. Unable to persuade express companies to go his way, he established the Southern Indiana Express Company.[53]

But by far the most serious problem was Walsh's inability to obtain acceptable traffic arrangements with roads north of Terre Haute. Undaunted, he retaliated with characteristic defiance by building a third line to Chicago, paralleling the Chicago and

The handsome limestone station in Bedford, built in 1899 as part of John Walsh's improvement program for the Southern Indiana and his related quarries.   *Photo by Francis H. Parker*

Eastern Illinois Railroad north of Terre Haute and the New York Central, as well, north of Danville, Illinois. They were by far the largest cities on the route. Unusual in its day, the road offered only a rudimentary local passenger service north of Terre Haute.[54]

By 1905 Walsh's Southern Indiana Coal Company had acquired eight mines with known reserves of 150 million tons. He blanketed the area with a spider web of four parallel lines, so that it was almost impossible to ship without using SI rails. With this feverish activity, Linton's population nearly tripled in six years and numerous on-line villages took on new importance.[55]

Further good fortune arrived when the Clinton coal fields were opened north of Terre Haute in

1910. The SI was fast becoming the Cinderella of the industry.[56]

Walsh's active mind never stopped turning and his thirst for power was never fulfilled. He now considered the mineral springs industry and visualized competing with Indiana's famed French Lick Springs and West Baden resorts.

In about 1898, Walsh's new Southern Indiana Hotel Company purchased 1,125 acres at Indian Springs, a remote station 18 miles west of Bedford, and opened a large hotel. He next turned to Trinity Springs, three miles away, and began to connect the two by rail.[57]

Despite his vast empire, Walsh's ambition drove him relentlessly. He decided to extend his Trinity Springs branch to Louisville, and started work on

The St. Joseph Valley Railway operated an incredible fleet of motor cars. These units were pictured about 1910 on the Angola public square. Each carried 20 passengers. The road used 11 models from 10 manufacturers. *Richard S. Simons collection*

---

an Indianapolis branch that would leave the main line at Blackhawk, 13 miles from Terre Haute.[58]

As Walsh stretched his empire further and his finances thinner, occasional rumblings could be heard. Eyebrows were raised over his lavish spending. Dissatisfaction arose when he failed to meet payrolls and bond interest. But his charismatic charm melted the doubts with assurance that the problems were only temporary.

Then, late in 1905, Walsh's empire collapsed. His Chicago National and Home Savings Banks failed. All rail and hotel construction stopped abruptly. The Indianapolis line was the major casualty. For many decades, the arrow-straight grade could be

seen shooting across Clay County with culverts in place, underpasses built, and bridge substructures completed. In Indianapolis, a 75-acre terminal site had been purchased for this unnecessary road, which would have been the fifth to connect Indianapolis with the southwestern Indiana coal fields.[59]

Walsh was unable to disengage himself from his difficulties and in 1908, at age 70, he was sentenced to five years in Leavenworth Penitentiary for violating national banking laws. Charges included overstating deposits, falsifying bank officers' liabilities, issuing dummy notes, personally borrowing beyond the legal maximum, and underreporting loans. Bank deposits secured most of his $15,000,000 holdings, and to maintain public confidence the Chicago Clearing House Association assumed the debt.[60]

Another bankruptcy followed and the road emerged in 1910 as the Chicago, Terre Haute and Southeastern Railway.[61] In 1921 the fuel-hungry Chicago, Milwaukee and St. Paul Railway leased and later merged the struggling road after looking enviously at the output of its 48 mines. From 1922 to 1945, it dominated Indiana's coal hauling, originating more than 7,000,000 tons in a single year.[62] It is the sole rail carrier serving the vast Crane Naval Surface Warfare Center, which was established during World War II. It also brought a glimmer of fame to Westport, which became the easternmost point in the United States from which a single company operated to the Pacific Coast; no other western railroad penetrated east of Chicago.[63]

In 1973 service began to Louisville on trackage rights over the former Monon south of Bedford. Following the Milwaukee Road's bankruptcy, CP (Canadian Pacific) Rail's Soo Line purchased its assets and continued to operate into Louisville.[64]

Although Walsh's limitless ambition ruined him, he left a legacy that in unexpected ways still benefits southern Indiana.

THE ST. JOSEPH VALLEY RAILWAY: MONEY BUILDS A RAILROAD PLAYTHING

Typical of the rugged individualism that marked some of the nation's best-known railroad builders, Herbert E. Bucklen of Elkhart marched to the beat of his own drummer. The St. Joseph Valley Railway, which he built and operated with absolute authority, extended across northeastern Indiana from Elkhart to Columbia, Ohio, hardly a demand route of travel. Between terminals it touched only two towns of more than 700 population and was squeezed in by parallel trunk lines on both sides, usually within 12 miles. Its chance of survival was slim and it held on only because of Bucklen's tenacity and his enormous wealth.[65]

Born in 1905, dead by 1918, the line became a legend in its own time.[66] Its relaxed operating practices, deplorable safety record, wandering right-of-way, and bewildering conglomeration of motive power—probably unequaled in America—lent it a sort of comic opera reputation.

Nevertheless, Bucklen had good intentions when he built it. He planned to close the 75-mile gap that separated interurban lines built east from Chicago and west from Toledo. But try as he might, he failed by 13 miles to reach Pioneer, Ohio, where the Toledo road ended, although it had graded part of the route to Columbia, Ohio, which was the end of the Valley line. Except for the nine miles between Elkhart and Bristol, it was never electrified.[67]

Probably more than any other Indiana railroad builder, Bucklen represented the colorful, entrepreneurial type who dared to dream and translate his dreams into reality. Independently wealthy from profitable Arnica Salve, a patent medicine, he embodied affluent if perhaps eccentric independence during the days before heavy government restraint.

Construction began in 1903 at Lagrange, which was midway on the line and was to become the operating headquarters. By 1905, trains were shuttling ten miles to Shipshewana and construction gangs continued to work on isolated segments until the line was completed to Elkhart in 1911. The corporate name was St. Joseph Valley Traction Company.[68]

Beginning in 1907, Bucklen pushed eastward from Lagrange to Angola. But it was slow going. In 1911 he reached Berlein, eight miles east of Angola, and then spent four more sinkhole-plagued years struggling to reach Columbia, where all operations ceased. This section was the St. Joseph Valley Railway, which leased the traction line west of Lagrange for $1 per year. For operational purposes, they were one.[69]

Bucklen financed the line almost 100% from his own pocket. He owned all but 102 of the traction company's 1,102 shares and held the $240,000 in bonds issued from a $700,000 authorization. When he died, the road owed his estate nearly $900,000, an amount that exceeded its physical assets.[70]

Although the Valley line was a typical traction road with trolley wires, interurban cars, and city street right-of-way for nine of its 70 miles, it also was a steam railroad. In addition to steam, it used nearly every other type of motive power known in its day, plus a hodgepodge of freight and passenger car styles almost unique in midwestern railway annals. These included gasoline-electric cars, a storage battery unit, and gasoline cars. Some were chain driven. Some, like a sprinter in a race, took off only after the motorman placed a shotgun shell in a chamber over the engine, struck it with a ball peen hammer, and started the car.[71]

The original car was a gasoline-electric motor unit, said to be one of the first in the country. But it was so crammed with equipment that no room remained for either passengers or freight. So Bucklen bought a trailer unit and ran it as a two-car train, supplementing it with steam locomotive power.[72]

To meet schedules after the road was extended to Angola, Bucklen acquired two gasoline cars, which were little more than oversized automobiles mounted on flanged wheels. The public immediately dubbed one the "tax collector" because Bucklen had rushed it into service to meet a subsidy deadline. The smaller car seated 20, the larger seated 25. Side panels could be removed in summer to convert them into open cars—a sort of primitive air conditioning.[73]

Still pioneering, Bucklen next turned to a new type of gasoline car and within a few years had bought eight. The smaller units could run 20 mph; the larger one, if urged, could cruise at 30.[74]

In 1913 Bucklen tried something different. He bought a storage battery car guaranteed to run 150 miles on a charge but it developed the exasperating habit of expiring a few miles before reaching its home terminal after a trip slightly shorter than the guaranteed mileage. Bucklen sued the manufacturer but lost.[75]

The battery car soured Bucklen, so he returned to gasoline locomotion, buying a formidable 150-horsepower unit. It had the misfortune of colliding with a motor speeder carrying Herbert E. Bucklen, Jr., flipping on its side and stopping with the front end hanging precariously over an embankment. Four persons were injured.[76]

The road's only passenger fatalities occurred in 1916 when a freight train rear-ended a standing passenger car at Inverness, northwest of Angola. Two persons died and 25 were injured. The car, according to an Interstate Commerce Commission investigation, carried more than three and one-half times its seating capacity of 21; a rear light was missing; the freight engine brakes were out; there was no standard clock anywhere on the line; and the following train had left its terminal three minutes behind the passenger car instead of the minimum required five minutes. Bucklen, seriously ill, never learned of the wreck. He died 12 days later.[77]

With Bucklen also went the railroad, for his heirs lacked his love for the iron horse and immediately moved to collect the money owed the estate. In less than a year, the road entered bankruptcy. A Chicago scrap dealer bought it for $390,000 but resold 15 miles between Lagrange and Orland to a new locally owned company. Traffic proved sparse and after three years, the last segment of the Valley line went to its final resting place.[78]

THE CINCINNATI, BLUFFTON AND CHICAGO: BAD LUCK DOWNS AN UNNECESSARY RAILROAD

During the era when the railroad was the only kid on the transportation block, many unnecessary roads were built. Some duplicated existing lines, some met a scarcely existing need, and some failed to follow logical traffic patterns.

The Cincinnati, Bluffton and Chicago Railroad fell into all three categories. If the road's promoters actually intended to connect the two end cities of its corporate title, it would have been the fourth such line; scarcely a transportation necessity. Its complete route, however, linked only Portland and Huntington, 52 miles apart. Between terminals, only Bluffton had more than a few hundred residents.[79]

The road's initials inspired its popular name— Corned Beef and Cabbage—by which it has been known since birth.[80]

During its turbulent 14-year existence—second shortest of any twentieth-century Indiana railroad —the CB&C suffered nearly every physical and financial hardship known to railroading. It was in receivership much of the time. It was the subject of litigation that reverberated all the way to the Indiana Supreme Court. It came within two days of missing a subsidy deadline. A broker walked away with the proceeds of a $300,000 bond issue, leaving the company without the money and with compensation claims from the purchasers. A parallel railroad removed the line's tracks in a contract dispute. An unattended locomotive backed off the end of the track in Huntington and into a grocery store, dropping into the basement and leaving not much more than the pilot and smokestack exposed to greet the wrecking crew.[81] When a rival road at Portland attempted to block a crossing site, CB&C crews overturned a boxcar blockade and completed their work amid a fistfight.[82] The 1913 flood heavily damaged its Wabash River bridge north of Bluffton.[83] The steel and concrete replacement bridge collapsed with fatal results shortly after it was completed.[84]

In only 14 years, what more could go wrong with a little railroad?

The CB&C first saw daylight in 1903 when it was completed between Bluffton and Pennville. The following year it was extended to Portland and in 1908 entered Huntington.[85]

The first blow in a long series of misfortunes fell in 1907. That year a Cleveland broker sold a $300,000 bond issue and kept the money. Although he went to prison in 1910, that didn't improve the road's financial condition, since it had to assume both liability for the bonds and loss of the proceeds.[86]

There was one bright spot, however. Huntington had voted a subsidy of nearly $100,000 for extension of the road and location of its shops. The company struggled valiantly to meet the deadline and managed to slide under the wire by a mere two days. That was in 1908.[87]

But the same year, creditors threw the company into receivership. Two years later the road was ordered sold under a court order, which the Indiana Supreme Court later overthrew.[88]

The lower court had decreed that the road always be operated as a steam line, and in 1911, when efforts were being made to convert it to an electric traction system, this became a political issue.[89]

The Erie Railroad donated 14 miles of its right-of-way to the parallel CB&C with the understanding that its rails would be available as a second track between Huntington and Uniondale. When repeated protests that the CB&C failed to build to adequate standards brought no response, Erie crews moved in without further notice and removed the tracks in four communities. This forced the CB&C to seek donations of right-of-way nearby.[90]

During construction, the railroad bought a gravel deposit at Twin Hills near Pennville and built a one-and-a-half-mile track to haul it to the main line. When the road refused to pay the owner, he went to court and received a judgment, but instead of receiving cash, he wound up the reluctant owner of the branch line.[91]

In 1912 the receiver attempted to cut losses by buying three gas-electric cars from the Barber Car Company of York, Pennsylvania. At 40 feet, they were the longest cars the company produced and had 100 horsepower motors. But the cars proved troublesome and were unsuccessful in holding down the road's four round trips daily.[92]

Toward the end, repeated efforts to sell the road failed. Finally in 1917, only nine years after completion, the railroad was sold for salvage for $310,000, a figure far less than the original cost of construction plus the outstanding debt.[93]

14

Railroad Towns and Cities

IN A SENSE, *most* towns in Indiana are railroad towns, their growth coinciding with the growth of the railroads during the nineteenth century. Some, however, owe their economic livelihood directly to the railroad. These are the terminals, division points, or shop towns where railroad employment was a significant part of the economy. The following Indiana towns have truly been railroad towns at some point in their history.

Bedford

A center of the limestone industry, Bedford was served at its peak by the Monon main line and the Monon's former narrow-gauge branch to Switz City, plus a B&O branch connection from Rivervale and the Bedford Belt. Its primary railroad importance was as headquarters of the Indiana Southern (later Milwaukee), with a ten-stall roundhouse, main repair shops (served by transfer table), and principal depot, all built of native limestone.

All that remains in 1996 is the former Milwaukee (now Soo Line) from Terre Haute, and the CSX (former Monon) from New Albany, forming a single through line used primarily by Soo Line freights to Louisville. Main line tracks still lead down the center of a street through the town square. Limestone depots from both the Monon and the Southern Indiana remain, though not in railroad use.

Bloomington

Best known as a university town, Bloomington was also a Monon division point, 104 miles from the southern terminal in Louisville. McDoel yards on the southern edge of town were named for W. H. McDoel, energetic Monon president from 1899 to 1909. It was expanded in 1910 and again in the 1920s, with a 14-stall roundhouse.[1] Bloomington

was also served by the Illinois Central line to Indianapolis, and by an Illinois Central branch to limestone quarries at Victor. In 1996 the former IC is still in service as Indiana Rail Road, and a disconnected fragment of the Monon (later CSX) line remains in service only seven miles north to Ellettsville. The Illinois Central passenger station and the freight station (now on the National Register of Historic Places) remain in non-railroad uses.

Elkhart

Elkhart was an important New York Central division point serving the "Old Road" and the shorter "Air Line" from the east, the Chicago line to the west, and the Michigan Division from Louisville to Benton Harbor, as well as a branch to Mishawaka. Shops and roundhouse were moved to Elkhart from Goshen by 1870.[2] In 1903 the LS&MS built the second largest railroad yard in the U.S. at Elkhart, with separate eastbound and westbound humps.[3] Two new roundhouses were built, servicing 160 locomotives per day. In 1902 the LS&MS had 636 engineers and firemen working out of Elkhart, and by 1912 it was said that over 40% of the workmen in town were employed by the Lake Shore.[4]

Today the Elkhart yard, rebuilt in the late 1950s, is the key Conrail classification yard for the Chicago gateway. Amtrak shares the Elkhart LS&MS depot, while the National New York Central Museum occupies the former LS&MS freight depot just across the tracks.

Evansville

Evansville was the terminus of the Chicago and Eastern Illinois main line from Chicago, and a division point on the Louisville and Nashville line to St. Louis. It was also served by an Illinois Central line from Mattoon, Illinois, a Southern Railway branch from Huntingburg, and New York Central lines from Terre Haute and from Mt. Carmel, Illinois, plus three local lines, the Evansville and Ohio Valley, the Evansville, Suburban and Newburgh, and the Evansville Belt.

Evansville was unique in Indiana in possessing two major terminal depots, each with platforms terminating behind the head houses. The L&N had a magnificent stone romanesque-style depot, built in 1902, reached by a 1.6-mile branch from the main line at Howell, where the railroad had built its division point yards and roundhouse (and the town of Howell itself) in the 1880s.[5] On the other side of downtown, the C&EI terminated at a neoclassical brick depot built in 1905 to replace an equally imposing 1882 structure.[6] The C&EI depot was vacated before World War II, and C&EI trains then reached the L&N depot via $1\frac{1}{2}$ miles of street track in Division Street. Both buildings were later demolished, the C&EI depot in the 1960s and the L&N depot in 1985, despite placement on the National Register of Historic Places. Four columns from the C&EI depot form the "Four Freedoms" monument on the waterfront.[7]

The C&EI moved its yard and roundhouse from a cramped downtown location to a site at the northern edge of town in 1928. In 1973 a two-mile bypass was built north of town, connecting the former C&EI to the L&N over portions of the former New York Central line from Illinois. The Division Street connection was abandoned. Today CSX traffic uses this route into Howell Yard, while NS, Indiana Southern, and Evansville Terminal Company operate the former Southern, NYC (E&I), and IC branches into the city.

Fort Wayne

Fort Wayne was a major Pennsylvania Railroad division point, about halfway between Chicago and Crestline, Ohio. A PRR line from Richmond and PRR subsidiary GR&I from Michigan joined the main line here. The Nickel Plate and the Wabash both had east-west lines through Fort Wayne, and the Nickel Plate had a division point here. The Nickel Plate built through the city on the right-of-way of the old Wabash and Erie Canal, which had brought the first railway locomotive to Fort Wayne by boat in 1852. A NYC branch ran north to Michigan, a Nickel Plate branch (former LE&W) ran south to Muncie and beyond, and the short-lived Cincinnati, Findlay and Fort Wayne ran east. There were also local switching roads.

The Pennsylvania's Piqua or East yard was southeast of downtown, and included a large roundhouse and a hump yard. A coaling tower, built in 1902 and described at the time as the largest coaling stage ever built, spanned 12 tracks at the yard, and permitted main-line trains to take on coal without uncoupling the locomotives. A portion of the Piqua yard remains in service as the hub for the Norfolk Southern Triple Crown network. The Nickel Plate West Wayne yard and roundhouse, west of the St. Mary's River, were replaced in 1951 by a new East Wayne yard and engine terminal between Fort Wayne and New Haven. The Wabash maintained a roundhouse south of downtown near the General Electric factory, and the New York Central had a small yard and roundhouse along Clinton Street across the St. Mary's from downtown.

In 1857, the PFtW&C purchased the existing Wayne Car and Engine Works and expanded them gradually into the largest shops on the western end of the Pennsylvania system.[8] In the latter 1800s the shops employed more than 1,000 men, and Fort Wayne became known as the Altoona of the West because of its key position on the great Pennsylvania system.

Beginning in 1867 the Fort Wayne shops built hundreds of locomotives, and over 12,000 freight cars, with car construction continuing until at least World War I.[9] The Wabash also built locomotives at its Fort Wayne shop in early years, while the Bass Foundry, opened in the late 1850s, was claimed to be the world's leading producer of railroad wheels and axles by 1880.[10]

The PRR and Wabash elevated their lines through Fort Wayne in 1912, as did the NKP in 1955.

PRR successor Conrail is only a minor player in Fort Wayne today, but the city is a major terminal for NS, and the hub of its innovative RoadRailer system. The former PRR and NYC passenger depots survive in non-railroad uses, and several railroad historical groups are active.

Frankfort

Frankfort was on the Indianapolis line of the Monon, and a junction point for PRR lines from Indianapolis, Logansport, and Terre Haute. Its main railroad significance, however, was as a division point for the Clover Leaf and later for the

Nickel Plate. The Clover Leaf line between Toledo and St. Louis crossed the Lake Erie and Western line between Peoria and Sandusky, and after both lines were merged into the Nickel Plate in 1923 Frankfort became a principal classification yard and engine terminal for both lines.

Frankfort today is served by NS, Conrail, and CERA. In 1996 the former LE&W, PRR, and Monon passenger depots remained, as did a concrete coal tower, turntable, and part of the former Nickel Plate roundhouse.

Garrett

Garrett was founded with the coming of the Baltimore, Pittsburgh and Chicago (B&O) railroad in 1874. It was a town totally dependent on the railroad, laid out by railroad engineers and named for railroad president John W. Garrett. Garrett was intended from the start to be a division point, 151 miles east of Chicago and 128 miles west of Willard, Ohio.[11] Shops and a roundhouse were built. The depot, with its division offices, was expanded in 1910, and a new and larger roundhouse built. By 1913 the shops employed some 1,300 men, out of the town's total population of 5,000.

In 1996 the CSX main line to Chicago remains active, but the last major shop structure, the brick roundhouse, was demolished in 1968, and the depot was demolished in 1996. A relocated freight station survives. Amtrak service ended in 1995 but was reinstated in late 1996.

Hammond

Hammond became a railroad town by virtue of its location athwart most eastern routes into Chicago. It was platted in 1875, six years after George Hammond of Detroit moved a slaughterhouse there and built a large fleet of railroad refrigerator cars to ship the dressed beef to market. By that time four railroads had built through the site, to be joined by seven more by 1908. The Michigan Central opened Gibson yards in 1906, followed soon after by the 80-acre Erie yards and the 48-acre Monon yards.[12]

The B&O, NYC, PRR, and EJ&E ran along the lakeshore. In downtown Hammond the Indiana Harbor Belt, Erie, Michigan Central, Nickel Plate, Monon, and C&O all converged, forming a barrier of intersecting tracks. Several roads officially terminated in Hammond, but most trains continued into Chicago over other lines.

The Standard Steel Car Company, later Pullman-Standard, came to Hammond in 1906. The huge plant on the southeast side soon became the city's largest industry, employing 3,500 by 1912.[13] It closed operations in 1981, soon after delivering Amtrak's "Superliners," leaving 2,000 out of work.

Today Conrail, CSX, NS, EJ&E, CSS&SB, and IHB all operate one or more lines through Hammond. The gash through downtown Hammond has been closed by the abandonment of the former Erie, Monon, and C&O. Amtrak uses the lakefront corridor with a station in Whiting.

Huntington

When the Chicago and Atlantic (Erie) was built across Indiana in 1883, Huntington was selected as a division point, lying halfway between Chicago and Marion, Ohio. Division offices, roundhouse, and repair shops were here, employing 600 men at their peak. Huntington was also a station on the Wabash Railroad, and it became the western terminus of the short-lived Cincinnati, Bluffton and Chicago Railroad.

With the demise of the Erie Lackawanna, Huntington is again a one-railroad town, on the busy Detroit–St. Louis line of the Norfolk Southern. The former Wabash passenger and freight depots remain, in non-railroad uses.

Indianapolis

When the Madison and Indianapolis reached Indianapolis in 1847, the city rapidly became a focus for rail construction in Indiana. By 1853 lines radiated from the city in seven directions. Seven more were built by 1900, and two final lines were added by 1918. In addition the city became the hub of the Indiana interurban network in the early twentieth century, with 13 lines radiating from the Indianapolis Traction Terminal.

By the peak years Indianapolis was a division point for Pennsylvania, New York Central, and B&O lines. All passenger service came together at the Indianapolis Union Depot, while freight was interchanged via the Indianapolis Belt Railway, circling the city from northeast to northwest and linking all the connecting railroads. Shops and facilities originally clustered near the Union Depot, on the eastern and southeastern sides of the original mile-square plat, or to the east and west of the river. As the city grew the shops and yards moved out with it, taking advantage of locations accessible to the Belt

For many years a mainstay of Lafayette's economy, and source of the Purdue nickname "Boilermakers," the Monon shops repaired diesel locomotives when this photo was taken in 1949.   *Richard S. Simons collection*

Beech Grove shops were built near Indianapolis between 1906 and 1914 as the main locomotive shops for the CCC&StL (The Big Four). They are now Amtrak's national car repair facility.   *Jay Williams collection*

Railway. Brightwood, platted in 1872, became the site of the Big Four's Brightwood yard and repair shops after 1877.[14] By 1910 450 men worked here.[15] In later years the Brightwood roundhouse was the terminal for Big Four freight locomotives, while passenger locomotives were maintained at the Shelby Street roundhouse, closer to Union Station on an earlier railroad repair shop site.

The Panhandle's yards and shops were located south of Washington Street west of the Belt crossing and employed 700 men in 1910.[16] After World War I the new Hawthorne hump yard and engine terminal were built east of the belt, with a connecting spur to the Richmond line. The Vandalia had a roundhouse at the river west of Union Station. Moorefield, west of the river, had shop facilities for the B&O, employing 110 men in 1910.[17] The Lake Erie and Western roundhouse, originally south of

Washington Street at Pogue's Run, was moved north to E. 28th Street by 1898. By 1915 the Monon had acquired this roundhouse, and the Nickel Plate later built another roundhouse for itself across the tracks from the Monon roundhouse.

Indianapolis was headquarters for the Big Four system, and between 1906 and 1914 they erected central locomotive shops for the system in the Indianapolis suburb of Beech Grove. Capable of completely rebuilding or even building new locomotives, by 1910 600 men worked there.[18] During their World War II peak, the shops employed over 5,000 people.[19] With the elimination of steam power and successive railroad consolidations, employment dropped significantly. In 1975 Amtrak purchased the facility, which remains their national center for passenger car repair.

In 1873 the Indianapolis Car Works opened on

Martindale Avenue in what was then the northeast edge of town. By 1887 it was replaced by a much larger plant, named the Indianapolis Car and Manufacturing Co., connected to the Belt Railway off Kentucky Avenue. It was renamed the Indianapolis Car and Foundry Co. by 1898.

Indianapolis in 1997 is served by Conrail's St. Louis line and by three shorter Conrail branches, as well as the Conrail-owned belt line. Conrail's major yard is at Avon, built west of Indianapolis in 1960. A CSX line from Cincinnati now terminates in Indianapolis, as do short lines Indiana Southern (former PRR), Indiana Rail Road (former IC), and Louisville and Indiana (former PRR). A new Port Authority purchased the former Nickel Plate line to the north and hosts the annual Fairtrain service between Fishers and the Indiana State Fairground. Amtrak currently provides limited service to Chicago and Washington.

Freight houses remained centrally located until abandoned in the 1970s and 1980s. The 1888 Indianapolis Union Station and its 1916–1922 train shed were restored in 1986 as a festival marketplace and hotel, but have had financial problems in the 1990s. Most of the railroad corridors established by 1853 still exist in central Indianapolis, although the Lafayette road's connection along the canal, long since replaced as a through route, was removed in the 1980s as part of the state office reconstruction project.

Jeffersonville—Clarksville—New Albany

The New Albany and Salem began operation north from New Albany in 1851, the same year the Jeffersonville Railroad began construction from Jeffersonville to Indianapolis. By the peak years, the adjacent communities were served by Pennsylvania and B&O lines to the north, the Monon to the northwest, and the Southern to the west. Two bridges crossed the Ohio from Jeffersonville to Louisville. The Big Four bridge carried NYC trains, which reached Jeffersonville over the B&O, and the Panhandle bridge carried Pennsylvania trains. From New Albany the Kentucky and Indiana bridge carried Monon, Southern, and B&O trains to Louisville. Both the B&O and the Pennsylvania had branches connecting Jeffersonville and New Albany.

From 1860 to 1879 the Jeffersonville Railroad and its successor JM&I built 25 locomotives at its Jeffersonville shops, including the Reuben Wells,

built for the Madison incline in 1868. In adjacent Clarksville the Ohio Falls Car Company was founded in 1864. Reorganized in 1876 after a disastrous 1872 fire, it included at least 17 brick buildings on a large site. It produced thousands of cars during the rest of the century, and continued car production until 1932 after its sale to American Car and Foundry in 1899. Although adapted to other uses the complex remains today, designated as the Ohio Falls Car and Locomotive Company Historic District.

Jeffersonville today is served by the Louisville and Indianapolis, by the recently constructed MG Railroad to the Clark Maritime Center, and by a CSX branch from New Albany through to Charleston. North of Jeffersonville the Southern Indiana, a latecomer, connects Watson and Speed. The L&I uses the former Panhandle bridge to Louisville, while the Big Four bridge, its approaches removed, is vacant. In New Albany the NS and CSX converge to cross the K&IT bridge, with the Soo Line sharing trackage rights on CSX. The original New Albany depot of the NA&S, the oldest depot in Indiana, was demolished in 1995.

Lafayette

Lafayette was served by four major railroads, the Monon, Wabash, New York Central, and Lake Erie and Western (NKP), plus the Lafayette Union Railway. NYC and Lake Erie and Western shared the NKP tracks from Lafayette Junction on the east side through town to Templeton, 20 miles west, and operated a joint passenger station in Lafayette. Until 1956 the New York Central used steam helpers on the grades in both directions out of the Wabash River valley, cutting off at Altamont, 3.7 miles east of Lafayette depot, or at Summit, 1.8 miles west.[20]

Lafayette was a division point for the Monon and home to its main repair shops. In 1892 Lafayette voted a donation of $100,000 and 40 acres of land to the Monon Railroad, and induced them to move their main shop facilities from New Albany. The new shops, including $13\frac{1}{2}$ miles of track, were completed in 1895, and contributed the name "Boilermakers" to the Purdue football team.[21] Until 1994 the Monon main line ran down the center of 5th Street through downtown Lafayette. The former Monon depot on 5th Street is now a theatre.

The Wabash line from Detroit to St. Louis cut diagonally across the city. The Lafayette railroad relocation project, opened in 1994, has rerouted Monon (now CSX) trains along the riverfront, and will also reroute the Wabash (now NS) trains, once a connection is completed through the former Monon shops site. The former NYC/LE&W depot has also been relocated to the riverfront site, to become an Amtrak and bus depot. The Kankakee, Beaverville and Southern operates the former NYC/LE&W line to the west.

Logansport

Logansport was an important junction, division point, and shop town for the Pennsylvania Railroad. From Logansport, Pennsylvania Panhandle lines radiated west, north, and east, while Vandalia lines went north, northeast, and south. The Panhandle and Vandalia had separate depots, yards and roundhouses in Logansport, while the Wabash had its own facilities. The major Panhandle yards, with separate humps for eastbound and westbound classification, were located southeast of town, across the Wabash River. The Panhandle shops built locomotives here in the nineteenth century, one of which still survives. In later years Logansport was a major junction for PRR passenger trains, which would arrive from Chicago and split for departure in three different directions. It was estimated that at one time there were 2,500 railroad employees in Logansport.

Logansport today is on the NS (former Wabash) main line between Detroit and St. Louis, and is served by short lines TP&W to Illinois, A & R to Winamac, and Winamac Southern to Bringhurst and Kokomo. A fragment of Vandalia and Eel River track in town is maintained by the Logansport and Eel River Railroad, which offers switching and occasional passenger excursions. A former Vandalia yard office, relocated twice, now occupies the forwmer Panhandle depot site. The Panhandle erecting shop and transfer table serves in 1996 as a car repair shop for Transco Railway Products.

Michigan City

Michigan City was reached by the Michigan Central from Detroit in 1850, and became the northern terminus of the New Albany and Salem in 1853. In its peak years Michigan City was traversed by the Michigan Central, the Pere Marquette, and the CSS&SB electric line, whose main shops are still located here. The city was also the terminus for branches of the LE&W and Monon.

The firm of Haskell and Barker began freight car construction in Michigan City in 1852, and had already produced 15,000 cars by 1871. By 1910 3,500 men were producing 10,000 cars annually. With 34 buildings on 116 acres of land it claimed to be the largest freight car plant in the world.[22] It was sold to Pullman in 1922 and continued production, in steel, until 1971. A remaining building of the Haskell and Barker complex is proposed for redevelopment into a railroad museum.

Michigan City retains all its former railroad lines except the Monon branch. It is traversed today by CSX, by the CSS&SB, and by an Amtrak-owned line into Michigan (the former MC), and is the terminus of an NS line from Argos.

Peru

Peru was a division point for both the Wabash and the C&O, and the terminus of the Winona Railroad, a former interurban converted to internal combustion freight service. Peru was the principal division point on the Chesapeake and Ohio Chicago division. It divided the Miami subdivision to the south and the Wabash subdivision to the north.[23] The C&O had a large roundhouse and shop, shared by the NKP until 1952.[24] The Wabash division point led to creation of a 9½-mile line between Peru and Chili and rerouting of Eel River line trains through Peru until 1902 when the Eel River was sold to the Pennsylvania.

Peru is served today by the NS former Wabash line. The C&O is gone and the Central of Indianapolis (former NKP) is out of service in both directions from Peru. The C&O coaling tower and restored C&O depot remain as of 1996.

Princeton

Princeton was laid out in 1814, and grew following completion of the Evansville and Crawfordsville in 1854. In 1882 the Louisville, New Albany and St. Louis built east-west through the center of Princeton, and in 1891–94 a successor built shops and division point facilities on the southern edge of town, served by a new bypass line around Princeton. By 1914 the Southern Railway shops employed 350 people.[25]

Today CSX and NS share a right-of-way past the

A row of car wheels, neatly lined up outside the old Ohio and Mississippi shop buildings in Washington, mark the city as a key division point and repair site on the Baltimore and Ohio line to St. Louis.   *Richard S. Simons collection*

restored depot once used by both lines. The former Southern shops, partly intact, are used by a private firm.

Richmond

Richmond's first railroad was the Indiana Central in 1853. It became a major Panhandle division point, with the east-west main line joined by lines from Cincinnati, Chicago, and Fort Wayne. Because of its junction status, Richmond had an imposing Pennsylvania depot and train shed. Engine facilities and yards, originally located near the depot, were moved in 1918–1922 to new and larger facilities east of town. Richmond was also a stop on the C&O between Cincinnati and Chicago.

Today the former PRR main line and Fort Wayne branch are gone, while the NS operates the remaining PRR lines as part of its own busy Chicago-Cincinnati line. The PRR depot, though empty, is the center of the designated Railroad Historic District. The former C&O right-of-way north of Richmond is to become a bicycle trail, while CSX continues to operate to the south.

Terre Haute

Terre Haute was a major shop town for the Vandalia, with a large roundhouse and repair shops just across the tracks from the imposing union station where the Vandalia and C&EI crossed. The three-story Romanesque depot, built in 1892, was surmounted by a high tower and had 500-foot-long train sheds stretching south and north from the railroad crossing. The Big Four had its own roundhouse and depot nearby, and later moved the roundhouse to Duane yards in northern Terre Haute. Around 1911 the Pennsylvania built a new yard and roundhouse on the east side, with a cutoff to the former Vandalia line to Logansport. A Milwaukee yard, depot, and roundhouse were in the southern part of the city, and a Milwaukee Road belt line bypassed the east side of the city. The car plant of the Terre Haute Car and Manufacturing

Co. was located at Crawford Street, and was later absorbed by American Car and Foundry.

Conrail today operates one main line through Terre Haute, using the former NYC east of Terre Haute and the PRR to the west. CSX operates the former C&EI line, while the Soo Line arrives from the north via CSX trackage rights and operates the former Milwaukee Road belt and lines to the south.

Tipton

Tipton was connected by rail to Indianapolis and Peru by 1854. Its importance as a railroad town, however, came as a division point on the LE&W and its predecessors, first completed in 1876. Tipton remained a division point for the Nickel Plate until 1933.[26]

Tipton today retains service from NS, CERA, and the Port Authority line to Indianapolis, currently (1996) with no interchange in Tipton.

Washington

The broad-gauge Ohio and Mississippi was completed through Washington in 1857. In 1888 Washington became the major division point between Cincinnati and St. Louis, when the city attracted railroad facilities away from Vincennes. The town contributed $72,000 and 70 acres of land, on which the O&M built a roundhouse, machine shop and other buildings, replacing shops in both Vincennes and Cochrane (west of Aurora).[27]

By its peak years the shops, by now under the B&O, included an enlarged roundhouse, car shops, and transfer tables. A New York Central branch came through town from north to south, but Washington was primarily a B&O town.

CSX still operates through Washington but the former NYC, now Indiana Southern, has been relocated west of town. The B&O depot and part of the roundhouse survive, and the shop buildings, including one displaying an intricate "O&M" stone monogram, are occupied in 1996 by Rescar Industries, Inc., a railroad car repair company.

15

Notable Bridges

Indiana Rail Road's Tulip Trestle (Richland Creek Viaduct) is easily the state's most spectacular railroad bridge. Like similar spans, it crosses a minor but deeply entrenched stream that requires a bridge all out of proportion to the amount of water that flows beneath it.

Located eight miles northeast of Bloomfield, near the village of Tulip, the trestle is a sensational sight when it bursts into view along a county road. It stretches 2,295 feet (originally 2,215) between valley walls at a height of 157 feet above Richland Creek. The Indianapolis Southern Railroad built the bridge in 1906 while constructing its Indianapolis–Switz City line. A similar but shorter 880-foot viaduct bridges Shuffle Creek, northeast of Unionville on the same railroad, at a height of 80 feet.[1]

When the Baltimore and Ohio Railroad realigned its Cincinnati–St. Louis route in 1901, it bridged Laughery Creek east of Osgood at a height of 109 feet. This was then the state's highest railroad bridge.[2] The B&O also operated over a high-level steel bridge on its Brazil branch, 1¾ miles north of Brazil.[3]

The Monon Railroad had three notable high bridges. The 60-foot-high Deer Creek span, one mile east of Delphi, was described as the state's second highest at one time and at 1,278 feet was the longest on the Monon system. A similar bridge spanned Wildcat Creek at Owasco but it measured only 853 feet. The line was abandoned in 1992.[4] The Paoli Trestle carried French Lick branch trains over a deep valley at the north edge of Paoli. Built in 1904, it was 100 feet high and 870 feet long, replacing a curving 1,600-foot wooden trestle as part of a line relocation. It was razed after the railroad abandoned the branch in 1981.[5]

Four massive rail bridges span the Ohio River: two at Jeffersonville, one at New Albany, and one near Evansville. Multiple railroads used all but one at various times.[6]

The 2,525-foot Big Four bridge, built in 1893, is the newest of the three that connects with Louisville, and is the farthest upstream. It was rebuilt in 1929.[7] Curiously, the owner and user of the bridge had no approach tracks and reached it over trackage rights while the tracks' owner crossed the river on a different bridge. The Big Four Railway (later New York Central) arrived on Baltimore and Ohio Railroad tracks from North Vernon but it owned two-thirds interest in the bridge until 1927, when it bought the balance from the Chesapeake and Ohio Railway.[8] With most of the North Vernon branch abandoned and the approaches removed, the isolated bridge now stands bizarrely 77.5 feet above pool stage.[9]

One and one-half miles downstream, the Jeffersonville, Madison and Indianapolis Railroad, later the Pennsylvania Railroad, built a bridge in 1870 and rebuilt it in 1919. It stretches 5,218 feet at a height of 106.7 feet above pool stage. Rebuilt as a doubletrack structure, it includes what was then the longest simple riveted-truss span ever built, 643'10½". It used all but one of the original piers.[10] The B&O used it until 1887 and the Monon also used it during most of the 1880s. Until 1921, the PRR operated a commuter service over it.[11] It is now the Louisville and Indiana Railroad bridge.[12]

Three miles downstream, the Kentucky and Indiana Terminal Railroad bridge carried trains of its three owners, the Monon, B&O, and Southern. The present structure, which for a time also had carried automobile traffic, was built in 1913, although an earlier bridge had been built in 1886. The 2,713-foot span stands a maximum of 100.1 feet above pool stage.[13]

The Louisville and Nashville Railroad, later Seaboard System and now CSX, opened a bridge down-

stream from Evansville in 1885. Its successor, which stretches 12,123 feet including approaches and stands 82.7 feet above pool stage, was completed in 1932. Illinois Central Railroad and Indiana Hi-Rail trains also have used it.[14]

Thirty-four bridges crossed the Wabash River, ranging from small headwater spans to long, massive structures in the lower reaches. Approximately 20 remain in use.[15] To permit navigation, some Wabash River bridges were movable. The Big Four bridge at Terre Haute originally had a short draw span. Surviving swing spans (now in fixed position) include the B&O Wabash River crossing at Vincennes and the NYC and Southern Railway Wabash River bridges in Gibson County. The Illinois Central, now Evansville Terminal, bridge near Grayville, Illinois, was a swing span in 1918 when a train

skidded onto it before it was locked into place. The weight of the locomotive, tender, and two coal cars transformed the span into a giant teeter-totter. Engineers lashed the locomotive to the bridge, lifted train and span by crane, and supported it with falsework. The effort was successful and the bridge remains in use.[16]

Movable bridges were also common in northwestern Indiana near Lake Michigan. Four rail lines ran parallel along Lake Michigan across the mouth of the Indiana Harbor Canal when it was built in the early twentieth century, and each had to provide movable bridges to accommodate shipping. The Chicago, Lake Shore and Eastern, the B&O, the LS&MS, and the Pennsylvania, totaling 12 tracks among them, each had to construct bridges. A swing bridge and a rolling-lift bridge, both now fixed, remain on the Norfolk Southern in Hammond, crossing the Grand Calumet. A New York Central (now Amtrak) swing span crosses Trail Creek in Michigan City, also now fixed in position.

Timber pile trestles were common on early railroads and persisted on light traffic branches. A 600-foot survivor stands on the abandoned Blooming-

This Wabash River bridge opposite Grayville, Ill., became a giant teeter-totter in 1918 when a train ran onto it before the swing span was locked firmly in place. Cranes raised the bridge with locomotive intact and returned it to its normal alignment. Previously an Illinois Central branch, it is now operated by Evansville Terminal Company.   *Richard S. Simons collection*

ton Southern Railroad one mile north of Victor, where the Victor Oolitic Stone Company uses it on its yard track, and the B&O used a high, curving 190-foot trestle on its former Bedford branch.[17] The Monon operated main-line trains over Paisley Trestle near Cedar Lake, a 963-foot floating structure that crossed a "bottomless" bog and was supported only by friction. A 1948 track relocation eliminated it.[18]

Early railroads sometimes used covered wooden bridges of the type associated with country roads. At least 32 are known to have been built, and there is speculation that twice that number may have been in service. They were favorites of the Ohio and Mississippi Railroad, later B&O and CSX, which built three across Hogan Creek in Dearborn County and one each in Ripley and Knox counties. At least 14 additional counties had covered bridges built by as many railroads. The last in use was on a Monon branch which crossed West Fork of White River west of Bloomfield. It was in service until 1935 and stood for two more years until a flood destroyed it.[19]

Railroad Covered Bridges

Railroad	Location	Stream	Year Built
BALTIMORE & OHIO RR (CSX)			
Cincinnati & Ipls Junction Ry	Brownsville	E Fork, Whitewater River	c. 1854
Ohio & Mississippi Ry	Aurora	Hogan Crk	c. 1855
Ohio & Mississippi Ry	Aurora	Hogan Crk	1868
Ohio & Mississippi Ry	5 mi W of Aurora	South Hogan Crk	c. 1855
Ohio & Mississippi Ry	3 mi NE of Osgood	Laughery Crk	c. 1854
Ohio & Mississippi Ry	Vincennes	Wabash R	1854
CHICAGO & EASTERN ILLINOIS RR (CSX)			
Evansville & Illinois RR	N edge of Evansville	Pigeon Crk	1850
Evansville & Crawfordsville RR	Hazleton	White R	1853
Evansville & Crawfordsville RR	Hazleton	White R	1868
ILLINOIS CENTRAL RR (INDIANA RR)			
Indiana & Illinois Southern Ry	Riverton	Wabash R	1886
LOUISVILLE & NASHVILLE RR (CSX)			
St Louis & Southeastern Ry	Evansville	Pigeon Crk	c. 1870
MONON RR (CSX)			
Bedford & Bloomfield RR	Elliston	W Fork, White R	1884
Bedford & Bloomfield RR	3 mi NW of Bedford	Salt Crk	1894
Louisville, New Albany & Chicago Ry	French Lick	French Lick Crk	1894
NEW YORK CENTRAL RR (CONRAIL)			
Cincinnati, Wabash & Michigan RR	Wabash	Wabash R	—
Cincinnati, Wabash & Michigan Ry	Ovid	Fall Crk	—
Cleveland, Columbus, Cincinnati & Ipls RR	Pendleton	Fall Crk	c. 1854
Ipls, Cincinnati & Lafayette RR	Shelbyville	Blue R	c. 1854
NEW YORK, CHICAGO & ST LOUIS RR (NORFOLK SOUTHERN)			
Ipls, Peru & Chicago RR	Ipls	Fall Crk	—
Ipls, Peru & Chicago RR	Ipls	Fall Crk	1880
Ipls, Peru & Chicago RR	Kokomo	Wildcat Crk	1850

Railroad	Location	Stream	Year Built
PENNSYLVANIA RR (CONRAIL)			
Columbus & Shelby RR	Lewis Crk	Just N of Lewis Crk	c. 1854
Columbus & Shelby RR	Flat Rock	Flat Rock R	c. 1854
Jeffersonville, Madison and Ipls RR	3 mi N of Crothersville	Muscatatuck R	1869
Logansport, Crawfordsville & Southwestern Ry	2 mi SE of Roseville	Big Raccoon Crk	1865
Logansport, Crawfordsville & Southwestern Ry	1/2 mi N of Jessup	Little Raccoon Crk	1865
Cincinnati & Chicago RR	Anderson	W Fork, White R	1855
Pittsburg, Cincinnati & St Louis Ry	Richmond	E Fork, Whitewater R	1852
Pittsburg, Cincinnati & St Louis Ry	Cambridge City	W Fork, Whitewater R	1852
WABASH RR			
Toledo, Wabash & Western RR or predecessor	Attica	Wabash and Erie Canal	c. 1854
Toledo, Wabash & Western RR or predecessor	Attica	Wabash R	after 1851

SOURCE: Gould, *Indiana Covered Bridges thru the Years*.

The men who blasted through a shale and sandstone ridge five miles east of Shoals during a 1901 B&O line relocation dropped their work long enough to be photographed inside the partly completed 1,160' Willow Valley Tunnel.   *Otto White from Robert F. Smith collection*

16

Tunnels

AS FAR BACK AS 1852, Hoosiers blasted tunnels through unwelcome terrain. In what is perceived as a flat state, 18 railroad tunnels have been drilled. If laid end to end, they would extend nearly four miles.[1]

First attempts were in what is now Clifty Falls State Park during efforts to reroute Indiana's first rail line and ease the 5.89% grade out of the Ohio River valley. Financial obstacles forced the Madison and Indianapolis Railroad to halt the project, but not before two tunnels had been built. One was a 600-foot bore, still intact, which is included in park tours. The second was blasted shut in the late 1880s to remove a safety hazard.[2]

Almost before conversation about these ill-fated tunnels died down, the Ohio and Mississippi Railroad (later part of the B&O and still later of CSX), built two tunnels as it pushed westward from Cincinnati to St. Louis in 1857.[3] The Lawrence County village that grew up between them appropriately was named Tunnelton. The Big or Ritner Tunnel, in daily use, measures 1,731 feet and is the state's third longest.[4] The second tunnel, named Little, extended 1,700 feet; it was daylighted in 1899.[5] At the same time, workmen drilled the 1,160-foot Willow Valley Tunnel east of Shoals to straighten the route and eliminate seven stream crossings.[6]

Indiana's most prolific tunnel builders, however, were the Southern Railway, now Norfolk Southern, and its predecessors. They built nine tunnels, half the state's total, including the Edwardsville or Duncan Tunnel, Indiana's longest, between New Albany and Georgetown. It was built in 1881 and measures 4,295 feet.[7]

Prior to this, however, three tunnels had been drilled east of the Edwardsville Tunnel but at a higher elevation. Although completed, they were never used and today are slowly disintegrating.[8] But as the track proceeded westward, it found the rugged terrain demanding more tunnels. The 700-foot Marengo Tunnel, 2½ miles east of Temple, and the 769-foot Patton, three miles west of English, remain in service. The 325-foot Georgetown Tunnel, 2½ miles west of Georgetown, was daylighted in 1945, and the 570-foot Depauw, two miles east of the town of Depauw, was bypassed in 1983.[9]

When the Southern built its French Lick branch, completed in 1907, it drilled 2,217 feet through a hill about four miles south of French Lick to create the state's second longest tunnel. Named Barton, it is now used by the French Lick, West Baden and Southern Railway tourist line.[10]

The four remaining tunnels are located in Monroe, Greene, and Martin counties. The Monon's narrow-gauge Bedford–Switz City branch ran through a 1,362-foot tunnel that was built in 1877 west of Owensburg. It was widened in 1894 to accommodate standard-gauge track, but most of the line was abandoned in 1935.[11]

The Evansville and Richmond Railroad, later the Milwaukee Road and now the Soo Line, bored a 1,106-foot tunnel in 1890, two miles northwest of Indian Springs. It remains in service but is little known because of its isolated location on the Crane Naval Surface Warfare Center grounds.[12]

Indianapolis Southern Railway, later Illinois Central Railroad, Illinois Central Gulf Railroad, and now Indiana Rail Road, drilled a 500-foot tunnel nine miles northeast of Bloomington in 1903. It is Indiana's shortest currently in use. At the same time, the railroad began to blast a 1,200-foot tunnel near Stanford, southwest of Bloomington, but a line change left it incomplete.[13]

Pullmans were named in series according to their interior accommodations. Heavyweight-era Butler University was rebuilt in the 1930s as an air-conditioned 12-section 2 double-bedroom car. *Jay Williams collection*

┼┼┼┼┼┼┼┼┼┼┼┼┼ **I7** ┼┼┼┼┼┼┼┼┼┼┼

Pullman Service

UNTIL THE AIRPLANE AND AUTOMOBILE burst upon the scene, the train was the only way to go. Overnight travelers turned to sleeping cars after they first appeared in 1837, but not until George M. Pullman entered the business in 1859 did they come into their own.[1] After he gained a monopoly in 1899, Pullman became a generic term meaning sleeping car and his company's standards of service approached luxurious perfection.[2]

Early cars contained mostly open sections where heavy curtains provided privacy, but by the late 1930s private-room cars were showing up. They were engineering marvels of comfort and space utilization. Each cubic inch served its specialized purpose. Each room had its individual toilet and wash basin, which disappeared into the wall or converted into a seat when not in use. Hollow walls became suit or shoe lockers. Deeply upholstered chairs vanished at night under beds that swung out from the walls. Thick carpets muffled all sounds.[3]

During the 1920s the Pullman Company operated more than 9,800 cars, which became rolling hotels for more than 50,000 passengers each night. Unlike most passenger cars, which stayed on a single railroad, Pullmans traveled interline routes that connected major city pairs throughout the country. One line rode six railroads to reach its destination.[4]

Trains carrying Pullman cars spun such a dense web through Indiana that they served more than 450 cities and towns. Nine Hoosier cities originated Pullman cars, which often were parked for occupancy before 10 p.m. in preparation for being whisked away by a through train arriving in the wee hours. Scores of additional stations benefited by being located on a through route that connected such cities as Chicago or St. Louis with New York. More than 200 lines that served Indiana originated in Chicago and approximately 120 more called

such cities as St. Louis, Detroit, or Louisville their homes.[5]

Spirited demand led to many route choices. At various times at least 14 combinations of railroads connected Chicago and New York and 11 joined Chicago and Boston. Five went to Buffalo and three each to Toronto and Montreal. All served Indiana stations.[6] The East's Big Two, New York Central and Pennsylvania, fielded a dazzling parade of trains carrying sleeping cars. The New York Central liked to show off its flagship Twentieth Century Limited, as well as such glamour trains as the Commodore Vanderbilt, Lake Shore Limited, and Fifth Avenue Special. To meet the competition, the Pennsylvania sent out its premier trains: Broadway, Pennsylvania, and Manhattan Limiteds, the General, and the Admiral. All stopped at Fort Wayne and most also served such intermediate stations as Valparaiso, Plymouth, and Warsaw. So heavy was the demand for sleeping car space that the New York Central, Pennsylvania, and Baltimore and Ohio operated Pullman car–only trains under such famous names as Twentieth Century, Broadway, and Capitol Limited.[7]

Not only could Hoosiers board night trains for the nation's largest cities, they could ride cars that terminated at such unlikely points as Oil City or Sharon, Pennsylvania, Kingston, New York, Galion, Ohio, or Fairmont, West Virginia.[8] Northern Michigan resorts attracted huge numbers of Hoosiers and the Pennsylvania, Pere Marquette (later Chesapeake and Ohio), and Big Four (later New York Central) individually or jointly operated Pullmans to Traverse City, Harbor Springs, and other resorts.[9] Obscure railroads such as the Cincinnati, Findlay and Fort Wayne carried Pullmans between Findlay and Fort Wayne, en route to Chicago, and the equally obscure 43-mile Chicago, Indiana and Eastern started sleeping cars at Muncie on their way to Chicago.[10]

The PENNSYLVANIA RAILROAD
offers you a Selection of Pullman Room Accommodations.

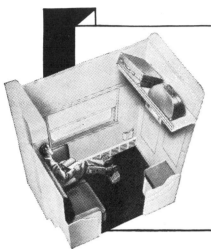

Roomette

FOR 1 PERSON

← In daytime service with bed folding into wall, providing passenger plenty of space.

Roomette in night-time service. A real bed affording all the comforts of home.

This accommodation affords complete privacy, including individual toilet and lavatory.

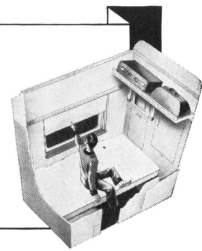

Duplex

FOR 1 PERSON

Upstairs and downstairs "Duplex" single rooms, complete with individual toilet facilities. Illustration shows them prepared for both day and night-time occupancy. Roomy sofa becomes a comfortable bed at night.

Double Bedroom

FOR 1 OR 2 PERSONS

As with all private rooms, individual toilet and lavatory are included. Illustrations show this type of room prepared for day and night-time occupancy. The sofa becomes a bed at night, over which there is a comfortable berth.

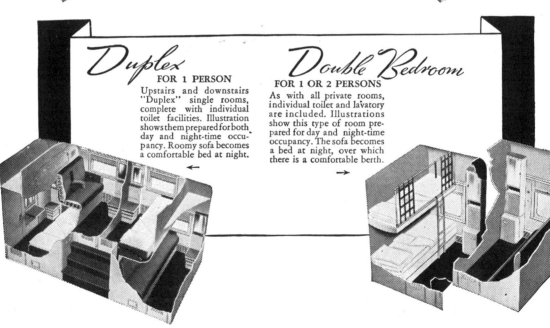

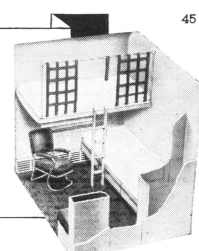

Compartment

FOR 1 OR 2 PERSONS

The Compartment sofa makes down into a bed, with an upper berth above it. →

← Compartment in daytime service with its comfortable sofa and a lounge chair. It, too, has its own individual toilet facilities.

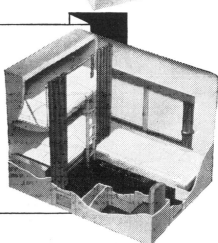

Drawing Room

FOR 1, 2 OR 3 PERSONS

← Complete with every personal facility, the spacious Drawing Room affords a living room atmosphere in day service.

Folding bed is let down at night. The sofa becomes a bed, and the upper bed, easy of access, is equally inviting. Private toilet facilities. →

Master Room

FOR 1 OR 2 PERSONS

↓ Four arm chairs for day service. Connecting room has private shower and lavatory facilities.

At night, two folding 6'4" beds. Roomy locker → provides ample space for clothes.

Comparable rates for illustrated types of Pullman accommodations between certain principal cities shown as an example. Consult page 42 of this time-table for rates applicable between other points.

BETWEEN				AND CHICAGO				
	Lower	Room-ette	Duplex Room	BEDROOM 1 Person	BEDROOM 2 Persons	Compart-ment *	Draw-ing Room **	Master Room *
New York	6.95	9.75	11.15	12.50	13.90	19.65	24.30	28.90
Philadelphia	6.40	8.95	10.20	11.45	12.75	17.95	23.10	27.75
Baltimore	6.40	8.95	10.20	11.45	12.75	17.95	23.10	27.75
Washington	6.40	8.95	10.20	11.45	12.75	17.95	23.10	27.75
Harrisburg	5.80	8.10	9.25	10.40	11.55	16.20	20.80	24.30

*for two persons
**for two or more persons

Fares shown subject to 15% Federal Tax.

Pullman Reservations in WARTIME...

Demands of the armed forces and increased business travel due to the war have placed a heavy burden on Pullman equipment. If you cannot get the accommodation you desire, may we ask you to take what is available. And we also ask that you cancel your reservations at once if you decide to postpone your trip. Someone else may have urgent need of your space.

By the late 1930s, private accommodations were replacing conventional open-section, upper and lower berth sleeping cars. They ranged from one-person roomettes and duplex rooms to compartments, drawing rooms, and master bedrooms. *Richard S. Simons collection*

Another fleet roamed through Dixie with separate cars for four cities in Georgia and five in the Carolinas. Other Pullmans were destined for such Florida resorts as Palm Beach, Miami, St. Petersburg, and Pensacola. Through sleeping cars also connected Indiana cities with New Orleans, including one that originated in Indianapolis.[11]

Among the more improbable lines through Indiana were those that connected Jacksonville, Florida, and West Yellowstone, Montana, via a six-railroad combination; a U-shaped route between Galion, Ohio, and Chicago, via Indianapolis; and a Minneapolis-Columbus, Ohio, line through Peoria and Indianapolis.[12]

In a burst of postwar optimism that failed to foresee the burgeoning air age, the three major eastern roads inaugurated a transcontinental sleeping car service through Indiana in March 1946. This was about the time C&O's Robert R. Young introduced his famous ad, "A Hog Can Cross the Country without Changing Cars, but You Can't,"[13] NYC and PRR inaugurated New York Pullmans to both Los Angeles and San Francisco, and the B&O and PRR originated similar service in Washington, D.C. These trains stopped conveniently in Fort Wayne, South Bend, and Gary and in such smaller communities as Columbia City and Syracuse.[14] Separate sleeping cars from New York and Washington traveled to seven cities in Texas and two in Oklahoma, as well as to Mexico City. Hoosiers could step aboard in Richmond, Indianapolis, Vincennes, and other cities.[15]

Indianapolis originated 32 Pullman cars to 19 destinations. Competition was fierce. Many duplications resulted because no road dared turn its back on a competitor. Both NYC and PRR originated Pullmans to Columbus, Ohio, Detroit, Evansville, Grand Rapids, Jacksonville, Florida, New York City, St. Louis, Washington, and, with the Monon, to Chicago.[16] The Evansville service was 32 miles

longer on NYC, which sent its trains roundabout via Paris, Illinois, but it chose to compete, regardless. Other originating Pullmans carried passengers to Miami, Peoria, Toledo, Cleveland, Pittsburgh, and New Orleans.[17]

Evansville travelers could choose among three Pullman routes to Chicago: C&EI or Big Four through Danville, Illinois, or Illinois Central via Mattoon, Illinois. The Big Four brought Pullmans to remote villages by stopping at Tab, Handy, Free, and Ade along the state's western border. A circuitous Evansville route to Cincinnati, established in 1872, dispatched cars via Terre Haute, and a joint C&EI-Wabash service via Danville, Illinois, carried Pullmans to Detroit.[18]

Individual cars connected Fort Wayne with Chicago, Pittsburgh, and Cleveland, and Richmond originated sleeping cars to Chicago, New York City, and, in summer, Michigan. Terre Haute had its own Chicago Pullman on the C&EI and South Bend enjoyed a Detroit sleeping car that ran to Pine on the 11-mile grandiosely named New Jersey, Indiana and Illinois Railroad before it was turned over to the Wabash.[19] As early as 1869 a through sleeping car originated in Jeffersonville and traveled to New York City via Columbus, Rushville, and Richmond.[20]

Two roads through Muncie went head-to-head for Chicago business. C&O's night train picked up a parked sleeper and the PRR-controlled Chicago, Indiana and Eastern Railway originated a train that crept through such rural towns as Matthews, Fairmont, and Swayzee before arriving at Converse, where a PRR train from Columbus, Ohio, picked up the waiting Pullman.[21]

The nationally patronized twin spas of French Lick and West Baden enjoyed Pullman service completely disproportionate to their size. Through cars operated from Chicago, Boston, and Louisville, and by two routes each from New York City and St. Louis.[22]

Indiana Cities Originating Sleeping Cars

Originating and Terminating Cities	Railroad	Remarks
Evansville and		
Chicago	Chicago & Eastern Illinois	est. 1872
Chicago	Big Four/New York Central	est. by 1913
Chicago	Illinois Central (Peoria, Decatur & Evansville)	1890s
Cincinnati	C&EI/Pennsylvania	est. 1872
Detroit	C&EI/Wabash	
Louisville	Louisville & Nashville	
Peoria	IC (PD&E)	1890s
St Louis	L&N	
Fort Wayne and		
Chicago	Pennsylvania	1920s–30s
Cleveland	Nickel Plate	1930s–50s
Pittsburgh	PRR	
French Lick and		
Boston	Monon/NYC	
Chicago	Monon	
Louisville	Monon	
New York City	Monon/NYC	
New York City	Monon/PRR	
St Louis	Monon/B&O	
St Louis	Southern	
Indianapolis and		
Chicago	Monon	One car originated at Boulevard Stn. (38th St.)
Chicago	NYC	
Chicago	Peoria & Eastern/C&EI	Operating in 1884
Chicago	PRR	
Cleveland	NYC	
Columbus, OH	NYC	Via New Castle and Springfield, OH
Columbus, OH	PRR	
Detroit	NYC	
Detroit	PRR/Wabash	
Evansville	NYC	Via Paris, IL
Evansville	PRR/C&EI	
Grand Rapids	Big Four (NYC)/Pere Marquette (C&O)	In 1890s. Via Marion, Elkhart, and Benton Harbor, MI
Grand Rapids	PRR	Via Richmond & Ft Wayne
Jacksonville, FL	NYC/Southern	Via Chattanooga
Jacksonville, FL	PRR/L&N/Central of Georgia/Georgia Southern and Florida/Atlantic Coast Line	Via Birmingham
Louisville	PRR	
Mackinaw City	PRR	Via Richmond and Ft Wayne (seasonal)
Miami, FL	PRR/L&N/ACL/Florida East Coast	Via Birmingham (seasonal)

Originating and Terminating Cities	Railroad	Remarks
Indianapolis and (cont.)		
New Orleans	IC	Began operation 1911
New York City	NYC	Via Cleveland
New York City	PRR	Via Pittsburgh
Northport, MI	PRR	Via Richmond (seasonal)
Peoria	Peoria & Eastern (NYC)	
Pittsburgh	PRR	
St Louis	NYC	
St Louis	PRR	
St Louis	ID&W/Clover Leaf	Operating in 1896
Toledo	NYC	
Traverse City, MI	PRR	Via Richmond and Ft Wayne (seasonal)
Washington, DC	B&O	Via Cincinnati
Washington, DC	NYC/C&O	Via Cincinnati
Washington, DC	PRR	Via Pittsburgh
Jeffersonville and		
New York City	PRR	Via Columbus, Shelbyville and Richmond. Began operation by 1869
Muncie and		
Chicago	C&O	
Chicago	CI&E/PRR	Via Converse
Richmond and		
Chicago	PRR	Via Logansport. Operated in 1920s and '30s
Mackinaw City	PRR	Seasonal
New York City	PRR	Operated during 1890s and 1920s
St Louis	PRR	
South Bend and		
Detroit	NJI&I/Wabash	
Terre Haute and		
Chicago	C&EI	

SOURCES: Maiken, *Night Trains; Official Guide of the Railways;* public time tables.

18

Motor Trains

IN THE EARLY 1920s, Indiana extensively expanded its highway system. Buffeted by the proliferation of paved roads and the cars to ride on them, rail passenger boardings dropped alarmingly. Short-haul runs were the most vulnerable, and deep cost cutting emerged as the only means of survival. This called for replacing steam locomotives with a variety of self-propelled motor cars, which lowered operating and maintenance costs and required fewer crew members. They often were known affectionately as "Doodlebugs."

Although passenger travel declined steadily, trains remained vital mail and express haulers, particularly to small towns which had no alternative in the pre–private delivery system days. Virtually all mail moved by rail and much sorting was done en route in railway post office cars.

As early as 1905, the St. Joseph Valley Railway used motor cars, and by 1913 the Cincinnati, Bluffton and Chicago and the Chicago, Terre Haute and Southeastern Railways also had placed cars in service. But these early units usually were small, often rough riding, and resembled city streetcars or buses on flanged wheels. Some carried as few as 16 passengers.[1]

After World War I, motor cars matured, both in capacity and performance, and Class I roads rushed to buy them as they sought to keep marginal runs operating. One manufacturer, Electro-Motive Corp., claimed that costs fell 36% when rail cars were substituted for locomotive-powered trains.[2]

This later generation of motor car usually resembled a passenger-mail-express combine. Larger cars could pull one or two coaches. Ten roads in Indiana, including the two largest, New York Central and Pennsylvania, used them on runs ranging from seven to 265 miles. A cumulative total of at least 116 daily runs served approximately 460 Hoosier cities and towns and traveled 2,450 route miles, which equaled 30% of the state's mileage. On many lines, they were the last passenger trains to survive.[3]

Motor cars came in many varieties, including storage battery and gasoline-mechanical units. Larger cars, however, usually were gasoline-electrics in which a gasoline engine drove a generator, which in turn drove the electric motors that propelled the car. Ultimately they dominated the field.[4]

Not only were motor cars operated in Indiana, they also were manufactured here. The most popular design in America had its genesis in Wabash.[5] Two other plants turned out a few units; two built demonstrators but evidently did not go into pro-

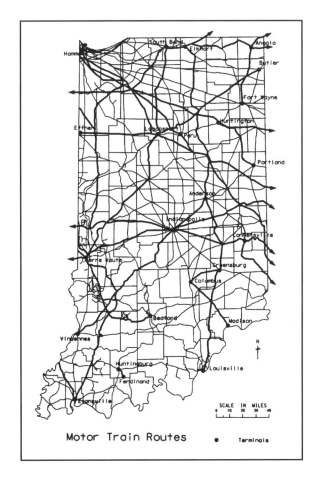

Motor Train Routes   •   Terminals

PRR car 4641 is northbound at Culver in 1932 en route from Logansport to South Bend, towing a baggage-mail combine. Gas-electrics like this 1928 Brill car served secondary passenger runs starting in the 1920s. Depot was built in 1925; it is now a community center.   *Photo by L. W. Rice—M. D. McCarter collection*

duction. One factory provided car bodies and another supplied engines to many railroads.[6]

With 29 runs at various times, the New York Central led the "Doodlebug" parade. It operated on three routes from Indianapolis, two from Evansville, and one each from Anderson, Greensburg, Connersville, Elkhart, Fort Wayne, and South Bend.[7]

But its lead was slim. The Pennsylvania operated at least 26 motor cars at various times over six of its seven lines out of Logansport, as well as on two routes out of Terre Haute, and one each from Indianapolis and Columbus. In addition to Logans-

port, Indianapolis and Terre Haute were the principal Indiana Class I railroad operating bases.[8]

The Chesapeake and Ohio Railway operated the state's longest motor train run, between Cincinnati and Hammond, and the Baltimore and Ohio Railroad operated on two routes out of Indianapolis. The Milwaukee Road connected Terre Haute and Bedford and a predecessor covered six miners' runs with motor cars. The Erie also operated motor units. The era closed in Indiana when the Milwaukee Road in July 1950 and the Baltimore and Ohio at about the same time made their last runs.[9]

During the earlier motor car period, the Cincin-

Gas-electrics like this Big Four car at Jonesboro on the Anderson-Goshen line in 1936, served secondary passenger runs starting in the 1920s. *Photo by C. E. Williams—M. D. McCarter collection*

nati, Bluffton and Chicago Railroad used three 40-passenger cars to operate eight schedules on its Huntington-Portland line.[10]

Nationally noted among motor car operators, however, was the St. Joseph Valley Railway, which connected Elkhart and Columbia, Ohio.[11] Its equipment was described as the "most outrageous, bizarre collection of rail cars ever assembled."[12] During its brief existence, the road purchased 17 rail cars from seven manufacturers.[13]

The seven-mile Ferdinand Railroad operated a gasoline car in the 1920s and the Chicago, Terre Haute and Southeastern Railway, a Milwaukee Road and Soo Line predecessor, covered six short miners' runs north of Terre Haute with a storage battery car it purchased from Thomas A. Edison's Federal Storage Battery Company.[14] The Chicago, Attica and Southern Railroad, a 141-mile line in western Indiana, used an Auto-Railer to move small shipments, but it offered no passenger service.[15]

Although mechanical deficiencies handicapped the industry's efforts, much of its limited success belongs to the Service Motor Truck Company of Wabash. Like the more prominent Mack and White truck manufacturers, Service in 1920 entered the field to meet pent-up demand created during

World War I. After a questionable start with uncomfortable vehicles that resembled buses rather than rail coaches, Service began a collaboration with J. G. Brill Company of Philadelphia, a national leader in streetcar production. With Brill providing the body, Service produced a 40-passenger car which weighed 50% more than earlier models and looked like a railroad car.[16]

Easily the most popular model until the Budd Company created the rail diesel car (RDC) in 1949, Service turned out its gas-mechanical Model 55 with Brill bodies until Brill, recognizing the potential, acquired Service in 1923 and became a fully integrated producer. It continued production until 1937.[17]

During its brief period in the rail car field, Service, and its successor, Brill, supplied approximately 150 Model 55s to nearly 40 railroads in the United States, Canada, Australia, and South Africa. They ranged from short lines to the giant Pennsylvania Railroad, New York Central, Missouri Pacific, Great Northern, and Canadian National systems. The Model 55 was the leading product of an industry leader.[18]

Indiana Truck Company in Marion and Studebaker Corporation in South Bend each built a few rail cars but they found only four customers.[19] Buckeye Manufacturing Company of Anderson, builder of Lambert automobiles, and Power Car Company of Indianapolis attempted to enter the rail car field, but there is no evidence that they built more than a single demonstrator.[20] Wayne Works in Richmond, a school bus body manufacturer, provided car bodies for the Illinois Terminal interurban lines and the famous "Galloping Geese" of the Rio Grande Southern Railroad in Colorado.[21] Midwest Engine Corporation of Indianapolis supplied power plants for Service cars and their Brill successors that went to at least 33 railroads.[22]

Motor Trains

Route	No. of Stations*	Daily Runs	Mileage per Run*	Total Daily Mileage*	Representative Year**
BALTIMORE & OHIO RR					
Ipls-Decatur, IL	13 (27)	2	77 (153)	154 (308)	1949
Ipls-Springfield, IL	11 (29)	2	77 (195)	154 (390)	1940
Ipls-Tuscola, IL***	11 (19)	2	77 (117)	154 (234)	1928
Ipls-Hamilton, OH	9 (11)	2	79 (99)	158 (198)	to Aug. 1950
CHESAPEAKE & OHIO RY					
Cincinnati, OH-Hammond	39 (46)	2	235 (265)	470 (530)	1929-31
Cincinnati, OH-Peru	23 (29)	2	132 (162)	264 (528)	1931-32
CHICAGO, TERRE HAUTE & SOUTHEASTERN RY					
Terre Haute-St Bernice	6	2	22	44	1913-16
Terre Haute-West Dana	7	2	28	56	1913-16
West Clinton-West Dana	3	2	8	16	1913-16
CHICAGO, MILWAUKEE, ST PAUL & PACIFIC RR					
Terre Haute-Bedford	24	2	82	164	1927-50
CINCINNATI, BLUFFTON & CHICAGO RR					
Huntington-Portland	16	8	52	416	1912-17
ERIE RR					
Huntington-Chicago***	28 (32)	2	122 (143)	244 (246)	c. 1929
Huntington-Marion, OH***	9 (25)	2	37 (127)	74 (254)	c. 1928

Route	No. of Stations*	Daily Runs	Mileage per Run*	Total Daily Mileage*	Representative Year**
FERDINAND RR					
Ferdinand-Huntingburg***	2	—	7	—	c. 1928
NEW YORK CENTRAL RR					
Columbus-Greensburg	8	5	26	130	1925
Connersville-Cincinnati, OH***	15 (22)	2	43 (69)	86 (138)	1931
Elkhart-Grand Rapids, MI***	3 (25)	2	15 (113)	30 (226)	—
Evansville-Paris, IL	1 (6)	2	30 (123)	60 (246)	1937
Ft Wayne-Jackson, MI	12 (22)	2	53 (100)	106 (200)	1929
Greensburg-Anderson	8	2	58	116	1941
Ipls-Mattoon, IL	18 (28)	2	80 (128)	160 (256)	1929
Ipls-St Louis, MO	18 (46)	1	80 (252)	80 (252)	1940-41
Ipls-Terre Haute	15	2	72	144	1941-48
Ipls-South Bend	21	2	171	342	1936
Ipls-Springfield, OH	15 (25)	2	78 (140)	156 (280)	1930s-40s
Louisville, KY-Anderson	12 (13)	2	136 (139)	272 (278)	1940-41
South Bend-Streator, IL	15 (29)	4	81 (152)	324 (608)	1929
Terre Haute-Evansville	31	4	135	540	1930
Washington-Evansville	15	2	58	116	1930
PENNSYLVANIA RR					
Columbus-North Madison	12	4	43	172	1931
Frankfort-South Bend***	15	2	104	208	1930
Ipls-Vincennes***	27	—	118	—	—
Logansport-Bradford, OH	24 (29)	2	93 (114)	186 (228)	1930
Logansport-Chicago, IL	16 (21)	2	91 (117)	182 (234)	1931
Logansport-Butler	24	2	93	186	1920s
Logansport-LaOtto	17	2	74	148	1929
Logansport-South Bend	9	2	69	138	1940s
Logansport-Effner	13	2	61	122	1920s
Terre-Haute-Decatur, IL	2 (20)	2	6 (94)	12 (188)	1930
Terre Haute-Peoria, IL	2 (35)	4	6 (174)	12 (348)	1930
Terre Haute-Frankfort	18	2	78	156	1930
ST JOSEPH VALLEY RY					
Angola-Columbia, OH	3 (4)	6	9 (10)	54 (60)	1915-18
Elkhart-Angola	26	4	60	240	1911-18
Elkhart-Lagrange	16	4	32	128	1911-18
Lagrange-Angola Junction	9	4	26	104	1907-08

* First figure is Indiana only. Figure in parentheses is interstate total.
** Representative years of service; not necessarily end years.
*** No. of stations and service frequency extrapolated from various time tables.

SOURCE: *Official Guide of the Railways;* public time tables.

╫╫╫╫╫╫╫╫╫╫╫ **19** ╫╫╫╫╫╫╫╫╫╫╫

Special Passenger Services

COMMUTERS

No Indiana city has supported commuter service, but frequent all-stop rush-hour trains have carried Hoosiers across state lines to Chicago, Cincinnati, and Louisville. The Pennsylvania Railroad, which traveled over three different routes, the New York Central Railroad, and the Chicago, South Shore and South Bend Railroad all have operated heavy Chicago commuter schedules, but only the South Shore remains. The Grand Trunk Western Railway, Erie Railroad, and Baltimore and Ohio Railroad each operated a round trip on rush-hour schedules but they were not true commuter runs because of infrequency of service and longer distances. Both the Big Four Railway, later the New York Central, at Cincinnati, and the Pennsylvania at Louisville operated commuter service.[1]

As early as 1893 the Pennsylvania operated a commuter train between Hebron, Crown Point, and Chicago, 52 miles and 18 trains daily between East Chicago and Chicago, 23 miles. By 1909 the Hebron train had been discontinued but the East Chicago runs had been increased to 22 and the terminal was pushed eastward three miles to Clarke Junction in Gary. By 1916, however, these trains ran on two routes, either westward through Hegewisch, Illinois, or northwest on the main New York line. A balanced schedule at intervals through the day prevailed rather than traditional rush-hour concentrations.[2]

The Pennsylvania eventually eliminated this service but inaugurated two round trips between Valparaiso and Chicago on 44 miles of the main line. In the mid–1950s, four stations were added to bring the total to 13, including one that had service in one direction only. Trains covered the distance in a minimum of 65 minutes. In 1979 Conrail, the Pennsylvania's successor, turned the service over to Amtrak, which discontinued it in 1991.[3]

New York Central, the other heavy Indiana player serving Chicago, operated 26 trains between Chesterton, Gary or Indiana Harbor, and Chicago through the 1930s and continued minimal srevice through the mid–1950s. Maximum distance was 41 miles and it required at least one hour and 20 minutes. Trains made up to 17 intermediate stops.[4]

Survivor among the commuters is the South Shore Line, which as a tax-supported commuter transportation district operates following bankruptcies by private companies. Originally a conventional Midwest interurban line, it has evolved into a heavy-duty electric railroad and in 1996 operated 40 trains daily between South Bend, Michigan City or Gary, and Chicago. In 1992 the South Shore extended its line to the Michiana Regional Airport to make it one of the few rail/air terminals in the country. Trains cover the 89.7 miles in as little as $2\frac{1}{4}$ hours.[5]

During World War I the Grand Trunk Western Railway operated a commuter train from Valparaiso, 56 miles; the Erie Railroad operated over the 69 miles from North Judson; the Michigan Central Railroad operated over the 142 miles from Kalamazoo, Michigan, and the Baltimore and Ohio Railroad ran over the 151 miles from Garrett. During the 1880s and 1890s, local accommodation trains on rush-hour schedules were operated by the Monon between Frankfort and Indianapolis, by the O&M (B&O) between Osgood and Cincinnati, B&O between Walkerton Junction and Chicago, Michigan Central between New Buffalo, Michigan, and Chicago, and Vandalia (PRR) between Edwardsport and Vincennes. In 1900, the Erie also operated a Rochester-Chicago rush-hour train. These did not meet the strict definition of commuter trains, however, because they operated over longer distances and made fewer stops.[6]

In the opposite corner of the state, the Big Four Railway operated commuter schedules between

Sometimes termed the country's last interurban, the South Shore line has been upgraded to a heavy duty electrified railroad. Offering frequent commuter service between South Bend and Chicago, its high-speed coaches carry more than 3,000,000 passengers a year. A separate corporation operates freight service. *Northern Indiana Commuter Transportation District*

Cincinnati and Aurora, 29 miles, and Cincinnati and Brookville, 44 miles, as early as 1909. Twenty-three daily trips traveled the Aurora line, although most were shuttles on the 6.7-mile branch that connected with the Cincinnati-Chicago line at Lawrenceburg Junction. As automobiles proliferated, service decreased steadily, and by 1931 had been discontinued. The Big Four also had operated a nine-stop service from Brookville, which traditionally consisted of six daily trips. It was discontinued by 1934.[7]

In the Falls Cities area, the Pennsylvania, successor to the Jeffersonville, Madison and Indianapolis Railroad, operated a commuter service that began in 1867 between Jeffersonville, New Albany, and Louisville. By 1909 it operated 19 round trips at hourly intervals between Louisville and Jeffersonville and nearly an equal number between Jeffersonville and New Albany. The service was discontinued in 1921.[8]

JOINT PASSENGER SERVICES

City pairs with a community of interest were not always connected by rails of a single company, so two railroads sometimes offered a joint service.

Others met the same need by operating on trackage rights over a second company's line and paying a fee. Either arrangement added to travelers' convenience by eliminating change of trains.

Joint services through Indiana connected Chicago with the South via Evansville, Chicago with Detroit over two separate routes, Chicago with Cincinnati, Fort Wayne with Cincinnati, and Indianapolis with French Lick, Fort Wayne, and South Bend.[9] These were in addition to joint runs during the state's infancy when the rail network was not yet well developed.

The glamour service was the Dixie fleet that the Chicago and Eastern Illinois Railroad carried for 287 miles between Chicago and Evansville, where it turned the trains over to the Louisville and Nashville Railroad for the remaining ten miles in Indiana. The L&N and connecting roads then provided continued service to Miami or Jacksonville, Atlanta, New Orleans, or Nashville.[10]

The fleet has a venerable heritage that goes back to 1908, when the Dixie Flyer was placed in service, followed by the all-Pullman Dixie Limited to Palm Beach.[11] The Dixie Flyer to Jacksonville followed by 1916 and the Dixieland and Dixie Flagler to Miami, Dixie Mail to Nashville, and Dixie Express to New Orleans came later. Although the Flagler was an all-coach train, it offered most comforts of first-class travel.[12]

Attrition set in during the late 1940s and by the late 1950s only two trains remained. The Chicago-Miami New Dixieland made its last run on November 29, 1957, and the Dixie Flyer was discontinued in 1965. Joint service continued, however, with the Georgian to Atlanta, but it too was gone by 1968.[13]

Two joint routes in different eras carried through trains between Chicago and Detroit. A Wabash Railroad predecessor operated over the Chicago and Atlantic Railroad (later the Erie) to Newton in northern Wabash County, where it continued to Detroit over its own rails. The 296-mile service began in 1887 after the Wabash leased the Eel River Railroad for a segment of its St. Louis-Detroit route but was discontinued when the Wabash opened its direct line across northern Indiana, which saved 24 miles, in 1893.[14]

About 40 years later, the Pennsylvania Railroad operating west of Fort Wayne and the Pennsylvania-controlled Wabash to the east inaugurated a joint Chicago-Detroit service. They scheduled three daily round trips, including two of the fastest runs in America, which required operating speeds of 90

mph.[15] The late afternoon Detroit Arrow—the westbound later was named the Chicago Arrow—covered the 141 miles between Chicago's Englewood suburban station and Fort Wayne in 115 minutes. The service continued until September 1949.[16]

The Monon Railroad north of Indianapolis and the Cincinnati, Indianapolis and Western Railroad, a Baltimore and Ohio Railroad predecessor beyond, inaugurated a joint Chicago-Cincinnati service by early in the century. At 308 miles, the route was the longest of four that connected the terminal cities and the roads pushed hard to be competitive. Like its two principal competitors, it offered three round trips daily but discontinued service in 1938.[17]

The Monon, jointly with the Pennsylvania, inaugurated an Indianapolis–French Lick Springs service in 1925 through Gosport Junction. During the pre-auto age, these resorts, with their luxurious hotels, attracted the affluent and the famous from throughout the country and brought them in the comfort of sleeping and parlor cars and the elegance of diners. Trains departed both terminals each morning and afternoon and when a New York Pullman was added to one consist the train was named the French Lick New Yorker. Service on the 120-mile route was eliminated in 1931.[18]

The Big Four Railway, later New York Central, and the Lake Erie and Western Railroad, later the Nickel Plate, Norfolk and Western and Norfolk Southern, offered inter-line service from Indianapolis to both Fort Wayne and South Bend and also from Fort Wayne to Cincinnati. They were inaugurated while New York Central controlled both roads. The Cincinnati trains operated on the Big Four to Connersville and northward beyond on the LE&W. Established in 1902, they continued until the mid-teens and by 1913 operated the unusual daily schedule of one trip southbound but two northbound.[19] Since they served a recreation area, trains stopped at four camps along the Whitewater River. Departing Fort Wayne in the morning and Cincinnati in both morning and late afternoon, they made the 177-mile run under the accurate but unromantically descriptive names of "Fort Wayne and Cincinnati Express" and "Cincinnati and Fort Wayne Express."[20]

The Indianapolis-Fort Wayne service operated over the Big Four to Muncie and the LE&W beyond to Fort Wayne. The 120-mile route was inaugurated in 1902 and discontinued about 1908.[21]

Indianapolis-South Bend schedules sent trains out of South Bend in the morning and out of

Indianapolis in the late afternoon. The 150-mile trip was 22 miles shorter than on the Big Four's own line through Anderson and Goshen. The joint service operated over the LE&W to Walkerton and on an NYC-controlled road the remaining 20 miles to South Bend. All three inter-line routes offered parlor car service.[22]

MINERS' TRAINS

Trains that carried miners to and from work were once a way of life in southwestern Indiana coal fields, and despite the automobile's impact, one survived until 1959.

The Pennsylvania Railroad and the Chicago, Terre Haute and Southeastern Railway, which preceded the Soo Line and the Milwaukee Road, were the state's predominant operators, but the Chicago and Eastern Illinois Railroad, the Monon Railroad, and the Central Indiana Railway played lesser roles. The Pennsylvania operated two trains out of Terre Haute and the CTH&SE operated five.[23]

The CTH&SE operated three round trips north of Terre Haute and two to the south. Using motor cars to the north in 1916, it ran short-distance trains between Terre Haute's north side and stations as far as West Dana. Running times varied from 19 minutes to one hour 20 minutes and distances from eight to 24 miles.[24] As mine activity shifted, constant schedule changes reflected the transient nature of an extractive industry. By 1931 a single round trip between Terre Haute and Clinton Yard was the lone survivor and it weathered 25 years of discontinu-ance efforts until Talleydale Mine, last on the line, closed and the Indiana Appellate Court granted the railroad's petition.[25]

Brazil also was a miners' train center. The Pennsylvania operated two daily round trips as early as 1909 on its ten-mile Center Point branch but they were gone by 1925.[26] The Central Indiana also operated miners' trains on the Brazil end of its line.[27]

South of Terre Haute, the CTH&SE operated two daily round trips to Sullivan as early as 1910 but discontinued these by 1925.[28] Other Greene-Sullivan County coal field trains connected Jasonville with Latta, Linton, and Hawton. The C&EI also operated miners' trains between the early 1900s and 1915 on a branch from Shelburn to Hymera.[29]

The Monon also entered this field from the east with a train that originated at Switz City and served such mines as Victoria, Little Betty, Vandalia 29, Little Giant, and Shirley Hill.[30] The Pennsylvania operated a Bushrod-Dugger train as early as 1893 but this was discontinued on December 27, 1923.[31] It also operated miners' trains between Bicknell and Vincennes, which were in service as early as 1893 but had disappeared by 1918. Other Pennsylvania trains ran in the Bicknell area over the 3.8-mile Knox Coal Company branch and the 1.6-mile Columbia branch.[32]

In addition to the coal mine runs, the CTH&SE and its successor, the Milwaukee Road, operated passenger trains between Bedford and Oolitic to serve the limestone industry as early as 1916, but these were discontinued sometime after spring 1928.[33]

Several major catastrophes marked early railroading in Indiana, some resulting in heavy loss of life. This Clover Leaf locomotive lies partly buried after a derailment at Marion in 1902. *Richard S. Simons collection*

20

Disasters

DESPITE an exemplary safety record, railroads have suffered occasional high-fatality disasters. In Indiana, collisions, washouts, explosions, and derailments have caused double-digit fatalities at least 13 times. Other misfortunes have taken lesser tolls. They were in addition to the nation's worst interurban disaster, which took 41 lives in 1910 near Kingsland.[1]

By the end of the Civil War, three major disasters had occurred in Indiana. On June 27, 1859, a Michigan Southern and Northern Indiana Railroad (later New York Central and Conrail) express train from Chicago crashed through a rain-weakened culvert on the South Bend–Mishawaka boundary. The usually dry ravine had become a raging torrent, and 40 passengers died, some by drowning.[2]

On September 17, 1861, a Cincinnati-bound troop train on the Ohio and Mississippi Railroad (later B&O and CSX) derailed while crossing Beaver Creek near Willow Valley in Martin County. As the cars piled up, 40 died and 100 were injured.[3]

On October 31, 1864, a Chicago-bound train carrying 508 passengers, including many soldiers on furlough, collided head-on with a freight train eight miles southeast of Lafayette on the Lafayette and Indianapolis Railroad (later New York Central and Conrail). The death toll was 30; 35 were injured.[4]

While approaching the depot in Lafayette on May 8, 1893, a Big Four train derailed when the brakes failed. Ten persons were killed, all train crew or depot bystanders.[5]

The crash that lives in history as the "Purdue Wreck" occurred on October 31, 1903, at 18th Street in Indianapolis where Methodist Hospital now stands. A special train carrying nearly 1,000 passengers on the Big Four Railway was headed for the annual Indiana-Purdue football game in Indianapolis. It collided with coal cars being switched on the main track and 17 persons died and 150 were injured. Among the victims was future governor Harry G. Leslie, a grid player, who was presumed dead and was taken to a morgue, where an attendant noticed his hand move. Leslie recovered but his injuries plagued him the rest of his life. Crews of both trains claimed the right-of-way and they were largely exonerated because of ambiguous rules.[6]

Three years later, on the stormy night of November 12, 1906, a B&O (now CSX) freight train took a siding approximately three miles south of Chesterton to meet a Chicago-bound passenger train. The train's lights to indicate a second section were dark and the freight train left the siding to collide with the following train. The toll was 44 killed and approximately 150 injured. The first passenger train's engineer was blamed for ignoring the absence of a warning whistle signal which the freight train should have given.[7]

On successive January days in 1907, the Big Four (later New York Central and Conrail) suffered two catastrophes, one under baffling circumstances. On January 19, at 2:15 a.m., a Chicago-Indianapolis passenger train sped past a red signal at Fowler and rammed a freight train pulling into a siding. The death toll was 29. Although fog had obscured signals, both crews were found to have violated rules.[8]

The following day, in one of Indiana's most puzzling disasters, 28 persons died and 39 were injured. A Big Four freight train carrying 500 kegs of rifle powder waited on a siding at Sandborn, northwest of Terre Haute, for a passenger train to overtake it. As the train passed the powder car, a tremendous explosion excavated a crater three feet deep, blew the 41-ton locomotive off the track, and caused heavy damage up to one-half mile away. Investigators never were able to find a cause.[9]

On November 13, 1912, a Cincinnati, Hamilton and Dayton Railroad (later B&O and CSX) passenger train from Cincinnati collided with a freight train standing on a siding at Arlington Avenue in Indianapolis. Because a trainman neglected to close a switch, 15 died.[10]

In both 1918 and 1921, the Michigan Central Railroad was involved in disastrous collisions in northwestern Indiana. On June 22, 1918, a Hagenbeck-Wallace circus train stopped for an emergency inspection as it left MC rails at Ivanhoe on Gary's west side. Behind it rushed an empty returning troop train which rammed the flimsy cars and ignited them. Sixty-eight died and more than 135 were injured in the state's worst rail catastrophe. Investigation revealed that the engineer had dozed while he passed two warning signals.[11]

Three years later, on February 27, 1921, the Michigan Central's Canadian thundered eastward toward Porter, where its main line to Detroit crossed the New York Central's main line to New York. Misinterpreting two warning signals, the Canadian's engineer entered the crossing at a speed estimated at 55 mph or more. A moment later, the New York Central's westbound Interstate Express, which had been cleared to cross, struck the Canadian at 50 mph. The death toll was 37.[12]

Twenty-nine died and 40 were injured near Terre Haute during the early hours of a foggy September 14, 1944. The Chicago and Eastern Illinois Railroad's Dixie Flyer, a premier train of its Florida fleet, and a northbound mail train collided head-on following disregard of signals.[13]

One of the strangest deadly wrecks occurred on June 8, 1925, at Converse, where a Chesapeake and Ohio Railway coal train crept through a narrow underpass that was being repaired. Some track crewmen stepped to the right to let the train pass; others stepped to the left. Suddenly a car derailed and several overturned. As if fate had made the decision, the coal cascaded down on the men who had stepped to the right and 12 died. Not a man who stepped to the left was injured.[14]

But the most bizarre—and luckiest—wreck occurred four miles northeast of Marion on the night of March 21, 1916. A devastating tornado lifted the Clover Leaf route's queen of the rails, the Commercial Traveler, off the track and deposited it in a field. In this uniquely Hoosier incident, there were no fatalities and only nine were injured, most of them superficially.[15]

Additional high-fatality disasters include:

January 31, 1884, Indianapolis, Monon, bridge collapse, six fatalities.

October 10, 1887, Kouts, Chicago and Atlantic (Erie), rear-end collision, nine fatalities.

March 10, 1897, Hazleton, Chicago and Eastern Illinois, washout, six fatalities.

August 14, 1911, Fort Wayne, Pennsylvania, sideswipe, four fatalities.

January 18, 1993, Gary, South Shore Line, collision on gantlet track, seven fatalities.[16]

Personalities

HOOSIERS HAVE MADE an indelible impact on many facets of the railroad industry. At least four headed major rail companies, two owned or promoted railways, and one was a nationally prominent labor leader and five-time presidential candidate. Another became an internationally known engineer.

W. W. ATTERBURY

William Wallace Atterbury became president of the powerful Pennsylvania Railroad after he had directed rail transportation in France during World War I.[1]

Born in New Albany in 1866, he was one of 12 children of an attorney who gave up his practice to become a Presbyterian Church home missionary.[2] Following graduation from Yale University in 1886, he became an apprentice in the Pennsylvania Railroad shops at Altoona, Pennsylvania, and began to climb the corporate ladder. After several promotions, he became assistant engineer of motive power in the Northwest system in 1892 and later returned to Indiana, where he served as master mechanic at Fort Wayne. Returning east, he became general manager of lines east of Pittsburgh and moved through successive vice presidencies. The American Railway Association elected him president in 1916.[3]

Selected to answer Gen. John J. Pershing's call for "the ablest man in the country" to direct French railway operations during World War I, Atterbury entered service in 1917 and was discharged a brigadier general.[4] Five European governments decorated him for his achievements.[5]

Returning to the Pennsylvania, he was elected president in 1925 and served until he resigned because of ill health in 1935. During his administration the railroad electrified its New York–Washington route and added air, bus, and truck lines to augment its rail service.[6]

Atterbury's first wife, who died in 1910, was Minnie Hoffman of Fort Wayne. He died in 1935.[7] Camp Atterbury, the huge World War II installation near Edinburg, was named for him.[8]

GEORGE A. BALL

One of five brothers who founded the glass manufacturing empire that is now Ball Corporation, George A. Ball spent most of his adult life in Muncie. Almost by accident, he acquired a 28,000-mile, $3 billion railroad empire[9] for the bargain price of $274,682.[10]

Ball and a partner he later bought out attempted to rescue the Van Sweringen brothers of Cleveland, when their overextended empire crumbled in 1935. Acquiring control, Ball offered the brothers a ten-year repurchase option but both died within little more than a year and Ball found himself owning a holding company which controlled a vast empire of railroads, warehouses, grain elevators, shipping companies, export businesses, coal mining companies, hotels, and valuable commercial real estate.[11]

Rail holdings revolved around the Nickel Plate, Chesapeake and Ohio, and Pere Marquette and, additionally, the Erie, Missouri Pacific, Chicago and Eastern Illinois, and the Wheeling and Lake Erie. Stock control varied between 43 and 57%. Lesser holdings were in Denver and Rio Grande Western, Texas and Pacific, International-Great Northern and Western Pacific. The lines blanketed 24 states and one Canadian province.[12] Ball placed the properties in a charitable trust where they remained until Robert R. Young acquired a major interest on his way to controlling the C&O and later the New York Central.[13]

Ball dropped out of sight as a rail tycoon until

nearly a decade later when he emerged as president of the Muncie and Western Railroad. In contrast to his former empire, Ball now headed a road only 4.77 miles long. He died in 1955.[14]

AMBROSE E. BURNSIDE

Born near Liberty in 1824, Ambrose E. Burnside led a distinguished, if turbulent, career as a Civil War commander, governor, U.S. senator, and railroad promoter. Appointed to the U.S. Military Academy at West Point, he served briefly in the armed forces but resigned to manufacture in Rhode Island a breech loading rifle he had invented. The venture failed after the War Department refused to grant him a contract, and he moved to Chicago for employment by the Illinois Central Railroad.[15]

When the Civil War began, Burnside was appointed commander of a regiment of Rhode Island militia and within a year was promoted to major general. Eight months later he was named Army of the Potomac commander but was relieved following the disastrous battle at Fredericksburg, Virginia. He continued in military service, however, and captured Cumberland Gap and fought at Knoxville, Tennessee.[16] Resigning in 1865, he returned to Indiana and gained control of the 26-mile Martinsville and Franklin Railroad, which had been idle after a lease had expired in 1858. Burnside rebuilt the road, extended it to an important junction at Fairland, and it resumed operations in 1866. It later became part of the New York Central system.[17]

Burnside also promoted the Indianapolis and Vincennes Railroad and its connection, the Cairo and Vincennes Railroad, which were projected to form part of a through route from Indianapolis to the Gulf of Mexico. Although the plan did not materialize, the I&V operated for many years as part of the Pennsylvania Railroad[18] and the C&V became part of the Wabash Railway[19] and later the New York Central. Burnside also was active in the Chicago and Great Eastern Railway, which became the Pennsylvania's important Chicago-Logansport line.[20]

After his railroad ventures, Burnside returned to Rhode Island where he served three terms as governor, following by one in the U.S. Senate. He died in office in 1881.[21] His name has been preserved in the distinctive side whiskers he wore, which, by transposition, are called "sideburns."

EUGENE VICTOR DEBS

Eugene Debs, the great labor leader, was born in Terre Haute in 1855. He represented the left wing of the labor movement, in contrast to the conservative craft union policies of the Railroad Brotherhoods and the AFL.

Debs began his career in the Terre Haute railroad shops and became a fireman on the Terre Haute and Indianapolis. He helped to organize a lodge of the Brotherhood of Locomotive Firemen, was made secretary, and was soon appointed editor of the Brotherhood's magazine. In 1880 he was elected national secretary and treasurer of the firemen's union. Elected as a Democrat to the Indiana General Assembly, he fought unsuccessfully in 1885 for a bill making railroad companies responsible for injuries to employees.[22]

Concluding that craft unions like the four railroad brotherhoods could not be effective in meeting the combined power of employers, Debs helped to organize the American Railway Union, based on an industry-wide model. After a successful strike against the Great Northern in April 1894, membership rose to 150,000.

In June 1894 the ARU took on the Pullman Company, which had cut wages and locked out workers at its plant in Chicago. ARU members refused to handle trains carrying Pullman cars, and the Pullman strike escalated into a major struggle between the union and the railroads. By late June every road in the Midwest was paralyzed, and the railroads appealed to President Cleveland on the grounds that U.S. mails were being disrupted. Cleveland ordered the U.S. Army to protect the trains, over the strong objections of Governor John P. Altgeld of Illinois. In the violence that followed, 22 people were killed, Debs was arrested, and the ARU was effectively broken.

Debs came out of jail a convert to socialism and was welcomed by a crowd of 100,000 in Chicago. For three decades he would run as Socialist party candidate for president, once attracting 900,000 votes while in a federal penitentiary. He died in 1926.[23]

EDWIN J. PEARSON

The son of a railroad superintendent, Edwin J. Pearson was born in Rockville in 1863. Carrying on the family railroad tradition, he worked as a rodman for the Missouri Pacific Railroad during summer vacations. Following graduation from Cornell University as a civil engineer, he was employed by the Northern Pacific Railway and successively served as division engineer, division superintendent, assistant general superintendent, and chief engineer.[24]

He left Northern Pacific in 1905 to help locate the Milwaukee Road's Pacific Coast extension across the Continental Divide. In 1911 he returned to the Missouri Pacific as vice president and in 1915 he became executive vice president of the Texas and Pacific Railway. The following year he moved to the New York, New Haven and Hartford Railroad, a leading New England system, as vice president, and a year later became its president. Although dominant in southern New England, the New Haven had suffered financial reverses, but Pearson stabilized the road, which paid its first dividend in 15 years. He died in 1928.[25]

ROOSEVELT FAMILY

Two members of the distinguished Roosevelt family served as Monon Railroad presidents. James, father of President Franklin D. Roosevelt, served in 1883–84 and continued as a director as late as 1889.[26] Born in 1828 in Hyde Park, New York, he was a career railroader who served as general manager of a Western Maryland Railway component, president of a Baltimore and Ohio Railroad ancestor, and president of the Southern Railway Security Company, which was instrumental in developing railroads in the Southeast. A Harvard law school graduate, he died in New York City in 1900.[27]

Frederick A. Delano, uncle of President Franklin Delano Roosevelt, was born in Hong Kong in 1863, was graduated from Harvard University, and began his railroad career with the Chicago, Burlington and Quincy.[28] He served as Monon president from December 1913 to August 1914.[29] Beginning in the Burlington's engineering department, he advanced to general manager but left in 1905 to head the Wheeling and Lake Erie Railroad. He also served as president of the Wabash Pittsburgh Terminal Railway and its parent Wabash Railroad before becoming Monon president. During World War I, he served in the Army Corps of Engineers on the staff of Gen. W. W. Atterbury and was discharged as a colonel.[30]

After the war, Delano served as chairman of the Federal Reserve Bank board in Richmond, Virginia, on the Smithsonian Institution executive committee, and on the Brookings Institution board. He died in 1953.[31]

SIR HENRY W. THORNTON

A Logansport native who was born in 1871, Henry W. Thornton served as the first president and chairman of Canadian National Railways, a vast coast to coast system which the Canadian government established in 1922. A $1.8 billion empire, it included hotels, steamships, and express and telegraph operations, which required the services of 115,000 employees. Earlier he had been general manager of Britain's Great Eastern Railway and had been knighted by the British crown.[32]

Graduated as a civil engineer by the University of Pennsylvania in 1894, Thornton stood 6 feet 4 inches and weighed 260 pounds. He starred in football. After a year as football coach at Vanderbilt University in Nashville, Tennessee, he turned to railroading, beginning as a draftsman for the Pennsylvania Railroad.[33]

Thornton advanced steadily to division superintendent and in 1911 was appointed general superintendent of the Pennsylvania's subsidiary Long Island Rail Road, which was New York's sprawling commuter system. In 1914 he became general manager of the Great Eastern Railway of England and during World War I he steadily moved upward to deputy director general of railroad movements. In 1918 he was named inspector general of transportation and promoted to major general. The British government knighted him in 1919 and he also was decorated by the United States, France, and Belgium.[34]

In 1922 when the Canadian government consolidated many small, weak and redundant roads into the Canadian National Railways, it looked for a strong leader to combat financial, physical, and morale problems. Sir Henry took the job and during ten years at the throttle, he welded the properties together, created an efficient operating organization, and improved morale. In six years, net revenue increased nearly 30-fold. Sir Henry speeded passenger trains, inaugurated the first coast to coast service, installed telephones on moving trains, and connected U.S. and Canadian capitals with through service.[35]

With the Depression, however, revenues fell rap-

Sir Henry Thornton, a Logansport native, shaped the Canadian National Railway system after he had helped guide British railways during World War I. He is one of more than a half-dozen Hoosiers who have left their marks on railroading world-wide.   *Richard S. Simons collection*

idly, the Liberal government which had appointed Sir Henry was voted out, and the financial drain threatened Canada's credit. Under relentless grilling by a study commission, he resigned. Broken in health, drained of spirit and impoverished, he moved to New York City, where he died in 1933.[36]

But his likeness remains in the form of bas relief plaques mounted by railway labor in at least seven stations, including Montreal's Central Station and others from Halifax and Toronto to Winnipeg and Vancouver.[37]

HARRY VON WILLER

Harry Von Willer, last president of the Erie Railroad before it merged to become the Erie-Lackawanna, was born in Greensburg in 1896 but the family soon moved to Indianapolis. He attended Purdue University but was forced to withdraw following the sudden death of his father, a New York Central conductor.

Returning to Indianapolis, Von Willer became a clerk in the Big Four (later New York Central) freight office, moved to a similar position with the Erie, and rose to vice president of traffic. After becoming president in 1956, he helped develop the joint facilities plan with the Delaware, Lackawanna and Western Railroad, which led to merger of the two companies.[38]

GEORGE W. WHISTLER

Born in Fort Wayne in 1800, George Washington Whistler acquired an international reputation as a civil engineer. Son of Major John Whistler, commandant of the Fort Wayne garrison, Whistler entered the U.S. Military Academy at West Point, and later became a professor there. He left to become a civil engineer with pioneer components of the Pennsylvania, Erie, Baltimore and Ohio, and Boston and Albany Railroads.[39]

In 1839, as Russia planned a 420-mile Moscow-St. Petersburg railroad, Czar Nicholas I turned to America for engineering expertise. He named Whistler consulting engineer for the line, which opened in 1842. Whistler died in St. Petersburg seven years later.[40]

His son, James A. McNeill Whistler, won worldwide acclaim as an artist and was best known for a portrait named "Arrangement in Gray and Black," popularly known as "Whistler's Mother."[41]

Notes

2. BEGINNINGS: 1830–1860

1. Elmer G. Sulzer, "Locomotives for the Madison Hill; Motive Power on the Madison & Indianapolis Railroad," *Railway & Locomotive Historical Society Bulletin* 123, p. 24.

2. John F. Stover, *Iron Road to the West: American Railroads in the 1850s* (New York: Columbia University Press, 1973), p. 180.

3. Daniel L. Schodek, *Landmarks in American Civil Engineering* (Cambridge: MIT Press, 1987), p. 36.

4. Carter Goodrich, *Government Promotion of American Canals and Railroads 1800–1890* (New York: Columbia University Press, 1960), p. 54.

5. Jack Gieck, *A Photo Album of Ohio's Canal Era 1825–1913* (Kent, Ohio: Kent State University Press, 1988, p. 3.

6. John F. Stover, *History of the Baltimore and Ohio Railroad* (West Lafayette: Purdue University Press, 1987), p. 27.

7. Jacob P. Dunn, *Greater Indianapolis* (Chicago: Lewis Publishing Co., 1910), p. 143.

8. Indiana *House Journal,* 1834–35, pp. 346–47, as quoted in Charles R. Poinsatte, *Fort Wayne during the Canal Era, 1828–1855* (Indianapolis: Indiana Historical Bureau, 1969), pp. 256–57.

9. Goodrich, *Government Promotion of American Canals and Railroads,* p. 140.

10. Victor M. Bogle, "Railroad Building in Indiana, 1850–1855," *Indiana Magazine of History* 58, no. 3 (Sept. 1962), p. 213.

11. Sulzer, "Locomotives for the Madison Hill," p. 23.

12. Paul Trap, "The Detroit & Pontiac Railroad," R&LHS *Railway History* 168 (Spring 1993), pp. 17–50.

13. Sulzer, "Locomotives for the Madison Hill," p. 30.

14. Ibid., p. 27.

15. Goodrich, *Government Promotion of American Canals and Railroads,* p. 141.

16. Alvin F. Harlow, *The Road of the Century: The Story of the New York Central* (New York: Creative Age Press, 1947), p. 358.

17. Dunn, *Greater Indianapolis,* p. 148.

18. Ibid., p. 149.

19. Ibid., p. 146.

20. Sulzer, "Locomotives for the Madison Hill," pp. 41–42.

21. Bogle, "Railroad Building in Indiana," p. 215.

22. Ared Maurice Murphy, "The Big Four Railroad in Indiana," *Indiana Magazine of History* 21 (June–Sept. 1925), p. 121.

23. Harlow, *Road of the Century,* pp. 379–81.

24. Murphy, "The Big Four Railroad in Indiana," p. 145.

25. H. C. Bradsby, *History of Vigo County* (Chicago: S. B. Nelson), 1891, p. 566.

26. Dunn, *Greater Indianapolis,* p. 152.

27. Harlow, *Road of the Century,* p. 253.

28. Abraham E. Weaver, *A Standard History of Elkhart Co.* (Chicago: American History Society, 1916), p. 170.

29. Ibid., p. 171.

30. Poinsatte, *Fort Wayne during the Canal Era,* p. 261.

31. Goodrich, *Government Promotion of American Canals and Railroads,* p. 141.

32. George H. Burgess and Miles C. Kennedy, *Centennial History of the Pennsylvania Railroad Company, 1846–1946* (Philadelphia: Pennsylvania Railroad, 1949), p. 77.

33. The mileage was New York—2,685; Ohio—2,453; Illinois—1,884; Pennsylvania—1,581; and Indiana—1,406. Bogle, "Railroad Building in Indiana," p. 220.

34. Poinsatte, *Fort Wayne during the Canal Era,* pp. 255-256.

35. Stover, *History of the Baltimore and Ohio Railroad,* p. 86.

36. William Swartz, "The Wabash Railroad," R&LHS *Railway History* 133 (1975), p. 34.

37. Burgess and Kennedy, *Centennial History of the Pennsylvania Railroad Company,* p. 178.

38. Ira Ford, ed., *History of Northeastern Indiana* (Chicago: Lewis Publishing Co., 1920), p. 573.

39. Ibid., p. 343.

40. John A. Rehor, *The Nickel Plate Story* (Milwaukee: Kalmbach Books, 1965), p. 98.

41. Ibid., p. 100.

42. Fort Wayne *Daily Times,* Nov. 2, 1854, celebrating completion of railroad from the east, quoted in Poinsatte, *Fort Wayne during the Canal Era,* p. 269.

43. Dunn, *Greater Indianapolis,* p. 152.

44. Quoted in ibid., p. 256.

45. Ibid., p. 153.

46. John H. White, Jr., "Once the Greatest of Builders: The Norris Locomotive Works," R&LHS *Railway History* 150 (Spring 1984), p. 17.

47. Richard S. Simons, "Indiana's Railroad Tunnels," *National Railway Bulletin* 55, no. 5 (1990), p. 13. (*National Railway Bulletin* is published by the National Railway Historical Society, Philadelphia.)

48. Harlow, *Road of the Century,* p. 259.

49. Stover, *History of the Baltimore and Ohio Railroad,* p. 31.

50. Robert Brown, "Pioneer Locomotives of America," *Railway & Locomotive Historical Society Bulletin* 101 (Oct. 1959), p. 40.

51. Harlow, *Road of the Century*, p. 268.

52. Ibid., p. 357.

53. Stover, *History of the Baltimore and Ohio Railroad*, p. 86.

54. T. D. Clark, "The Lexington and Ohio Railroad—A Pioneer Venture," *Kentucky State Historical Society Register*, Jan. 1933, p. 16.

55. Dunn, *Greater Indianapolis*, p. 143.

56. Sulzer, "Locomotives for the Madison Hill," p. 24.

57. Burgess and Kennedy, *Centennial History of the Pennsylvania Railroad Company*, p. 247.

58. Col. Morris, quoted in Murphy, "The Big Four Railroad in Indiana," p. 119.

59. Burgess and Kennedy, *Centennial History of the Pennsylvania Railroad Company*, p. 246.

60. Sulzer, "Locomotives for the Madison Hill," p. 27.

61. Francis Anthony Chevalier de Gerstner, "Letters from the United States of America on Internal Improvements, Steam Navigation, Banking, & etc.," tr. and ed. Frederick C. Gamst, R&LHS *Railway History* 163 (Autumn 1990), p. 45.

62. Gary W. Dolzall and Stephen F. Dolzall, *Monon: The Hoosier Line* (Glendale, Calif.: Interurban Press, 1987), p. 32.

63. Murphy, "The Big Four Railroad in Indiana," p. 118.

64. Report of Mar. 6, 1849, quoted in ibid., p. 118.

65. Sulzer, "Locomotives for the Madison Hill," p. 24.

66. Murphy, "The Big Four Railroad in Indiana," p. 145.

67. Dunn, *Greater Indianapolis*, p. 143.

68. John H. White, Jr. *Cincinnati Locomotive Builders* (Washington: Museum of History and Technology, Smithsonian Institution, 1965), p. 6.

69. Brown, "Pioneer Locomotives of America."

70. Sulzer, "Locomotives for the Madison Hill," p. 42.

71. William D. Edson, "Panhandle Locomotives," R&LHS *Railway History* 141, p. 56.

72. White, *Cincinnati Locomotive Builders*, p. vii.

73. Ibid., pp. 147–160.

74. Charles E. Fisher, "Locomotive Builders of the United States," *Railway & Locomotive Historical Society Bulletin* 58 (May 1942), p. 62.

75. Sulzer, "Locomotives for the Madison Hill," pp. 31–32.

76. Ibid., p. 40.

77. Ibid.

78. Ibid.

79. Horace Porter, "Railway Passenger Travel, 1825–1880," *Scribner's*, Sept. 1988; reprinted by *Americana Review*, 1962, unpaged.

80. Quoted in Dunn, *Greater Indianapolis*, p. 146.

81. Ibid., p. 150.

82. Ibid., p. 153.

3. EXPANSION AND CONSOLIDATION: 1860–1900

1. *Chicago Daily Tribune*, 20, 21 Oct. 1874; and *Valparaiso Messenger*, 27 Oct. 1874.

2. Allen W. Trelease, *The North Carolina Railroad, 1849–1871, and the Modernization of North Carolina* (Chapel Hill: University of North Carolina Press, 1991), p. 327.

3. Robert F. Smith, *From the Ohio to the Mississippi* (Cincinnati: Mt. Airy Printing Co., 1965).

4. B. A. Botkin and Alvin F. Harlow, eds., *A Treasury of Railroad Folklore* (New York: Crown Publishers, 1953), p. 110.

5. E. G. Campbell, *The Reorganization of the American Railroad System, 1893–1900* (New York: AMS Press, 1968; first published 1938), pp. 10–11.

6. Figures from *Poor's Manual of the Railroads of the United States*, reported in Emma Lou Thornbrough, *Indiana in the Civil War Era 1850–1880* (Indianapolis: Indiana Historical Society, 1965), p. 361.

7. Ibid., p 361.

8. *History of LaPorte County*, 1880, p. 597.

9. George W. Hilton, *American Narrow Gauge Railroads* (Stanford, Calif.: Stanford University Press, 1990), p. 111.

10. National Park Service, *The Evolution of Transportation in Western Pennsylvania* (Special History Study, NPS, U.S. Dept. of Interior, May 1994), pp. 102–107.

11. George W. Hilton, *American Narrow Gauge Railroads* (Stanford, Calif.: Stanford University Press, 1990), p. 103.

12. David McLellan and Bill Warrick, *The Lake Shore & Michigan Southern Railway* (Polo, Ill.: Transportation Trails, 1989), p. 45.

13. Alvin F. Staufer, *New York Central's Early Power: 1813–1916* (Medina, Ohio: Alvin Staufer, 1967), p. 214.

14. Sanborn maps, various.

15. George W. Hilton, *Monon Route* (Berkeley: Howell-North Books, 1978), p. 105.

16. Ibid., p. 109.

17. George Vaughn, "Design and Maintenance of Track Tanks," *Railway Age Gazette*, Apr. 13, 1913, pp. 893–896.

18. Trelease, *The North Carolina Railroad, 1849–1871*, p. 315.

19. Campbell, *The Reorganization of the American Railroad System*, p. 12.

20. Goodrich, *Government Promotion of American Canals and Railroads*, p. 254, citing Goodrich, "Local Government Planning of Internal Improvements," *Political Science Quarterly* 66 (1951), pp. 432–34.

21. Ibid., p. 261.

22. Dunn, *Greater Indianapolis*, p. 258.

23. Ibid., p. 261.

24. Goodrich, *Government Promotion of American Canals and Railroads*, p. 240.

25. Trelease, *The North Carolina Railroad*, p. 315.

26. Staufer, *New York Central's Early Power*, p. 198.

27. *Daviess County Democrat*, July 29, 1871, cited in Smith, *From the Ohio to the Mississippi*.

28. Maury Klein, *History of the Louisville & Nashville Railroad* (New York: Macmillan, 1972), p. 191.

29. Ibid., p. 318.

30. *Central Headlight* 20, no. 3, fourth quarter, 1990 (bulletin of the New York Central System Historical Society).

31. Dunn, *Greater Indianapolis*, p. 152.

32. Burgess and Kennedy, *Centennial History of the Pennsylvania Railroad Company*, p. 292.

33. Ibid., p. 293.

34. Jeremy Atack and Jan K. Brueckner, "Steel Rails and American Railroads, 1867–1880," *Explorations in Economic History* 19 (Oct. 1982): pp. 339–59.

35. Ibid.

36. Murphy, "The Big Four Railroad in Indiana," p. 21.

37. Dolzall and Dolzall, *Monon: The Hoosier Line*, p. 42.

38. Burgess and Kennedy, *Centennial History of the Pennsylvania Railroad Company*, p. 718.

39. William S. Young, "Extra 1 South," *Railroading* 26 (Feb. 1969), p. 11.

40. *Locomotive*, June 9, 1860, cited in Harlow, *Road of the Century*, p. 371.

41. John H. White, Jr., *The Great Yellow Fleet: A History of American Railroad Refrigerator Cars* (San Marino, Calif.: Golden West Books, 1986), fig. 4.34.

42. McLellan and Warrick, *The Lake Shore & Michigan Southern Railway*, p. 99.

43. David G. Blaine, "The Westinghouse Air Brake Story," *Trains*, Oct. 1975, pp. 44–53.

44. Merle Rice, ed., *History of the Pennsylvania Railroad's Fort Wayne Shops* (Fort Wayne: Fort Wayne Public Library, 1966), p. 16.

45. John H. White, Jr., "Railroad Car Builders of the United States," R&LHS *Railway History* 138 (1978), pp. 5–29.

46. John H. White, Jr., *The American Railroad Freight Car* (Baltimore: Johns Hopkins University Press, 1993), p. 143.

47. White, "Railroad Car Builders of the United States," p. 11.

48. *Cincinnati Commercial*, Sept. 6, 1880, cited in Smith, *From the Ohio to the Mississippi*.

49. Cited in Rice, *History of the Pennsylvania Railroad's Fort Wayne Shops*, pp. 20–21.

50. Horace Porter, "Railway Passenger Travel, 1825–1880," *Scribner's*, Sept. 1888, unpaged.

51. Harlow, *Road of the Century*, p. 395.

52. McLellan and Warrick, *The Lake Shore & Michigan Southern Railway*, pp. 79, 100.

53. Ibid., p. 100, 103.

54. Walter G. Berg, *Buildings and Structures of American Railroads* (New York: John Wiley, 1893. Repr. Newton Gregg, c. 1977), pp. 252, 286.

55. *The Evolution of Transportation in Western Pennsylvania*, NPS, May 1994, p. 92.

56. *The Official Guide of the Railways and Steam Navigation Lines of the United States, Puerto Rico, Canada, Mexico, and Cuba* (New York: National Railway Publication Co., June 1893).

57. White, *The American Railroad Freight Car*, p. 128.

58. Ibid., p. 60.

59. Ibid., p. 129.

60. Ibid.

61. Ibid.

62. Ibid.

4. THE ERA OF DOMINANCE: 1900–1930

1. Elmer G. Sulzer, *Ghost Railroads of Indiana* (Indianapolis: V. A. Jones, 1970), p. 8.

2. Ibid.

3. Jerry Marlette, *Electric Railroads of Indiana* (Indianapolis: Hoosier Heritage Press, 1980), p. 8.

4. George W. Hilton and John F. Due, *Electric Interurban Railways of America* (Stanford, Calif.: Stanford University Press, 1960), p. 275.

5. Marlette, *Electric Railroads of Indiana*, p. 17.

6. In addition to the Marlette and Hilton books cited above, the later years of the Indiana Interurbans are described in George K. Bradley, *Indiana Railroad: The Magic Interurban* (Chicago: Central Electric Railfans' Association, 1991).

7. Harlow, *Road of the Century*, p. 376.

8. Sulzer, *Ghost Railroads of Indiana*, p. 53.

9. Simons, "Indiana's Railroad Tunnels," and USGS 7.5 minute quadrangle map, Huron, Indiana.

10. Dunn, *Greater Indianapolis*, p. 153.

11. Cleland B. Wyllie, "Route of the Freight 400's," *Trains*, Jan. 1947, p. 21.

12. Indiana Railroad Commission Report, 1912.

13. Clifton J. Phillips, *Indiana in Transition: The Emergence of an Industrial Commonwealth, 1880–1920* (Indianapolis: Indiana Historical Bureau and Indiana Historical Society, 1968), p. 260.

14. Railroad Commission of Indiana, *Fourth Annual Report*.

15. Railroad Commission Report, 1912, p. 14.

16. Ibid.

17. *Richmond Palladium*, 25 Mar. 1921, p. 10.

18. John A. Droege, *Freight Terminals and Trains* (New York: McGraw-Hill, 1912).

19. Michael W. Blaszak, "Change on the Harbor: Whither the Indiana Harbor Belt?" *Trains*, Mar. 1986, p. 27.

20. Ibid.

21. Letter from James Alexander, 1/6/96.

22. Vaughn, "Design and Maintenance of Track Tanks," pp. 893–96.

23. Letter from James Alexander, 1/6/96.

24. Donald J. Heimburger, *Wabash* (Forest Park, Ill.: Heimburger House Publishing, 1984), p. 22.

25. Ibid., p. 4.

26. Ibid., p. 170.

27. Sulzer, *Ghost Railroads of Indiana*, p. 222.

28. Staufer, *New York Central's Early Power*, p. 270.

29. Ibid., p. 219.

30. Al Armitage, "NYC H–5 Mikado," *Mainline Modeler*, June 1994, p. 60.

31. McLellan and Warrick, *The Lake Shore & Michigan Southern Railway*, p. 72.

32. Rehor, *The Nickel Plate Story*, p. 407.

33. David P. Morgan, "M–300 to M–10000: The Formative Years," *Trains*, Nov. 1963, pp. 38–43.

34. John Riddell, "Canadian National's 30-foot twin hoppers," *RMC*, Oct. 1996, p. 61.

35. Burgess and Kennedy, *Centennial History of the Pennsylvania Railroad Company*, p. 774.

36. Riddell, "Canadian National's 30-foot twin hoppers," p. 61.

37. White, *The American Railroad Freight Car*, p. 597.

38. Ibid.

39. Burgess & Kennedy, *Centennial History of the Pennsylvania Railroad Company*, p. 770.

40. Ibid., p. 751.

41. Ibid.

42. Ibid.

43. Ibid., p. 752.

44. Stover, *History of the Baltimore and Ohio Railroad*, p. 226.

45. Francis H. Parker, *Indiana Railroad Depots: A Threatened Heritage* (Muncie: Ball State University, 1989), p. 10.

46. Marion County Historical Survey, p. 168.

47. Dunn, *Greater Indianapolis*, pp. 257–63.

48. 1911 Indiana Railway Commission Report.

49. Lucius Beebe, *20th Century* (Berkeley: Howell-North, 1962), p. 39.

50. Ibid., pp. 49, 174.

51. *Official Guide of the Railways*, Feb. 1922; Harry Stegmaier, *Baltimore & Ohio Passenger Service, 1945–1971. Vol. 1: The Route of the National Limited* (Lynchburg, Va.: TLC Publishing, 1993), p. 9.

52. Beebe, *20th Century*, p. 49.

53. Rehor, *The Nickel Plate Story*, p. 210.

54. *Pullman Facts for 1929*—The Pullman Co.

55. R. Lyle Key, Jr., *Midwest Florida Sunliners* (Godfrey, Ill.: RPC Publications, 1970), p. 6.

56. Ibid., p. 78.

57. Ibid., p. 77.

58. Ibid., p. 8.

59. Rehor, *The Nickel Plate Story*, p. 155.

60. Ibid., p. 212.

61. 1911 Indiana Railway Commission Report.

62. Indiana Railroad Commission Report for 1909.

63. Droege, *Freight Terminals and Trains*, p. 165.

64. Ibid.

65. Ibid.

66. D. H. Dinan, "Main Tracking of Freight Trains," *Railway Age*, Feb. 13, 1926, p. 441.

67. Richard Saunders, *The Railroad Mergers and the Coming of Conrail* (Westport: Greenwood Press, 1978), p. 29.

68. Ibid., p. 4.

69. Phillips, *Indiana in Transition*, p. 259.

70. Ibid.

71. Ibid., p. 261.

72. Burgess and Kennedy, *Centennial History of the Pennsylvania Railroad Company*, p. 535.

73. Stover, *Iron Road to the West*, p. 192.

74. Ibid., p. 196.

5. THE ERA OF TRANSITION: 1930–1960

1. Hilton, *Monon Route*, p. 197.

2. Ibid., p. 210.

3. Jeremy Taylor, "Gravity Switching by the New York Central on the Eve of Marger, Part 2" *Central Headlight* 20, no. 4, 1990, p. 31.

4. Jeremy Taylor, letter to author, 8/29/1994.

5. Jeremy Taylor, "Gravity Switching by the New York Central on the Eve of Marger, Part 3," *Central Headlight* 21, no. 2, 1991, p. 17.

6. Ibid.

7. Ibid.

8. Ibid.

9. Rehor, *The Nickel Plate Story*, p. 360.

10. Michael W. Blaszak, "The J: A Centennial History (2)," *Trains*, Sept. 1989, p. 31.

11. Heimburger, *Wabash*.

12. Brian Hollingsworth, *The Illustrated Encyclopedia of the World's Steam Passenger Locomotives* (New York: Crescent Books, 1982), p. 158.

13. Richard Adams, "Pennsylvania 4–8–2," *Mainline Modeler*, Jan. 1987, p. 25.

14. Donald Heimburger, "B&O Steam Days," *S Gaugian*, Sept.–Oct. 1981, p. 35.

15. Victor Baird photo collection.

16. Hollingsworth, *The Illustrated Encyclopedia of the World's Steam Passenger Locomotives* p. 125.

17. Amtrak National Timetable, Spring/Summer 1996, p. 14.

18. Heimburger, *Wabash*, p. 256.

19. Robert A. Le Massena, "The Strange Story of Mr. Kiefer's superlative S class 4–8–4s," *Trains*, Mar. 1984, pp. 46–51.

20. David P. Morgan, *Diesels West* (Milwaukee, Wis.: Kalmbach Publishing, 1963), p. 47.

21. Brian Reed, ed., *Locomotives in Profile*, vol. 1 (New York: Doubleday, 1971), p. 35.

22. James E. Kranefeld, "Railroads on Parade at the World of Tomorrow," *National Railway Bulletin* 54, no. 4 (1989), p. 14.

23. Donald J. Bush, "Raymond Loewy and the World of Tomorrow," in Angela Schonberger, ed., *Raymond Loewy: Pioneer of American Industrial Design* (Berlin: Prestel, 1990).

24. Dolzall and Dolzall, *Monon: The Hoosier Line*, p. 77.

25. *Railway Age*, May 21, 1951, p. 84.

26. Ibid., p. 82.

27. Rehor, *The Nickel Plate Story*, p. 270.

28. Hilton, *Monon Route*, p. 185.

29. Burgess and Kennedy, *Centennial History of the Pennsylvania Railroad Company*, p. 747.

30. Thomas W. Dixon, *The Chesapeake & Ohio in Color, 1950–1975* (Lynchburg, Va.: TLC Publishing, 1992), p. 73.

31. Stover, *History of the Baltimore and Ohio Railroad*, p. 338.

32. Hilton, *Monon Route*, p. 317.

33. NYC Annual Report, 1953, p. 32.

34. Robert J. Yanosey, *Pennsy Diesel Years* (Edison, N.J.: Morning Sun Books, 1988), p. 148.

35. Louis A. Marre, "All About Sharks," *RMC*, May 1972, pp. 34, 37, quote p. 35.

36. David Ingles, "Landmark Locomotives: EMD's GP7," *Trains*, June 1995, p. 48.

37. Patrick C. Dorin, *The Grand Trunk Western Railroad* (Seattle: Superior Publishing, 1977).

38. Sulzer, "Locomotives for the Madison Hill."

39. J. David Ingles, "Too Big, Too Early, Too Different," *Trains*, Jan. 1996, pp. 60–65.

40. Gordon Chappell, *Steam over Scranton: The Locomotives of Steamtown* (Washington, D.C.: National Park Service, Special History Study, 1991), p. 295.

41. David R. Sweetland, *New York Central Steam* (Edison, N.J.: Morning Sun Books, 1992), p. 128.

42. Don Ball, *America's Colorful Railroads* (New York: Bonanza, 1978, p. 85.

43. David R. Sweetland, *Pennsy Steam Years* (Edison, N.J.: Morning Sun Books, 1992), p. 128.

44. Stover, *History of the Baltimore and Ohio Railroad*, p. 339.

45. Ibid., p. 342.

46. Victor Baird, New Haven, Ind., catalog of photographs, July 1995.

47. John L. Gorsky, "Milwaukee Junction 1960," *National Railway Bulletin* 56, no. 1 (1991), pp. 4–11.

48. Rehor, *The Nickel Plate Story*, p. 360.

49. *The Evolution of Transportation in Western Pennsylvania*, NPS, May 1994, p. 118.

50. Rehor, *The Nickel Plate Story*, p. 256.

51. Linn H. Westcott, "Begin CTC," *Trains*, Sept. 1947, p. 14.

52. George S. Rainey, *Demise of the Iron Horse* (Berne: Economy Printing, 1969), p. 35.

53. Patrick Dorin, *The Chesapeake & Ohio Railway* (Seattle: Superior Publishing, 1981), p. 116.

54. Rehor, *The Nickel Plate Story*, p. 256.

55. Simmons-Boardman map, 1950.

56. S. Kip Farrington, *Railroading from the Rear End* (New York: Howard McCann, Inc., 1946), p. 264.

57. *Indianapolis Star Sunday Magazine*, Feb. 25, 1951, pp. 24–25.

58. Key, *Midwest Florida Sunliners*, p. 12.

59. Short note, no author, *Trains*, June 1941, p. 50.

60. Hilton, *Monon Route*, p. 191.

61. Stegmaier, *Baltimore & Ohio Passenger Service, 1945–1971. Vol. 1: The Route of the National Limited* p. 2.

62. Rehor, *The Nickel Plate Story*, p. 373.

63. *Railway Age*, Apr. 23, 1951.

64. S. Kip Farrington, *Railroads at War* (New York: Coward-McCann, 1944), pp. 98–105.

65. Rehor, *The Nickel Plate Story*, p. 264.

66. *Railway Age,* Jan 15, 1951.

67. Short note, no author, *Central Headlight*, fourth quarter, 1990, p. 11.

68. *Railway Age,* Jan 8, 1951.

69. Freeman Hubbard, "Will 'Piggyback' make the boxcar obsolete?" *Railroad Magazine*, Feb. 1958, p. 28.

70. Ibid., p. 29.

71. Michael W. Blaszak, "Intermodal: Railroading's Indispensable Adaptation," *Pacific RailNews*, Sept. 1996, p. 30.

72. Short note, no author, *Central Headlight*, fourth quarter, 1990, p. 11.

6. RAILROADS RECONFIGURED: 1960 TO THE PRESENT

1. "The Railway Market," *Railway Age,* Feb. 1995, p. 8.

2. Stegmaier, *Baltimore & Ohio Passenger Service, 1945–1971. Vol. 1: The Route of the National Limited* p. 4.

3. Roger Bradley, *Amtrak: The US National Railroad Passenger Corporation* (Poole, Dorset: Blandford Press, 1985), p. 29.

4. McLellan and Warrick, *The Lake Shore & Michigan Southern Railway*, p. 85.

5. Quoted in Saunders, *The Railroad Mergers and the Coming of Conrail*, p. 270.

6. Bradley, *Amtrak*, p. 27.

7. Harold A. Edmonson, ed., *Journey to Amtrak: The Year History Rode the Passenger Train* (Milwaukee: Kalmbach Books, 1972), pp. 102–104.

8. Patrick C. Dorin, *The Domeliners* (Seattle: Superior Publishing, 1978), pp. 197, 198; various Amtrak timetables.

9. Not shown is the brief rerouting of the Floridian onto the former C&EI during 1975, which did not appear in any Amtrak time table (Dolzall and Dolzall, *Monon: The Hoosier Line*, p. 173).

10. 1995 Indiana Rail Plan, p. 262.

11. "High Speed Group Touts Amtrak, Florida Plans," *Trains*, Sept. 1996, p. 19.

12. News Release, Amtrak and MDOT, Friday, Oct. 11, 1996.

13. Blaszak, "Intermodal," p. 33.

14. News Release, Oct. 15, 1996.

15. "CSX, Norfolk Southern Agree on Division of Conrail." Press release, CSX Corporation and Norfolk Southern Corporation, Richmond and Norfolk, Va., April 8, 1997.

16. Indiana Department of Transportation (henceforth INDOT) abandonment reports.

17. 1975 State rail plan, p. 9.

18. Edward A. Lewis, *The "DO" Lines* (Strasburg: The Baggage Car, 1977), p. 7.

19. Blaszak, "Intermodal," p. 33.

20. *Railway Age*, Apr. 1995, p. 1.

21. Ibid.

22. Ibid.

23. Edward A. Lewis, *American Shortline Railway Guide*, 4th ed. (Waukesha, Wis.: Kalmbach Books, 1991), p. 125.

24. Indiana Code, Title 8–9–2–4; Lawrence Johnson, "Answering the Call," *Trains*, Nov. 1994, p. 75.

25. "Railroads Haul Profits in Utility-Owned Coal Cars," *Progressive Railroading*, Jul. 1996, p. 43.

26. Bruce P. Curry, "Short Line Fever," *Railroad Model Craftsman*, Feb. 1979, p. 66. Booz-Allen and Hamilton, *Piggyback: The Efficient Alternative for the 80's* (a report for Transamarica Interway, New York, Mar. 1980), p. xv.

27. Jim Panza, "Railbox Boxcar," *Railroad Model Craftsman*, Aug. 1984, p. 101.

28. Curry, "Short Line Fever," pp. 62–69.

29. David G. Casdorph, "Modern Auto Racks," *Railroad Model Craftsman*, May 1993, p. 87.

30. Simons, "Indiana's Railroad Tunnels," p. 17.

31. Bill Stephens, "Automotive Artery, *Trains*, Jan. 1996, pp. 42–55.

32. *Official Guide of the Railways*, Apr. 1967.

33. Blaszak, "Intermodal: Railroading's Indispensable Adaptation," p. 30.

34. Booz-Allen Hamilton, *Piggyback: The Efficient Alternative for the 80's*, p. 6.

35. *Railway Age*, Apr. 8, 1921.

36. Jim Hediger, "New York Central's Flexi-Van Flatcar," *Model Railroader*, Feb. 1992, p. 96.

37. Blaszak, "Intermodal," p. 35.

38. Ibid., p. 36.

39. *Railway Age,* Oct. 1994.

40. Rich Wallace, "Why Does J. B. Hunt Ride the Rails?" *Pacific Rail News,* Sept. 1996, p. 41.

41. *Railway Age,* Oct. 1994, p. 34.

42. Blaszak, "Intermodal," p. 37; Booz-Allen Hamilton, *Piggyback,* p. 6.

43. Kevin Keefe, "A Horse of a Different Color: Norfolk Southern's Triple Crown Service leads the RoadRailer revolution," *Trains,* June 1989.

44. Keith Thompson, "Tracking Freight Cars: AEI tags and readers," *Trains,* Jan. 1996, p. 86.

45. Cincinnati Chapter NRHS, *The Cincinnatian,* Oct. 1996, p. 4.

46. "Michigan's High Speed Rail Program," news release, Oct. 11, 1996.

47. TRAIN-IT, bi-weekly publication of AAR.

7. RAILROAD PRESERVATION

1. *RR Gazette,* June 14, 1901, p. 415.

2. John F. Hamilton, "The Chicago Chapter of the R & LHS and Its First Railfan Excursion," R&LHS *Railway History* 169 (Autumn 1993), pp. 69.

3. Swartz, "The Wabash Railroad," and R. Simons's photo files.

4. *Passenger Train Journal,* Nov. 1979.

5. *Railfan & Railroad,* Oct. 1991, p. 48.

6. Roger Kirkpatrick, Marietta, OH, unpublished catalog, Oct. 15, 1995.

7. Parker, *Indiana Railroad Depots: A Threatened Heritage,* p. 1.

8. Francis H. Parker, author's unpublished list, 1996.

8. MAJOR RAILROADS IN INDIANA

1. *Official Guide of the Railways,* various; Sulzer, *Ghost Railroads of Indiana,* p. 236.

2. *Official Guide of the Railways,* various.

3. Graydon M. Meints, *Michigan Railroads and Railroad Companies* (East Lansing: Michigan State University Press, 1992), p. 172.

4. Ibid., pp. 4, 172.

5. Ibid., p. 5.

6. Harlow, *Road of the Century,* p. 254.

7. Meints, *Michigan Railroads and Railroad Companies,* p. 5; *Official Guide of the Railways,* various.

8. New York Central time table, May 1913, table 3.

9. William D. Edson, *Railroad Names* (Potomac, Md.: author, 1993), pp. 94, 102; Harlow, *Road of the Century,* p. 76.

10. Harlow, *Road of the Century,* pp. 265–70, 279.

11. John Martin Smith, *History of DeKalb County, Indiana* (Auburn, Ind.: Natmus, Inc., 1992), pp. 356–57; Association of American Railroads, *Quiz on Railroads and Railroading,* no. 79.

12. Harlow, *Road of the Century,* p. 235.

13. Meints, *Michigan Railroads and Railroad Companies,* pp. 176, 183.

14. *Travelers Official Railway Guide of the United States and Canada* (reprint, New York: National Railway Publication Co., 1968), table 152.

15. McLellan and Warrick, *The Lake Shore & Michigan Southern Railway,* p. 79.

16. Harlow, *Road of the Century,* p. 413.

17. *Official Guide of the Railways,* June 1916, pp. 265–66.

18. Ibid., Aug. 1947, pp. 174, 182; Hollingsworth, *The Illustrated Encyclopedia of the World's Steam Passenger Locomotives,* p. 124.

19. Hollingsworth, *Illustrated Encyclopedia of the World's Steam Passenger Locomotives,* p. 168; Harlow, *Road of the Century,* p. 421.

20. Conrail, Freight Schedules, Dec. 1, 1993.

21. *Official Guide of the Railways,* Aug. 1947, p. 194.

22. Ibid., Dec. 1964, p. 102; Conrail, Freight Schedules, Dec. 1, 1993.

23. Smith, *History of DeKalb County, Indiana,* pp. 375–77.

24. *Official Guide of the Railways,* June 1916, p. 268; ibid; Aug. 1947, p. 215.

25. Reports of INDOT, Railroad Division.

26. *Official Railway Guide,* June 1995, p. C119.

27. Information from Gale E. Shultz, Indiana Northeastern Railroad.

28. Information from Little River Railroad.

29. Henry V. Poor, *Manual of the Railroads of the United States* (New York: H. V. and H. W. Poor, 1897), pp. 104–105. (This book was published annually from 1868 until at least sometime in the teens.)

30. Ibid., 1908, p. 862.

31. Conrail, Freight Schedules, Dec. 1, 1993.

32. *Official Guide of the Railways,* various.

33. Reports of INDOT, Railroad Division; Conrail, Freight Schedules, Dec. 1, 1993.

34. Sulzer, *Ghost Railroads of Indiana,* pp. 147–48; Meints, *Michigan Railroads and Railroad Companies,* p. 182.

35. Sulzer, *Ghost Railroads of Indiana,* p. 147; *Official Guide of the Railways,* various.

36. Reports of INDOT, Railroad Division.

37. Meints, *Michigan Railroads and Railroad Companies,* p. 50; Harlow, *Road of the Century,* p. 391.

38. *Official Guide of the Railways,* June 1916, p. 311; May 1944, p. 183.

39. Information from Bee Line and Kankakee, Beaverville and Southern Railroads.

40. *Official Guide of the Railways,* June 1916, pp. 306, 308–11.

41. Murphy, "The Big Four Railroad in Indiana," pp. 113, 121, 131.

42. Ibid., p. 139; Harlow, *Road of the Century,* p. 388.

43. George H. Drury, *The Historical Guide to North American Railroads* (Waukesha, Wis.: Kalmbach Books, 1992), p. 214; Meints, *Michigan Railroads and Railroad Companies,* p. 53.

44. *Official Guide of the Railways,* June 1916, pp. 303–12 and Aug. 1947, pp. 186–91.

45. Conrail, Freight Schedules, Dec. 1, 1993.

46. Burgess and Kennedy, *Centennial History of the Penn-*

sylvania Railroad, p. 203; Murphy, "The Big Four Railroad in Indiana," pp. 139, 217–18, 220, 227.

47. *Official Railway Guide,* June 1995, p. B54.

48. Conrail, Freight Schedules, Dec. 1, 1993.

49. Murphy, "The Big Four Railroad in Indiana," pp. 161–62.

50. Ibid., p. 178.

51. Harlow, *Road of the Century,* p. 378.

52. Murphy, "The Big Four Railroad in Indiana," pp. 143, 155.

53. Ibid., pp. 196–97.

54. Ibid., p. 197.

55. Ibid., p. 214; Poor, *Manual of the Railroads of the United States,* 1889, p. 394.

56. *Official Guide of the Railways,* June 1916, p. 306, and Aug. 1947, p. 189.

57. Reports of INDOT, Railroad Division; information from Central Railroad of Indiana and Kankakee, Beaverville and Southern Railroad.

58. Murphy, "The Big Four Railroad in Indiana," pp. 193–94, 213.

59. *Connersville Weekly Times,* Jan 23, 1868.

60. Big Four time table, Oct. 1909, p. 24; Rehor, *The Nickel Plate Story,* pp. 110–11; *Official Guide of the Railways,* June 1916, p. 311, and various.

61. Sulzer, *Ghost Railroads of Indiana,* p. 96; information from Indiana Hi-Rail.

62. *Whitewater Valley Railroad Train Trip Guide*; Lewis, *American Shortline Railway Guide,* 4th ed., p. 123.

63. Poor, *Manual of the Railroads of the United States,* 1889, p. 399.

64. Ibid., 1889, p. 535; Murphy, "The Big Four Railroad in Indiana," p. 265.

65. Meints, *Michigan Railroads and Railroad Companies,* p. 53.

66. Harlow, *Road of the Century,* pp. 393–95.

67. *Official Guide of the Railways,* June 1916, pp. 306, 310; ibid., various.

68. Reports of INDOT, Railroad Division; Conrail, Freight Schedules, Dec. 1, 1993; Lewis, *American Shortline Railway Guide,* 4th ed., p. 50; Carthage, Knightstown and Shirley Railroad time table.

69. Murphy, "The Big Four Railroad in Indiana," p. 215.

70. *Official Guide of the Railways,* June 1916, p. 312; Big Four time table, Jan. 21, 1934, table 14.

71. Report of Indiana Department of Transportation, Railroad Division.

72. Murphy, "The Big Four Railroad in Indiana," pp. 194–96.

73. *Official Guide of the Railways,* June 1916, p. 310; Big Four time table, Jan. 21, 1934, table 15.

74. Reports of INDOT, Railroad Division; *Official Guide of the Railways,* various.

75. Murphy, "The Big Four Railroad in Indiana," p. 216.

76. Ibid., p. 268; Big Four time table, Oct. 1909, pp. 55–56; Harlow, *Road of the Century,* p. 391.

77. Big Four time table, Oct. 1909, pp. 55–56; Reports of INDOT, Railroad Division; Sulzer, *Ghost Railroads of Indiana,* p. 54.

78. Murphy, "The Big Four Railroad in Indiana," p. 368.

79. Big Four time table, Jan. 21, 1934, table 25, p. 11.

80. Report of INDOT, Railroad Division.

81. Oran Perry, "History of the Evansville and Indianapolis Railroad and Constituent Companies" (1917), pp. 1–27; Drury, *The Historical Guide to North American Railroads,* pp. 214–15.

82. Perry, "History of the Evansville and Indianapolis Railroad and Constituent Companies," pp. 2, 15; *Official Guide of the Railways,* June 1916, pp. 897, 899; Drury, *The Historical Guide to North American Railroads,* pp. 214–15; Edson, *Railroad Names,* p. 58.

83. Reports of INDOT, Railroad Division; information from Indiana Southern Railroad.

84. Sulzer, *Ghost Railroads of Indiana,* pp. 53, 231.

85. Murphy, "The Big Four Railroad in Indiana," pp. 236, 240, 242, 250–52.

86. *Official Guide of the Railways,* June 1916, p. 310; Reports of INDOT, Railroad Division.

87. *Official Guide of the Railways,* June 1917, p. 310 and Aug. 1957, p. 240; Amtrak timetable, Oct. 29, 1995, p. 17.

88. Report of INDOT, Railroad Division.

89. Meints, *Michigan Railroads and Railroad Companies,* pp. 5, 108–109; Harlow, *Road of the Century,* p. 235.

90. *Official Guide of the Railways,* June 1916, pp. 286–87, and Aug. 1947, pp. 175, 183.

91. *The Official Railway Guide,* Conrail ed., p. 6; Conrail, Freight Schedules, Dec. 1, 1993; INDOT, Railroad Division, 1987 Update, p. 40; Amtrak timetable, Oct. 29, 1995, p. 20.

92. Poor, *Manual of the Railroads of the United States,* 1889, p. 485.

93. Report of INDOT, Railroad Division.

94. Meints, *Michigan Railroads and Railroad Companies,* pp. 88–89, 136, 183.

95. Sulzer, *Ghost Railroads of Indiana,* pp. 149–51.

96. Meints, *Michigan Railroads and Railroad Companies,* p. 107.

97. *Official Guide of the Railways,* June 1916, p. 284.

98. Sulzer, *Ghost Railroads of Indiana,* p. 8; *Official Guide of the Railways,* various.

99. Bogle, "Railroad Building in Indiana," p. 212; Sulzer, *Ghost Railroads of Indiana,* p. 8.

100. Firm of Coverdale and Colpitts, *The Pennsylvania Railroad Company: Corporate, Financial and Construction History of Lines Owned, Operated, and Controlled to December 31, 1945. Vol. 3: Leased Lines West of Pittsburgh* (New York: Coverdale and Colpitts, 1947), pp. 8, 313, 364, 371.

101. H. W. Schotter, *The Growth and Development of the Pennsylvania Railroad Company* (Philadelphia: Allen, Lane & Scott, 1927), p. 84.

102. Burgess and Kennedy, *Centennial History of the Pennsylvania Railroad Company,* pp. 176–78.

103. *Official Guide of the Railways,* June 1916, pp. 486–87, and Aug. 1947, pp. 323–24.

104. Conrail, Freight Schedules, Dec. 1, 1993; Norfolk Southern Corporation Annual Report, 1994, pp. 6–7; *Fort Wayne Journal-Gazette,* June 30, 1995; Amtrak timetable, Oct. 28, 1990.

105. Burgess and Kennedy, *Centennial History of the Pennsylvania Railroad Company,* pp. 200–202; Coverdale and Colpitts, *The Pennsylvania Railroad Company,* vol. 3, p. 309.

106. Association of American Railroads, *Quiz on Railroads and Railroading*, no. 24.

107. *Official Guide of the Railways*, June 1916, p. 506; INDOT, Railroad Division.

108. Coverdale and Colpitts, *The Pennsylvania Railroad Company*, vol. 3, pp. 364–65, 368, 370–71.

109. Ibid., pp. 364–65, 375; *Travelers Official Railway Guide*, June 1868, table 144.

110. *Official Guide of the Railways*, June 1916, p. 496, and Aug. 1947, pp. 325–26; INDOT, Railroad Division.

111. Coverdale and Colpitts, *The Pennsylvania Railroad Company*, vol. 3, pp. 356–58, 366–68; *Travelers Official Railway Guide*, June 1868, table 144.

112. *Official Guide of the Railways*, June 1916, p. 498, and Aug. 1947, pp. 232–33.

113. INDOT, Railroad Division; *Official Guide of the Railways*, various; information from Honey Creek and Indian Creek Railroads and operator of Winamac Southern Railway.

114. Coverdale and Colpitts, *The Pennsylvania Railroad Company*, vol. 3, pp. 357–58; *Travelers Official Railway Guide*, June 1868, table 144.

115. *Official Guide of the Railways*, June 1916, p. 499, and Aug. 1947, p. 332.

116. INDOT, Railroad Division; *Official Railway Guide*, June 1995, p. B54.

117. Burgess and Kennedy, *Centennial History of the Pensylvania Railroad Company*, pp. 212–13; *Travelers Official Railway Guide*, June 1868, table 203; Poor, *Manual of the Railroads of the United States*, 1879, p. 692.

118. Association of American Railroads, *Quiz on Railroads and Railroading*, no. 80; Indiana Historical Society, *Indiana: A New Historical Guide*, p. 414; James Alexander, "The Locomotive Reuben Wells," *Milepost* 9, no. 4 (Oct. 1991), p. 4.

119. Simons, "Indiana's Railroad Tunnels," pp. 12–13.

120. INDOT, Railroad Division; Lewis, *American Shortline Railway Guide*, 4th ed., p. 151.

121. Burgess and Kennedy, *Centennial History of the Pennsylvania Railroad Company*, pp. 212, 214, 220–21, 380; *Travelers Official Railway Guide*, June 1868, table 203.

122. *Official Guide of the Railways*, June 1916, p. 500, and Aug. 1947, p. 333.

123. Information from Louisville and Indiana Railroad.

124. Sulzer, *Ghost Railroads of Indiana*, p. 83.

125. Ibid., p. 84.

126. Coverdale and Colpitts, *The Pennsylvania Railroad Company*, vol. 3, pp. 356–58, 369.

127. Ibid., p. 375; *Official Guide of the Railways*, June 1916, p. 500; Pennsylvania Railroad time table, Sept. 28, 1930.

128. Kenneth N. Rinker, letter in "The Readers' Viewpoint," *Railroad Magazine*, Nov. 1942, p. 142.

129. INDOT, Railroad Division.

130. Coverdale and Colpitts, *The Pennsylvania Railroad Company*, vol. 3, p. 202.

131. *Official Guide of the Railways*, June 1916, p. 506 and Aug. 1947, p. 331.

132. INDOT, Railroad Division.

133. Coverdale and Colpitts, *The Pennsylvania Railroad Company*, vol. 3, pp. 357, 364–66.

134. *Official Guide of the Railways*, June 1916, p. 499.

135. Lewis, *American Shortline Railway Guide*, 4th ed., p. 258.

136. Sulzer, *Ghost Railroads of Indiana*, p. 114; Coverdale and Colpitts, *The Pennsylvania Railroad Company*, vol. 3, p. 361, 370.

137. Chicago, Indiana and Eastern time table, n.d.; *Official Guide of the Railways*, June 1916, p. 499: INDOT, Railroad Division.

138. Coverdale and Colpitts, *The Pennsylvania Railroad Company*, vol. 3, pp. 364, 371–72; Burgess and Kennedy, *Centennial History of the Pennsylvania Railroad Company*, p. 556.

139. Ibid., pp. 203, 205; Coverdale and Colpitts, *The Pennsylvania Railroad Company*, vol. 3, p. 371.

140. *Official Guide of the Railways*, June 1916, p. 501, and Aug. 1947, pp. 325–26; INDOT, Railroad Division; Lewis, *American Shortline Railway Guide*, 4th ed., pp. 251–52.

141. Sulzer, *Ghost Railroads of Indiana*, pp. 230–231; *Official Guide of the Railways*, June 1916, p. 501.

142. Burgess and Kennedy, *Centennial History of the Pennsylvania Railroad Company*, pp. 195, 216–17, 220–21, Murphy, "The Big Four Railroad in Indiana," p. 196; *Encyclopedia Americana*, vol. 5, p. 24.

143. *Official Guide of the Railways*, June 1916, p. 503; Pennsylvania Railroad time tables, Sept. 28, 1930, table 51, and June 29, 1941, table 29.

144. INDOT, Railroad Division; Lewis, *American Short Line Railway Guide*, 1st ed. (Morrisville, Vt.: The Baggage Car, 1978), p. 42; subsequent editions of this book were retitled *American Shortline Railway Guide* with a different publisher. We also cite the 3rd (1986) and 4th (1991) editions. Information from Indiana Southern Railroad.

145. Sulzer, *Ghost Railroads of Indiana*, pp. 177, 229–30; INDOT, Railroad Division.

146. Coverdale and Colpitts, *The Pennsylvania Railroad Company*, vol. 3, pp. 359–60, 377–78.

147. Burgess and Kennedy, *Centennial History of the Pennsylvania Railroad Company*, p. 424.

148. *Official Guide of the Railways*, June 1916, p. 502; Pennsylvania Railroad time tables, Apr. 2, 1939, and Jan. 11, 1948.

149. INDOT, Railroad Division; information from Winamac Southern Railway.

150. Poor, *Manual of the Railroads of the United States*, 1889, p. 540.

151. Wabash Railway System, *Corporate and Financial History, as of December 31, 1939* (New York, 1940), p. 124; Richard S. Simons, "The Eel River and Its Railroad," *National Railway Bulletin* 53, no. 6 (1988), pp. 28–35; *Official Guide of the Railways*, June 1916, p. 503; Pennsylvania Railroad time table, Sept. 28, 1930.

152. INDOT, Railroad Division.

153. Burgess and Kennedy, *Centennial History of the Pennsylvania Railroad Company*, p. 542.

154. *Official Guide of the Railways*, various.

155. Rehor, *The Nickel Plate Story*, pp. 27, 40.

156. Taylor Hampton, *The Nickel Plate Road* (Cleveland: World Publishing Co., 1947), pp. 219, 297–98.

157. Compiled from various editions of *Official Guide of the Railways.*

158. *Moody's Transportation Manual* (New York: Moody's Investors Service, 1990), pp. 52–53.

159. Ibid., p. 43; *Official Guide of the Railways,* various.

160. Hampton, *The Nickel Plate Road,* p. 117.

161. *Official Guide of the Railways,* June 1916, p. 318, and Nov. 1949, p. 472.

162. Rehor, *The Nickel Plate Story,* pp. 231–39.

163. Norfolk Southern Corporation Annual Report, 1994, pp. 6–7.

164. Compiled from *Official Guide of the Railways,* various issues.

165. Rehor, *The Nickel Plate Story,* pp. 85, 93, 97–103.

166. Ibid., pp. 89–92.

167. Ibid., pp. 86–89.

168. Ibid., pp. 89–92.

169. Ibid., p. 91.

170. Ibid., pp. 109, 117.

171. Ibid., pp. 97–98.

172. Ibid., pp. 97, 100.

173. Ibid., p. 100.

174. *Indianapolis Star,* July 16, 1996, p. E2.

175. Rehor, *The Nickel Plate Story,* p. 103.

176. Ibid., p. 110; New York Central Lines time table, May 1913, pp. 53–72.

177. Lewis, *American Shortline Railway Guide,* 4th ed., p. 125; Indiana Department of Transportation, Railroad Division abandonment reports; information from Honey Creek Railroad.

178. Rehor, *The Nickel Plate Story,* pp. 147–48.

179. Hilton, *American Narrow Gauge Railroads,* pp. 101–11.

180. Rehor, *The Nickel Plate Story,* pp. 147–48.

181. Ibid., p. 158.

182. *Official Guide of the Railways,* Mar. 1978, p. 337; INDOT, Railroad Division abandonment reports; Lewis, *American Shortline Railway Guide,* 4th ed., pp. 54, 126.

183. *Official Guide of the Railways,* Jan. 1964, p. 149.

184. Swartz, "The Wabash Railroad," pp. 17–23.

185. Ibid., pp. 14–28.

186. Ibid., pp. 18–21.

187. *Historical Guide to North American Railroads,* pp. 341, 343–44.

188. *Official Guides,* various.

189. Swartz, "The Wabash Railroad," pp. 13–14.

190. Calculated from Wabash Railroad time table, Oct. 1932; *Illustrated Historical Atlas of the State of Indiana,* 1876.

191. Wabash Railway System, *Corporate and Financial History, as of December 31, 1939,* p. 124.

192. Ibid., p. 125; Simons, "The Eel River and Its Railroad," p. 32.

193. Wabash Railway System, *Corporate and Financial History, as of December 31, 1939,* p. 125.

194. *Official Guide of the Railways,* June 1916, p. 119; ibid., Aug. 1947, p. 240.

195. Bill Stephens, "Automotive Artery," *Trains,* Jan. 1996, pp. 42–55.

196. Simons, "The Eel River and Its Railroad," p. 31.

197. Sulzer, *Ghost Railroads of Indiana,* pp. 33–34; *Official Guide of the Railways,* June 1916.

198. Poor, *Manual of the Railroads of the United States,* 1903, p. 434.

199. *Official Guide of the Railways,* June 1916; Wabash Railroad time table, Oct. 1932, p. 7.

200. *Indianapolis Star Sunday Magazine,* Apr. 22, 1956, pp. 26–30; *Official Guide of the Railways,* July 1958, p. 257.

201. INDOT, Railroad Division.

202. Sulzer, *Ghost Railroads of Indiana,* p. 153; Wabash Railroad time table, Mar. 1916. Table 19.

203. Rehor, *The Nickel Plate Story,* p. 97; *Official Guide of the Railways,* various.

204. Ibid., pp. 89–91; ibid.

205. Sulzer, *Ghost Railroads of Indiana,* p. 36.

206. Ibid., p. 54; *Official Guide of the Railways,* Oct. 1966, p. 97.

207. Atlantic and Great Western Railroad employee time tables, various.

208. Compiled from *Official Guide of the Railways,* various.

209. Hilton, *Monon Route,* pp. 11, 15.

210. Ibid., p. 11.

211. Ibid., p. 27; Frank F. Hargrave, *A Pioneer Indiana Railroad: The Origin and Development of the Monon* (Indianapolis: William B. Burford Printing Co., 1932), p. 16. (Hargrave was a professor of economics at Purdue University).

212. Dolzall and Dolzall, *Monon: The Hoosier Line,* pp. 32, 35, 43, 56, 171–72.

213. *Official Guide of the Railways,* June 1916, pp. 552–54.

214. Dolzall and Dolzall, *Monon: The Hoosier Line,* pp. 171–72.

215. Hilton, *Monon Route,* pp. 14, 16, 23, 24, 27.

216. Ibid., p. 23.

217. *Lafayette Journal and Courier,* July 23, 1994.

218. Hargrave, *A Pioneer Indiana Railroad,* p. 108.

219. Hilton, *Monon Route,* pp. 39, 47.

220. Ibid., pp. 30, 43–44.

221. Ibid., pp. 46–50.

222. Ibid., pp. 109–10.

223. Ibid., p. 243; Dolzall and Dolzall, *Monon: The Hoosier Line,* pp. 150–51; *Official Guide of the Railways,* June 1916, p. 554; Pennsylvania Railroad time table, Sept. 28, 1930.

224. Hilton, *Monon Route,* pp. 110–13; *Indianapolis News,* Oct. 2, 1957; *Official Guide of the Railways,* June 1916, p. 554.

225. Hilton, *Monon Route,* p. 116; INDOT, Railroad Division.

226. Hilton, *Monon Route,* pp. 119, 155; *Indianapolis Star Sunday Magazine,* Mar. 27, 1960; Monon Railroad time table, Feb. 1918.

227. *Official Guide of the Railways,* June 1916, pp. 550, 554.

228. Dolzall and Dolzall, *Monon: The Hoosier Line*, pp. 35, 43–44, 48.

229. Hilton, *Monon Route*, pp. 90, 117.

230. Ibid., pp. 177–79; Dolzall and Dolzall, *Monon: The Hoosier Line*, pp. 62–64.

231. John W. Barriger, "The Monon Is a Guinea Pig," *Trains*, July 1947, pp. 15–19; Hilton, *Monon Route*, pp. 187–98.

232. Hilton, *Monon Route*, pp. 184–98.

233. Dolzall and Dolzall, *Monon: The Hoosier Line*, pp. 110, 114–17, 120–26; *Railway Age*, Feb. 4, 1952.

234. Dolzall and Dolzall, *Monon: The Hoosier Line*, pp. 171–72; INDOT, Railroad Division.

235. Compiled from *Official Guide of the Railways*, various.

236. Stover, *History of the Baltimore and Ohio Railroad*, pp. 85, 151–52, 210.

237. Ibid., pp. 6, 10–11, 25–27.

238. Ibid., pp. 359–72.

239. Ibid., pp. 85, 151.

240. Smith, *From the Ohio to the Mississippi*; Edson, *Railroad Names*, pp. 18, 108.

241. Smith, *From the Ohio to the Mississippi*; Simons, "Indiana's Railroad Tunnels," pp. 13–18.

242. *Official Guide of the Railways*, June 1916, p. 544, and Aug. 1947, p. 407.

243. Smith, *From the Ohio to the Mississippi*.

244. *Official Guide of the Railways*, June 1916, p. 545, and Aug. 1947, p. 406; INDOT, Railroad Division.

245. Sulzer, *Ghost Railroads of Indiana*, pp. 169–70.

246. Stover, *History of the Baltimore and Ohio Railroad*, pp. 151–53; Report of Railroad Commission of Indiana, 1908, p. 563.

247. Stover, *History of the Baltimore and Ohio Railroad*, p. 152; Smith, *History of De Kalb County, Indiana*, p. 382.

248. Ibid., pp. 384–88.

249. *Official Guide of the Railways*, June 1916, p. 533, and Aug. 1947, p. 400.

250. Stover, *History of the Baltimore and Ohio Railroad*, pp. 259–61; Edson, *Railroad Names*, pp. 38, 72.

251. Poor, *Manual of the Railroads of the United States*, 1900, p. 263; Edson, *Railroad Names*, p. 38; Stover, *History of the Baltimore and Ohio Railroad*, pp. 259–60.

252. Poor, *Manual of the Railroads of the United States*, 1888, p. 464; Edson, *Railroad Names*, pp. 38, 72; Stover, *History of the Baltimore and Ohio Railroad*, pp. 259–60.

253. *Official Guide of the Railways*, June 1916, pp. 550, 554; B&O time table, Jan. 14, 1951; Amtrak timetable, Apr. 27, 1986.

254. *Official Guide of the Railways*, June 1916, p. 550.

255. INDOT, Railroad Division; Sulzer, *Ghost Railroads of Indiana*, pp. 32–33.

256. Ibid., pp. 145–47; Edson, *Railroad Names*, pp. 38, 58.

257. Sulzer, *Ghost Railroads of Indiana*, pp. 145, 147.

258. Harold R. Sampson, *A Preliminary Historical Digest of the C&EI Railroad* (Glenwood, Ill.: HLW Industries, 1965).

259. Phillips, *Indiana in Transition*, p. 243; Edson, *Railroad Names*, p. 36.

260. *Official Guide of the Railways*, various.

261. Sampson, *A Preliminary Historical Digest of the C&EI Railroad*.

262. Ibid.

263. Ibid.

264. Ibid.

265. Phillips, *Indiana in Transition*, p. 242.

266. Sampson, *A Preliminary Historical Digest of the C&EI Railroad*.

267. *Official Guide of the Railways*, June 1916, pp. 896–97; Apr. 1943, p. 723; Aug. 1947, p. 774.

268. Sulzer, *Ghost Railroads of Indiana*, p. 40.

269. Sampson, *A Preliminary Historical Digest of the C&EI Railroad*; INDOT, Railroad Division; Lewis, *American Shortline Railway Guide*, 4th ed., p. 213; *Official Guide of the Railways*, Aug. 1950, p. 785.

270. Sampson, *A Preliminary Historical Digest of the C&EI Railroad*; INDOT, Railroad Division.

271. Sulzer, *Ghost Railroads of Indiana*, pp. 224–25.

272. Ibid., p. 225.

273. Ibid., p. 39; Sampson, *A Preliminary Historical Digest of the C&EI Railroad*; INDOT, Railroad Division; correspondence with Burt Etchison, Stewart Grain Company.

274. Sulzer, *Ghost Railroads of Indiana*, pp. 14–17.

275. Ibid., p. 17.

276. Ibid., pp. 17–19.

277. Ibid., pp. 23–25; *Official Guide of the Railways*, Apr. 1943, p. 63; INDOT, Railroad Division.

278. Perry, "History of the Evansville and Indianapolis Railroad," pp. 12–24; Sulzer, *Ghost Railroads of Indiana*, p. 229.

279. Ibid.; Sampson, *A Preliminary Historical Digest of the C&EI Railroad*.

280. Poor, *Manual of the Railroads of the United States*, 1891, p. 706; F. H. Johnson, "Brief Record of the Development of the Milwaukee Road" (pamphlet published by the Milwaukee Road, n.d., ca. 1945), pp. 16–17.

281. Richard S. Simons, "The Milwaukee Road in Indiana," *National Railway Bulletin* 45, no. 1, p. 5.

282. Ibid., p. 7; Sulzer, *Ghost Railroads of Indiana*, p. 99.

283. Simons, "The Milwaukee Road in Indiana," p. 10; seventh annual report of the Railroad Commission of Indiana, p. 651.

284. *Official Railway Guide*, July 1974, p. 147; *Historical Guide to North American Railroads*, p. 375; INDOT, Railroad Division; *Official Railway Guide*, June 1995, p. B64.

285. Fairfax Harrison, *A History of the Legal Development of the Railroad System of the Southern Railway Company* (Washington, D.C., 1901), p. 1336.

286. Ibid.; Poor, *Manual of the Railroads of the United States*, 1887, various pages; Richard E. Prince, *Southern Railway System, Steam Locomotives and Boats* (Green River, Wy.: Richard E. Prince, 1965), p. 22.

287. Harrison, *A History of the Legal Development of the Railroad System of the Southern Railway Company*, p. 1336; Poor, *Manual of the Railroads of the United States*, 1887.

288. Harrison, *A History of the Legal Development of the Railroad System of the Southern Railway Company*, p. 1336; Poor, *Manual of the Railroads of the United States*, 1889, p.

1032; Prince, *Southern Railway System, Steam Locomotives and Boats,* p. 22; Jerry Marlette, *Interstate: A History of Interstate Public Service Rail Operations* (Polo, Ill.: Transportation Trails, 1990), p. 20.

289. Simons, "Indiana's Railroad Tunnels," pp. 12–23; correspondence with office of chief engineer, Southern Railway, Mar. 23, 1948.

290. *Official Guide of the Railways,* June 1916, p. 1255, Oct. 1953, p. 526.

291. Harrison, *A History of the Legal Development of the Railroad System of the Southern Railway Company,* p. 1336.

292. George R. Wilson, *History of Dubois County from Its Primitive Days to 1910* (Jasper, Ind.: Published by the author, 1910), p. 395; *Official Guide of the Railways,* June 1916, pp. 1225–26; Southern Railway public time table, Jan. 1938; correspondence with R. Powell Felix, president (1995), Indiana Hi-Rail Corp., and G. Allen Barnett, president, Dubois County Railroad.

293. Harrison, *A History of the Legal Development of the Railroad System of the Southern Railway Company,* p. 1336; Poor, *Manual of the Railroads of the United States,* 1887, p. 1040; Edson, *Railroad Names,* p. 84.

294. *Official Guide of the Railways,* June 1916, p. 1225; Southern Railway public time table, Mar. 1940.

295. Harrison, *A History of the Legal Development of the Railroad System of the Southern Railway Company,* p. 1336; Poor, *Manual of the Railroads of the United States,* 1889, p. 1032.

296. *Official Guide of the Railways,* June 1916, p. 1255; Southern Railway Public Time Table, Jan. 1938.

297. R. Powell Felix correspondence; Hoosier Southern Railroad correspondence.

298. Poor, *Manual of the Railroads of the United States,* 1908, p. 499; George W. Hilton, "The Chicago, Cincinnati & Louisville Railroad," *Railway & Locomotive Historical Society Bulletin* 114 (Apr. 1966), p. 10.

299. Poor, *Manual of the Railroads of the United States,* 1903, p. 446; Hilton, "The Chicago, Cincinnati & Louisville Railroad," pp. 6–7.

300. Ibid., pp. 7–8.

301. Poor, *Manual of the Railroads of the United States,* 1910, p. 736; Hilton, "The Chicago, Cincinnati & Louisville Railroad," pp. 9–10.

302. Edson, *Railroad Names,* p. 36; Hilton, "The Chicago, Cincinnati & Louisville Railroad," pp. 8–9.

303. Ibid.

304. Ibid., pp. 10–11.

305. Chesapeake and Ohio Railway Company, Chicago Division, Employee Time Table no. 121, Mar. 30, 1930.

306. *Official Guide of the Railways,* June 1916, p. 569, and Sept. 1948, p. 486.

307. Hilton, "The Chicago, Cincinnati & Louisville Railroad," p. 11.

308. Amtrak timetables, various; INDOT, Railroad Division.

309. INDOT, Railroad Division; Bob Johnston, "At Last, a Transcontinental Passenger Train," *Trains,* July 1993, p. 30.

310. John F. Stover, *History of the Illinois Central Railroad* (New York: Macmillan, 1975), pp. 55–56, 200, 231–33, 265.

311. INDOT, Railroad Division; Lewis, *American Shortline Railway Guide,* 4th ed., pp. 122, 125; Joseph A. Batchelor, *The Indiana Limestone Industry* (Bloomington: Indiana University School of Business, 1944), p. 93.

312. Sulzer, *Ghost Railroads of Indiana,* p. 36.

313. Stover, *History of the Illinois Central Railroad,* p. 34.

314. Hilton, *American Narrow Gauge Railroads,* p. 389.

315. *Official Guide of the Railways,* June 1916, p. 1142; INDOT, Railroad Division.

316. Stover, *History of the Illinois Central Railroad,* pp. 231–33; Sulzer, *Ghost Railroads of Indiana,* p. 125.

317. Sulzer, *Ghost Railroads of Indiana,* pp. 123–26; Hilton and Due, *Electric Interurban Railways in America,* pp. 49–50.

318. *Official Guide of the Railways,* June 1916, p. 1147; Lewis, *American Shortline Railway Guide,* 4th ed., p. 125.

319. John C. Leffel, *History of Posey County, Ind.* (Chicago: Standard Publishing Co., 1913), p. 188; *Official Guide of the Railways,* June 1916, p. 1147; INDOT, Railroad Division.

320. Hilton, *American Narrow Gauge Railroads,* p. 390.

321. Stover, *History of the Illinois Central Railroad,* p. 265; Edson, *Railroad Names,* p. 72.

322. Illinois Central Railroad Historical Society, *Green Diamond* (n.d.), pp. 20–21.

323. *Official Guide of the Railways,* June 1916, p. 1145; *Bloomington Daily Telephone,* June 24, 1911.

324. Lewis, *American Shortline Railway Guide,* 4th ed., p. 122.

325. Illinois Central Railroad Historical Society, *Green Diamond* (n.d.), p. 23.

326. Ibid.; information from Thomas G. Hoback, president, Indiana Rail Road.

327. H. Roger Grant, *Erie Lackawanna* (Stanford, Calif.: Stanford University Press, 1994), p. 1.

328. Hilton, *American Narrow Gauge Railroads,* p. 392.

329. Grant, *Erie Lackawanna,* p. 6.

330. Ibid., p. 43.

331. Erie track chart provided by John R. Michael, Huntington, former Erie chief dispatcher.

332. Chicago and Atlantic employee time table no. 17, June 19, 1887.

333. Erie Lackawanna employee time table no. 4, Feb. 24, 1974.

334. *Official Guide of the Railways,* various.

335. Myron J. Smith, Jr., ed., *Huntington Area Centennials Historical Handbook* (Huntington, Ind.: Our Sunday Visitor, 1973), p. 58.

336. Sulzer, *Ghost Railroads of Indiana,* p. 39.

337. Grant, *Erie Lackawanna,* p. 99.

338. Edson, *Railroad Names,* pp. 34, 56.

339. Information from Laketon Refinery; *Official Railway Guide,* June 1995, p. C106.

340. *Official Guide of the Railways,* Apr. 1943, p. 452.

341. Meints, *Michigan Railroads and Railroad Companies,* pp. 19–20, 126; *1995 Indiana Rail Plan,* p. 34; *Official Guide of the Railways,* Aug. 1957, p. 524.

342. Meints, *Michigan Railroads and Railroad Companies,* pp. 20, 126.

343. Edson, *Railroad Names,* p. 38.

344. Hilton, "The Chicago, Cincinnati & Louisville Railroad," pp. 8–9.

345. Meints, *Michigan Railroads and Railroad Companies*, p. 126; *Official Railway Guide*, Dec. 1995, p. B64.

346. *Official Guide of the Railways*, June 1916, pp. 575–76; Amtrak timetable, fall-winter 1995.

347. Poor, *Manual of the Railroads of the United States*, 1884, p. 593, 1908, p. 437; Sulzer, *Ghost Railroads of Indiana*, p. 16.

348. *Official Guide of the Railways*, June 1916, p. 578, Dec. 1931, p. 507.

349. INDOT, Railroad Division.

350. *Official Guide of the Railways*, Oct. 1966, p. 745.

351. Meints, *Michigan Railroads and Railroad Companies*, pp. 11, 83, 124; Poor, *Manual of the Railroads of the United States*, 1882, p. 581.

352. Meints, *Michigan Railroads and Railroad Companies*, p. 84; *Dictionary of American Biography*, vol. 18, pp. 501–502.

353. "Railroad news," *Trains*, July 1995, p. 14.

354. *Official Guide of the Railways*, June 1916, pp. 87, 92, 369.

355. Kincaid A. Herr, *Louisville and Nashville Railroad 1850–1963* (Louisville: L&N Railroad, Publicity Dept., 1943), pp. 1, 63; *1995 Indiana Rail Plan*, p. 38.

356. Herr, *Louisville and Nashville Railroad*, pp. 63–64, 173; *Official Guide of the Railways*, July 1958, pp. 530, 531.

357. Herr, *Louisville and Nashville Railroad*, pp. 76–78.

358. Ibid., pp. 78–82.

359. *Official Guide of the Railways*, June 1916, pp. 1177, 1186, Aug. 1947, pp. 540, 541.

360. Edson, *Railroad Names*, pp. 84, 128.

9. HISTORIC SHORT LINES

1. Elmer G. Sulzer, *Indiana's Abandoned Railroads, No. I: Abandoned Railroads of Bedford* (Indianapolis: Council for Local History, 1959), p. 44. See also *Ghost Railroads of Indiana*.

2. Ibid.

3. Ibid., pp. 46–47.

4. Illinois Central Railroad Historical Society, *Green Diamond* (n.d.), p. 23; Batchelor, *Indiana Limestone Industry*, p. 93.

5. Information from Thomas G. Hoback, president, Indiana Rail Road; INDOT, Railroad Division

6. Sulzer, *Ghost Railroads of Indiana*, p. 74.

7. Hilton, *Monon Route*, pp. 86–87.

8. Sulzer, *Ghost Railroads of Indiana*, pp. 153–54.

9. Ibid., p. 153.

10. Poor, *Manual of the Railroads of the United States*, 1897, p. 124.

11. *Atlas of St. Joseph County*, 1911, pp. 42–43.

12. McLellan and Warrick, *The Lake Shore & Michigan Southern Railway*, p. 45.

13. *South Bend Tribune*, Apr. 28, 1994.

14. McLellan and Warrick, *The Lake Shore & Michigan Southern Railway*, p. 45.

15. Lewis, *American Short Line Railway Guide*, 1st ed., p.

42; Lucius Beebe, *Mixed Train Daily* (New York: E. P. Dutton, 1947), p. 305.

16. Lewis, *American Shortline Railway Guide*, 4th ed., p. 97.

17. Ibid.; *Official Guide of the Railways*, various.

18. Marlette, *Interstate: A History of Interstate Public Service Rail Operations*, p. 155; *Official Guide of the Railways*, various.

19. Beebe, *Mixed Train Daily*, p. 305; Lewis, *American Shortline Railway Guide*, 4th ed., p. 97.

20. Lewis, *American Shortline Railway Guide*, 4th ed., p. 42.

21. Ibid., 3rd ed., p. 85.

22. Ibid., 4th ed., p. 97.

23. Poor, *Manual of the Railroads of the United States*, 1885, p. 486.

24. Ibid., 1900, p. 333.

25. Ibid.

26. Sulzer, *Ghost Railroads of Indiana*, p. 53.

27. Lewis, *American Shortline Railway Guide*, 3rd ed. (1986), p. 126.

28. *Official Guide of the Railways*, various.

29. Correspondence with Richard P. Pearson, marketing director, and interview with Victor Sauerheber, operations director, Louisville, New Albany and Corydon Railroad.

30. Ibid.

31. *Official Guide of the Railways*, June 1916, p. 113.

32. Central Electric Railfans' Association, *Electric Railways of Indiana 104*, section 4, p. 25.

33. Lewis, *American Short Line Railway Guide*, 1st ed., p. 43.

34. *Official Guide of the Railways*, various.

35. Swartz, "The Wabash Railroad," p. 26.

36. *Official Guide of the Railways*, various.

37. Edson, *Railroad Names*, pp. 12, 40; Sulzer, *Ghost Railroads of Indiana*, p. 58.

38. Sulzer, *Ghost Railroads of Indiana*; Burgess and Kennedy, *Centennial History of the Pennsylvania Railroad*, p. 519.

39. Sulzer, *Ghost Railroads of Indiana*, pp. 58, 73.

40. Ibid., pp. 62–63.

41. Ibid., pp. 57–58.

42. Ibid., p. 58.

43. Ibid.

44. Ibid.

45. INDOT, Railroad Division.

46. *Railway Age*, Dec. 1, 1952.

47. *New York Times*, Dec. 24, 1953.

48. *Official Railway Guide*, July 1987, p. C82.

49. Sulzer, *Ghost Railroads of Indiana*, p. 14.

50. Ibid., pp. 14, 16.

51. Ibid., p. 23.

52. Ibid., pp. 23, 25.

53. Ibid., pp. 27–29.

54. Indiana Coal Association, *Report of Indiana Coal Production*, 1955, p. 25.

55. Sulzer, *Ghost Railroads of Indiana*, pp. 20, 22.

56. Ibid., p. 29.

57. Ibid., pp. 23, 30.

58. Ibid., p. 31.

59. *Official Guide of the Railways,* Apr. 1943, p. 63.

60. Sulzer, *Ghost Railroads of Indiana,* p. 31.

61. Lewis, *American Shortline Railway Guide,* 3rd ed., p. 12.

62. Ibid., 4th ed., p. 13.

63. Interview with Robert A. Shaw, retired general manager, Algers, Winslow and Western Railway, and his successor, Joe Huey.

64. Ibid.; *Official Guide of the Railways,* various.

65. Lewis, *American Shortline Railway Guide,* 3rd ed., p. 12.

66. Huey interview.

67. Interview with Keith Reibly, traffic manager, Peabody Coal Company, and Dan Taylor of Peabody.

68. Interview with Irvin Reiss, president, Meadowlark Farms; map of southwestern Indiana coal area, Geological Survey, 1979.

69. Interviews with Bill Pohlman and John Longfield, Breed plant managers.

70. Edson, *Railroad Names,* p. 146; Central Electric Railfans' Association, *Electric Railways of Indiana,* p. 23.

71. Ibid.

72. Ibid.

73. Edson, *Railroad Names,* p. 146.

74. Correspondence with Yankeetown Dock Corporation; *Operations Guide,* Amax Coal Industries.

75. *Operations Guide,* Amax Coal Industries.

76. Sulzer, *Ghost Railroads of Indiana,* pp. 43, 116, 188; Marlette, *Interstate: A History of Interstate Public Service Rail Operations,* p. 227.

77. William D. Middleton, *South Shore* (San Marino, Calif.: Golden West Books, 1970), pp. 9–11.

78. Ibid., pp. 25–26.

79. Ibid., pp. 35, 39.

80. Chicago SouthShore and South Bend Railroad, "Brief History of the South Shore Line" (handout, no date); Northern Indiana Commuter Transportation District, *South Shore Line.*

81. *Indiana Business Review,* Mar. 1984, pp. 3–4; information from John Parsons, marketing director, Northern Indiana Commuter Transportation District; *South Shore Line* time table.

82. Information from Chicago SouthShore and South Bend Railroad; Marlette, *Electric Railroads of Indiana,* p. 79.

83. Sulzer, *Ghost Railroads of Indiana,* pp. 116–18.

84. Hilton and Due, *Electric Interurban Railways in America,* pp. 285–86.

85. Ibid., p. 286.

86. Sulzer, *Ghost Railroads of Indiana,* pp. 117, 121; Hilton and Due, *Electric Interurban Railways in America,* p. 286.

87. Sulzer, *Ghost Railroads of Indiana,* p. 121.

88. Indiana Coal Association, *Report of Indiana Coal Production,* 1955, p. 29.

89. Sulzer, *Ghost Railroads of Indiana,* p. 43; Hilton and Due, *Electric Interurban Railways in America,* p. 286.

90. Sulzer, *Ghost Railroads of Indiana,* p. 48.

91. Ibid., pp. 48, 51.

92. Indiana Coal Association, *Report of Indiana Coal Production,* 1955, p. 30.

93. Hilton and Due, *Electric Interurban Railways in America,* p. 286.

94. Richard S. Simons, "The Southern Indiana," *National Railway Bulletin* 59, no. 2 (1994), pp. 31–32.

95. Hilton and Due, *Electric Interurban Railways in America,* pp. 100, 279.

96. Marlette, *Interstate: A History of Interstate Public Service Rail Operations,* pp. 49, 52–53.

97. Ibid., pp. 60–61.

98. Simons, "Southern Indiana," pp. 31–34.

99. Sulzer, *Ghost Railroads of Indiana,* pp. 183, 188–89.

100. Ibid., pp. 181, 183, 186, 188.

101. Ibid., pp. 181, 183, 186.

102. Ibid., p. 188.

103. Ibid.

104. Ibid.

105. Ibid., pp. 188–89.

106. Information from Naval Surface Warfare Center, Crane Division.

107. Ibid.; Dorothy Riker, *The Hoosier Training Ground* (Bloomington: Indiana War History Commission, 1952), pp. 290–91.

10. MODERN SHORT LINES

1. *Official Railway Guide,* various; Lewis, *American Shortline Railway Guide,* 4th ed., p. 288.

2. *Official Railway Guide,* various; INDOT, Railroad Division.

3. *Official Railway Guide,* various.

4. Interviews with Thomas G. Hoback, president, Indiana Rail Road; Phillip G. Wilzbacher, director of marketing, Indiana Southern Railroad; and Gordon R. Fuller, president, Toledo, Peoria and Western Railway.

5. *Indianapolis Star Sunday Magazine,* Sept. 1, 1974, p. 8.

6. Interviews with Hoback, Indiana Rail Road, and Wilzbacher, Indiana Southern Railroad.

7. Lewis, *American Short Line Railway Guide,* 1st, 3rd, and 4th eds., various pages.

8. *Official Railway Guide,* various.

9. Ibid.

10. Interview with Daniel R. Frick, an owner of A & R Railroad.

11. Smith, *History of DeKalb County, Indiana,* p. 417.

12. Ibid.; correspondence with Gedd Copenhaver, president, Auburn Port Authority.

13. Correspondence with Burt Etchison, Stewart Grain Company, Stewart.

14. Correspondence with Al Dewitt, Demeter Grain Company, Fowler.

15. *Official Railway Guide,* Jan. 1980, p. 121.

16. Ibid.; Edson, *Railroad Names,* p. 34.

17. Lewis, *American Short Line Railway Guide,* 1st ed., pp. 41–42.

18. Ibid.; Edson, *Railroad Names,* p. 56.

19. Interview with Tom Wilson, Wilson Fertilizer and Grain Company, Rochester.

20. Interview with Doug Jesch, vice president, Heritage Transport, Indianapolis.

21. Lewis, *American Shortline Railway Guide,* 4th ed., p. 117.

22. Ibid.

23. Ibid.

24. Correspondence with Gale E. Shultz, president, Pigeon River Railroad Company.

25. Lewis, *American Short Line Railway Guide,* 1st ed., p. 42; Edson, *Railroad Names,* p. 72.

26. Edson, *Railroad Names,* p. 72.

27. Shultz correspondence.

28. *Fort Wayne News-Sentinel,* Sept. 5, 1994.

29. Shultz correspondence.

30. Ibid.

31. Frick correspondence and interview.

32. Lewis, *American Shortline Railway Guide,* 4th ed., p. 131.

33. INDOT, Railroad Division; correspondence with F. R. Orr, president, KB&S Railroad; *Rail Classics,* Nov. 1994, pp. 16–23.

34. *Rail Classics,* Nov. 1994, pp. 16–23, Orr interview.

35. Orr correspondence.

36. Correspondence with Lori L. Day, general manager, Michigan Southern Railroad.

37. Lewis, *American Shortline Railway Guide,* 4th ed., p. 203; INDOT, Railroad Division.

38. Lewis, *American Shortline Railway Guide,* 4th ed., p. 203.

39. Shultz correspondence.

40. Interview with Jerry L. Ambrose, PSL employee; Edson, *Railroad Names,* p. 118.

41. Lewis, *American Shortline Railway Guide,* 3rd ed., p. 208.

42. Frick correspondence.

43. Interview with Henry E. Weller Jr., president, Central Railroad of Indianapolis.

44. *Official Guide of the Railways,* various.

45. Frick interview.

46. Frick correspondence; *Official Railway Guide,* various.

47. Lewis, *American Shortline Railway Guide,* 4th ed., p. 40.

48. Interview with Joseph A. Borinstein.

49. Lewis, *American Shortline Railway Guide,* 4th ed., p. 50; INDOT, Railroad Division; *Official Guide of the Railways,* June 1916, p. 310.

50. Lewis, *American Shortline Railway Guide,* 4th ed., p. 50.

51. INDOT, Railroad Division.

52. Lewis, *American Shortline Railway Guide,* 4th ed., p. 53; *Indianapolis Star Sunday Magazine,* Oct. 19, 1947.

53. Sulzer, *Ghost Railroads of Indiana,* p. 63; INDOT, Railroad Division; Edson, *Railroad Names,* p. 30.

54. Correspondence with Mark Brown, general manager, CI&W Railroad.

55. Interviews with Henry E. Weller Jr., president, Central Railroad of Indianapolis, and his successor, C. J. Burger.

56. Weller interview.

57. Ibid.

58. Correspondence with C. J. Corman via Wesley F. and Shirley Ross.

59. Interview with Raymond Pasko, manager, Morristown Grain Company, Inc.

60. Ibid.; INDOT, Railroad Division.

61. Interview with Thomas Rydman, president, Indian Creek Railroad.

62. Edson, *Railroad Names,* p. 68; *Official Railway Guide,* May 1982, p. 247.

63. Lewis, *American Shortline Railway Guide,* 4th ed., pp. 125–26; correspondence with R. Powell Felix, president, Indiana Hi-Rail Corporation.

64. Felix correspondence.

65. Lewis, *American Shortline Railway Guide,* 3rd ed., p. 103.

66. Ibid., 4th ed., pp. 125, 213.

67. Felix correspondence.

68. Interview with Tim Yeager, assistant vice president, Indiana Hi-Rail Corporation.

69. *Rand McNally Handy Railroad Atlas,* 1988, p. 18.

70. Lewis, *American Shortline Railway Guide,* 3rd ed., p. 104; Edson, *Railroad Names,* p. 72.

71. *Official Guide of the Railways,* June 1916, p. 310.

72. Lewis, *American Shortline Railway Guide,* 4th ed., p. 147.

73. Correspondence with John R. Hillis, president, Logansport and Eel River Shortline.

74. Lewis, *American Shortline Railway Guide,* 4th ed., pp. 251–52; correspondence with John C. Carvey, Indianapolis, THB&E attorney.

75. *Historical Guide to North American Railroads,* pp. 324–26.

76. *Official Railway Guide,* Dec. 1995, p. C116.

77. Correspondence with Gordon R. Fuller, president, TP&W Railway.

78. Ibid.; Edson, *Railroad Names,* p. 146; *Historical Guide to North American Railroads,* p. 325; Robert C. Reed, *Train Wrecks* (New York: Bonanza Books, 1968), pp. 30–33; Moody's Transportation news reports, Mar. 12, 1996, p. 4851.

79. Weller and Burger interviews.

80. Weller interview.

81. Ibid.

82. Correspondence with G. Allen Barnett, president, Dubois County Railroad; Wilson, *History of Dubois County,* p. 394.

83. Barnett correspondence.

84. Interview with J. H. Marino, president, RailAmerica.

85. Correspondence with general manager, Hoosier Southern Railroad.

86. Correspondence with Thomas B. McOwen, president, Indiana and Ohio Railroad.

87. Lewis, *American Shortline Railway Guide,* 4th ed., pp. 123–25; interview with Phillip G. Wilzbacher, director of marketing for Indiana Southern Railroad, also a RailTex road.

88. *Official Railway Guide,* July 1987, p. C84; Dec. 1995, p. C104.

89. Illinois Central Railroad Historical Society, *Green Diamond* (n.d.), pp. 20, 23–24.

90. Gary W. Dolzall and Stephen F. Dolzall, "High Times on the Hi-Dry," *Trains,* June 1988, pp. 25–27; "Arrivals & Departures," *Trains,* Oct. 1989, p. 10.

91. Interview with Thomas G. Hoback, president, Indiana Rail Road.

92. Ibid.

93. Wilzbacher interview.

94. *Official Railway Guide*, May 1977, p. 170, May 1988, p. B64.

95. Correspondence with John K. Secor, president, Louisville and Indiana Railroad.

96. Burgess and Kennedy, *Centennial History of the Pennsylvania Railroad Company*, p. 213; correspondence with Cathy S. Hale, general manager, Madison Railroad.

97. Hale correspondence; interview with William G. Prime, board of directors, Madison Railroad; Lewis, *American Shortline Railway Guide*, 4th ed., p. 151.

98. Burgess and Kennedy, *Centennial History of the Pennsylvania Railroad Company*, p. 213; Prime interview.

99. Correspondence and interview with Carl Skaggs, terminal manager, MG Rail; Lewis, *American Shortline Railway Guide*, 3rd ed., p. 135, 4th ed., p. 160.

100. Yeager interview; Marino interview; Felix interview.

101. Yeager interview; Felix correspondence.

102. Correspondence with Donald R. Snyder, port director, Southwind Maritime Centre.

11. BELT LINES AND TERMINAL RAILROADS

1. Charles S. Roberts, *B&O West End* (Baltimore, Md.: Barnard, Roberts, 1991), p. 122.

2. Ibid., pp. 122–23.

3. Ibid., p. 122.

4. B&OCT Employe Time Table, Apr. 25, 1954, pp. 16–18; *Moody's Transportation Manual*, 1990, p. 266; information from CSX headquarters.

5. Blaszak, "Change on the Harbor: Whither the Indiana Harbor Belt?" pp. 22–24.

6. Ibid., p. 24; *Official Guide of the Railways*, Oct. 1966, p. 101.

7. Interview with G. J. Purgert, superintendent, Chicago Short Line Railway; Lewis, *American Shortline Railway Guide*, 4th ed., p. 61.

8. Blaszak, "Change on the Harbor: Whither the Indiana Harbor Belt?" pp. 23–27.

9. Michael W. Blaszak, "The J: A Centennial History (1)," *Trains*, Aug. 1989, p. 35.

10. Ibid., p. 30.

11. Poor, *Manual of the Railroads of the United States*, 1910.

12. Blaszak, "The J: A Centennial History (1)," p. 34.

13. *State Rail Plan*, 1985, p. 326.

14. Interview with C. H. Allen, general manager, Indiana Harbor Belt Railroad.

15. Blaszak, "Change on the Harbor: Whither the Indiana Harbor Belt?" pp. 22–27.

16. Ibid., pp. 25–27.

17. Ibid., p. 24.

18. Ibid., pp. 27–37.

19. Ibid., p. 36; Allen interview.

20. Poor, *Manual of the Railroads of the United States*, 1905, p. 397; Edson, *Railroad Names*, p. 34; *Atlas of St. Joseph County*, p. 34.

21. Edson, *Railroad Names*, p. 72; *Atlas of St. Joseph County*, p. 34.

22. *Moody's Transportation Manual*, 1990, p. 385.

23. Ibid.; Edson, *Railroad Names*, p. 60.

24. Poor, *Manual of the Railroads of the United States*, 1910, p. 832; information from Howard R. Pletcher, Fort Wayne, Indiana.

25. *Moody's Transportation Manual*, 1990, p. 63.

26. Coverdale and Colpitts, *The Pennsylvania Railroad Company*, vol. 3, pp. 360, 368.

27. Maps, Kokomo, Indiana, various; interviews with Henry E. Weller, Jr., and C. J. Burger, successive presidents of Central Railroad of Indianapolis.

28. *Commemorative Book of Tippecanoe County, 1826–1976*, p. 23.

29. *Moody's Transportation Manual*, 1978, p. 1919.

30. *Souvenir of Elwood*, 1893, pp. 32–33; Poor, *Manual of the Railroads of the United States*, 1910, p. 792.

31. Coverdale and Colpitts, *The Pennsylvania Railroad Company*, vol. 3, p. 361.

32. Ibid., pp. 364, 370.

33. Anderson city map.

34. *Moody's Transportation Manual*, 1981, p. 863.

35. John Nehrich, "Mather Patent Box Car," *Mainline Modeler*, Nov. 1986, pp. 34–35; typewritten manuscript from Muncie and Western Railroad.

36. Typewritten manuscript from Muncie and Western Railroad.

37. Richard S. Simons, "Muncie's Own Railroad," *National Railway Bulletin* 57, no. 2 (1992), pp. 11–13.

38. Sanborn fire insurance maps, 1892, 1896.

39. Railroad Commission of Indiana Annual Report, 1906, p. 261; Poor, *Manual of the Railroads of the United States*, 1905.

40. Staufer, *New York Central's Early Power*, p. 273.

41. New York Central annual report, 1953, p. 195.

42. Edson, *Railroad Names*, p. 32.

43. Dunn, *Greater Indianapolis*, p. 256.

44. Ibid.

45. Ibid.

46. Hilton, *Monon Route*, p. 51.

47. Ibid.

48. Dunn, *Greater Indianapolis*, p. 256.

49. Edson, *Railroad Names*, p. 156; Poor, *Manual of the Railroads of the United States*, 1885, p. 616.

50. Poor, *Manual of the Railroads of the United States*, 1908, p. 474; Batchelor, *Indiana Limestone Industry*, pp. 36–37.

51. Batchelor, *Indiana Limestone Industry*, pp. 36–37, 66.

52. Edson, *Railroad Names*, pp. 20, 36, 38.

53. INDOT, Railroad Division.

54. Harlow, *Road of the Century*, p. 395.

55. New York Central Railroad annual report, 1953, p. 277.

56. Burgess and Kennedy, *Centennial History of the Pennsylvania Railroad Company*, p. 215.

57. Schotter, *Growth and Development of the Pennsylvania Railroad Company*, p. 128.

58. Burgess and Kennedy, *Centennial History of the Pennsylvania Railroad Company*, p. 215.

59. Smith, *From the Ohio to the Mississippi.*
60. Hilton, *Monon Route,* p. 77.
61. Ibid., pp. 116–17.
62. Smith, *From the Ohio to the Mississippi;* Poor, *Manual of the Railroads of the United States,* 1897, p. 182.
63. Hilton, *Monon Route,* p. 79.
64. Ibid., pp. 77, 116–17.
65. Indiana Railroad Commission annual report, 1906, p. 261.
66. Hilton, *Monon Route,* p. 117.
67. Robert L. Hundman, "Construction at Louisville, Ky," *Mainline Modeler,* June 1990, pp. 36–37.
68. Hilton, *Monon Route,* p. 98.
69. Poor, *Manual of the Railroads of the United States,* 1897, p. 182.
70. Indiana Railroad Commission annual report, 1906, p. 261.
71. Sampson, *A Preliminary Historical Digest of the C&EI Railroad,* p. 18.
72. Herr, *Louisville and Nashville Railroad,* pp. 77–78.
73. Ibid., pp. 252–53.

12. MAJOR ABANDONMENTS

1. Compiled from reports of INDOT, Railroad Division.
2. Compiled from Sulzer, *Ghost Railroads of Indiana,* pp. 11, 261–62.
3. *1995 Indiana Rail Plan,* pp. 17–18; Sulzer, *Ghost Railroads of Indiana,* p. 8.
4. Sulzer, *Ghost Railroads of Indiana,* pp. 78, 83–84.
5. Ibid., p. 40; Coverdale and Colpitts, *The Pennsylvania Railroad Company,* vol. 3, pp. 358, 366.
6. Sulzer, *Ghost Railroads of Indiana,* p. 261.
7. Ibid.
8. Ibid., pp. 261–62.
9. Ibid., p. 262.
10. *Official Guide of the Railways,* various; INDOT, Railroad Division, various.
11. *Official Railway Guide,* Dec. 1995, p. B54.
12. Grant, *Erie Lackawanna,* pp. 208–13.
13. Reports of INDOT, Railroad Division, various.
14. *Official Railway Guide,* 1980s, various.
15. Reports of INDOT, Railroad Division, various.
16. Ibid.
17. Ibid., 1984, 1987, 1988.
18. Ibid., 1978, 1980; Sulzer, *Ghost Railroads of Indiana,* p. 99.

13. CASE HISTORIES

1. Proceedings of Supreme Court of Indiana, vol. 155, pp. 433–61.
2. S. H. Church, *Corporate History of the Pennsylvania Lines West of Pittsburgh,* vol. 2 (Baltimore: Friedenwald Co., 1905), pp. 537–38.
3. Ibid., p. 539.
4. Swartz, "The Wabash Railroad."
5. Wabash Railroad time table, Jan. 1, 1899, p. 13.

6. *Peru Evening Journal,* June 4, 1898; ibid., June 16, 1900; Wabash Railroad time table, Jan. 1, 1899, p. 11; Simons, "The Eel River and Its Railroad," p. 31.
7. Wabash Railway System, *Corporate and Financial History, as of December 31, 1939,* p. 125.
8. *Logansport Pharos,* Sept. 22, 1891.
9. Ibid.
10. *Peru Journal,* Sept. 24, 1891.
11. *Logansport Journal,* Sept. 26, 1891.
12. *Peru Journal,* Sept. 1891.
13. *Logansport Pharos,* Sept. 25, 1891.
14. *Peru Journal,* Sept. 1891.
15. *Huntington Herald,* Sept. 25, 1891.
16. Proceedings of Supreme Court of Indiana, vol. 155, p. 435.
17. Ibid., p. 436.
18. Ibid., p. 438.
19. Ibid., pp. 46–61.
20. Wabash Railway System, *Corporate and Financial History, as of December 31, 1939,* p. 125.
21. Simons, "The Eel River and Its Railroad," p. 34.
22. Church, *Corporate History of the Pennsylvania Lines,* p. 614.
23. *Official Guide of the Railways,* various.
24. Wabash Railway System, *Corporate and Financial History, as of December 31, 1939,* p. 125; Sulzer, *Ghost Railroads of Indiana,* p. 188.
25. INDOT, Railroad Division.
26. Hilton, *American Narrow Gauge Railroads,* p. 101; Rehor, *The Nickel Plate Story,* p. 143.
27. Rehor, *The Nickel Plate Story,* p. 121.
28. Ibid., p. 123.
29. Ibid.
30. Ibid., p. 126.
31. Ibid., pp. 119, 135–36.
32. Hilton, *American Narrow Gauge Railroads,* p. 475.
33. Rehor, *The Nickel Plate Story,* p. 141.
34. Ibid., p. 144.
35. Ibid., p. 146.
36. Ibid., p. 147.
37. Ibid.
38. Ibid.
39. Ibid.
40. Ibid., p. 148.
41. Ibid., p. 151.
42. Ibid., p. 152.
43. Ibid., pp. 155–56.
44. Ibid., p. 166; Indiana Coal Association, *Report of Indiana Coal Production,* 1955.
45. Rehor, *The Nickel Plate Story,* pp. 168, 82.
46. Ibid., p. 385; Richard S. Simons, "The Clover Leaf Route," *National Railway Bulletin* 43, no. 1 (1978), p. 25; Lewis, *American Shortline Railway Guide,* 4th ed. pp. 54, 126; INDOT, Railroad Division.
47. Poor, *Manual of the Railroads,* 1891, p. 706.
48. *Milwaukee Employes' Magazine,* May 1922, p. 16.
49. Simons, "The Milwaukee Road in Indiana," p. 4.
50. Poor, *Manual of the Railways,* 1905, p. 376; ibid., 1903, p. 428–31; ibid., 1899, p. 350.

51. *Indianapolis News,* Aug. 20, 1908, p. 1; James M. Guthrie, *History of Lawrence County* (Bedford, Ind., 1958), p. 180.

52. Batchelor, *Indiana Limestone Industry,* pp. 36–37, 66.

53. Guthrie, *History of Lawrence County,* pp. 89, 106, 114, 181.

54. Johnson, *Development of the Milwaukee Road,* p. 16; Simons, "The Milwaukee Road in Indiana," p. 5; *Official Guide of the Railways,* various.

55. Simons, "The Milwaukee Road in Indiana," p. 5; *Indianapolis News,* Dec. 21, 1905.

56. *Milwaukee Employes' Magazine,* May 1922, p. 16.

57. Guthrie, *History of Lawrence County,* p. 181.

58. Ibid., p. 93; *Indianapolis News,* Dec. 21, 1905, p. 8.

59. *Indianapolis News,* Mar. 3, 1906, p. 1; ibid., Dec. 21, 1905, p. 8.

60. Ibid., Mar. 3, 1906.

61. Johnson, *Development of the Milwaukee Road,* p. 19.

62. Chicago, Milwaukee and St. Paul Railway annual report, 1921; *Milwaukee Employes' Magazine,* May 1922, p. 12; Indiana Coal Association, *Report of Indiana Coal Production,* 1955.

63. Simons, "The Milwaukee Road in Indiana," pp. 4, 10.

64. *Milwaukee Road Magazine,* Mar. 1973, pp. 10–13; *Official Guide of the Railways,* May 1988.

65. Joseph A. Galloway and James J. Buckley, *The St. Joseph Valley Railway* (Chicago: Electric Railway Historical Society, 1955), p. 6.

66. Ibid., pp. 7, 27.

67 Traction line gap calculated from Indiana highway map and Ibid., p. 2.

68. Ibid., pp. 7, 10.

69. Ibid., pp. 15, 21, 29.

70. Ibid., p. 29.

71. Simons, "St. Joseph Valley Railway," *National Railway Bulletin* 52, no. 1 (1987), pp. 28–32.

72. Ibid., pp. 29–30.

73. Galloway and Buckley, *The St. Joseph Valley Railway,* pp. 18, 35.

74. Ibid., pp. 18–19.

75. Ibid., p. 24.

76. Ibid.

77. Report of Interstate Commerce Commission, Jan. 29, 1917; Galloway and Buckley, *The St. Joseph Valley Railway,* p. 25.

78. Galloway and Buckley, *The St. Joseph Valley Railway,* pp. 27, 29.

79. *Official Guide of the Railways,* June 1916; U.S. census reports.

80. Sulzer, *Ghost Railroads of Indiana,* p. 101.

81. *Indianapolis News,* Nov. 10, 1917.

82. Sulzer, *Ghost Railroads of Indiana,* p. 102.

83. Ibid., p. 108.

84. Ibid.

85. Ibid., pp. 102–103.

86. *Indianapolis News,* Nov. 10, 1917.

87. Sulzer, *Ghost Railroads of Indiana,* p. 103.

88. Ibid., p. 106; *Indianapolis News,* Nov. 10, 1917.

89. *Indianapolis News,* Nov. 10, 1917.

90. Sulzer, *Ghost Railroads of Indiana,* p. 103.

91. Ibid., p. 106.

92. Edmund Keilty, *Interurbans without Wires* (Glendale, Calif.: Interurban Press, 1979), p. 63; *Official Guide of the Railways,* June 1916.

93. *Indianapolis News,* Nov. 10, 1917.

14. RAILROAD TOWNS AND CITIES

1. Dolzall and Dolzall, *Monon: The Hoosier Line,* p. 51.

2. McLellan and Warrick, *The Lake Shore & Michigan Southern Railway,* p. 71.

3. Ibid., p. 72.

4. Ibid., p. 77.

5. Darryl E. Bigham, *An Evansville Album: Perspectives on a River City* (Bloomington: Indiana University Press, 1988), p. 15.

6. Ibid., pp. 25, 77.

7. Ibid., p. 25.

8. Rice, ed., *The History of the Pennsylvania Railroad's Fort Wayne Shops,* p. 4.

9. Ibid., p. 12.

10. Michael C. Hawfield, *Fort Wayne Cityscapes: Highlights of a Community's History* (Northridge, Calif.: Windsor, c. 1988), p. 66.

11. Craig Leonard, *Garrett Railroad Museum, Museum Planning Study* (Bluffton, Ind.: Restoration/Preservation/ Architecture, Inc., 1980), p. 1.

12. Warren A. Reeder Jr., "Hammond, Indiana: From the Beginning to the Bicentennial of the American Revolution," *Hammond, Indiana's Bicentennial Yearbook* (Hammond: Rand McNally, 1976), p. 72.

13. Ibid., p. 71.

14. Phillips, *Indiana in Transition,* p. 366.

15. Dunn, *Greater Indianapolis,* p. 267.

16. Ibid.

17. Ibid., p. 266.

18. Ibid., p. 267.

19. Historic Sites and Structures Inventory, *Decatur, Perry and Franklin Townships, Marion County,* Historic Landmarks Foundation of Indiana, 1992.

20. Bill Harvey, "Lafayette, Indiana: NKP and NYC Operation," *Mainline Modeler,* Nov. 1988, pp. 68–71.

21. Hilton, *Monon Route,* p. 52.

22. John H. White, Jr., "Railroad Car Builders of the United States," R&LHS *Railway History* 138 (1978), pp. 5–29.

23. Dixon, *The Chesapeake & Ohio in Color, 1950–1975,* p. 69.

24. Rehor, *The Nickel Plate Story,* p. 364.

25. *Gibson County, Warrick County: Interim Report,* 1984, p. xvii.

26. Rehor, *The Nickel Plate Story,* p. 227.

27. Smith, *From the Ohio to the Mississippi.*

15. NOTABLE BRIDGES

1. Illinois Central Railroad Historical Society, *Green Diamond* (n.d.), pp. 20, 23.

2. *Osgood Journal,* May 23, 1901.

3. Sulzer, *Ghost Railroads of Indiana,* p. 32.

4. Hilton, *Monon Route,* p. 48; Linn H. Westcott, "The Monon System and Its Traffic," *Trains,* July 1947, p. 28; INDOT, Railroad Division.

5. *Indianapolis News,* 1904; INDOT, Railroad Division; Westcott, "The Monon System and Its Traffic," p. 32.

6. U.S. Army Corps of Engineers, *The Ohio River,* pp. 264, 266, 269, 271; Smith, *From the Ohio to the Mississippi;* Sulzer, *Ghost Railroads of Indiana,* p. 125.

7. U.S. Army Corps of Engineers, *The Ohio River,* pp. 264, 266, 269; Marlette, *Interstate: A History of Interstate Public Service Rail Operations,* p. 77.

8. Harlow, *Road of the Century,* p. 395.

9. U.S. Army Corps of Engineers, *The Ohio River,* p. 264; INDOT, Railroad Division.

10. U.S. Army Corps of Engineers, *The Ohio River,* p. 266; Lewis C. Baird, *History of Clark County* (Indianapolis: B. F. Bowen & Co., 1909), p. 368; Burgess and Kennedy, *Centennial History of the Pennsylvania Railroad Company,* p. 548.

11. Smith, *From the Ohio to the Mississippi;* Hilton, *Monon Route,* p. 77, 80; Marlette, *Interstate: A History of Interstate Public Service Rail Operations,* p. 14.

12. *Official Railway Guide,* p. C106.

13. Hilton, *Monon Route,* p. 117; U.S. Army Corps of Engineers, *The Ohio River,* p. 269; Marlette, *Interstate: A History of Interstate Public Service Rail Operations,* pp. 20, 81. (Hilton gives the construction date as 1911; Dolzall and Dolzall, *Monon: The Hoosier Line,* p. 43, give it as 1910; Marlette gives the opening date as Dec. 1, 1913.)

14. Herr, *Louisville and Nashville Railroad,* p. 252; U.S. Army Corps of Engineers, *The Ohio River,* p. 271; Sulzer, *Ghost Railroads of Indiana,* p. 125; *Official Railway Guide,* May 1988, p. C102.

15. Compiled from *Official Guide of the Railways,* various, and Indiana State Highway maps.

16. *Indianapolis Star Sunday Magazine,* Apr. 11, 1954, pp. 18–19.

17. Information from Thomas G. Hoback, president, Indiana Rail Road; Clay W. Stuckey, "A Minor Historical Ambiguity Clarified" (MS., Bedford, Ind., 1986), pp. 1–7.

18. Hilton, *Monon Route,* pp. 197, 203–209.

19. George E. Gould, *Indiana Covered Bridges thru the Years* (Indianapolis: Indiana Covered Bridge Society, 1977), pp. 24–27, 50–55, 57–58, 60–64.

16. TUNNELS

1. Simons, "Indiana's Railroad Tunnels," pp. 12–13.

2. "John Brough's Folly, 1852–54: Pioneer Railroading in Clifty Canyon" (DNR brochure, n.d.).

3. Smith, *From the Ohio to the Mississippi.*

4. Correspondence with C. B. Harveson, chief engineer, maintenance, Baltimore & Ohio Railroad, Mar. 13, 1948.

5. *Seymour Weekly Democrat,* Nov. 16, 1899.

6. *Railroad Gazette,* Feb. 3, 1899.

7. Correspondence with H. L. Rose, assistant vice-president, Southern Railway, Oct. 3, 1988.

8. Correspondence with chief engineer, Southern Railway, Mar. 23, 1948.

9. Ibid.; H. L. Rose correspondence, Oct. 3, 1988.

10. Correspondence with chief engineer, Southern Railway, Mar. 23, 1948 (some sources give the tunnel name as "Burton"); correspondence with G. Alan Barnett, president, French Lick, West Baden and Southern Railway, Oct. 20, 1989.

11. Sulzer, *Ghost Railroads of Indiana,* p. 163; Hilton, *Monon Route,* pp. 110, 155.

12. Harry Q. Holt, *History of Martin County* (Oxford, Ind.: Richard B. Cross Co., 1966), p. 101.

13. Illinois Central Railroad Historical Society, *Green Diamond* (n.d.), pp. 20–21.

17. PULLMAN SERVICES

1. Association of American Railroads, *Quiz on Railroads and Railroading,* no. 43.

2. Peter T. Maiken, *Night Trains: The Pullman System in the Golden Years of American Rail Travel* (Chicago: Lakme Press, 1989), p. 8.

3. Ibid., p. 9; Pennsylvania Railroad time tables, various in 1930s, 1940s.

4. Maiken, *Night Trains,* pp. 8, 137.

5. Ibid., various pp.; *Official Guide of the Railways,* various; individual railroad time tables, various.

6. Maiken, *Night Trains,* pp. 172–73; *Official Guide of the Railways,* various; individual railroad time tables, various.

7. New York Central, Pennsylvania Railroad, and Baltimore & Ohio Railroad time tables, various; *Official Guide of the Railways,* various.

8. Ibid.

9. Maiken, *Night Trains,* p. 81; Pennsylvania Railroad time tables, various.

10. Sulzer, *Ghost Railroads of Indiana,* p. 147; Chicago, Indiana and Eastern time table, n.d.

11. Maiken, *Night Trains,* pp. 172–73; Pennsylvania Railroad time table, Apr. 25, 1937; Big Four time table, Jan. 21, 1934; *Bloomington Daily Telephone,* June 24, 1911.

12. Maiken, *Night Trains,* pp. 137, 161; Big Four time table, Sept. 27, 1946.

13. *New York Times,* Mar. 4, 1946.

14. *Official Guide of the Railways,* June 1946, pp. 174, 188, 264–67, 331–32, 403, 411.

15. Ibid., pp. 175, 192, 267, 333, 404–405, 418.

16. Maiken, *Night Trains,* pp. 79–81.

17. Pennsylvania Railroad time table, Sept. 28, 1930; Big Four time table, Apr. 27, 1930; Maiken, *Night Trains,* p. 81; *Bloomington Daily Telephone,* June 24, 1911.

18. Sampson, *A Preliminary Historical Digest of the C&EI Railroad;* Maiken, *Night Trains,* p. 82; Big Four time table, Jan. 21, 1934.

19. Maiken, *Night Trains,* pp. 82–83; *Official Guide of the Railways,* Jan. 1930, p. 380.

20. Coverdale and Colpitts, *The Pennsylvania Railroad Company,* vol. 3, p. 375.

21. C&O time table, Oct. 12, 1916; CI&E time table, n.d.

22. Maiken, *Night Trains,* p. 82.

18. MOTOR TRAINS

1. Edmund Keilty, *The Short Line Doodlebug* (Glendale, Calif.: Interurban Press, 1988), pp. 53–54.
2. Edmund Keilty, *Interurbans without Wires*, p. 21.
3. Compiled from *Official Guide of the Railways* and time tables of individual railroads, various.
4. Keilty, *Interurbans without Wires*, p. 13.
5. Ibid., p. 145.
6. Ibid., pp. 145–47, 173, 187; Keilty, *The Short Line Doodlebug*, pp. 12, 103, 105, 123.
7. *Official Guide of the Railways*, New York Central and Big Four time tables, various.
8. Pennsylvania Railroad time tables, various.
9. Chesapeake and Ohio Railway, Baltimore & Ohio Railroad, Milwaukee Road time tables, various.
10. *Official Guide of the Railways*, June 1916, p. 556; Keilty, *The Short Line Doodlebug*.
11. Sulzer, *Ghost Railroads of Indiana*, pp. 130, 143–44.
12. Keilty, *The Short Line Doodlebug*, p. 52.
13. Ibid., pp. 53–54.
14. Ibid.; Keilty, *Interurbans without Wires*, p. 73; *Official Guide of the Railways*, June 1916, p. 513.
15. Sulzer, *Ghost Railroads of Indiana*, p. 29.
16. Keilty, *Interurbans without Wires*, pp. 88, 145.
17. Ibid., pp. 88, 101.
18. Ibid., pp. 93–101.
19. Keilty, *The Short Line Doodlebug*, pp. 12, 103, 105, 123.
20. Keilty, *Interurbans without Wires*, pp. 173, 187.
21. Keilty, *The Short Line Doodlebug*, pp. 30, 33.
22. Ibid., various pages; Keilty, *Interurbans without Wires*, pp. 94–101.

19. SPECIAL PASSENGER SERVICES

1. *Official Guide of the Railways*, June 1916, May 1944; New York Central Railroad Employe Time Table no. 37a, Western Division, June 25, 1933.
2. *Official Guide of the Railways*, June 1893, pp. 355, 362, Apr. 1909, p. 467, and June 1916, p. 499.
3. *Central States Guide*, Sept. 1925, p. 127-a; *Official Guide of the Railways*, June 1959, p. 301; Amtrak time-tables, various.
4. New York Central Railroad Employee Time Table, various in 1930s.
5. South Shore Line time table, Feb. 18, 1996; information from John Parsons, marketing director, Northern Indiana Commuter Transportation District.
6. *Official Guide of the Railways*, June 1916, pp. 92, 144, 286, 533; Jan. 1885, 1896, 1900.
7. Ibid., June 1916, pp. 309, 311; Big Four time table, Jan. 31, 1934.
8. Marlette, *Interstate: A History of Interstate Public Service Rail Operations*, p. 14; *Official Guide of the Railways*, Apr. 1909, p. 476.
9. *Official Guide of the Railways*, various.
10. Ibid., May 1944, p. 715 and Aug. 1955, p. 789.

11. Sampson, *A Preliminary Historical Digest of the C&EI Railroad*, p. 18.
12. *Official Guide of the Railways*, June 1916, p. 893, May 1944, p. 715, Aug. 1955, p. 789.
13. Ibid., various.
14. Chicago and Atlantic Railroad Employe Time Table, June 19, 1887; Poor, *Manual of the Railroads in the United States*, 1903, p. 434; Wabash Railroad time table, Jan. 1, 1899 and Sept. 1924; Erie Railroad time table, May 1897.
15. Pennsylvania time table, Apr. 25, 1937; Swartz, "The Wabash Railroad."
16. Pennsylvania time table, Apr. 2, 1939, and Sept. 25, 1949.
17. *Official Guide of the Railways*, June 1916, pp. 306, 498, 554, 569; Hilton, *Monon Route*, p. 155. (Dolzall and Dolzall, *Monon: The Hoosier Line*, p. 30, give the end of Chicago-Cincinnati service in 1927).
18. Hilton, *Monon Route*, p. 136.
19. Rehor, *The Nickel Plate Story*, p. 110; New York Central Lines time table, May 1913; Big Four Route time table, Oct. 1909.
20. Big Four Route time table, Oct. 1909.
21. Rehor, *The Nickel Plate Story*, pp. 109–10, 113.
22. New York Central time table, May 1913; *Official Guide of the Railways*, June 1916, p. 315; Rehor, *The Nickel Plate Story*, pp. 110, 114.
23. Sulzer, *Ghost Railroads of Indiana*, pp. 58, 207.
24. *Official Guide of the Railways*, June 1916, p. 513.
25. Ibid., Dec. 1931, p. 1071; Simons, "The Milwaukee Road in Indiana," p. 10.
26. *Official Guide of the Railways*, Apr. 1909, p. 478; *Central States Guide*, Sept. 1925, p. 127-a.
27. Sulzer, *Ghost Railroads of Indiana*, p. 58.
28. *Official Guide of the Railways*, effective Sept. 4, 1910; *Central States Guide*, Sept. 1925, p. 45.
29. Sulzer, *Ghost Railroads of Indiana*, p. 225.
30. Ibid., p. 226.
31. *Official Guide of the Railways*, June 1893, p. 362; Sulzer, *Ghost Railroads of Indiana*, p. 230.
32. *Official Guide of the Railways*, June 1893, p. 362, and June 1918, p. 475; Bernice Mason, *Bicknell, Indiana, Centennial Historical Book* (Vincennes: Vincent Printing, 1969).
33. *Official Guide of the Railways*, June 1916, p. 513; Milwaukee Road time table, Apr. 1928.

20. DISASTERS

1. Hilton and Due, *Electric Interurban Railways in America*, p. 88.
2. *South Bend Tribune*, Mar. 4, 1990. Robert Shaw, *Down Brakes: A History of Railroad Accidents, Safety Precautions and Operating Practices in the United States of America* (London: PRM Publishers, 1961), p. 476, lists fatalities as 34.
3. Smith, *From the Ohio to the Mississippi*. (Shaw, *Down Brakes*, p. 476, lists fatalities as 28.)
4. "Historical News by the Indiana Historical Commission," *Indiana Magazine of History* 18 (March 1922), p. 118.
5. *Marion Daily Chronicle*, May 9, 1893.

6. Shaw, *Down Brakes*, pp. 347–48; Robert W. Topping, *A Century and Beyond: The History of Purdue University* (West Lafayette: Purdue University Press, 1988), pp. 156–57.

7. Shaw, *Down Brakes*, p. 372; Second Annual Report of the Railroad Commission of Indiana, pp. 194–96.

8. *World Almanac*, 1992, p. 541 (Second Annual Report of the Railroad Commission of Indiana, pp. 196–202, lists fatalities as seven).

9. *Marion Leader-Tribune*, Jan. 20, 1907; Second Annual Report of the Railroad Commission of Indiana. (Commission report lists 15 fatalities.)

10. *Indianapolis News*, Nov. 13, 1912.

11. Wesley S. Griswold, *Train Wreck!* (Brattleboro, Vt.: Stephen Greene Press, 1969), pp. 104–106; Shaw, *Down Brakes*, p. 296.

12. Shaw, *Down Brakes*, pp. 134–36.

13. Ibid., p. 484; *Marion Chronicle*, Sept. 15, 1944; *Marion Leader-Tribune*, Sept. 15, 1944.

14. *Marion Chronicle*, June 9, 1925.

15. Ibid., Mar. 22, 1916.

16. Contemporary newspapers, various.

21. PERSONALITIES

1. *National Cyclopaedia of American Biography*, vol. 26, p. 105.

2. Burgess and Kennedy, *Centennial History of the Pennsylvania Railroad Company*, p. 589.

3. Ibid., pp. 589–90.

4. Ibid., p. 590.

5. *National Cyclopaedia of American Biography*, vol. 26, p. 106.

6. Ibid.

7. Ibid.

8. May E. Arbuckle in *The Hoosier Training Ground*, pp. 20–21.

9. Frederic A. Birmingham, *Ball Corporation, the First Century* (Indianapolis: Curtis Publishing Co., 1980), pp. 120–21; "'Pittance' Wins Industrial Empire," *Literary Digest,* Dec. 19, 1936, p. 43.

10. *Saturday Evening Post*, Feb. 6, 1937, p. 5.

11. *Literary Digest,* Dec. 19, 1936.

12. Hampton, *The Nickel Plate Road*, p. 319.

13. *Business Week*, May 1, 1937, p. 18.

14. *Official Guide of the Railways*, May 1944, p. 1125; *Who's Who in America*, vol. 3.

15. *National Cyclopaedia of American Biography*, vol. 4, p. 53.

16. *Encyclopedia Americana*, vol. 5, p. 24.

17. Murphy, "Big Four Railroad in Indiana," pp. 194–96.

18. Burgess and Kennedy, *Centennial History of the Pennsylvania Railroad Company,* pp. 216–18.

19. Edson, *Railroad Names*, p. 26.

20. Harlow, *Road of the Century*, pp. 382–83.

21. *Encyclopedia Americana*, vol. 5, p. 24.

22. Phillips, *Indiana in Transition*, p. 258.

23. Stewart H. Holbrook, *Dreamers of the American Dream* (Garden City, N.Y.: Doubleday, 1957), p. 307.

24. *National Cyclopaedia of American Biography*, vol. 23, pp. 21–22.

25. Ibid.

26. Dolzall and Dolzall, *Monon: The Hoosier Line*, p. 48; Hilton, *Monon Route*, p. 80.

27. *National Cyclopaedia of American Biography*, vol. 24, pp. 11–12.

28. Ibid., vol. 40, pp. 464–65.

29. Hilton, *Monon Route*, p. 23.

30. *National Cyclopaedia of American Biography*, vol. 40, pp. 564–65.

31. Ibid.

32. *American Magazine*, Nov. 1925, p. 29.

33. *Dictionary of American Biography*, vol. 9, p. 501; *Toronto Star,* Feb. 28, 1925; *Living Age*, Dec. 1928, p. 273.

34. *Dictionary of American Biography*, vol. 9, p. 501.

35. Ibid.; speech by John W. Barriger, at Portland, Maine, Nov. 21, 1944, pp. 19–20.

36. *Indianapolis Star Sunday Magazine*, Oct. 4, 1981, p. 17.

37. *Canadian National Magazine*, Jan. 1951, p. 32; correspondence with Brian P. Moreau, public affairs representative, Canadian National Railways.

38. Grant, *Erie Lackawanna*, pp. 75–79.

39. *National Cyclopaedia of American Biography*, vol. 9, pp. 48–49.

40. Ibid., p. 49.

41. Rockwell Kent, *World Famous Paintings* (New York: Wise & Co., 1947), Plate 91.

Select Bibliography

Abbey, Wallace W. "The Road of Efficiency Plus." *Trains,* February 1953, pp. 24–28.

Atack, Jeremy, and Jan K. Brueckner. "Steel Rails and American Railroads, 1867–1880." *Explorations in Economic History* 19 (October 1982), pp. 339–59.

Batchelor, Joseph A. *The Indiana Limestone Industry.* Bloomington: Indiana University School of Business, 1944.

Bain, William E. *B&O in the Civil War; from the papers of William Prescott Smith.* Denver: Sage Books, 1966.

Beebe, Lucius. *Mixed Train Daily.* New York: E. P. Dutton, 1947.

Berg, Walter G. *Buildings and Structures of American Railroads.* New York: John Wiley, 1893. Reprint, Newton Gregg, 1977.

Bigham, Darrel E. *An Evansville Album.* Bloomington: Indiana University Press, 1988.

Blaine, David G. "The Westinghouse Air Brake Story." *Trains,* October 1975, pp. 44–53.

Blaszak, Michael W. "Change on the Harbor: Whither the Indiana Harbor Belt?" *Trains,* March 1986, pp. 22–39.

Blaszak, Michael W. "The J: A Centennial History." *Trains,* August 1989, pp. 26–35; September 1989, pp. 28–41.

Blaszak, Michael W. "Intermodal: Railroading's Indispensable Adaptation." *Pacific RailNews,* September 1996, pp. 26–37.

Bogle, Victor M. "Railroad Building in Indiana, 1850–1855." *Indiana Magazine of History* 58, no. 3 (September 1962), pp. 211–232.

Botkin, B. A., and Alvin F. Harlow, eds. *A Treasury of Railroad Folklore.* New York: Crown Publishers, 1953.

Bradley, George K. *Indiana Railroad: The Magic Interurban.* Chicago: Central Electric Railfans' Association, 1991.

Bradley, Roger. *Amtrak: The US National Railroad Passenger Corporation.* Poole, Dorset: Blandford Press, 1985.

Bradsby, H. C. *History of Vigo County.* Chicago: S. B. Nelson, 1891.

Brown, Robert. "Pioneer Locomotives of America." *Railway and Locomotive Historical Society Bulletin* no. 101, October 1959.

Burgess, George H. and Miles C. Kennedy. *Centennial History of the Pennsylvania Railroad Company, 1846–1946.* Philadelphia: The Pennsylvania Railroad Company, 1949.

Campbell, E. G. *The Reorganization of the American Railroad System, 1893–1900.* New York: AMS Press, 1968 (first published 1938).

Central Electric Railfans' Association. *Bulletins.* Chicago.

Chappell, Gordon. *Steam Over Scranton: The Locomotives of Steamtown.* National Park Service, Special History Study, 1991.

Chicago, Milwaukee and St. Paul Railroad. *Annual Reports.*

Clark, T. D. "The Lexington and Ohio Railroad—A Pioneer Venture." Kentucky State Historical Society *Register,* January 1933, pp. 9–28.

Collias, Joe. *The Search for Steam.* Forest Park, Ill.: Heimburger House, 1972.

Cottman, George S. "Internal Improvements, Part IV—Railroads." *Indiana Magazine of History* 3, no. 4 (December 1907).

Coverdale and Colpitts, firm of. *The Pennsylvania Railroad Company: Corporate, Financial and Construction History.* 1947.

Crosby, John R. "Second Engine 28." *Trains,* March 1975, pp. 42–51 (Broadway Limited, Chicago-Fort Wayne, WW II).

Daniels, Wylie J. *The Village at the End of the Road.* Indianapolis: 1938.

Dilts, James D. *The Great Road: The Building of the Baltimore & Ohio: The Nation's First Railroad 1828–1853.* Stanford, Calif.: Stanford University Press, 1994.

Dixon, Thomas W. *Chessie: The Railroad Kitten.* Sterling, Va.: TLC Publishing Co. 1988.

Dixon, Thomas W. *The Chesapeake & Ohio in Color—1950–1975.* Lynchburg, Va.: TLC Publishing Co., 1992.

Dixon, Thomas W. "C&O Brill Gas Electric Cars." *Mainline Modeler,* January 1989, pp. 38.

Dolzall, Gary W., and Stephen F. Dolzall. *Monon: The Hoosier Line,* Glendale, Interurban Press, 1987

Dorin, Patrick C. *The Chesapeake and Ohio Railway.* Seattle: Superior Publishing, 1981.

Dorin, Patrick C. *The Grand Trunk Western Railroad.* Seattle: Superior Publishing, 1977

Dorin, Patrick C. *The Domeliners.* Seattle: Superior Publishing, 1973.

Droege, John A. *Freight Terminals and Trains.* New York: McGraw Hill, 1912.

Drury, George H. *The Historical Guide to North American Railroads.* Waukesha, Wis.: Kalmbach Books.

Dunn, Jacob P. *Greater Indianapolis.* Chicago: Lewis Publishing Co., 1910.

Edmonson, Harold A., ed. *Journey to Amtrak: The Year History Rode the Passenger Train.* Milwaukee: Kalmbach Books, 1972.

Edson, William. "Panhandle Locomotives." *Railway and Locomotive Historical Society Bulletin* no. 141, 1979, pp. 34–56.

Edson, William D. *Railroad Names.* Potomac, Md., 1993.

Encyclopedia Americana. Danbury, Conn.: Grolier, Inc., 1992.

Farrington, S. Kip, Jr. *Railroads at War.* New York: Coward-McCann, 1944.

Fisher, Charles E. "The 'Clover Leaf.'" *Railway and Locomotive Historical Society Bulletin* no. 97 (October 1957), pp. 72–75.

Fisher, Charles E. "Locomotive Builders of the United States." *Railway and Locomotive Historical Society Bulletin* no. 58 (May 1942), pp. 55–68.

Ford, Ira, ed. *History of Northeast Indiana; LaGrange, Steuben, Noble and DeKalb Counties.* Chicago: Lewis Publishing Co., 1920.

Galloway, Joseph A., and James J. Buckley. *The St. Joseph Valley Railway.* Chicago: Electric Railway Historical Society, 1955.

Gamst, Frederick C., ed. "Letters from the United States of America on Internal Improvements, Steam Navigation, Banking, & c., written by Anthony Chevalier de Gerstner during his sojourn in the United States, 1839. Translated from the German. *Railway and Locomotive Historical Society Bulletin* 163, Autumn 1990, pp. 28–73.

Gieck, Jack. *A Photo Album of Ohio's Canal Era 1825–1913.* Kent, Ohio: Kent State University Press, 1988.

Goodrich, Carter. *Government Promotion of American Canals and Railroads 1800–1890.* New York: Columbia University Press, 1960.

Goodrich, Carter. "Local Government Planning of Internal Improvements." *Political Science Quarterly,* 66 (1951), 411–45.

George E. Gould. *Indiana Covered Bridges thru the Years.* Indianapolis: Indiana Covered Bridge Society, 1977.

Grant, H. Roger. *Erie Lackawanna.* Stanford, Calif.: Stanford University Press, 1969.

Griswold, Wesley S. *Train Wreck.* Brattleboro, Vt.: Stephen Greene Press, 1969.

Halberstadt, Hans, and April Halberstadt. *The American Train Depot & Roundhouse.* Osceola, Wis.: Motorbooks International, 1995.

Hampton, Taylor. *The Nickel Plate Road.* Cleveland: World Publishing Company, 1947.

Harlow, Alvin F. *The Road of the Century: The Story of the New York Central.* New York: Creative Age Press, 1947.

Harrison, Fairfax. *A History of the Legal Development of the Railroad System of the Southern Railway Company.* Washington, D.C., 1901.

Harvey, Bill. "Lafayette, Indiana: NKP and NYC Operation." *Mainline Modeler,* November 1988, pp. 68–71.

Harwood, Herbert H., Jr. *Impossible Challenge: The Balti-more and Ohio Railroad in Maryland.* Baltimore: Barnard, Roberts, 1979.

Heimburger, Donald J. *Wabash.* Forest Park, Ill.: Heimburger House, 1984.

Henderson, Ralph. "Problems of our First Railroad." *Indiana History Bulletin* 30, no. 6. Indianapolis: June 1953.

Herr, Kincaid A. *Louisville and Nashville Railroad 1850–1963.* Public Relations Department, L&N Railroad, Louisville, 1943.

Hilton, George W. *Monon Route.* Berkeley, Howell-North Books, 1978.

Hilton, George W. "Pere Marquette." *Trains.* August 1945, pp. 8–21.

Hilton, George W. "The Chicago, Cincinnati & Louisville Railroad." *Railway and Locomotive Historical Society Bulletin* 114, April 1966, pp. 6–13.

Hilton, George W. *American Narrow Gauge Railroads.* Stanford, Calif.: Stanford University Press, 1990.

Hilton, George W., and John Due. *The Electric Interurban Railways in America.* Stanford, Calif.: Stanford University Press, 1960.

Hinderer, Carl E. "The Evansville Route." MS. 20 pp text plus illustrations, n.d. [post–1987].

Hirsimaki, Eric E., Bruce K. Dicken, and James M. Semon. *Reflections: The Nickel Plate Years: Lake Erie & Western District.* Cleveland: The Nickel Plate Road Historical & Technical Society, Inc., 1982.

Hungerford, Edward. *Men of Erie.* New York: Random House, 1946.

Hungerford, Edward. *The Story of the Baltimore & Ohio Railroad, 1827–1927.* New York: G. P. Putnam's Sons, 1928.

Husband, Joseph. *The Story of the Pullman Car.* Chicago: 1917 (reprint).

Illinois Central Historical Society, *Green Diamond.* n.d.

Indiana Coal Association, Annual Reports, Indianapolis.

Indiana Department of Transportation, Railroad Division, Abandonment Reports.

Indiana Department of Transportation. *1995 Indiana Rail Plan.* prepared by Department of Geography and Transportation Research Center, Indiana University, Bloomington, July 1995.

Indianapolis Star Sunday Magazine.

Ivey, Paul Wesley. *The Pere Marquette Railroad Company.* Grand Rapids, The Black Letter Press, 1970.

Johnson, Eric C. A. *Reflections on America's First Union Depot; Indianapolis Union Station.* 1978.

Jones, Robert E. "Train Time at Hammond." *Trains,* Sept. 1985, pp. 46–50A (Steam era and 1985).

Keefe, Kevin P. "Beech Grove: Central's Pride Is Amtrak's Inheritance." *Passenger Train Journal,* November 1978, pp. 20-29.

Keilty, Edmund. *Interurbans Without Wires.* Glendale, Calif.: Interurban Press, 1979.

Keilty, Edmund. *The Short Line Doodlebug.* Glendale, Calif.: Interurban Press, 1988.

Klein, Maury. *History of the Louisville & Nashville Railroad.* New York: Macmillan, 1972.

Lewis, Edward A. *American Shortline Railway Guide*. Waukesha, Wis., Kalmbach Books, 1991. 1st, 3rd, 4th and 5th eds.

Lewis, Edward A. *The "DO" Lines*. Strasburg, Pa.: The Baggage Car, 1977.

McLellan, David, and Bill Warrick. *The Lake Shore & Michigan Southern Railway*. Polo, Illinois: Transportation Trails, 1989.

McMillan, Joe, and Robert P. Olmsted. *The Peoria Way*. McMillan Publications, 1984.

Maiken, Peter T. *Night Trains—The Pullman System in the Golden Years of American Rail Travel*. Chicago: Lakme Press, 1989.

Marlette, Jerry. *Electric Railroads of Indiana*. Indianapolis: Hoosier Heritage Press, 1980.

Marlette, Jerry. *Interstate*. Polo, Ill.: Transportation Trails, 1990.

Meints, Graydon M. *Michigan Railroads and Railroad Companies*. East Lansing: Michigan State University Press, 1992.

Middleton, William D. *South Shore*. San Marino, Calif.: Golden West Books, 1970.

Moody's Transportation Manuals, Moody's Investment Service, New York.

Murphy, Ared Maurice. "The Big Four Railroad in Indiana." *Indiana Magazine of History* 21 (June and September 1925), pp. 109–273.

National Cyclopaedia of American Biography.

National Park Service. *The Evolution of Transportation in Western Pennsylvania*. Special History Study, NPS, U.S. Dept of Interior, May 1994.

National Railway Bulletin. National Railway Historical Society, Philadelphia.

New York Central Railroad. *Annual Reports*.

Norfolk Southern Railway. *Annual Reports*.

Official Railway Guide. K-III Directory Corporation, New York.

Olmsted, Robert P. *The Streator Connection*. Woodridge, Ill.: McMillan Publications, 1982.

Phillips, Clifton J. *Indiana in Transition: The Emergence of an Industrial Commonwealth, 1880–1920*. Indiana Historical Bureau and Indiana Historical Society, 1968; chapter 6, "The Evolution of a Modern Transportation System," pp. 224–270.

Pinkepank, Jerry. "The Kankakee Belt Is Back in Business." *Trains*, February 1969, pp. 20–23.

Poinsatte, Charles R. *Fort Wayne During the Canal Era: 1828-1855*. Indiana Historical Bureau, 1969.

Poor, Henry V. *Manual of the Railroads of the United States*.

Porter, Horace. "Railway Passenger Travel, 1825–1880." *Scribner's*, September 1888 (reprinted by Americana Review), no page numbers.

Prince, Richard E. *Steam Locomotives and Boats; Southern Railway System*. Green River, Wy.: Richard E. Prince, 1965.

Railroad Commission of Indiana, Annual Reports.

Railway and Locomotive Historical Society Bulletin.

Rainey, George S. *Demise of the Iron Horse*. Berne: Economy Printing, 1969.

Reeder, Warren. *Hammond Bicentennial Yearbook*. 1976.

Rehor, John A. *The Nickel Plate Story*. Milwaukee: Kalmbach Books, 1965.

Rice, Merle, ed. *History of the Pennsylvania Railroad's Fort Wayne Shops*. Fort Wayne Public Library, 1966.

Sampson, Harold R. *A Preliminary Historical Digest of the C&EI RR*. Glenwood, Ill.: HLW Industries, 1965.

Saunders, Richard. *The Railroad Mergers and the Coming of Conrail*. Westport: Greenwood Press, 1978.

Schodek, Daniel L. *Landmarks in American Civil Engineering*. Cambridge: MIT Press, 1987.

Schotter, H. W. *The Growth and Development of The Pennsylvania Railroad Company*. Philadelphia: Allen, Lane & Scott Press, December 1927.

Shaffer, Frank E. "Pullman Prolificacy." *Trains*, October 1967, pp. 24–28 (Eastern Pullman service in 1927).

Shaw, Robert B. *Down Brakes*. London: PRM Publishers, 1961.

Simons, Richard S. "The Clover Leaf Route." *National Railway Bulletin* 43, no. 1 (1978), pp. 16–27.

Simons, Richard S. "Indiana's Railroad Tunnels." *National Railway Bulletin* 55, no. 5 (1990), pp. 12–23.

Simons, Richard S. "The Eel River and its Railroad." *National Railway Bulletin* 53, no. 6 (1988), pp. 28–35.

Simons, Richard S. "Muncie's Own Railroad." *National Railway Bulletin* 57, no. 2 (1992), pp. 10–15.

Simons, Richard S. "St. Joseph Valley Railway." *National Railway Bulletin* 52, no. 1 (1987), pp. 28–36.

Simons, Richard S. "The Milwaukee Road in Indiana." *National Railway Bulletin* 45, no. 1 (1980), pp. 4–10.

Smith, John Martin. *History of DeKalb County, Indiana*. Auburn, Ind.: Natmus, Inc., 1992.

Smith, Robert F. *From the Ohio to the Mississippi*. Cincinnati: Mt. Airy Printing Co., 1965.

Staufer, Alvin F. *New York Central's Early Power: 1813–1916*. Alvin Staufer, 1967.

Staufer, Alvin F. *Pennsy Power: Steam and Electric Locomotives of the Pennsylvania Railroad 1900–1957*. Alvin Staufer, 1962.

Stegmaier, Harry. *Baltimore & Ohio Passenger Service, 1945–1971 - Volume 1: The Route of the National Limited*. Lynchburg, Va.: TLC Publishing, 1993.

Stilgoe, John R. *Metropolitan Corridor: Railroads and the American Scene*. New Haven, Yale University Press, 1983.

Stover, John F. *History of the Baltimore and Ohio Railroad*. West Lafayette, Purdue University Press, 1987.

Stover, John F. *History of the Illinois Central Railroad*. New York: Macmillan, 1975.

Stover, John F. *Iron Road to the West: American Railroads in the 1850s*. New York: Columbia University Press, 1973.

Sulzer, Elmer G. *Ghost Railroads of Indiana*. Indianapolis: V. A. Jones, 1970.

Sulzer, Elmer G. *Indiana's Abandoned Railroads. Part I— Abandoned Railroads of Bedford*. Indianapolis, Council for Local History, 1959.

Sulzer, Elmer G. "Locomotives for the Madison Hill: Motive Power on the Madison & Indianapolis Railroad." *Railway and Locomotive Historical Society Bulletin* 123, pp. 23–43.

Swartz, William. "The Wabash Railroad." *Railway and Locomotive Historical Society Bulletin* 133, 1975.

Sweetland, David R. *Pennsy Steam Years.* Edison, N.J.: Morning Sun Books, 1992.

Sweetland, David R. *New York Central Steam.* Edison, N.J.: Morning Sun Books, 1992.

Taylor, Jeremy. *Conrail Commodities.* Telford, Pa.: Silver Brook Junction Publishing Co., 1994.

Thornbrough, Emma Lou. *Indiana in The Civil War Era, 1850–1880.* Indiana Historical Bureau and Indiana Historical Society, 1965. Chapter 8, "The Transportation Revolution," pp. 318–361.

Trains Magazine, Waukesha, Wis.

Trap, Paul. "The Detroit & Pontiac Railroad." *Railway & Locomotive Historical Society Bulletin* 168, Spring 1993, pp. 17–50.

Trelease, Allen W. *The North Carolina Railroad 1849–1871 and the Modernization of North Carolina.* Chapel Hill: University of North Carolina Press, 1991.

Turner, Charles W. *Chessie's Road.* Richmond, Va.: Garrett and Massie, 1956.

United States Army, Corps of Engineers. *The Ohio River.* Washington: U.S. Government Printing Office, 1935.

Vaughn, George. "Design and Maintenance of Track Tanks." *Railway Age Gazette,* April 13, 1913, pp. 893–896.

Weaver, Abraham E., ed. *A Standard History of Elkhart Co.* Chicago: American History Society, 1916.

Weber, Thomas. *The Northern Railroads in the Civil War: 1861- 1865.* Columbia: King's Crown Press, 1952.

White, John H. *A Short History of American Locomotive Builders.* Washington, Bass Inc., 1982.

White, John H. *Cincinnati Locomotive Builders.* Washington: Museum of History and Technology, Smithsonian Institution, 1965.

White, John H. "Once the Greatest of Builders: The Norris Locomotive Works." *Railway and Locomotive Historical Society Bulletin* 150, Spring 1984, pp. 17–52.

White, John H., Jr. *The American Railroad Freight Car.* Baltimore: Johns Hopkins University Press, 1993.

White, John H., Jr. "Railroad Car Builders of the United States." *Railway and Locomotive Historical Society Bulletin* 138, 1978, pp. 5–29.

White, John H. *The Great Yellow Fleet: A History of American Railroad Refrigerator Cars.* San Marino, Calif.: Golden West Books, 1986.

White, John H. *The John Bull; 150 Years a Locomotive.* Washington, D.C.: Smithsonian Institution Press, 1981.

Wyllie, Cleland B. "Route of the Freight 400s." *Trains,* January 1947, pp. 14–25 [GTW].

Young, William S. "Extra 1 South." *Railroading,* no. 26, February 1969.

Index

Boston, Mass., 122, 239, 242
BPM Rail, 170
Bradford (Monon), Ind., 131
Brazil, Ind., 25, 139, 142, 168, 170, 171, 172, 186, 189, 205, 231, 253
Breed Generating Station, 175
Breyfogle, Dr. William L., 168
Bridges: Covered, 131, 234; Ohio River, 200–203, 231–35
Bridgeton, Ind., 168, 171
Brightwood (Indianapolis), 200
Bringhurst, Ind., 118
Brill, J. G. Company, 248
Bristol, Ind., 174, 219
Brookston, Ind., 129
Brookville, Ind., 107, 190, 251
Brotherhood of Locomotive Firemen, 258
Browns, Ill., 190
Buckeye Manufacturing Company, 248
Bucklen, Herbert E., 168, 219, 220
Budd Company, 248
Buffalo & Mississippi RR, 11
Buffalo, N. Y., 99, 109, 119, 126, 198, 211, 214, 215
Burlington Northern Santa Fe, 189
Burnside, Gen. Ambrose E., 108, 118, 258
Bushrod, Ind., 253
Butler, Ind., 14, 100, 117, 119, 125, 126, 211, 212

Cairo, Ill., 104, 108, 152, 170
Cairo & Vincennes RR, 108
Cairo, Vincennes & Chicago RR, 258
Calumet region, 104, 108, 194
Cambridge City, Ind., 107, 117, 123
Cambridge City Car Co., 32
Camp Atterbury, 117, 257
Canada, 109, 126, 211, 257
Canada & St. Louis Ry, 104
Canadian National Railways, 78, 161, 162, 248, 259
Cannelton, Ind., 149, 178, 188, 190
Carbon, Ind., 168, 171
Car leasing, 169
Car retarder, first mechanical system, 196
Carroll, Charles, 6
Carthage, Ind., 108, 181, 186, 187, 188
Carthage, Knightstown & Shirley RR, 92, 108, 186
Cars, Steel, 48
Cavanaugh, Ind., 196
CCC&StL. See Cleveland, Cincinnati, Chicago & St. Louis
Cedar Lake, Ind., 133, 234
Central Canal, 9
Center Point, Ind., 118, 253
Central Indiana Ry, 167, 168, 170–72, 186, 205, 253
Central Indiana & Western RR, 172, 181, 186
Central Properties, 186, 187
Central Railroad of Indiana, 106, 181, 186, 190
Central Railroad of Indianapolis, 124, 183, 186, 187–90, 197, 199, 216
Centralized Traffic Control, 68
Charlestown, Ind., 136, 178, 179
Chatsworth, Ill., 189
Chesapeake & Ohio Ry, 150–52, 159, 161; Abandonments, 161, 187, 206, 207; Controls Chicago, South Shore & South Bend RR, 176; Disaster at Converse, 256; Motor trains, 246, 248; Ohio River bridge, 200, 231; Van Sweringen empire, 257
C&O of Indiana, 150
Chessie System, 77

Chesterton, Ind., 250, 255
Chesterfield, Ind., 11
Chicago, Ill.: Abandonments, 205, 206; Bank failures, 218; Bypass routes, 104, 110, 189; Chicago–New York service, 101, 115, 156; Cincinnati, Lafayette & Chicago RR reaches, 106; Commuter trains, 176, 250; Erie RR (Western & Atlantic) reaches, 156; Grand Central station, 194; Grand Trunk RR (Chicago & Grand Trunk) reaches, 162; Illinois Central RR, 106, 152; Joint passenger services, 106, 126, 152; Michigan Central RR reaches, 99, 109; Michigan Southern RR reaches, 99; Nickel Plate RR reaches, 119; Pere Marquette Ry reaches, 157; Pittsburgh, Ft. Wayne & Chicago RR reaches, 111; Pullman services, 117, 239, 242; Toledo, O., interurban line projected to, 219; Union Stock Yards, 195, 196
Chicago & Alton RR, 216
Chicago & Atlantic Ry, 25, 127, 157, 252, 256
Chicago, Attica & Southern RR, 139, 142, 160, 167, 172, 205, 207, 247
Chicago & Block Coal RR, 142
Chicago, Burlington & Quincy RR, 189, 259
Chicago and Calumet Terminal RR, 194, 195
Chicago & Cincinnati RR, 150
Chicago, Cincinnati & Louisville RR, 41, 150, 159
Chicago, Detroit & Canada Grand Trunk Junction RR, 162
Chicago, Danville & Vincennes RR, 139, 142
Chicago & Eastern Illinois RR, 28, 73, 109, 139–43, 234; Abandonments, 207; Brazil branch, 139; Chicago, Attica & Southern RR, 172; Disasters, 256; Dixie Fleet, 166, 252; Evansville Belt Ry, 203; Miners' trains, 253; Mount Vernon branch, 188, 192; Pullman service, 242; Terre Haute & Logansport RR leased, 118; Van Sweringen empire, 257
Chicago & Grand Trunk Ry, 25, 162
Chicago & Great Eastern Ry, 24, 114, 115, 205, 258
Chicago & Great Southern Ry, 25, 142
Chicago & Great Western RR, 194
Chicago, Hammond & Western RR, 194, 195, 196
Chicago Heights, Ill., 143
Chicago & Indiana RR, 157, 183, 184, 185
Chicago & Indiana Air Line Ry, 176
Chicago & Indiana Coal Ry, 25, 142, 172
Chicago, Indiana & Eastern Ry, 117
Chicago, Indiana & Southern RR, 41, 104, 196, 242
Chicago & Indianapolis Air Line Ry, 25
Chicago Junction, O., 137
Chicago Junction Ry, 195, 196
Chicago & Lake Huron RR, 24
Chicago, Lake Shore & Eastern Ry, 195, 233
Chicago, Lake Shore & South Bend Ry, 176
Chicago & Northwestern Ry, 196
Chicago River & Indiana RR, 195
Chicago, Rock Island & Pacific RR, 110, 142, 196
Chicago Short Line Ry, 195
Chicago & South Bend RR, 196
Chicago & South Eastern Ry, 171
Chicago, South Shore & South Bend RR, 176–78, 191, 250, 256
Chicago, St. Louis & Pittsburgh RR, 114, 197
Chicago Terminal Transfer RR, 194
Chicago, Terre Haute & Southeastern Ry, 143, 200, 219, 245, 247, 248, 253
Chicago & Wabash Valley Ry, 41, 132, 152
Chicago & Western Indiana RR, 150, 183
Chicago & West Michigan Ry, 25, 161
Chili, Ind., 126, 212, 213
Cincinnati, O.; B&O service, 231; Cincinnati-Chicago service, 106, 115, 122, 124, 132, 150, 189; Cincinnati-Indianapolis

service, 106; Commuter trains, 250, 251; Joint passenger services, 124, 252; Motor trains, 246; Northern Michigan service, 117; Pullman services, 242

Cincinnati, Bluffton & Chicago RR, 41, 167, 174, 205, 207, 220–21

Cincinnati & Chicago RR, 14, 114

Cincinnati, Findlay & Ft. Wayne Ry, 135, 139, 167, 174, 205, 239

Cincinnati, Hamilton & Dayton Ry, 135, 137–39, 150

Cincinnati, Hamilton & Indianapolis RR, 138

Cincinnati & Indiana RR, 106

Cincinnati & Indianapolis Junction RR, 23, 138

Cincinnati, Indianapolis, St. Louis & Chicago RR, 105

Cincinnati, Indianapolis & Western RR, 132, 138, 152

Cincinnati, Lafayette & Chicago RR, 25, 106

Cincinnati & Martinsville RR, 106, 108

Cincinnati, Peru & Chicago Ry, 14

Cincinnati & Richmond RR, 114

Cincinnati, Richmond & Ft. Wayne RR, 24, 117

Cincinnati, Richmond & Muncie RR, 150

Cincinnati, Rockport & Southwestern RR, 24, 147

Cincinnati & Southern Ohio River Ry, 108

Cincinnati & Western Indiana RR, 150

Cincinnati & Terre Haute RR, 24, 108, 109

Cincinnati, Wabash & Michigan RR, 24, 25, 108

Civil War, 22

Clark Maritime Centre, 192

Clarke Junction, Inc., 195, 250

Clarksville, Ind., 227

Claytor, W. Graham Jr., 174

Cleveland, O., 99, 242, 257

Cleveland, Cincinnati, Chicago & St. Louis RR, 26, 42, 99, 168; Acquires OI&W RR, 109; Acquires Terre Haute–Evansville line, 109, 139, 143; Acquires VG&R RR, 108, 123; Cairo, Ill., line, 104, 108, 109; Central Railroad of Indianapolis, 187, 199; Central Indiana Ry, 171; Commuter trains, 250, 251; Disasters, 255; First Big Four, 105; Joint passenger service, 124, 252; Leased to New York Central, 106; Michigan Division, 108; Mileage in Indiana, 99, 104; Ohio River bridge, 108, 200, 231; Pullman service, 239, 242; Second Big Four, 105

Cleveland, Indiana & St. Louis Ry, 170

Cleveland, Painesville & Ashtabula RR, 99

Clifty Falls State Park, 115, 237

Clinton Yard, Ind., 253

Cloverdale, Ind., 133

Clover Leaf line (TStL&KC), 214, 215, 216, 256

Clover Leaf Steamboat Line, 214

Clymers, Ind., 118

CN North America, 161

Coal carriers, 118, 119, 156, 174, 178, 181, 189, 196, 206, 215, 219

Coal fields, 104, 118, 131, 132, 133, 143, 156, 171, 172, 217, 218, 253

Coal mines, 109, 118, 142, 191, 253

Cochrane, Ind., 136

Coldwater, Mich., 184

Columbia, O., 174, 205, 219, 247

Columbia branch (Knox county), 253

Columbia City, Ind., 14, 119, 242

Columbian Exposition of 1893, 27, 38

Columbus, Ind., 10, 12, 115, 117, 192, 205, 242, 246

Columbus, O., 104, 114, 115, 117, 242

Columbus, Chicago & Indiana Central Ry, 24, 114

Columbus, Hope and Greensburg RR, 108

Columbus, Piqua and Indiana RR, 115

Columbus & Shelby RR, 12, 117

Commuter service, 109, 231, 250–51

Connersville, Ind., 23, 107, 122, 123, 124, 188, 246

Connersville & New Castle Junction RR

Conrail, 76; Abandonments 104, 115, 117, 118, 157, 183, 184, 206; Commuter ser-vice, 250; Detroit-Chicago line, 101; Erie-Lackawanna included, 157, 181; Indianapolis-Evansville ser-vice, 181; NS acquires Ft. Wayne line, 122; spinoffs, 180, 181, 185

Consolidated Grain & Barge Company, 192

Continental Steel Corporation, 197

Converse, Ind., 117, 242, 256

Cook Transit Company, 178

Corman, R.J. RR, 187

"Corned Beef & Cabbage Line." See Cincinnati, Bluffton & Chicago

Corydon, Ind., 167, 169

Corydon Junction, Ind., 169

Corydon Scenic RR, 92, 170

Cottage Grove, Ind., 150

Covington, Ind., 126, 142

CP Rail, 159

Crane, L. Stanley, 174

Crane Naval Surface Warfare Center (Crane Naval Ammunition Depot), 179, 219, 237

Crawford, Henry, 171

Crawfordsville, Ind., 106, 109, 118, 129, 133

Crawfordsville & Wabash RR, 11, 129

Crescent Navigation Company, 178

Crown Point, Ind., 114, 250

CSX, 77, 181; abandonments, 206

C&EI. See Chicago & Eastern Illinois

Danville, Ill., 104, 108, 109, 125, 139, 142, 185, 217, 242

Dayton, Oh., 105

Dayton & Union RR, 105

Debs, Eugene V., 258

Decatur, Ind., 117, 183, 184, 206

Deer Creek bridge (Monon), 231

Defense, Department of, 167, 179

Delano, Frederic A., 133, 259

Delaware, Lackawanna & Western RR, 157

Delaware Otsego Corporation, 189

Delphi, Ind., 133, 231

Delphos, O., 124, 213, 216

Depauw Tunnel, 237

Depew, Chauncey, 196

Depots, 34; Fort Wayne, 50, 98; Gary, 50; Indianapolis Union, 98; New Albany & Salem, 98; Richmond, 50; South Bend, 50

Designated Operator Lines, 80

Detroit, Mich., 125, 126, 211; Joint passenger service, 126, 127, 252; Pullman service, 126, 239, 242; Trackage rights, reached by, 127

Detroit, Butler & St. Louis RR, 125, 211

Detroit, Eel River & Illinois RR, 24, 119, 211

Dining cars, first, 33

Disasters, 255–56

Disko, Ind., 157

Dixie fleet (C&EI), 142, 252

Dolly Madison Industries, 169

Douglas, O., 124, 188

Dubois, Ind., 188, 190

Dubois County RR, 149, 190

Duffey, Ike, 171, 172

Dugger, Ind., 118, 174, 253

Dreyfus, Henry, 58
Dykeman, Judge D.D., 212

East Chicago, Ind., 194, 195, 196, 233, 250
East Chicago Belt RR, 195, 196
East Gary, Ind., 110
East St. Louis, Ill., 124, 213
Eaton & Hamilton RR, 114
Edinburg, Ind., 10, 115, 116, 205, 257
Edwardsport, Ind., 250
Edwardsville Tunnel, 237
Eel River RR, 125, 126, 127, 157, 211–13, 252
Effingham, Ill., 154, 190
Effner, Ind./Ill., 117, 189
Egg transportation, 179
Elgin, Joliet & Eastern Ry, 195, 196, 207
Elkhart, Ind., 12, 99, 100, 110, 167, 168, 185, 205, 222; Conrail, 101; Motor trains, 246, 247; Old road, 99, 100, 101; St. Joseph Valley Ry, 174, 219
Elkhart: NYC Museum, 95
Elkhart & Western RR, 25, 168, 175, 185
Elkhart Yard, 55
Elnora, Ind., 143, 191, 216
Elwood, Ind., 197
Elwood, Anderson & Lapel RR, 197
Emporia, Ind., 108, 181, 186, 187, 188
Englewood (Chicago), Ill., 252
English, Ind., 237
Enos Coal Corp., 174
Erie & Kalamazoo RR, 6
Erie Canal, 6
Erie RR, 127, 156–57; Chesapeake & Ohio paired track, 150; Cincinnati, Bluffton & Chicago RR; paired track, 221; Commuter trains, 250; Disaster at Kouts, 256; Motor trains, 246, 248; Trackage rights to Wabash RR, 119; Van Sweringen control, 257; Von Willer, Harry, 261; Whistler, George W., 261
Erie Lackawanna RR, 73, 157; Abandonment, 183, 184, 206, 207; Short lines, 181, 185
Erie Western Ry, 157, 183, 184, 185
Essroc Materials, 178
Evans Transportation Company, 169
Evansville, Ind., 13, 71, 109, 142, 143, 147, 149, 178, 188, 205, 222; Bridge, Ohio River, 203, 233; C&EI RR, 139; Illinois Central RR, 154; Interurban lines, 176; Joint passenger services, 252; L&N RR, 166; Motor trains, 246; New York Central lines, 104, 108, 109; Pullman services, 242, 243; Southern Railway, 149
Evansville Belt Ry, 203
Evansville & Crawfordsville RR, 13, 23, 118, 139, 142
Evansville & Eastern Electric Ry, 178
Evansville & Indianapolis RR, 25, 142
Evansville, Indianapolis & Terre Haute Ry, 42, 109, 139
Evansville Local Trade RR, 149
Evansville, Mt. Carmel & Northern RR, 41, 108
Evansville Museum of Arts and Science, 95
Evansville & Ohio Valley Ry, 41, 154, 167, 176, 178, 207
Evansville Rys, 178
Evansville & Richmond RR, 25, 143, 200, 216, 237
Evansville, Rockport & Eastern Ry, 147, 149
Evansville, Suburban & Newburgh Ry, 41, 167, 176, 178, 207
Evansville Terminal Company, 154, 190, 233
Evansville &Terre Haute RR, 139, 142
Evansville, Terre Haute & Chicago RR, 24

Fairland, Ind., 108, 258
Fairland, Franklin & Martinsville RR, 108, 118

Fairmount, Ind., 117, 242
Fair Oaks, Ind., 142, 172
Fairtrain, 123
Fast Freight Lines, 29
"Fast Mail" on LS&MS, 101
Federal Steel Company, 195
Ferdinand, Ind., 167
Ferdinand RR (Ry), 41, 81
Ferdinand & Huntingburg RR, 169
Ferdinand Station, Ind., 147
Ferries, car, 154, 166, 178
Findlay, O., 139, 174, 205, 214, 239
Findlay, Ft. Wayne & Western Ry, 139, 174
Findley, Mich., 104
Fisher, Ill., 152
Fishers, Ind., 123
"Fishing Line." See Grand Rapids & Indiana
Flexi-van, 70, 85
Florida, through cars & trains to, 106, 116, 119k, 139, 142, 186
Fort Branch, Ind., 142
Fort Madison, Iowa, 189
Fort Recovery, O., 187
Fort Wayne, Ind., 31, 123, 223; Disaster, 256; Joint passenger operations, 107, 124, 252; Motor trains, 246; NYC branch, 101; Nickel Plate Road, 119, 122; Norfolk Southern, 122; Norfolk & Western Ry, 115; Track elevation, 42, 55; Pennsylvania Railroad, 110, 126; Pittsburgh, Ft. Wayne & Chicago RR, 110; Pullman service, 239, 242, 243; Switching roads, 197; Triple Crown Service, 126; Wabash RR, 125, 126, 212; Whistler, George W., 261
Ft. Wayne and Jackson RR, 101
Ft. Wayne, Jackson & Saginaw RR, 24, 101
Ft. Wayne Railway Historical Society, 95
Fort Wayne Rolling Mill Company, 197
Ft. Wayne, Terre Haute & Southwestern, 167, 168, 171
Ft. Wayne Union Ry, 197
Fowler, Ind., 255
Frankfort, Ind., 118, 119, 124, 187, 213, 214, 216, 223, 250
Frankfort & Kokomo RR, 25, 213
Franklin, Ind., 10, 11, 108, 192
Franklin Park, Ill., 195, 196
Frankton, Ind., 187
Free, Ind., 185, 242
Freeland Park, Ind., 142
Freight Services; Erie Flying Saucer, 70; NYC Pacemaker, 70
Fremont & Indiana RR, 24
French Lick, Ind., 131, 147, 190, 217, 237; Abandonment, 206; Car storage, 169; Dubois County RR, 149, 190; Joint passenger operations, 118, 252; Pullman operations, 133, 242, 243
French Lick, West Baden & Southern Ry, 149, 169, 237
Frick, Daniel family, 183, 185, 186
Fulton County RR, 184

Galion, O., 105, 239, 242
"Galloping Geese," 248
Garrett, Ind., 137, 224, 250
Garrett, John W., 137
Garrett Railway Museum, 95
Gary, Ind.; Commuter trains, 176, 194, 195, 196, 256
Gary, Judge Elbert, 195
Gas-Electric cars, 48
General Electric Company, 191
Gentryville, Ind., 149
Georgetown Tunnel, 237
Gibson, Ind., 196
Gifford, Benjamin J., 152

Pullman services, 156, 242, 243–44; Short lines, 113; Union Depot, 14, 15, 20, 194, 199, 200; Union RR, 200; Union RR Transfer & Stockyard Company, 200; Union Stockyards, 194, 200; White River Ry, 200

Indianapolis & Bellefontaine RR, 11, 15, 18
Indianapolis Belt Ry, 28, 52, 105, 199
Indianapolis Car Company, 32, 224
Indianapolis Children's Museum, 91, 96, 115
Indianapolis & Cincinnati RR, 13, 22, 106, 108
Indianapolis, Cincinnati & Lafayette RR, 26, 106, 107
Indianapolis, Crawfordsville & Danville RR, 24, 118
Indianapolis, Decatur & Springfield RR, 138
Indianapolis, Decatur & Western Ry, 138
Indianapolis, Delphi & Chicago RR, 24, 129
Indianapolis & Frankfort RR, 41, 119
Indianapolis & Madison RR, 115
Indianapolis, Peru & Chicago Ry, 126
Indianapolis Southern Ry (RR), 41, 154, 231, 237
Indianapolis & St. Louis RR, 24, 106, 118
Indianapolis Terminal Corporation, 191
Indianapolis Traction Terminal, 42
Indianapolis Union Station, 35, 42
Indianapolis Union Ry, 14
Indianapolis & Vincennes RR, 24, 106, 117, 118, 258
Ingleton, Ind., 147
Insull, Samuel, 176
Interstate Commerce Commission, 39, 54
Interstate Public Service Company, 178, 179, 201
Interurbans, 41
Inverness, Ind., 220
Ivanhoe, Ind., 256

Jackson, Mich., 101, 109, 110, 205
Jacksonville, Fla., 150, 242, 252
Jasonville, Ind., 253
Jasper, Ind., 147
Jefferson Proving Ground, 192
Jeffersonville, Ind., 11, 192, 194, 227; Commuter trains, 252; Interurban line, 176; Ohio River bridges, 108, 136, 194, 200, 201, 203, 231; Pullman service, 242, 244
Jeffersonville RR, 11, 115, 116, 192, 205
Jeffersonville, Madison & Indianapolis RR, 30, 114, 115, 117, 201, 231, 251
JK Line, 157, 181, 183, 185, 186
Joint Passenger Service, 251–53
Joliet, Ill., 110, 195
Joliet & Northern Indiana RR, 110
Jonesville, Mich., 101
Joslyn Stainless Steels, 197
Judyville, Ind., 142

Kalamazoo, Mich., 101, 109, 110, 250
Kankakee, Ill., 104, 106, 185
Kankakee, Beaverville & Southern RR, 104, 106, 124, 181, 183, 185
"Kankakee Belt RR," 104
Kendallville, Ind., 114
Kensington, Ill., 176
Kentland, Ind., 104
Kentucky Derby, 131
Kentucky & Indiana RR Co., 136, 147, 203
Kentucky & Indiana Terminal RR, 203, 231
Kindill Company (coal mining), 174
Kingan & Company, 200
Kingsland, Ind., 255
Kirk Yard, 195

Kirk Yard Junction, 195
Knightstown, Ind., 11, 108
Knox, Ind., 119
Knox Coal Company, 253
Kokomo, Ind., 115, 119, 186, 190, 197
Kokomo Belt RR, 197
Kokomo Rail Company, 187, 190
Kouts, Ind., 256
Kuhler, Otto, 58

LaCrosse, Ind., 114, 139, 142, 143, 161, 172, 205; CA&S RR, 143; PM Ry, 157, 159
Ladoga, Ind., 171
Lafayette, Ind., 5, 11, 13, 71, 106, 122, 124, 125, 129, 227; Disasters, 255; Kankakee, Beaverville & Southern RR, 126, 185; Lafayette Union Ry, 197; RR relocation, 71
Lafayette, Bloomington & Mississippi Ry, 126
Lafayette & Indianapolis RR, 11, 15, 16, 22, 106, 255
Lafayette, Muncie & Bloomington RR, 24, 123
Lagrange, Ind., 114, 219, 220
Lake Erie, Evansville & Southwestern Ry, 24, 149
Lake Erie & Ft. Wayne RR, 197
Lake Erie & Louisville RR, 117
Lake Erie, Wabash & St. Louis RR, 13, 125
Lake Erie & Western RR, 106, 107, 119, 122, 123, 197; Joint passenger operations, 124, 252, 253
Lake Shore RR, 99
Lake Shore & Michigan Southern RR, 26, 27, 99, 100, 104, 157, 168, 169, 186, 233; Chicago, Indiana & Southern RR, control of, 104; Elkhart & Western RR, acquired, 169; Formation of, 99; Fort Wayne, Jackson & Saginaw RR, 101; Indiana, Illinois & Iowa RR, control, 104; Monon charter, use of, 129; Sturgis, Goshen & St. Louis Ry control, 104; Switching roads, 196; Vanderbilt acquires control, 99
Laketon, Ind., 157, 184
Laketon Refining Co., 157, 184
Land grants, 114
Lapel, Ind., 172, 186, 187, 197
LaPorte, Ind., 12, 14, 99, 161
La Salle & Chicago RR, 194
Latta, Ind., 253
Laughery Creek, 231
Lawrenceburg, Ind., 12, 13, 26, 189
Lawrenceburg Junction, Ind., 108, 251
Lawrenceburg & Indianapolis RR, 8, 106
Lawrenceburg & Upper Mississippi RR, 12
Lebanon, Ind., 119, 121
Leesburg, Ind., 179
Leroy, Ill., 126, 152
Leslie, Gov. Harry G., 255
Lexington & Ohio RR, 6
Liberty, Ind., 258
Liberty Center, O., 188
Lima, O., 187
Limedale, Ind., 118, 189
Limestone carriers, 118, 137, 143, 167; Bedford district, 143, 200; Bloomington district, 152, 156
Lincoln City, Ind., 149, 190
Lincoln, President Abraham, 22
Linden Railway Museum, 95
Linton, Ind., 217, 253
Litchfield, Mich., 184, 185
"Little Giant." See TC&StL RR
Little River RR, 98, 104, 184
Little Tunnel, 237

RR, 122, 123; Muncie Belt Ry, 199; Muncie & Western RR, 198, 199, 208, 258; NKP relocation, 55; Pennsylvania Railroad, 131; Pullman service, 239, 242, 244

Nashville, Tenn., 166, 252
National Homes Corp., 197
National Railway Historical Society, 91, 97
National Road, 5
Naval Surgace Warfare Center, Crane, 179
New, Sen. Harry S., 168
New Albany, Ind., 11, 20, 129, 136, 147, 203, 227; Atterbury, Wallace W., 257; Bridges, 194, 203, 231; Commuter trains, 251; Tunnels, 237
New Albany Belt & Terminal RR, 203
New Albany & Salem RR, 11, 12, 129
New Albany & St. Louis Air Line Ry, 147
New Buffalo, Mich., 161, 250
Newburgh, Ind., 176, 178
New Castle, Ind., 109, 114, 115, 122, 124, 181, 187, 188
New Castle & Richmond RR, 12
New Castle & Rushville RR, 123
New Harmony, Ind., 152, 154
New Haven, Ind., 126
New Haven & Lake Erie NG RR, 94
New Jersey, Indiana & Illinois RR, 41, 81, 170, 197, 242
New Orleans, La., 142, 150, 156, 242, 252
New Paris, O., 114
Newton, Ill., 188, 190
Newton, Ind., 127, 157, 251
New York Central RR, 99–110, 181, 234, 258; Abandonments, 104, 106, 181, 183, 205, 208; "Air Line," 100, 101; Auburn, Ind., 183; Central Indiana Ry acquired, 170, 186; Chicago-Cairo, Ill., line, 104, 108, 126, 181; C&EI RR line acquired, 109; Commuter Trains, 250; Disasters, 256; Fort Wayne Union Ry, 197; Michigan Central RR leased, 100; Motor trains, 245, 248, 249; New York–California service, 101; Nickel Plate Road control, 119, 123; Passenger service, joint, 104, 124; Penn Central merger, 181; StJSB&SRR acquisition, 110; Switching roads, 195; Vanderbilt control, 100
New York Central & Judson River RR, 109
New York City, 116, 211, 239, 242, 252
New York, Chicago & St. Louis. See Nickel Plate Road
New York, Susquehanna & Western RR, 170, 189
New York, New Haven & Hartford RR, 259
Nickel Plate Road (NYC&StL), 25, 119–24, 181, 234; Abandonments, 181; Ball, George A., 257; Elwood, Anderson & Lapel RR acquired, 197; Mergers, 119, 124, 216
Niles, Mich., 109, 110
Noble, Governor Noah, 9
Noblesville, Ind., 11, 123, 171
Norfolk Southern Ry, 77, 119, 122, 123, 124, 147, 174; Short lines, 149, 170, 180, 187, 188, 190
Norfolk & Western Ry, 123, 206; Erie RR, control of, 157; NKP RR acquired, 119, 181, 216; PRR line acquired, 122, 181; Wabash RR acquired, 119, 125, 181
North Indianapolis, 200
North Judson, Ind., 25, 104, 150, 157, 184, 185, 186, 250
North Madison, Ind., 5, 9, 20
North Manchester, Ind., 157, 184
North Vernon, Ind., 108, 115, 136, 186, 192, 200, 231
Northern Indiana RR, 11, 14
Northern Indiana Commuter Transportation District (South Shore Line), 176

Oakland City, Ind., 174
Oakland City Jct., Ind., 174

Ohio & Erie Canal, 6
Ohio Falls Car Co., 33, 50
Ohio & Indiana RR, 13, 111
Ohio, Indiana & Western RR, 109
Ohio & Mississippi RR, 13, 22, 24, 108, 135, 136, 147, 200, 237; Bridges, 201, 203, 234; Commuter trains, 250; Disasters, 255
Ohio River; Bridges, 166, 191, 194, 200–203, 231; Rail/boat service, 106, 178; Southern Railway, 147
Oklahoma, through cars from New York City, 106, 114, 242
Oil City, Pa., 239
Old Ben Coal Co, 174
Old Point Comfort, Va., 150
"Old Road" of MS&NI, 101
Oliver Chilled Plow Company, 196
Oliver family, 168
"Onion Belt" RR. See Chicago & Wabash Valley
Oolitic, Ind., 216, 253, 200
Orland, Ind., 220
Orleans, Paoli & Jasper Ry, 131
Orr, F.R., 185
Osgood, Ind., 136, 231, 250
Osseo, Mich., 101
Otter Creek Jct., Ind., 142
Owasco, Ind., 231
Ownsboro, Ky., 178
Owens-Brockway Glass Container plant, 186
Ownsburg, Ind., 237
Ownsville Terminal Company, 192

Paisley Trestle, 234
Palm Beach. Fla., 242, 252
Pan-American Exposition
Panhandle Ry See Pittsburgh, Cincinnati, Chicago & St. Louis
Panic of 1837, 9
Panic of 1857, 13
Panic of 1873, 24, 200
Panic of 1893, 194
Paoli, Ind., 231
Paris, Ill., 171, 242
Parlor car service, 107, 124
Passenger services, joint, 107, 132, 251–53
Passenger Trains; Admiral, 239; Amtrak, 75; Bluegrass, 60; Broadway Limited, 52, 239; Canadian, 256 ; Capitol Limited, 52, 60, 137, 239; Chicago Arrow, 252; Cincinnati & Ft. Wayne Express, 252; Columbian Express, 38; Commercial Traveler, 52, 124, 215, 256; Commodore Vanderbilt, 239; Detroit Arrow, 46, 252; Diplomat, 60; Dixie Flagler, 252; Dixie Limited, 53; Dixie Flyer (C&EI), 53, 142, 252, 256; Dixie Flyer (IC), 156, 252; Erie Limited, 52; Exposition Flyer, 38; Fort Wayne & Cincinnati Express, 252; French Lick New Yorker, 252; Hoosier, 60; Interstate Express, 256; James Whitcomb Riley, 69, 106; Jeffersonian, 69; Lake Shore Limited, 52, 239; Liberty Limited, 52, 60; Manhattan Limited, 52, 239; Maple Leaf, 69; Mercury, 69; Metropolitan Express, 52; Michigan Central Limited, 52; Mohawk, 52; National Limited, 52, 60; New York & Chicago Limited, 38; Nickel Plate Limited, 52; Old Dominion Limited, 150; "Old Nellie," 131; Pacemaker, 69; Pennsylvania Limited, 52, 239; Pennsylvania Special, 46; Spirit of St. Louis, 60; Southwestern Limited, 38, 52; South Wind, 69; St. Louisian, 52; Sunset Limited, 150; Thoroughbred, 60; Tippecanoe, 60; Trail Blazer, 69; Train of Tomorrow, 60; Twentieth Century Limited, 40, 52, 69, 72, 101, 239; Whippoorwill, 60, 70; Wabash Cannon Ball, 126, 212; Wolverine, 52; World's Fair Special, 38
Patton Tunnel, 237
PCC&StL. See Pittsburgh, Cincinnati, Chicago & St. Louis

Valparaiso, Ind., 24, 114, 119, 162, 205, 239, 250
Van Buren, Ind., 188
Vandalia RR, 110, 114, 117, 118, 250; Terre Haute shops, 37
Vanderbilt, "Commodore" Cornelius, 27, 100, 109, 213
Vanderbilt interests, 119
Vanderbilt, William, 162
Van Sweringen, M.J. and O.P., 216, 257
Veedersburg, Ind., 142, 172
Venango River Corp., 176
Vernon, Greensburg & Rushville RR, 108, 123
Vernon, Ind., 9
Victor, Ind., 156, 168, 234
Victor Oolitic Stone Co., 168, 234
Villard, Henry, 194
Vincennes, Ind., 13, 108, 117, 118, 126, 136, 184, 242, 250
Von Willer, Harry, 261

Wabash, Ind., 212, 245
Wabash & Erie Canal, 6, 9, 11, 13, 109, 125, 129
Wabash & Erie RR, 188
Wabash National Corporation, 197
Wabash & Ohio RR, 188
Wabash RR (Ry), 124, 129, 181, 212, 213, 234, 258; Abandon-
    ments, 184, 185, 206, 210; Delano, Frederick A., 259; Eel
    River line, 157; New Haven cutoff, 41; Passenger service,
    joint, 252; Pullman services, 242; Short lines, 170, 184, 185,
    188, 197; Subsidiaries, early, 123
Wabash River, 108, 133, 154, 172, 220, 233
Wabash, St. Louis & Pacific RR (Ry), 119, 154, 211, 213
Wabee Lake, 168
Wagner Palace Car Co., 33
Walkerton, Ind., 104
Walkerton Junction, Ind., 250
Wallace, Governor James, 5
Wallace Junction, Ind., 132
Walsh, John R., 143, 200, 216, 217, 218, 219
Warsaw, Ind., 108, 179, 205, 239
Washington, D.C., 242
Washington, Ind., 42, 109, 135, 216 230
Waterloo, Ind., 101
Watson (Watson Jct.), Ind., 136, 178, 179, 203
Waukegan, Ill., 195
Waveland, Ind., 170, 171
Wayne Works, 248
Weaver Popcorn Company, 188

Weehawken, N.J., 126, 211, 212
Wellsboro, Ind., 161
West Baden Springs, Ind., 131, 147, 217, 242
West Dana, Ind., 253
Western Indiana RR, 195
West Lebanon, Ind., 126, 152
West Melcher, Ind., 139
Westport, Ind., 143, 216, 219
West Shore RR, 211
Westville, Ind., 129
West Yellowstone, Mont., 242
Wheatfield, Ind., 104,
Wheeling & Lake Erie Ry, 257, 259
Whistler, George W., 261
Whistler, James A. McNeill, 261
White River, 131, 168, 191, 234
White River Railway, 200
White River Valley line, 200
Whitewater Canal, 9, 107
Whitewater Valley RR, 92, 106, 107
Whiting, Ind., 194, 195, 196
Wildcat Creek, 231
Wilkinson, Ind., 188
Willard, O., 137
Willow Valley, Ind., 237, 255
Winamac, Ind., 115, 183, 186
Winamac Southern Ry, 115, 118, 181, 183, 186, 189, 190
Winona Assembly, 179
Winona Interurban Ry, 126, 179, 213
Winona RR, 167, 176, 179, 210
Winona Service Company, 179
Winona & Warsaw Ry, 179
Wolcottville, Ind., 185
Woodburn, Ind., 188
Woodville, O., 188
Worthington, Ind., 109, 191
Wren, O., 183

Yankeetown, Ind., 176
Yankeetown Dock Corporation, 167, 174, 176
Yeddo, Ind., 142
Young, Robert R., 242

Zearing, Ill., 104

RICHARD S. SIMONS is author of *The Rivers of Indiana* and was a contributing editor of *Popular Mechanics Picture History of American Transportation*.

■

FRANCIS H. PARKER is professor and former department chair of urban planning at Ball State University. He is the author of *Indiana Railroad Depots: A Threatened Heritage*.

Railroad names remain on the landscape—sometimes literally, as with this Nickel Plate boundary post.